STATE AND COMMONWEALTH

STATE AND COMMONWEALTH

The Theory of the State in Early Modern England, 1549–1640

NOAH DAUBER

PRINCETON UNIVERSITY PRESS
PRINCETON AND OXFORD

Published by Princeton University Press,
41 William Street, Princeton, New Jersey 08540
In the United Kingdom: Princeton University Press,
6 Oxford Street, Woodstock, Oxfordshire OX20 1TR
press.princeton.edu

Library of Congress Cataloging-in-Publication Data

Names: Dauber, Noah, author.
Title: State and commonwealth : the theory of the state in early modern England,
    1549–1640 / Noah Dauber.
Description: Princeton : Princeton University Press, 2016. | Includes bibliographical
    references and index.
Identifiers: LCCN 2016001828 | ISBN 9780691170305 (hardback)
Subjects: LCSH: Political science—Great Britain—History—16th century. | Political
    science—Great Britain—History—17th century. | Great Britain—Politics and
    government—1558–1603. | Great Britain—Politics and government—1603–1649. |
    State, The. | BISAC: POLITICAL SCIENCE / History & Theory. | POLITICAL
    SCIENCE / General.
Classification: LCC JA84.G7 D29 2016 | DDC 320.10942/09031—dc23 LC record available
    at http://lccn.loc.gov/2016001828

British Library Cataloging-in-Publication Data is available

This book has been composed in Sabon Next LT Pro

Printed on acid-free paper. ∞

Printed in the United States of America

10 9 8 7 6 5 4 3 2 1

TO MY PARENTS

CONTENTS

ACKNOWLEDGMENTS

My first debt is to Richard Tuck. I have been studying the history of political thought and discussing it with him since the middle of my undergraduate years, and his example of formulating a position, thinking about it, and rethinking it over decades has made it possible and pleasurable to think of it as my life's work. The earliest inklings of the approach taken in this book probably came from reading bits and pieces of Gierke's *Natural Law and the Theory of Society* and discussing them with him in those first years, and there are echoes of countless other conversations throughout this book. In graduate school, he introduced me to Istvan Hont, whose generosity and company I treasured then and for years afterward, and whose memory remains a constant reminder of the importance of serious scholarship in the history of political thought. When we first met, we discussed at some length the work of Horst Dreitzel, whose approach to the history of ideas has influenced mine ever since.

I owe my appreciation of the sophistication of the medieval Aristotelian commentary tradition to Christoph Flüeler, Lidia Lanza, and Marco Toste, and I would like to acknowledge the Swiss National Science Foundation for its support of the time I spent working with those scholars at the University of Fribourg. Our work together is most obviously reflected in chapter 3, but it has changed my understanding of the arc of the history of political thought more generally and has convinced me that there is still much more to say about the continuities between medieval and early modern political thought.

This book began to take definite shape during the semester I spent at Cambridge in the spring of 2014, and I thank my colleagues there for their wonderful generosity and hospitality. In particular, I am grateful to Annabel Brett, John Robertson, and Richard Serjeantson and the conveners and attendants of the wonderful Political Thought Work-in-Progress series, especially Hugo Drochon. Thankfully, Isaac Nakhimovsky and Karuna Mantena, longtime friends and colleagues, were in Cambridge at the same time, and they made hard work a pleasure. Another longtime friend, Leah Whittington, was a great help in the final stages of the book process; I cannot be more thankful for her friendship and for our ongoing dialogue.

At Colgate University, I have been blessed by wonderful colleagues. Many thanks especially to Melissa Kagle, Valerie Morkevicius, and Illan Nam for their friendship and intellectual companionship in general and particularly during the writing of this book. I also wish to thank my research assistants at Colgate, above all Ranissa Adityavarman, Lumbardh Halitjaha, and Skylar Salim. The support of the Colgate Research Council, which made research trips to England possible on a number of occasions, is much appreciated. Thanks are also due to the staff of the library at Chatsworth House, Derbyshire, and to Frank Reynolds of the Ulster University Library, who went above and beyond in helping me track the influence of Carlo Sigonio on William Harrison. Finally, I thank the anonymous readers for Princeton University Press for their thoughtful and detailed comments.

This book is dedicated to my parents, whom I cannot thank enough for their endless support. I would also like to thank my brothers, Jeremy and Andrew; my sisters-in-law, Miri and Sara; and above all my nieces and nephews for distraction and delight. They are a whole of which I am but a part.

ABBREVIATIONS

BL	British Library
C	*Code of Justinian*
Cowper	Thomas Starkey, *England in the Reign of King Henry the Eighth. . . . A Dialogue between Cardinal Pole and Thomas Lupset, Lecturer in Rhetoric at Oxford*. Edited by J. Meadows Cowper and Sidney J. H. Herrtage. London: Published for the Early English Text Society by N. Trübner, 1871.
CR	Philipp Melanchthon, *Opera Quae Supersunt Omnia*. Edited by Karl Gottlieb Bretschneider and Heinrich Ernst Bindseil. 28 vols. Halle: Schwetschke, 1834–1860 (= *Corpus Reformatorum*, vols. 1–28).
D	*Digest of Justinian*
Dialogue	Thomas Starkey, *A Dialogue between Pole and Lupset*. Edited by T. F. Mayer. London: Offices of the Royal Historical Society, University College London, 1989.
EL	Thomas Hobbes, *The Elements of Law, Natural and Politic*. 2nd ed. Edited by Ferdinand Tönnies. New York: Barnes and Noble, 1969.
LL	Francis Bacon, *The Letters and the Life of Francis Bacon*. Edited by James Spedding. 7 vols. London: Longman, 1861.
Orations	Edward VI's 55 Latin orations, written under the instruction of John Cheke. BL Add. 4724.
SC	John Case, *Sphaera Civitatis*. Oxford, 1588.
Weinberger	Francis Bacon, *The History of the Reign of King Henry the Seventh*. Edited by Jerry Weinberger. Ithaca, NY: Cornell University Press, 1996.

STATE AND COMMONWEALTH

INTRODUCTION: STATE, REPUBLIC, AND COMMONWEALTH

The name that we most commonly use today for political organization, "the state," is ambiguous, meaning either the nation or the administrative staff. The early modern predicament was far worse. The Latin terms *civitas* and *respublica* had many more meanings. John Case wrote in the *Sphaera Civitatis*, the most extensive work of political theory in Elizabethan England, that *respublica*, translated then and now as "commonwealth," could mean four distinct things: the public use of goods, the multitude of citizens, the union of the multitude, or the order and organization of government.[1] The confusion was apparent to him in 1588, and the concept has become only blurrier in hindsight. He thus stipulated that what he meant by *respublica* was what we would call the state in the narrow sense, namely, the organization of sovereignty and the magistrates.[2] But he fully recognized that most of these other meanings were acceptable, reflecting in part the usage of his day, where the English words "commonweal" and "commonwealth" corresponded to his "public use of goods" and to the "union of the multitude."[3]

If everyone had only agreed with Case's recommendations to use *respublica* for the state, *civitas* for society understood as a community, and *multitudo* for society understood as a collection of individuals, the history of state and society in early modern England would be far easier to tell. Instead, "commonwealth" in English and *respublica* in Latin were frequently used for all of the meanings and often in contexts that blended them. The scholarship on the period has traced the stories of some of these meanings, though not often in connection with each other. The story told here builds on the multiple meanings to tell the double history of the commonwealth as state and society in early modern England, such that the state, understood more narrowly

---

1 Case, *SC*, 228; Case, "Sphaera Civitatis," 3.4.4.

2 Case, *SC*, 228–9: ordo & descriptio imperii.

3 Case was uncomfortable with the use of *respublica* for the "multitude of the citizens," which presumably was insufficiently communal to be thought of, in his view, as a *respublica*. And for the community or union of the multitude he preferred *civitas*, presumably in order to keep his definitions straight. Ibid.

as the order of magistracies and their activities, is viewed against the background of the broader understanding of the commonwealth as a whole.

The early modern usage of "commonwealth" that has been most fully explored is its meaning as a union or community of the people. Over the centuries the classical *respublica* had become identified with the medieval society of orders and was said by the theologians to be sustained by the virtues of charity and justice.[4] The commonwealth in this sense was a normative vision of society as a cooperative whole composed of harmonious interrelated parts. As the Henrician propagandist Thomas Starkey wrote in his *Dialogue between Reginald Pole and Thomas Lupset*:

> in a cuntrey, cyty, or towne, ther ys perfayt cyvylyte, ther ys the true commyn wele, where as al the partys, as membrys of one body, be knyt togyddure in perfayt love and unyte; every one dowyng hys offyce and duty, aftur such maner that, what so ever state, offyce, or degre, any man be of, the duty therto perteynyng wyth al dylygence he besyly fulfyl, and wythout envy or malyce to other accomplysch the same.[5]

Geographically, there could be communities or commonwealths of this sort at the level of "cuntrey, cyty, or towne," as Starkey said. The term "country" could mean various things by the sixteenth century, but probably referred here to rural communities in opposition to the urban communities of the city or town.[6] Starkey and others often did not distinguish clearly between the sense of the commonwealth as a community and as an order of offices. The country and city commonwealths of the period understood office holding to be woven into the fabric of society. Governing was thus said to be the social role of the nobility and gentry in a rural commonwealth. William Tyndale explained that the reason that there were landlords and that tenants paid rent was so that landlords would keep order among tenants. "If thy tenant shall labour and toil all the year round to pay thee thy rent and when he had bestowed all his labour, his neighbour's cattle shall devour his fruits, how tedious and bitter shall his life be?"[7] Starkey noted that the nobility and gentry were responsible for "the admynystratyon of justyce to the hole commynalty." Thus they were supported "in pompe and plesure" by the "labur and travayle of the pore commynalty."[8] In exchange for being

---

4 Jones, *Tudor Commonwealth*, 7–9; Wood, *The 1549 Rebellions*, 144–5.

5 Starkey, *Dialogue*, 37 (Cowper, 54–5). Starkey's *Dialogue* is quoted throughout the book from Thomas Mayer's edition and cited as *Dialogue*, but the page numbers in Cowper's edition have been provided for ease of reference.

6 Hughes, *Politics, Society, and Civil War*, 112.

7 Tyndale, *Obedience of a Christian Man*, 62–3; Jones, *Tudor Commonwealth*, 18.

8 Starkey, *Dialogue*, 37 (Cowper, 55).

guided by the nobility, the commonalty were "wyth commyn quyetness" to "apply themselfys to theyr laburys and paynys," being sure to give "reverently to theyr pryncys and lordys al humbul servyce and meke obedyence requyryd to theyr state and degre."[9] The growth in the incorporations of towns in England from the mid-sixteenth century led to a parallel but distinct sense of what it meant to live in a commonwealth. The citizens of the urban settlements developed an increasing self-consciousness of a political culture of "civility" and a notion of their towns as "city commonwealths."[10]

Talk of commonwealth ballooned with the coming of the Reformation to England. Thomas Cromwell, the secretary of the Privy Council under Henry VIII, encouraged the appeal to the ideal of commonwealth by his propagandists in order to justify the sweeping changes brought by the government's declaration of supremacy and the beginning of the Reformation of England.[11] Commonwealth took on the overtones of the national Reformed or Reforming community, as it had for continental Reformers like Philipp Melanchthon and Martin Bucer. The Reformation in England and on the Continent was portrayed as consistent with the broader movement of social reform championed by Christian humanists of the previous generation, chiefly Erasmus and Thomas More. The commonwealth of the Reformers was thus part of a broader attempt to institute a Christianized vision of the classical *respublica*. This ideal of the commonwealth as Christian community was used strategically from above and below to further the interests of all sorts of people, featuring in the literature of agrarian complaint, in the programs of rural rebels, and in learned treatises and sermons on obedience.[12] The social and economic legislation of the period, whether initiated by the government or by business interests, often claimed to be furthering the "commonweal."[13] The commonalty insisted on it in a popularizing key, emphasizing that the common good should take into account the well-being of everyone, including the lower sorts.[14] In response, the sermons on obedience exhorted them to heed the lessons of the book of Romans and bear in mind the "great chain of being."[15] The political uses of the language of commonwealth were extremely localized, and regional variants have begun to be identified.[16]

---

9 Ibid.

10 Withington, *Politics of Commonwealth*, 12.

11 Zeeveld, *Foundations of Tudor Policy*, 114–5.

12 McRae, *God Speed the Plough*, chap. 1; Shagan, *Popular Politics and the English Reformation*; Wood, *The 1549 Rebellions*, 146.

13 Elton, *Reform and Renewal*, chap. 5, esp. 111, 122.

14 Shagan, *Popular Politics and the English Reformation*, 273–80.

15 Cf. Fletcher and MacCulloch, *Tudor Rebellions*, 10–1.

16 These were determined by the particular hierarchies and political traditions of local communities, such as the "medieval social apartheid" longed for by the not quite elite rebels

While it is widely recognized that "commonwealth" became a watch-word for the cause of reform at this time in England, there has not been extensive study of the reception of the Reformers as readers of the classical idea of commonwealth in the double sense of state and society, of *respublica* and *civitas*, as Case would have put it. While this is changing, in the work of social and political historians, commonwealth has often been understood in the context of the rural community, in which government has been understood in the manner portrayed by the official preachers in their sermons and homilies on obedience.[17] Government was, as Starkey said, the role of the landlords, and the obedience owed them as officials was just another reflection of a hierarchical society in which everyone "was expected to obey their immediate superior."[18] In this view, the emergence of the state as a bureaucratic, impersonal institution was one of gradual differentiation of officialdom from society, freed from the logic of hierarchy and obedience. The historians of political thought have told a very different story. Emphasizing the classical idiom of the textual treatment of commonwealth (*respublica*), rather than the social setting, has resulted in a more purely political treatment of commonwealth, in which the history of commonwealth *is* the story of sovereignty, of the impersonal unity and the specialized institutions that compose the state as opposed to society.

THE HISTORY OF POLITICAL THOUGHT AND THE EARLY MODERN STATE IN ENGLAND

Commonwealth as a Theory of the State

In the history of political thought, the official Tudor use of commonwealth has been treated as a theory of the state, rather than of society or of state-society relations. Quentin Skinner argued that the commonwealth theories of Cromwell's and Somerset's day could be understood as part of a reconstructed history of the foundations of the modern state, which was at once participatory and modernizing. This was in keeping with the work of Hans Baron, who described a civic humanism in Quattrocentro Italy that provided an alternative to the history of the state as a forward march to the "Prussian" model, the bureaucratic apparatus described by Max Weber,

---

in East Anglia in 1549. MacCulloch, *Suffolk and the Tudors*, 305–6. This is also suggested by Withington's account of Ludlow and Cambridge. It seems, for instance, that the university community had quite a different view of civic participation than the corporation of the town and presumably than both factions in Ludlow. Withington, *Politics of Commonwealth*, chap. 4, esp. 92–3.

17 For the existence of an official view, see Wrightson, "Two Concepts of Order," 22.

18 Fletcher and MacCulloch, *Tudor Rebellions*, 10–1.

or as a Whiggish struggle between absolutism and constitutionalism.[19] In Skinner's elaboration of this alternative history of the state, developed since the 1970s, the commonwealth thinking of this period plays an important, if supporting role. Its importance is not so much that it is a perfect exposition of the ideal of the free state, the keystone of his theory of the neo-Roman or republican tradition, but that the Tudor use of commonwealth appears to combine clearly the statism of the Henrician royal supremacy, the Eltonian bureaucratic revolution of Thomas Cromwell, and the classical thinking about participation, which would support the notion of the continuities between Quattrocentro civic humanism and European state formation on a grand scale.

For Skinner, the Quattrocentro idea of the free state combined two ideas that are central to the idea of the modern state: the Weberian definition of the state as the monopoly on the use of legitimate force, which is equated with national sovereignty, and the impersonality of the state in which "governmental authority" is distinguished from "the powers of particular rulers or magistrates."[20] Skinner found support for his understanding of national sovereignty in Gordon Zeeveld's 1948 study, *Foundations of Tudor Policy*, which argued that Starkey's vision of the state combined the positivism implied by Melanchthonian adiaphorism with Marsilius's theory of conciliar church government to produce a more consensual theory in which statute was the product of the king-in-parliament.[21] It was later argued that this embrace of indifferentism was not unique to Melanchthon or to Starkey,[22] but the broader argument that conciliarism and adiaphorism combined in Henry's reign in such a way that the use of statute can be understood as a reflection of a modernizing national state, free to legislate for itself on the basis of some degree of popular sovereignty, was influential for both G. R. Elton and Skinner.[23] Taking a firm line on whether Parliament was to be seen as the meeting of the estates of the realm as a king's council or a genuine political institution, Elton argued that in the 1530s Parliament became a fully political institution. Despite being populated by landlords, Elton argued, it had been effectively representative of the entire political nation for a long time, but in the 1530s it became an effective political organization, an equal partner in the emerging understanding of the English state as king-in-parliament, which depended on the king, the

19 Hankins, "The 'Baron Thesis' after Forty Years."

20 Skinner, "From the State of Princes," 2:382.

21 Zeeveld, *Foundations of Tudor Policy*, chap. 6.

22 McConica, *English Humanists*, 160: "It is the 'adiaphoristic principle' attributed by Zeeveld to Starkey, which, however, was instinctive to the whole approach of Erasmus and his followers, including many others besides Melanchthon." Skinner, *Foundations*, 2:104, noted that the doctrine appeared before Starkey in the work of John Frith and Robert Barnes. Mayer, "Starkey and Melanchthon on Adiaphora."

23 Skinner, *Foundations*, 2:103–8; Elton, *Reform and Renewal*, chap. 4.

Lords, and the Commons for the production of far-reaching statutes like the acts of supremacy, such that "for the first time, it could be truly said that acts of Parliament were omnicompetent in England."[24] It was in this era that "the king was no longer in the position of a man who owned a court and could use it as he willed, but in that of a member of the assembly who had to manage things 'politically.'"[25] Skinner agreed that this understanding of statute anticipated the omnicompetent parliamentary sovereignty of the modern state (he quoted Zeeveld's summary of Starkey: "The voice of parliament had become the voice of God").[26]

For Skinner, there was no real break between Italian civic humanism and the new oligarchical form; he maintained that Starkey's thinking was in keeping with civic humanism. His account of the mid-Tudor commonwealth's men, perhaps in part because they served as a foil to the Italian republicans, implied that there was a conservative version of republican "political participation," which he characterized as the "maintenance of 'degree'" or "order." For other scholars, like Whitney Jones, the maintenance of degree was a social and economic matter of vocation and the division of labor. Skinner's interpretation was more overtly political; according to him, "order" amounted to a socially stratified vision of office holding, in which it was argued that the nobility should hold office and attain "honour, glory, and fame," rather than those deemed to possess sufficient virtue, as in the republican view.[27] Just as an emerging territorial unitary sovereignty could be comprehended within the overarching philosophy of liberty in the Italian city-republics, where it took on the meaning of independence and self-rule,[28] so it could be understood in England (and elsewhere) under the overarching philosophy of hierarchical order.[29] In Skinner's account broader structural ideas like sovereignty, the nation, or the common good were colored by these more specific ideologies. The idea of the sovereign nation that accompanied the legislative capacity of the king-in-parliament, for example, did not issue directly in the modern liberal nation understood as a democratic body but, in keeping with the "apocalyptic nationalism" of the day, as "the elect people of England."[30]

The interpretation of Tudor commonwealth in terms of citizenship and sovereignty represented a break from its treatment in earlier twentieth-century studies, where it was depicted as an ideal of Christian community

24 Elton, "Body of the Whole Realm," 22–3, 33, 50.

25 Ibid., 52.

26 Skinner, *Foundations*, 2:104; Zeeveld, *Foundations of Tudor Policy*, 155.

27 Ibid., 1:234.

28 Skinner has articulated at great length how liberty could encompass various ideals; see esp. Skinner, *Liberty before Liberalism*.

29 Skinner, *Foundations*, 1:235–42.

30 Ibid., 2:107.

and a corresponding social program championed by clergy and government men alike. For some interpreters, the ideal was the very modern product of the Reformation in England, while for others, it represented the continued force of the communal obligations of the Middle Ages. In 1900 A. F. Pollard argued that there had been a "commonwealth party" of preachers and administrators surrounding Edward Seymour, the Duke of Somerset, who were concerned above all with implementing a progressive social vision.[31] Approximately twenty-five years later, R. H. Tawney addressed commonwealth in the context of the debate over the modernity of the social teaching of the church.[32] Even after Zeeveld's interpretation of Cromwell's embrace of commonwealth as a slogan for the project of Henrician supremacy, Jones continued to carry the standard for the interpretations of Pollard and Tawney, arguing that the commonwealth agenda was not a radical expression of a new kind of national sovereignty, but an increasing shouldering of the burdens of the traditional norms of a universal morality, which had been handled by the church prior to the Reformation.[33] He argued that while Cromwell's propagandists may have used commonwealth as a cover for the centralization of power under Henry, the commonwealth party that surrounded Somerset in 1548–9 offered a social vision sympathetic to the poor and oppressed. Like Tawney, Jones treated the question of whether such views were modernizing or not with some care and attempted to identify which bits of legislation were nostalgic and which forward-looking. He concluded that, regardless, it was empathy with the poor that defined their approach: "Whether their ideals and ideas be interpreted as looking back nostalgically to medieval values and assumptions or forward to mercantilism, all those who would check the unbridled operation of private profit to the common hurt were denounced as rabble-rousing Anabaptists by those who felt their interests to be opposed."[34]

Elton was impatient with what he took as a naive socialist idealization of traditional economic life and a grasping for a prehistory of the welfare state. Elton was completely unconvinced that there was a "commonwealth party" around Protector Somerset and argued that the heroes championed by Pollard and company needed to be treated far more critically.[35] In Elton's view, they scarcely had a political analysis, let alone a coherent program. They had, by and large, a poor grasp of economic realities and were more interested in railing against sin than in ameliorating the plight of the poor. Hugh Latimer's preaching, for instance, was "at best only a general outburst of grieved

---

31 Elton, "Reform and the 'Commonwealth-Men' of Edward VI's Reign," 235.

32 Tawney, *Religion and the Rise of Capitalism*.

33 Jones, *Tudor Commonwealth*, 13, 29, 277.

34 Ibid., 39.

35 Elton, *Reform and Renewal*, 7; Elton, "Reform and the 'Commonwealth-Men' of Edward VI's Reign."

spleen, devoid of either a reforming programme or any rational understanding of what had gone wrong. . . . Lechery, he argue[d], leads to covetousness because lechers need cash. So that [was] what was wrong with England."[36] Like M. L. Bush, Elton praised what he took to be the more objective or rational analysis of England's economic problems and favored Sir Thomas Smith's analysis to those of Latimer, Thomas Lever, and John Hales.[37] "It is this line of thought and action that now merits better attention: the succession of men who thought coolly, secularly and constructively about the problems of the common weal and who faced the practical tasks involved in turning aspiration into action. They, rather than the laudators of a glorious past that had never been and the lamenters over man's fallen nature, were the true reform party of the sixteenth century."[38]

That the ideal of commonwealth represented a new way of thinking of politics, rather than a conservative version of civic humanism unaltered in its essentials, has been argued by Thomas Mayer in his study of Starkey. Mayer depicted Starkey's thought as representative of an Italian perspective that had already broken with the spirit, if not quite the language, of civic humanism: "Starkey was in Padua precisely when Florentine refugees and Venetian patricians on the defensive blended their two distinct civic humanisms into a new oligarchical form which could suit English circumstances much better than older republican varieties."[39]

The mind-set of the Venetian patricians and some of the Florentine refugees after the Venetian defeat at Agnadello in 1509, which Starkey exemplified, is extremely rich:

> Ultimately, the strain produced a complex reaction known variously as Italian Evangelism or the party of the *spirituali*. It was born in the circles in which Pole moved during Starkey's two residences. In the course of his first visit, this group wove concern for personal salvation (symbolized by belief in *sola fide*), humanism in the narrower sense of linguistic method, and various varieties of republicanism into something new, which then came to define a broad party of reform by the time of Starkey's second stay in the early 1530s. Evangelicals like Contarini who chose to remain in the world continued to espouse loyalty to republican or civic humanist ideals, but often in muted form. In Padua, where public life was no longer the arena for the exercise of *virtù* it had once been, republicanism was first transmuted into new theories of courtly behaviour and then went underground once more and

---

36 Elton, "Reform and the 'Commonwealth-Men' of Edward VI's Reign," 241.
37 Bush, *Government Policy of Protector Somerset*, 40.
38 Elton, "Reform and the 'Commonwealth-Men' of Edward VI's Reign," 253.
39 Mayer, *Thomas Starkey and the Commonweal*, 44.

emerged in the form of conciliarism, as it had done already in the fifteenth century. Republicanism or conciliarism also frequently reinforced the call for reform of the institutional church generated by a quest for a more personal religion.[40]

Starkey's politics in Mayer's description thus have a particular class character; Starkey's idea of commonwealth was a thinking through of what government by the nobility would require institutionally and educationally. Mayer's account nevertheless shares elements with Skinner's "aristocratic republicanism."[41] Starkey, like Pole, was republican on this view, in the strict sense of opposing tyranny, and Mayer associated his circle with Baron's tradition of new Guelphism: they showed their hostility to the large imperial monarchies through their opposition to Caesar in their classical scholarship. Starkey's account of citizenship, aristocratic or not, still meant participation, the choice of the active life versus the life of retirement. Precisely what this sort of participation meant, and even what retirement was, however, changed, and for Mayer this was much of what the lessons of Agnadello were about. The celebration of courtly life by Castiglione was in part a compromise between the poles of retirement and participation, while conciliarism was the more active approach, the reform approach.

The extent to which there was an English state differentiated from society in the sixteenth century, and thus whether the civic humanist understanding really could have constituted a theory of the state under the Tudors in practice, has been a matter of some debate. On the one hand, it has been argued that such idioms were employed in the self-understanding of one of Elton's "points of contact" at the very heart of the Tudor centralizing government: the Privy Council. Building on the work of John Guy, who argued that the practice of counsel was valorized and idealized in Tudor England, Stephen Alford examined closely the counselors of Edward VI, many of whom became Elizabeth's counselors as well. In a number of studies, Alford found that the counselors to Edward VI and to Elizabeth early in her reign were deeply influenced by the classical heritage.[42] Alford has argued that the "Cambridge connection"—that is, the leaders who had studied and taught in Cambridge, including John Cheke, Thomas Smith, Roger Ascham, Walter Haddon, Thomas Wilson, and Richard Rainolde—thought of their work as counselors in terms of the ideal of the *vir civilis* described by Skinner.[43]

40 Ibid., 45.

41 Ibid., 56.

42 Alford, *The Early Elizabethan Polity*, 20–3; Alford, *Kingship and Politics in the Reign of Edward VI*, 44–5; Alford, *Burghley*, 16–18, 142.

43 Alford, *Kingship and Politics*, 203.

There are several difficulties in identifying the republic with the political institutions and practices of the Tudor state. The central institutions, as Alford explained, functioned as much like personal rule as like an impersonal state, and the classical idioms were used in the contexts of both personal service and impersonal office holding. Thus William Cecil freely used the neo-Roman language of the *vir civilis* when he and Sir Thomas Smith were serving the young King Edward in a personal rather than in a public function. Alford correspondingly distinguished between the institutionalized *council* of Elton's Tudor revolution and the informal *counsel* of the king's household.[44] In keeping with Patrick Collinson's analysis of monarchical republicanism, the spirit of the institutionalization was not that of an oppositional project bent on popular sovereignty, but in Alford's eyes was a remedy for the evident weaknesses in the English monarchy and a hope to secure a Protestant England from those weaknesses, especially the threat of a succession crisis.[45]

It may be for reasons such as these that Skinner seemed to be more comfortable with thinking of republicanism as an oppositional philosophy until the Interregnum. While Skinner acknowledged the use of classical sources in the Elizabethan era, the full Roman ideal that he reconstructed pointed ahead to the modern state; the ideal of citizenship in the free state was not simply marked by the consciousness of a national community, a realm, combined with some level of intersubjectivity through counsel, a combination that many historians of monarchical republicanism have settled on.[46] On the contrary, it included features that have customarily been attributed to the liberal nation-state: the protection of individual liberties,[47] the promotion of popular sovereignty,[48] and the articulation of a distinction between state and society.[49] It was thus in the context of civil war and commonwealth that Skinner argued that these neo-Roman ideas came alive, albeit only as a full-blooded statement of the ideal.[50]

Court and Commonwealth

At first glance, the language of commonwealth seems to have faded from view under the Stuarts. As Phil Withington showed, the overt classical language of commonwealth had come to be seen in Jacobean court circles as

44 Alford, *Kingship and Politics*, chap. 3.
45 Ibid., 64.
46 For the relevant literature, see McDiarmid, "Introduction," 3–4.
47 Skinner, "Classical Liberty," 320–2.
48 Ibid., 332–42.
49 Skinner, "From the State of Princes," 382: "the republican theorists no longer equate the idea of governmental authority with the powers of particular rulers or magistrates"; and 386: "they constitute the earliest group of political writers who speak with full self-consciousness of a categorical distinction between states and governments."
50 Skinner, *Liberty before Liberalism*, 9–16.

vaguely absurd, the discourse of city officials who were overly impressed with themselves. Such talk was satirized by Ben Jonson in his *Bartholomew Fair*, in the character of Adam Overdo, "the Cicero-quoting citizen-magistrate."[51] In its place, there was a "new humanism" at the court that drew more heavily on Tacitus, Machiavelli, and Guicciardini than before, though also on new commentaries on Aristotle, as I argue here.[52] It has also been suggested that there was a new language of "improvement," which reflected a market-oriented attitude at odds with the traditional talk of commonwealth.[53] Nevertheless, there were by all accounts "survivals" of the language of commonwealth.[54] Not all of the courtiers were self-conscious about its use, and Archbishop Laud, as has been long recognized, used it widely.[55]

That the old classical idiom was still used to describe the state has been argued above all in the case of Francis Bacon. Markku Peltonen wrote that there was a "continuance of the classical humanist vocabulary" in this period and that the theory of the state retained its participatory character. He concluded that it was thus "misleading to describe this shift, as many scholars have done, as a complete change from a Ciceronian humanism to a Tacitean one."[56] Bacon, he noted, used the Machiavellian language of civic greatness, *grandezza*, in the context of Anglo-Scottish union and stressed the superiority of the "armed citizen" over the professional soldier.[57] Richard Serjeantson argued that Bacon's understanding of *grandezza* was very much that of the expanding state, linking it to his plans for an English empire ranging from the archipelago of the "British" islands to the Netherlands on the Continent.[58] On the other hand, Johann Sommerville challenged the notion that classical political thought amounted to a participatory theory of the state under the Stuarts. In his view, the various Latin tags were not meant as an idealization of Roman politics, but rather served royal government. "Virtue is the true nobility" (*Virtus vera nobilitas*) "was not a republican party slogan. Indeed, if anything it had anti-republican or at least anti-aristocratic connotations, suggesting that old noble families could not expect rewards or power except for service to king and country."[59] When considering the expansion of the fiscal-military state in the 1630s, Sommerville insisted that it be understood in terms of a conflict between the ideologies of absolutism and of limited government (i.e., accountability to the people, the ancient constitution).

51 Withington, *Politics of Commonwealth*, 60–1.
52 Cf. Tuck, *Philosophy and Government*; Salmon, "Seneca and Tacitus."
53 McRae, *God Speed the Plough*, chap. 5; Wrightson, *Earthly Necessities*, 203–15.
54 Wrightson, *Earthly Necessities*, 202.
55 Tawney, *Religion and the Rise of Capitalism*, 170–5.
56 Peltonen, *Classical Humanism and Republicanism*, 7–15.
57 Ibid., 309–10.
58 Serjeantson, "Francis Bacon, Colonisation, and the Limits of Atlanticism."
59 Sommerville, "English and Roman Liberty," 209–10.

For Sommerville, contributing to the postrevisionist view of the causes of the civil war, this participatory view of the Stuart state would occlude the mounting sense of ideological conflict, which led to the war. The structural weakness of the state—the dependency of the center on the localities—rose to the level of political conflict because it was understood in ideological terms. The English state was envisioned by the lawyers as a community of free Englishmen insisting on traditional common-law rights. Absolutist ideology, by contrast, failed to describe the reality of government and in so doing contributed to the crisis. "Whatever the theoretical merits of absolutist doctrine, it misdescribed English political practice, for the king and his subjects were in fact bound together by mutual dependencies." As a matter of fact, "the king could govern effectively only with the assistance of the nobility and landed gentry."[60]

The ideological account offered by Sommerville emphasized the weakness of the state as much as its strength. For scholars interested in tracing the development of the modern state, like Richard Tuck, and who see it as emerging in the "English Revolution," among other sites, this account of conflict over the constitution fails to explain how the idea of the state became adapted to the growth of the fiscal-military state—including the power to tax and spend at will. In Tuck's view such expansion required successful justification of the state's authority to decide what was required in moments of necessity. This in turn depended on three innovations: a new sense of the self, that of the Renaissance skeptic and the "scientific" postskeptic who was ready to give up his own judgment in favor of that of the state; a new understanding of how the state was related to society, representation, and unitary sovereignty; and a new sense of what the state was for, namely, self-preservation, necessity, or interest. Historically, these innovations were driven, respectively, by Renaissance skepticism, a rejection of Calvinist ecclesiology, and a new reason for the state, but they all merged (and were translated into juridical language) in the early Enlightenment "modern natufral law" of Grotius and Hobbes. Tuck called this abdication of private judgment for the judgment of the sovereign "representation."[61]

Though it was in the English Revolution that Tuck found a practical expression of the principle of representation (in the arguments of Henry Parker and Nathaniel Bacon on the non-presbyterian side of Parliament in the 1640s and in the insistence by John Lilburne and the Army Council that the Parliament be representative and elected on a regular basis), it was in the philosophy of Thomas Hobbes that he found the most sophisticated account of it as a theory of the state.[62] The full recognition of the threat of private judgment

60 Sommerville, *Royalists and Patriots*, 55.
61 Tuck, *Philosophy and Government*.
62 Ibid., 235, 243.

implies that collective judgment can only be secured through a "political" transformation of society, not through a direct mirroring of society in the state. The common designation of a person or an assembly as the sovereign, as the representative of the people in Hobbesian language, transforms the underlying body from a "multitude" to a "people." It is the transference of decision-making power that is crucial to Hobbesian representation (Tuck called it "the cession of judgement") rather than the representation of particular interests. It has long been maintained that the way in which Hobbes understood this transition from the "multitude" to a "people" and the erection of a sovereign expressed his way of thinking about the relationship of state and society. Tuck has continued to argue for representation, even suggesting that Hobbes found classical inspiration of his own sort for this end in Aristotle's description of extreme democracy. He thus traced a parallel Hobbesian history of the reception of classical thought in which this sort of extreme democracy became identified by French and Italian sixteenth-century scholars with the plebiscitary voting assemblies of the Roman republic and then with Hobbes himself.[63]

Reflecting on this material, scholarly work in the history of political thought has begun to question the idea that the relationship between state and society was understood either as the product of the intersubjectivity stemming from active participation or as the decisionistic unitary sovereignty of representation. Kinch Hoekstra questioned the idea that the formation of the state in Hobbes amounts to the decisionistic union of wills of this kind and thus that the state constitutes a distinct unified will completely apart from society. He argued that the basis of Hobbes's union is the voluntary subjection of individuals to the de facto powers that be, in keeping with their natural will to preserve themselves.[64] De factoism allows for an understanding of the state in which interests (albeit of a quite basic kind) are taken into account in the formation of the state. Such bare interests, I think it is fair to say, concerned with security and stability, are still essentially of a political kind. The extent to which the political represents a transformation of the social or a reflection of it in early modern political thought has been explored by Annabel Brett, who has reconstructed a range of early modern views in which society (*civitas* or *multitudo*) was understood to be related to the state (*respublica*). She showed that there was a tension between those who understood the state to be the "order of command and obedience" and those who maintained that "order just *is* the commonwealth."[65] For most of the sources she examined, order meant "ordination to a head" or the erection of a political power. The thinkers of the second scholastic, such as Suárez

63 Tuck, "Hobbes and Democracy."
64 Hoekstra, "Lion in the House."
65 Brett, *Changes of State*, 122.

and Soto, imagined that society was composed of individuals endowed with natural liberty, but society was only given form as a body politic through the subjection of the individuals to a common political power. On this account, the social is quickly absorbed into the political, and the original form of the body politic was a pure democracy, but the political power of the people was often transferred to a more restricted government. This transfer did not entail a full transformation of the people, since "the body of the people continues to play a regulatory role in the commonwealth even if it has totally alienated its power."[66] Hobbes, in Brett's reconstruction, was "deeply opposed" to this view. He adopted the juridical way of understanding the transfer of natural liberty to a government from the second scholastic, but made the moment of transfer also the moment of union, the creation of a people who did not exist prior to that moment. In Brett's summary, for Hobbes, "The city *is* the state."[67]

STATE AND COMMONWEALTH

The prevalence in the history of political thought of a more political interpretation is in part a natural outgrowth of its subject matter, since it is focused on explaining the nature and legitimacy of the specialized institutions of the state. This was reinforced by the focus in the historiography on the central institutions of the state, Parliament and the Privy Council. As the focus on the early modern state in England has shifted increasingly to the character of local administration, historians of political thought have begun to examine how classical texts informed practice.[68] Yet the sources in the history of political thought seem to fit uneasily with the portrait of local government being drawn by the social and institutional historians, in which offices were thought to be "envisioned as broader social roles."[69] In a summary of the work of many scholars on the tensions between state and society in local office holding, Braddick defines the delicate balance between the exercise of authority understood as an officer of the state and as a member of a community:

> Office not only reflected social status but also confirmed it and this was a motive, sometimes perhaps the chief one, for seeking office. Clearly, administrative tasks would be undertaken assiduously when and where assiduity would enhance local social standing. Where im-

66 Ibid., 127–8.

67 Ibid., 138–41.

68 This is above all the case for Markku Peltonen's pioneering exploration of the 1576 *Safegarde of Societie* written by John Barston, the town clerk of Tewksbury. Peltonen, *Classical Humanism and Republicanism*, 59–73. See also Goldie, "Unacknowledged Republic."

69 Braddick, *State Formation*, 77.

plementation of an administrative task was likely to be unpopular, active officeholders faced the prospect of losing rather than gaining prestige. Officeholding could become counter-productive, perhaps even wholely so. . . . These more informal expectations shaped the way in which offices were perceived and set limits to administrative action. In this way, the legitimation of offices gave political force to wider social values, such as neighbourliness, and local standards of order.[70]

It is my contention in this book that a detailed examination of the reception of the classical commonwealth in the wake of the Reformation in England will explain more clearly how these tensions between state and society were understood in their day. Given the extent of serious study of the classics at the time, the relevant source material is almost limitless. Rather than attempting a broad survey, I have chosen to study five cases in depth: the Reforming Christian commonwealth of the counselors who surrounded Edward VI; the vision of England as a society of orders in Thomas Smith's *De Republica Anglorum*; the Aristotelian monarchical republic of John Case's *Sphaera Civitatis*; the exploration of private and public in Jacobean England, especially in the *Essays* of Francis Bacon; and the penal state and the commonwealth of conscience in Thomas Hobbes's *Elements of Law*. The works studied were chosen for their importance to the scholarship in either social history or the history of political thought in the hopes of bringing the textual basis of the two fields into a single conversation while sketching a rough narrative arc across the period.[71] While I argue that the Reformers' understanding was deeply influential and set the terms in which commonwealth was discussed throughout the period, their works were often not the immediate sources for writers on the subject, and the models offered here are by no means straightforward rehearsals of their views. The works studied here are variations on a theme rather than instances of the same pattern.

In the early sixteenth century, the classical commonwealth seemed to offer a solution to the tensions between state and society. The elimination of self-love and the creation of a community based on the love of one's neighbor was the target of the Christian humanists, like Erasmus, Colet, and More, who hoped to realize a Christian version of the classical commonwealth in the years before the Reformation.[72] By the late 1520s, as Protestant and some

70 Ibid., 35.

71 As the review of the literature above shows, Smith and the "commonwealth party" of Edward VI's reign have long been important for social history in England, while Bacon and Hobbes have been at the heart of many accounts of the idea of the state in the history of political thought. John Case has been emerging recently as an important source for understanding how the Aristotelian tradition was applied in England. See Brett, *Changes of State*.

72 For an overview, McConica, *English Humanists*, chap. 2; Skinner, *Foundations*, 1:196–201, 213–21.

Catholic Reformers, like Melanchthon and Gasparo Contarini, considered the social and political implications of the doctrine of salvation by grace, there was an increasing sense of the inadequacy of political arrangements for the regeneration and sanctification required for genuine neighborly community.[73] Considering not only the coercive elements of social and political organization, but also the classical teachings on the voluntary social processes of virtue, the pursuit of honor, and friendship in light of this doctrine, the Reformers concluded (in line with Augustine and others) that all of these mechanisms for keeping order were similarly tainted with a concern for self-love.[74] The hope remained that people would come to love one another through reflection on the grace of God, but in the ordinary course of life the "hypocritical" conformity with the law, in which people often felt internally opposed to conformity, could be replaced by a spontaneous feeling of identification with the community by making it possible for "affection to overcome affection," in Melanchthon's phrase. The theologians identified the voluntary attachment of this somewhat lower sort with the kind of attachment the citizenry of the classical city-republics felt, as described by philosophers and historians of antiquity.[75] The process of overcoming affection by affection meant that the private and the public were not simply related in opposition; conformity with the law, if only of the "hypocritical" sort, could be achieved through the satisfaction of private needs.

The relevant categories for understanding the relationship between state and society were by the close of the sixteenth century the public and the private. The order of magistracies, the *ordo politicus*,[76] was certainly understood to be conceptually distinct from the populace, the *civitas*, and the theory of sovereignty played as important a role in the Reformers' struggles against imperial reaction as it did in the struggle of the Italian city-states for independence.[77] Yet, it was office used "indifferently" or publicly that really

73 There are other indications that elements of the relationship between state and commonwealth developed here may have been shared by Counter-Reformation thinkers. That both "Aristotelian" and "juridical" ways of approaching the state cut across the Protestant and Catholic divide has been explored by Brett, *Changes of State*. The summary of Jesuit social thinking in Höpfl, *Jesuit Political Thought*, chap. 12, suggests several important parallels, including on distributive justice (284), price stability and sumptuary laws (285), and the distribution of offices (288). These parallels will need to be kept in mind as broader attempts to synthesize the various accounts of the early modern state are undertaken.

74 Augustine, *City of God*, bk. 5.

75 See chapter 1 in this volume.

76 Huschke, *Ordo Politicus*, 109, 119.

77 This is perhaps most visible in the work of Bucer, who explained in his commentary on Romans that it is the possessor of *merum imperium* who ought to be respected as the authority in question in Romans 13. He specifically noted that this does not mean just the emperor in the case of the Holy Roman Empire, but also the cities and subordinate powers that

constituted the exercise of public authority. "Private" did not have the connotations of "individual" that it does today; it did not mean the closed domestic sphere in the bourgeois sense of the nineteenth century, our usual sense of the word.[78] Depending on the author, the understanding of the category of the private was individualized or identified with a group to various extents: some authors stereotyped "private" needs and associated them with occupational and status groups (Smith, Case); others thought of the interest of particular patronage networks or factions as private (Bacon); while still others saw the pursuit of private aims as genuinely more individualized, the concerns of particular people with their own salvific histories (Hobbes). In a more fundamental sense, however, all of the authors agreed that the private concerns were social, since they mostly consisted of externalized needs, requiring the recognition, esteem, or dignity provided by others.

Following the Reformation analysis of the classical commonwealth as an order of self-love, classical ethics and politics increasingly became a science of keeping order and a social psychology. Aristotelian distributive justice came to be understood as a means of maintaining order by distributing goods in accordance with the different degrees of the people. In Aristotle's analysis, treating people how they believed they deserved to be treated led to stability. These claims were in turn understood to be relative to one's particular class, as one's ideas about desert were informed by self-love, which magnified the significance of whatever qualities one already possessed. Thus the wealthy believed that goods should be distributed according to the criterion of wealth; the poor, according to the equality of persons; the aristocrats, according to virtue.[79] There was thus not one standardized psychology but a set of psychological profiles differentiated by class. By the late sixteenth century, the attitudes toward what one felt that one deserved were not only understood to be socially differentiated by social class, but in some accounts were thought to depend on one's atittudes toward what others deserved and were being given. The stability that was supposed to come with distributive justice was now understood to depend on whether one had cooperative or competitive attitudes toward the satisfactions of these needs. If attitudes were understood to be competitive and the goods positional, their satisfaction could not be approached straightforwardly without consideration of envy.

This disenchanted view of the classical commonwealth also meant that the Reformers were open to embracing the reconstruction of the particular

---

exercise such authority, "no less the ruler of a little town, than the prince of a great realm, as much in a small town and the greatest city." Bucer, *In Romanos*, 484: non minus regulus unius oppiduli, quam princeps ditionis ingentis, aeque exiguum municipium, atque civitas amplissima. Kroon, *Studien*, 4.

78 Habermas, *Structural Transformation*, 10–12, 36–7.

79 Aristotle, *Politics*, 4.11, 1295a35ff., and 7.8, 1328a36.

and very worldly ways in which the classical commonwealth worked. The Reformers showed great interest, for instance, in how the penal codes of antiquity were used to further conformity in religion and to further social policy, and they studied Roman law, Athenian law, Plato's *Laws*, and Cicero's forensic oratory in this connetion.[80] The mid- to late sixteenth-century studies by Carlo Sigonio on the institutions of Rome and by Piero Vettori on Aristotle's *Ethics*, *Politics*, and *Rhetoric* added still more detail to their understanding of the institutions of the ancient world and how classical ethics fit into that setting.[81] This amounted to a rich account of the classical *respublica* in all of its senses, where distributive justice was institutionalized in Roman hierarchical social structures, such as clientage, the system of orders, and the *cursus honorum*.

All of this empirical detail was reduced to two master strategies for achieving conformity with the law: reward and punishment, the honor system and the penal code. Outside of the household, the distribution of punishments was reserved to the state alone, and one of the central tensions in thinking about the use of classical commonwealth beginning with the Christian humanists was the consideration of whether the enforcement of the penal code by magistrates was preferable to the social processes for the maintenance of order. On the one hand, the use of the penal apparatus was in principle preferable since it was thought to be public, insulated from private quarrels and concerns. It was also held, for the same reasons, to be more effective and rigorous. On the other hand, it was widely recognized that in practice magistracy was often used for private purposes, and it was felt that incentivizing citizens to conform to the law through rewards was more in keeping with the Christian values of charity and brotherly love than using the fear of punishment.

Reward could mean material benefit, but it usually meant recognition, honor. Where the application of punishment was premised on the opposition of the private affections and the public good, the bestowal of reward assumed that the two could be reconciled in the satisfaction of private desires. This coordination between private needs and the public good depended on the unusual qualities of honor, "the most precious of all goods externall."[82] Honor as a source of public acclaim or recognition was the rare good that both pleased the beneficiary and reflected the pleasure of the benefactors. It was conducive to social solidarity because it reflected the preferences of society at large. It was understood that in practice this depended on maintaining a meaningful economy of honors, in which the distribution of official

80 See chapter 1 in this volume and the footnotes to Bucer, *De Regno*, where the parallels to Plato's *Laws* are documented.

81 See McCuaig, *Carlo Sigonio*; Tuck, "Hobbes and Democracy"; and chapters 2, 3, and 4 in this book.

82 Peltonen, *Duel in Early Modern England*, 37, citing Romei and Kepers, *The Courtiers Academie*.

recognition, whether through titles or offices, was thought to reflect broadly held values and in which everyone felt sufficient recognition for their role in society.

In practice, it is extremely difficult to ensure that a desirable good will not be the source of competition rather than cooperation and thus of disunity rather than unity. In the literature on honor in early modern England, it has been shown by Anna Bryson and Markku Peltonen that the impact of the Italian courtesy literature in England was to introduce an honor culture in which "extreme outward politeness was merely covering the intense rivalry between courtiers."[83] Bryson saw this two-sided nature of courtesy as a reflection of urbanity, an anonymous culture that is deeply competitive but also committed to the graces necessary for living together.[84] The rivalry for courtly honor often seemed like a parody of the commonwealth ideal, and Peltonen showed that "many aspects of the Elizabeth chivalric revival . . . should be seen rather as a partial reaction against this Italian culture in general and the private duel of honor in particular than as arguments in its favor."[85] Similar arguments about the rehabilitation of a more martial code of honor under Charles have also been made.[86] I show in this book that the battles between the chivalric and courtly theories of honor were but one aspect—though one of the most significant—of the broader coming to grips with whether the distribution of reward could be maintained in the wake of a greater and greater appreciation of the social psychology of competitive behavior.

"Reward" was, in sum, another way of saying a well-functioning social order, and the two were combined in one of the most frequently cited adages at the time, *honos alit artes*, "profit or advancement nourishes every faculty," in Thomas Smith's contemporary translation. A well-designed and well-maintained social order was the key to both stability and productivity, and the theorists of the classical commonwealth studied here understood from the wealth of scholarship that they were consuming and producing that there was nothing inevitable about it. The use of classical sources for the description of social order has often been thought to be idealizing, abstracting from the real economic and social forces of the day. Keith Wrightson has distinguished the "theorists of gentility," who defined the qualities of being a gentleman in terms of the "renewed classical ideals of citizenship," in opposition to a new approach under Elizabeth, where the society of the people was divided into degrees distinguished "less with function than with place, less with vocational and occupational differentials than with the

83 Peltonen, *Duel in Early Modern England*, 75.
84 Ibid., 68.
85 Ibid., 93.
86 Cust, *Charles I and the Aristocracy*.

bald facts of relative wealth, status, and power."[87] There were theorists of gentility in this vein, such as Sir Thomas Elyot, but I argue here that the understanding of society in classical terms was not in opposition to an appreciation of a broad range of economic or social forces. The visions of social order developed by Thomas Smith and John Case were at once idealizing—imagining England as resembling a particular golden moment of class harmony in the Roman republic—and realistic—imagining advances in the transition "from the language of 'estates' to 'classes'" or from "an organic commonwealth with a traditional hierarchy of tenurial status" to a "social order which combines reference to economic circumstances with a system of esteem."[88] This peculiar account of political development, which seems to point backward to classical citizenship and forward to a scale of esteem and wealth, was made possible by a view of legal history, popular among Protestants, that saw Roman history itself as marked by a development from a "curial" form of lordship to a freer society of citizens divided into orders. Emancipation from unfree tenure—the assurance of liberties understood as legal capacity—was thus coordinated with an account of classical citizenship.

Office, as already mentioned, could be both private and public, and in this analysis was at once responsible for meting out punishment to others while constituting a reward in the form of status for its occupant. The private use of office (and of the state more generally, such as the system of courts) has been emphasized by the social historians of politics who see the state as a "resource." Building on the work of Gerald Harriss in medieval history, Hindle argued that "[s]tate authority was manifested not only in initiatives of control by central agencies, but also as a popular resource for the peaceful ordering of society, which might be employed and promoted at highly localized levels. The state was a reservoir of authority on which the populace might draw, a series of institutions in which they could participate, in pursuit of their own interests."[89] Thus the state did not obviously serve one class or the other; it was rather a resource that could be used variously by different classes to different ends. Hindle showed, for example, that the court of the Star Chamber, usually thought of as one of the instruments of the king's prerogative for disciplining recalcitrant subjects, could be used by tenant farmers against their more prosperous landlords.[90] The use of government in new ways, such as the poor law, was both modernizing and an instrument of distinction. The experience of implementing the poor law was thus said to have contributed to the middling sort's "sense of social and moral

87 Wrightson, "Estates, Degrees, and Sorts," 38–43.
88 Ibid., 31; Cressy, "Describing the Social Order," 33.
89 Hindle, *State and Social Change*, 16.
90 Ibid., 70.

distance from the poor, excited their prejudices, bureaucratised the extension of neighbourly charity and taught them how to estimate the relative utility of the poor as an economic resource."[91]

The account offered in this book is in many ways very close to this picture of the state as a resource, which captures much of what the authors studied here felt about the use of the state. Yet, it differs in that many of the authors (though not all) imagined that a transformation of the private into the public was possible, and it would be due to such a transformation that society would become (if only in the activities of certain individuals) the state. This is theoretically possible in a participatory model of the civic humanist or republican sort, and Braddick imagines such a transformation taking place in his application of Weber's theory of legitimacy and Skinner's account of the participatory state to England. For Braddick, political power at the time was exercised through "a coordinated network of territorially bounded offices . . . recognisable to us as a kind of state," which he identified with Skinner's "impersonal order."[92] Though Braddick understood legitimacy broadly in Weberian terms, his account, in keeping with the use of the republican paradigm, gave it a more communicative definition.

Legitimation in Braddick's account depended largely on the deeper intersubjective or communicative understanding that was said to underlie the legal and procedural constraints at the heart of the operation of the central government's courts and councils, the legal validity of the commissions of local office holders, and the neighborliness that moderated the implementation of policy by local office holders.[93] There was such a communicative aspect in the performance of office holding in the localities, which could be seen in the resistance to the implementation of particular policies "as officeholders responded to perceived challenges and opportunities with initiatives of their own."[94]

The sources take a variety of positions (summarized below) on the relationship between state and society, between public and private. They are sophisticated and eclectic, draw on detailed historical scholarship, and are engaged in heated contemporary debates. At the risk of oversimplifying, it can perhaps be noted that the positions roughly fall into the two camps of reward and punishment and that a pendulum movement of a sort can be discerned as the promise of the honor system seems to fade and penal law is embraced, after which there is a return to the honor system as complaints mount about the rigor of the penal law. These swings are accompanied by

91 Wrightson, *Earthly Necessities*, 220.
92 Ibid., 19.
93 Ibid., 22–9. This communicative understanding of the legal basis of legitimacy resembles that of Habermas much more closely than that of Weber. For Habermas's critique of Weber's understanding of legal rationality, see Habermas, *Theory of Communicative Action*, 1:302.
94 Braddick, *State Formation*, 24.

similar swings between the sense of the inevitability of the opposition between private and public motives and a sense that the two can be coordinated. Both viewpoints shared a background understanding of the power
of distributivist thinking; they divided on whether the satisfaction of such
claims could really be the source of unity. Those who believed it was possible saw office holding less as the practice of communicative intersubjectivity than as the achievement of one's own consciousness of one's desert
as filtered through a shared consensus on order and distributive justice as
reflected in the social distribution of honor. This harmonization of one's
needs with the recognition of others that the satisfaction of those needs was
legitimate—for those who believed this was possible—established a commonwealth and legitimated the state.

———

This book picks up the story of state and commonwealth during Kett's Rebellion in Norfolk in the summer of 1549. For many writers, the rebellion
marked a moment of crisis not only for traditional tenurial arrangements
in the countryside, but for the popular commonwealth policies of Protector Somerset, who was governing during Edward VI's minority. In the first
chapter, I argue that the commonwealth had already years earlier come to
grips with the "realism" that some have portrayed as a turn to a more self-
interested political economy. The Cromwellians had largely depended on
the law, imagining a penal system that would ban idleness and maintain
just relationships between the classes of people. Participation in the state
was understood as serving in the magistracy and having the liberty to use
the law courts. In these years, the work of the continental Reformers became progressively better known in England, and their understanding of
penal law as the instantiation of divine law for a particular country was
adopted in some quarters. As Protector Somerset's reforms failed to take
hold, the Protestant analysis of the "hypocritical" participation of the nobility and gentry in government, who served for their own interests, threw
into relief the differences between the state administration as a public office
and as a private source of status. The motives for public service and for conformity with the law were well understood by the "Cambridge connection,"
including William Cecil, later Lord Burghley, a secretary to Protector Somerset; John Cheke, Edward's teacher; and Sir Thomas Smith, the clerk of the
Privy Council and then secretary of state to Somerset.[95] The extent of their
analysis, developed from their practical experiences, independent studies of
the classical sources, and Protestant teaching, is unfortunately obscured by
the bluntness of the propaganda efforts during the summer of crisis. But a

95 Hudson, *Cambridge Connection.*

fuller sense of it is reflected in Cheke's assignments to the young Edward and in Smith's *A Discourse of the Commonweal of This Realm of England*.

When the Protestants regained power after the short reign of Mary I (1553–8), many of Edward's counselors returned under Elizabeth, including Cecil, who became the secretary of state, and Smith, who became the ambassador to France, the chancellor of the Order of the Garter, the secretary of state, and the keeper of the privy seal. In the 1560s and 1570s, their commitment to the Reformation came under some pressure from Catholic criticism. Catholic propagandists abroad scoffed at the Protestant commitment to "liberty," which only seemed to result in periodic rebellion, and Catholics at home complained that the prosecution of recusancy showed that the Protestant leaders were not truly committed to liberty, but were rather "new men" committed to remaking the English government in their own image. It was in this context that Sir Thomas Smith offered a fresh account of political development in the form of a description of the Elizabethan state in his *De Republica Anglorum*, the subject of the second chapter. Most probably in his revisions in the 1570s, he suggested that England was a society of orders of the sort that Sigonio had described with reference to Rome. Smith carefully situated the "republic of the English" in a scheme of political development, drawing on Sigonio and the humanist lawyer Ulrich Zasius for background. Smith likened the English constitution to a moment of balance during the Roman republic after the curial institutions of the tyrants had faded away, but before the popular party gained the upper hand. This provided one of the most searching reconstructions of the relationship between the English state and society to date, largely collapsing the distinction between public, "indifferent," justice and private motivations for social distinction into the idea of fulfilling one's role in the *respublica* in keeping with one's order. He thereby offered an account of the "commonwealth" that was neither state nor society precisely and that depended on the active participation of a broad swath of the people, though in a differentiated way.

Elizabeth, as is well known, refused to marry. The fear of a succession crisis led her councillors to other expedients, such as envisioning a resort to councils in an interregnum. The ability to think broadly about the constitution of England as independent from the person of the monarch amounted to a new sort of political thinking: monarchical republicanism. By the late 1580s, this approach took on a heavier monarchical emphasis as presbyterians argued for a more popular approach to government—or rather were portrayed as doing so by their episcopalist opponents. The theory of commonwealth was adapted to these trends in the form of John Case's *Sphaera Civitatis*, a monumental commentary on Aristotle's *Politics* and the subject of the third chapter. The *Sphaera* offered an Elizabethan conformist Aristotelianism that carefully plotted a course between the more absolutist theories of Jean Bodin and the republican sympathies of Sigonio and Vettori.

To do so, it fell back on the older "natural law" reading of Aristotle, which portrayed social difference as the result of capacities rather than of the political distribution of goods due to the particular constitution. The idealizing and naturalizing of one's "suitability" for office made the persistence of the private in the conduct of public office less obvious, and the implication was that once commissioned, one simply *was* a public authority. In the end, Case allowed for the broad participation of Englishmen in government, but ruled out any doubt that England was a monarchy. Using a distinction between the form of sovereignty and the administration of government probably drawn from Bodin, he argued that England was a monarchy with a broad-based administration.

The notions of the public and the private only grew more important after James's accession in 1603, as the rivalry for place and the easy distribution of honors, including the sale of titles, threatened to undermine the view that the distinction was in line with distributive justice. Now, an office scarcely seemed like the reward for virtue. James had proposed—in line with the conformist theologians—a more hierarchical vision of the commonwealth, which nevertheless captured the aspirational and competitive desires of the lower sorts. He believed that the nobility as an exemplary class could model the correct behaviors of obedience and public service, which the lower sorts could emulate. Given the trials of Essex (and later himself and Buckingham) for corruption, the vogue for Italian-style courtesy that was sweeping the young nobility and gentry, and the general failure of the gentry to implement the commonwealth legislation that was put in place under the Tudors, Francis Bacon, whose work is the subject of chapter 4, was skeptical that a vision of state and commonwealth that placed its hopes in social distance and an exemplary class could really deliver the public-minded service and broader contentment needed. What he saw was envy, competitive and imitative behaviors of the wrong sort, and idleness. He argued throughout his *Essays* that the ideal type of behavior required true talent and the capacity to actually accomplish things; those who sought office to serve others, even if not from the nobility, were no less public-minded and their motivations no more private. The key was to devise systems of appointment and oversight that would ensure that office holders actually served to execute the laws necessary for the maintenance of the commonwealth, which would then ensure the contentment (and military preparedness and tax base) of the broader populace. The corresponding vision of the state was surprisingly open to both the private motivations of those seeking place and the private alliances of patron networks. In a monarchy, however, Bacon believed that stability required that those alliances be centered around the monarch and that the clients who served him be conversant with the law as far as possible.

The policies of Charles's personal rule provided the greatest challenge to the commonwealth vision of state and society, in which the private desire for the distributive good of honor was thought to generate sufficient voluntary compliance and contentment to maintain the society and provide for its defense. The functional breakdown of these years, when the idleness complained of during James's reign eventually became outright opposition but stopped along the way at the fairly widespread failure to comply with the orders of the council, meant that the premises of the commonwealth theory, especially with regard to the state, came under severe scrutiny. In the end, the theory survived civil war and continued as one of the explanations for public service well into the nineteenth, if not the twentieth, century. But during the personal rule, some commentators, perhaps Hobbes above all, came to believe that public behavior required exclusively the threat of penalty and that external conformity to the law could not be achieved through honor or material contentment, as had long been hoped and promised. Hobbes argued powerfully in a thoroughgoing critique that the pursuit of distributive justice would only result in discord rather than unity and that it was not true justice. True justice could only be achieved through a proper understanding of one's motives, which required a screening out of the motives for external conformity with the law, such as guilt or the desire to prove one's superiority, from those of spontaneous fellow feeling. Hobbes, I argue in chapter 5, thus drew on his understanding of the theory of sanctification and justification to develop a political theory that again split the difference between two rival groups, here between those supporters of the personal rule, who argued that the law was binding in conscience, and the puritan opposition, who believed that conscience provided a reason for noncompliance. Aside from emphasizing Hobbes's theological motivations, my account of Hobbes differs from the existing literature in emphasizing the importance for him of the conditions in the *respublica* after the transfer of power to the sovereign. While it would be impossible to deny the significance of Hobbes's formulation of his version of the juridical transfer of power in the history of political thought, I emphasize that, like Bacon, Hobbes understood the persistence of sovereignty to be a dynamic relationship between the state and society, requiring local (if perhaps not broad) participation. This vision of the state was continuous with Bacon's view; office holding was understood as a public service that needed oversight in order to ensure compliance. Yet, in the wake of the Petition of Right and of the extra-parliamentary levies, public service could no longer be represented in the factional way that Bacon had, and Hobbes's understanding of the state thus resembled that of Thomas Wentworth (the Earl of Strafford after 1640) and the country gentlemen (like his patron, the Earl of Newcastle) who wanted to be of service to the Crown. His vision of society was far less developed than his vision of the state, but I suggest that he thought of it as a sphere of voluntary relationships of the sort imagined by Reformed theologians in their revision of the Aristotelian theory of friendship. Yet, in his handling, these relationships were only made possible by the framework of the state, which ensured external conformity with the law and enabled one to evaluate one's motives in social relationships and approach others without the need to exert one's superiority or use others for one's own good.

The image of the state that emerges here, understood narrowly as the magistracies and the activities involving magistracies, was set firmly within a broader understanding of society, of commonwealth. The processes by which the state worked on the psychology of subject-citizens was not understood to be wholly different from those that worked on them outside of the state. All of these processes potentially mattered in the quest to achieve conformity with the law, social order, and the beginnings of sanctification. They could be said to differ inasmuch as fear differs from love, but they all fell under the greater heading of distributive justice, and they all attempted to work through an appeal to the emotions, affection overcoming affection. While the use of fear was reserved to the state, the use of love was not; rewards could be social or political. The state was thus understood to be impersonal and personal, as much the site of indifferent justice as personal patronage. The participation imagined here was not exclusively communicative, not always concerned with legislation or policy formation; it could be the bringing of lawsuits to enforce the conditions of one's lease or an avenue for exerting social distinction. It could be remarkably active in all the ways that the republicans noted, or it could be utterly vilified as a means for the poor to vent their ambition. It could be understood to be public or private or both simultaneously. It could be at once the work of a magistrate holding office and a client acting in the interests of his patron. And at times, the interests of the commonwealth, the community of the realm, meant not participating at all and leaving one's neighbor in peace. The offices of the state were public, but in the hope of keeping order, the state was in endless negotiations with the private lives of the citizenry. The state was still very much recognizable as the classical *respublica*, as *taxis* or *ordo*, the arrangement of offices in accordance with some view of distributive justice. But it was also the set of *formulae*, the legal actions that could call for justice from the magistrates, and the honors bestowed by the king in the Order of the Garter or on newly minted baronets. It was in the end a little bit of this and a little bit of that, all in accordance with the different sorts of people who lived in the commonwealth.

CHAPTER 1

THE REFORMERS' COMMONWEALTH

> You see, moreover, what a great difference there is between Scripture's view of man and that of philosophy or human reason. Philosophy looks at nothing except the external masks of men; the Holy Scriptures look at the deepest, incomprehensible affections. Since a man is governed by these, the Scriptures judge the acts according to the motivation behind the affections. . . . And as far as those who live outwardly good lives are concerned, is not one man drawn to these ways by an aversion for human affairs, another because [of] the fear of fate, another by ambition, and another by a love of tranquility? For these have been the causes for a better outward life formerly in the case of philosophers and they are now for many men.
>
> —Philipp Melanchthon, *Loci Communes Theologici*[*]

The mid-Tudor upheaval has been described as part of the transition from a medieval to a modern economy. It had several elements: the change from hereditary forms of tenure to contracts; depopulation; a transformation from an agricultural economy to an economy based on trade in wool; inflation, especially in the prices of foodstuffs; and the rise of a new class.[1] These changes were collectively discussed as the problem of "enclosure," which more specifically referred to the practice of landowners enclosing fields (with hedges for pasturage) that had previously been under cultivation. These issues were the subject of discussion and proposed reform from the 1530s onward.

With the death of Henry in 1547 and the coronation of nine-year-old Edward VI, the son of Jane Seymour, not only was economic reform given new impetus, but it was revisited in a new ideological context in which the social basis of participation in government—of the sort that Starkey was interested in investigating—became an open question. Edward's uncle Edward Seymour, the Earl of Hertford, became the Duke of Somerset and was

[*] Pauck, *Melanchthon and Bucer*, 35–6.
1 Bucer, *De Regno Christi*, xxii–xxiii.

named as lord protector of England by the executors of Henry's will. During Edward's minority, Somerset combined an aggressive foreign policy with a politics of "popularity" at home, in part, it seems, "to compensate for his structurally weak position as Lord Protector"[2] and in part out of genuine conviction. In 1547, he began an invasion of Scotland, which drew England into war with France as well. The methods of funding the wars were in tension with the popular politics of relieving the poor through various methods of price control. The Somerset government oversaw the passage of laws regulating the production of leather, malt, and steel; it combated fraud in the wool industry through the specification of measures; and it controlled the export of commodities. It also took steps to relieve the poor, doing away with compulsory purveyance, which required the provision of goods for the use of the military, and transferring tax revenues from town fee-farms to poor relief. A tax on sheep and woolen cloth combined both agendas of the government, raising revenue for the wars and serving as a disincentive for pasturage and enclosure.[3] In general, however, these popular measures were in tension with the chief method of raising revenue, the debasement of the currency.[4] This was offset to some extent by the revenue raised through the sale of church and chantry lands.

Somerset's measures did little to calm the tensions in the countryside or to resolve the issues of land tenure. In fact, the appointment of enclosure commissions in 1548 and 1549 and the rhetoric of the commonwealth men that preceded the commissions may have only fanned the flames of rebellion. In the 1530s, tenant farmers had begun speaking of the commonwealth in the manner that had been preached to them. They worried that their relatively independent way of life was under attack and that the better sort was willing to countenance "the destruction of another one of the orders—that of the commons."[5] John Hales's 1548 bill on the enclosures set out the theory in its classic form:

> for dyvers of your graces subiectes, called to the degree of nobilitie not considering that it hathe pleased almightie god to ordeyn them so farre to excell the comen sorte of people in the comen wwalthe as shepardes to the shepe, and to be particuler serveiours and overseers undre your maiestie of us your graces subiectes, to see that we shuld lyve here in this worlde a godlie and a quyet life, according to goddes worde and your graces Lawes, and to geve them sufficient possessions &

2 Shagan, *Popular Politics and the English Reformation*, 275.

3 Bush, *Government Policy of Protector Somerset*, 40–58; Shagan, *Popular Politics and the English Reformation*, 275–6.

4 Bush, *Government Policy of Protector Somerset*, 41.

5 Wood, *The 1549 Rebellions*, 5.

revenues for that purpose, by the rentes wherof they might quyetly and without bodely labour lyve and attend therunto, but thinking them-selfes onelye born to themselfes and little remembryng that these hon-ours estates & degrees cannot be mayneteyned and preserved wihout your poore subiectes, have somoche neglected ther vocations that they be become grasiers shepemasters and Toilours of the earthe hav-ing pulled downe a greate many Townshippes villages & houses of husbandrie and converting the ground which was wont to be occuped in husbandrie and tillage into pasture.[6]

The tenant farmers were especially concerned that their traditional rights to the use of the commons were being eroded and that the landlords were beginning to raise rents at the expiration of copyhold contracts.[7] They saw these developments in light of the commonwealth ideal that had been preached to them. The self-interest of which they accused the landlords was just what Hales, the instigator of the plan for the enclosure commissions, had suggested was the object of the commissions, namely, "to remove the self-love that is in many men."[8] These anxieties led to a series of revolts in En-gland, the best known of which is Kett's Rebellion in July 1549 in Norfolk. The rebellion began after a festival celebrating St. Thomas à Becket, when a mob began to pull down the enclosures of an unpopular lawyer, John Flow-erdew, who then bribed them to destroy those of Robert Kett instead. Kett, acquiescing to the destruction of the enclosures on his land, became the rebels' leader, ultimately heading an encampment of thousands on Mouse-hold Heath. After various statements of demands and discussions with the authorities, the rebellion was crushed by John Dudley, the Earl of Warwick, and some 3,500 rebels were killed.[9]

It is clear that Kett's Rebellion was a crisis for Somerset, who fell from power in its wake, but it is less obvious precisely what about his policies was so objectionable and the extent to which these objections reflected a rejec-tion of the ideal of commonwealth. Many have interpreted the comments of William Paget and the Privy Council in the fall of 1549 as a crisis of the commonwealth ideal generally. Some of the complaints preceding the fall of Somerset, especially those of Paget, suggest that the protector was too sympathetic to the people, that it was his policies, principally that of the en-closure commissions but also his liberal use of pardons throughout the cri-sis, that fueled the fires of rebellion.[10] According to a statement of the Privy

6 Lamond, *Discourse of the Common Weal*, xlvi.
7 Loach, *Edward VI*, 79.
8 Shagan, *Popular Politics and the English Reformation*, 278.
9 Santschi, "Obedience and Resistance," 133–6; Loach, *Edward VI*, 78.
10 Santschi, "Obedience and Resistance," 158.

Council in the fall of 1549, it was the protector, "mynding to follow his owne fantasyses," that had led to the uprisings, and William Paget reported to Somerset that some had been saying "that youe haue some greater enterpryse in your hedde, that leane so muche to the multitude."[11]

When these complaints are read along with the pamphlets and sermons exhorting obedience during and immediately after the rebellions, it seems that there was a new anxiety to reinforce hierarchy and to put forward a "vision of the body politic which was composed of interdependent but unequal parts."[12] Social commentary now stressed that it was the covetousness of the *people* that was the problem; Latimer and Lever, among others, worried that many were now reaching beyond their degree in dress and consumption. Lever preached that "dyvers members in dyvers place[s], having dyvers duties" should have "dyvers provision in feedyng and clothyng."[13] For many scholars, especially economic, social, and political historians, such comments amounted to a critique of the commonwealth ideal. A new "realism" has been perceived in Smith's writing above all.[14] Thus, for Hindle, "[i]n the years after Kett's rebellion in particular, the government sought to distance itself from what Sir Thomas Smith could by 1565 regard as the facile communism of the 'feigned commonwealth' *Utopia* 'such as never was nor never shall be.'"[15]

The new social history of politics has tended to identify commonwealth thinking with the policies of the Somerset regime in 1548–9 and the social commentary of those years that advocated for those policies.[16] On this view, the council perceived such thinking to be a dead end and chose to pursue instead paternalistic policies that "were palliative rather than ameliorative, their fundamental objective—social control rather than social justice."[17] These historians see an expansion of government under Elizabeth both in the expansion of statute to the regulation of personal conduct (the reformation of manners) and in the explosion of rates of participation of the middling sorts in government. These trends combined to constitute social control, because the policing of manners was effected by converting the middling sorts' desire for distinction into a willingness to regulate their own behavior and to police the lower sorts.

Yet studying the political thought of the mid-Tudor period—in preambles, draft bills, and full treatises—shows that the attempt to respond to the

11 Ibid., 153, 156–7.

12 Hindle, *State and Social Change*, 56.

13 Santschi, "Obedience and Resistance," 206, citing Lever, *A Fruitfull Sermon*, sig. Eiiv.

14 See the contrast between Hales and Smith in Outhwaite, *Inflation*, 17; Wood, *Foundations of Political Economy*, 164, 193; Bush, *Government Policy of Protector Somerset*, 64.

15 Hindle, *State and Social Change*, 56.

16 See the introduction to this book.

17 Hindle, *State and Social Change*, 63.

desire for distinction and the impulse to reform manners were both imagined within the context of the commonwealth, a classical ideal of society. The crisis of 1549 was not a crisis for the overarching goal of commonwealth, which was shared broadly, but for a specific version of commonwealth as championed by Hales, Bucer, and Somerset himself, in which it was attempted to give the state a larger role through the active use of magistrates, who were imagined as custodians of the divine law.

THE CONSERVATORS OF THE COMMONWEAL

Talk of the classical ideal of the commonwealth began to develop rapidly in England in the 1520s and 1530s as the Henricians began to think about the role of the nobility in the English commonwealth, which was inspired by a rush of Italian writing with classical overtones on the subjects of courtesy, true nobility, and gentlemanliness. This in turn generated a small flood of English publications and translations on the subject. The experience of Reginald Pole, Thomas Lupset, and Thomas Starkey in Padua yielded Lupset's *An Exhortacion to Yonge Men* and Starkey's *A Dialogue between Pole and Lupset* in 1529, though Starkey did not present his work publicly for some years. Sir Thomas Elyot published *The Gouernour* (1537), *Of the Knowledge That Maketh a Wise Man* (1533), a commonplace book (1534), and a Latin-English dictionary (1539). Castiglione's *Il Cortegiano* (1528) was imported from Italy and was being read in London by 1530. There were also plans for a more institutional approach to the education of the nobility: Thomas Denton, Nicholas Bacon, and Robert Carey drew up an (unrealized) proposal for an academy for noblemen, which would teach them the law along with Latin and French.[18]

Thomas Cromwell, the secretary of the Privy Council, at much the same time found the discussion of the commonwealth useful for justifying the legislative agenda of the government in social and economic policy, and he employed or encouraged several writers who made the improvement of the commonwealth their main theme, including Thomas Starkey, John Rastell, William Marshall, and Clement Armstrong.[19] Starkey's *Dialogue*, a fictionalized discussion between Pole and Lupset, was not published until the nineteenth century, but it circulated in manuscript and was echoed in several proposals and other works on the English commonwealth.[20]

---

18 Jayne, *Plato in Renaissance England*, 86–9; Fisher, "Thomas Cromwell, Humanism and Educational Reform." Mayer, *Starkey and the Commonweal*, 128–30, corrects the old view, adopted by Jayne, that this program of educating the nobility was aimed exclusively at the gentry.

19 For this group, see Jones, *Tudor Commonwealth*, 29ff.

20 Elton, "Reform by Statute," 244.

Much attention has been paid to Starkey's scheme for national government, but he held his ideas about local government to be essential for the realization of the commonwealth.[21] At the national level, Starkey's vision can certainly be characterized as monarchical republicanism, mixed monarchy, or aristocratic republicanism.[22] In the 1520s Pole, Lupset, and Starkey had all been in Padua, which was then part of the republic of Venice, and at the heart of the *Dialogue* was an adaptation of the contemporary call for the rehabilitation of the Venetian nobility in the wake of recent defeat.[23] The goal of the *Dialogue* was to call on the nobility to take up their proper role in government, with the more particular goal of urging Pole to take up the royal service being offered by Henry VIII.[24] This was to be achieved in England above all by the adoption of a system of councils similar to those in Venice, which dampened ambition and promoted quietness through bridling the prince.[25]

But local government, which was essential for the realization of Starkey's vision of the commonwealth as a populous and materially flourishing society, was almost lordship. Commonwealth required that everyone share their labor, abilities, and resources with everyone else.[26] But the overcoming of self-love could not be achieved by persuasion or exhortation alone; it required either the fear of punishment or the promise of reward, which Starkey maintained was consistent with classical ideas of the commonwealth, including Plato's.[27] Tranquility would be achieved in England when everyone was convinced that everyone else was acting for the common good by fulfilling their vocations energetically.

In this regard, Starkey broke with More's *Utopia*, though he had followed the diagnosis of the ills of England presented there quite closely.[28] He accepted the policies of the Utopians in some respects, but also modified them, considerably changing the character of the relationship of the state to commonwealth. More had suggested that it was crucial for productivity in the commonwealth for everyone to be assigned to the vocation that best suited their talents. Starkey agreed with this, but his understanding of "vocation" differed. More's vision of vocation, drawing on the Ciceronian idea of the *genus vitae*, was voluntary, and it was the interest and pleasure that stemmed from the choice of occupation that was clearly the engine of productivity

21 For the importance of the local in the realization of commonwealth, see Withington, *Politics of Commonwealth.*

22 Mayer, *Thomas Starkey and the Commonweal,* 127–8; see also the introduction to this volume.

23 Mayer, *Thomas Starkey and the Commonweal,* chap. 2.

24 Ibid., 36.

25 Starkey, *Dialogue,* 112, 121–2 (Cowper, 169, 182–4).

26 Ibid., 4 (Cowper, 5–6).

27 Ibid., 147.

28 Mayer, *Thomas Starkey and the Commonweal,* 36.

in *Utopia* (along with the curtailment of unnecessary needs).[29] The *genus vitae* was "the private determination of a career consistent with [one's] own nature, aptitude, and constitution" and harmonized with the good of the commonwealth. As Cicero wrote in *De Officiis*, and as was echoed by Erasmus and More, such a career was to be carefully chosen in line with one's own particular character or *ingenium* and lived with constancy, so that one's choices were a reflection of one's appreciation of one's own character.[30]

Starkey's vision of vocation was far more coercive, more in line with the recent municipal programs of poor relief in Ypres and Rouen, which distinguished between idleness and productivity and accordingly instituted greater penalties for begging.[31] Starkey recommended in the *Dialogue* that England implement the Ypres program,[32] and unlike More's *Utopia*, he specified that "every man that contentyth not hymselfe wyth hys owne mystere craft & faculty" must be punished.[33] Idleness was to be punished by banishment,[34] while negligence in one's occupation was to be fined.[35] Under these conditions, the lower sorts would be productive and provide sufficient material goods for everyone, while the nobility would ensure justice for everyone. The ecclesiastical courts were too lax,[36] and thus penal laws—including the regulation of personal conduct, such as drunkenness and gaming—needed to be upheld.[37] While regular lawsuits would be presided over by the nobility and gentry acting as justices of the peace (JPs),[38] the supervision of occupations and personal conduct would be performed by new local officers, called the conservators of the commonweal and modeled on the Roman censors.[39] There were some rewards for good actions. Starkey proposed that the councils distribute honors to placate the populace, and to promote productivity, rewards would be offered for excellent work in the crafts, as More suggested. There was, however, no provision for conciliar government at the local level; participation as under-officers was implied but not emphasized.

Starkey was aware that his coercive approach to the commonwealth barely seemed to fulfill the Christian ideal of a society in which neighborly love was realized, and he pinned his plans on the reform of the nobility

---

29 Douglas, "Talent and Vocation."
30 Ibid., 269; Cicero, *On Duties*, 1:30–4.
31 Davies, "Slavery and Protector Somerset," 540.
32 Starkey, *Dialogue*, 116–7 (Cowper, 176).
33 Ibid., 105 (Cowper, 158).
34 Ibid., 102–3 (Cowper, 155).
35 Ibid., 113–4 (Cowper, 171).
36 Ibid., 92–3 (Cowper, 139–40).
37 Ibid., 115–6 (Cowper, 171–2).
38 Ibid., 126–7 (Cowper, 190).
39 Ibid., 103, 106, 115, 136 (Cowper, 155, 159, 171, 204).

through public education and the restriction of expenditures, which he hoped would be sufficient to provide them with an expanded vision of the whole.[40] Even this, he admitted, would not be enough; the full realization of a Christian commonwealth of genuine love for one another required the working of grace ("hyt is not suffycent to bryng man to his perfectyon, but to that ys requyred a . . . celestial remedy . . . wych our Master Chryste cam to set and stablysch in the hartys of Hys electe pepul"),[41] and he explained that this would require the teaching of the gospel through well-educated preachers and the availability of the liturgy in English. Over time, these efforts could lead to the sanctification of the populace by allowing grace to do its work.

And so, by thys mean man fyrst inducyd by feare of punyschment and payne and by desyre of honest plesure and profyt by law prescrybd, schold be inducyed by lytl and lytl to thys perfectyon, that he for love only of vertue schold folow vertue, and for love of chryste, al plesure and payne set aparte schold folow chryst, and then at the last thys lyvyng in perfayt concord and cyvylyte schold attayne to the everlast-yng lyfe due to the nature of man ordeynyd to hym by the provydence of god in immortalyte.[42]

This is the position that "Pole" came to at the end of the *Dialogue*, and it was with this profession of *sola fideism* and the distinction between law and gospel that the work essentially came to rest. "Pole" wavered over the course of the *Dialogue* and earlier had stated the classical position that the formation of habits aided by the fear of punishment could bring one to love virtue for its own sake over time.[43] At the very end of the work, probably added later, Lupset's assertion that ambition "when men desyre honowre to theyr owne plesure or profyt" can be put aside by those "veray nobul hartys" that "ever desyre to governe and rule, to the commyn wele of the hole multy-tude" sounds oddly complacent and unworried, given the concerns over the corruption of the will aired throughout the book.[44]

A draft for an act written sometime after Starkey began working for Cromwell and that echoed Starkey's concerns, if not his solutions, illustrates many of the problems.[45] The draft called for the establishment of a court

---

40 Ibid., 124–5 (Cowper, 187).
41 Ibid., 138 (Cowper, 206–7).
42 Ibid., 141–2 (Cowper, 213).
43 Ibid., 97 (Cowper, 147).
44 Ibid., 142–3 (Cowper, 214–5).
45 Plucknett, "Some Proposed Legislation of Henry VIII." Elton considered the draft act on several occasions, including Elton, *Studies in Tudor and Stuart Politics and Government,*

of six judges, who would enforce the penal and popular statutes that had been enacted since 1485.[46] The draft called these judges "Conservators of the Commonweal," echoing a phrase of Starkey, though he envisioned the conservators as supervisors of lesser magistrates.[47] At the time there was no public prosecution for serious misdemeanors; the justices of the peace were empowered to investigate and try all misdemeanors, but this was considered insufficient. The enforcement of most misdemeanors depended on the bringing of civil suits by private individuals, called informers or promoters, who could bring actions of debt under the common law. If the court found in their favor, they could then, depending on the crime, keep or share with the government the statutory penalty. The draft act provided instead for a force of "sergeants" who would be authorized to seek out infractions of statutes and then bring the defendants to trial by jury in front of the court of conservators.[48]

The draft act shared Starkey's concern that the quality of justice needed to be improved, and there was a similar worry about "vexatious suits." But the approach to the law taken in the draft act was far closer to a position of "Lupset" that was shown to be erroneous by "Pole" in the *Dialogue*. In arguing for the nobility as the rightful administers of justice, the *Dialogue* committed to the notion that justice should be rendered as much as possible at the county level. "Pole" accordingly came out against what he perceived as the too frequent use of legal writs, which required that cases be heard in London, a well-known burden on defendants.[49] "Lupset," however, defended the use of writs:

> Syr as touching thys mater me thynke you dow amys, for you lay the faute wych ys in the party to the ordynance of the law for the parte ys to blame wych thys wyl vex hys adversary for hys plesure or profyt, but the ordynance of the law ys gretely to be alowyd, wych for bycause oft-tymys in the schyre by partys made by affectyon & powar materys are so borne & bolsteryd that justyce cannot have place, wyth indyfferency hath ordeynyd that by wryte the cause myght be removyd to London to indyfferent jugement, where as the partys be nother of both knowen nor by affectyon favoryd, therefore in the law touchyng thys behalfe I thynke there ys no faute at al.[50]

2:69–71, 245–6; Elton, *Reform and Renewal*, 140–1. See also Mayer, *Thomas Starkey and the Commonweal*, 201.

   46 Plucknett, "Some Proposed Legislation of Henry VIII," 125.
   47 Elton, *Studies in Tudor and Stuart Politics and Government*, 2:246.
   48 Plucknett, "Some Proposed Legislation of Henry VIII," 125–9.
   49 Starkey, *Dialogue*, 126–7 (Cowper, 190).
   50 Ibid., 78–9 (Cowper, 117).

The draft act, like "Lupset," was concerned to find "good and indiffer-
ente officers" to put "the said good and holsome Actis statuis and ordinancis
in a due charitable execucion." That is, it precisely specified the removal
of justice from the countryside to London for prosecution. The preamble
almost went out of its way to impugn the justice being served up by the
nobility in the localities: "the common weale of this his Realme susteyneth
and by a long tyme hathe susteyned no little hurte and dammage and sel-
dome is regardid or lokid unto in many and sundry partes of the Realme
aswell within liberties as without." The preamble emphasized that such centralized justice did not have a fiscal purpose—always a worry—and a clause
specified that the sergeants would pay back acquitted parties four times the
penalty.[51]

The draft act's approach was thus an adaptation both of Starkey's localized
penal approach to commonwealth and of Cromwell's preference for centralized new courts. The purview of Starkey's conservators included penal
laws of the sort that the draft act's conservators were charged with enforcing. But the method of prosecution imagined seems to have differed. Starkey's method was unspecified but was presumably some type of summary
judgment of the sort enjoyed by the justices of the peace outside of the
quarter sessions, since there was no mention of a trial of any kind, let alone
a trial by jury, and the punishment was specified as the imposition of fines.
Starkey's conservators were also responsible for the supervision of idleness
and occupation, tasks that were not assigned to the conservators in the draft
act.

THE REFORMATION AND THE PENAL LAW

Henry declared royal supremacy over the church in the early 1530s in a series of acts, and the government continued to offer defenses of this position
over the next few years. In the mid-1530s, these defenses used theological
ideas similar to those of the continental Reformers, and England was eagerly celebrated by the Reformers, who were hoping that England would
embrace their cause. This was especially true of Philipp Melanchthon and
Martin Bucer, who in the mid-1530s had high hopes of forming a league of
Protestant countries under a broad tent. Melanchthon dedicated the new
edition of his *Loci Communes* to Henry in 1535, and Bucer, who beginning
in 1535 followed the events in England closely, was thrilled when the English representatives to Schmalkalden, Edward Foxe and Nicholas Heath,
stopped at Strasbourg on the way, carrying with them *De Vera Obedientia* by

51 Plucknett, "Some Proposed Legislation of Henry VIII," 136.

the bishop of Winchester, Stephen Gardiner. Bucer hailed the work, which is the classic defense of Henrician supremacy, as part of a common project of reform, and arranged to have it printed at Strasbourg with an introductory letter of his own, which praised the efforts of the "true bishops," namely, Gardiner, Thomas Cranmer, Foxe, and Heath. In the same year, Bucer dedicated two of his own works, his commentaries on Romans and on the synoptic Gospels, to Cranmer and Heath, respectively.[52]

The English and continental Reformers shared a common Erasmian background, but this was fading for both parties by the 1530s as they moved further away from his more conservative vision of reform.[53] Erasmus had taught in his *Institutio Principis Christiani* (1516) that the Christian prince must rule in a Christian manner, that the state should be organized for the purpose of the common good or public peace, that the common good is moral or religious in nature, and that public peace requires true piety. The duty of princes was thus the moral and religious education of their subjects. Henry shared all of this and the broader Erasmian conception of the prince as following in the footsteps of the Old Testament kings, serving as Christ's representative, as the shepherd, the paterfamilias.[54] Though much of the Reformers' language would remain Erasmian, they were beginning to divide over the approach the magistrate should take in matters of religion. For Erasmus, the Christian magistrate had to use Christian means to achieve his ends. He summarized the approach in this passage in *Institution of a Christian Prince*:

> Authority is not lost to him who rules in a Christian way; but he maintains it in other ways, and indeed much more gloriously and more securely. You will be able to grasp that this is so from the following considerations. First, people you oppress with servitude are not really yours because it takes general agreement to make a prince. But in the end those are truly yours who obey you voluntarily and of their own accord. Next, when your subjects are compelled through fear, you do not possess even the half of them; their bodies are in your power, but their spirit is estranged from you. But when Christian charity binds

52 Gardiner and Janelle, *Obedience in Church and State*, xxv–xxvii.

53 Estes noted, "Melanchthon's views were hardly unique. The heavy reliance on Luther in the context of a continued adherence to the Erasmian ideal of a Christian commonwealth headed by a Christian magistrate who is responsible for the establishment of true religion and worship, and the routine use of the argument that true doctrine and worship are the best prophylaxis against disorder and rebellion, were typical of humanist[s]-turned-reformer[s] in the years immediately preceding and following the Peasants' Revolt." Estes, *Peace, Order, and the Glory of God*, 91.

54 Ibid., 57.

prince and people together, everything is yours whenever occasion demands.[55]

This embrace of peaceful methods, though self-evidently attractive, had started to founder in the 1520s as the Anabaptists challenged traditional sacramental practices and the peasants rose up in rebellion. Martin Luther and Melanchthon sided with the princes in sanctioning the use of violence, first in the instances of those whose behavior was outwardly seditious, but by the end of the decade they had come to believe that coercion could be used to enforce conformity in religious practice, regardless of the threat to external peace.[56] Many of the issues that would define the debate through the 1530s and 1540s, such as the expanding definition of treason and the use of the civil law as a means of justifying the penal law, were already emerging at this time.[57]

The Reformers increasingly took up the defense of the penal approach not only because of the threat of disorder from the Anabaptists, but because the introduction of the Reformation into civil law was beginning to be questioned on Erasmian grounds even by leading townsmen. In 1530 Erasmus himself had poured cold water on the approach of the Reformers in the cities: "I would prefer to bear the yoke of the most powerful emperor than of some evangelical magistrates, albeit of a humble sort."[58] Townsmen and city councillors, even in cities where the cause of the Reformation was very advanced, were relatively unconcerned about the lack of conformity in belief. In Bucer's Strasbourg, the city council had taken no steps against the Anabaptists who sought refuge there, and several leading citizens, including pastors and school headmasters, whom Bucer called "Epicureans," argued in a synod (called in 1533 to consider the question of the enforcement of conformity) that religious matters should be independent of governmental authority. Bucer strongly disagreed, arguing that the examples of Moses, Old Testament kings like Josiah, and Emperor Constantine showed that governmental authority could be used to enforce conformity.[59]

Furthermore, the Reformers responded that the civil—and penal—care of religion was a standard feature of ancient commonwealths. Bucer argued in his *Dialogi* of 1535, "Plato, Aristotle, Cicero, and others . . . really always give

55　Erasmus, *Collected Works*, 27:236.

56　Estes, *Peace, Order, and the Glory of God.*

57　Rowan, "Ulrich Zasius on the Death Penalty."

58　Erasmus, "Epistola contra Quosdam Qui se Falso Jactant Evangelicos," 1579B, cited in Kroon, *Studien*, 2: Malimque Caesaris potentissimi ferre jugum, quam quorundam Magistratuum Evangelicorum, quamvis humili sorte.

59　Estes, *Peace, Order, and the Glory of God*, 111–8.

the first place to the laws and ordinances of religion and worship."[60] Contrary to the claims of Erasmus and the Epicureans, the Reformers argued that the use of penal law was not opposed to the teaching of the New Testament or to the teachings of antiquity. The law of the Old Testament and the mercy of the New Testament were not in opposition; it was a form of mercy to punish injustice. This was also the teaching of antiquity, even of Plato, *the* utopian, who, Bucer added, taught that punishment was sometimes necessary to heal a sickness of injustice.[61]

For the Reformers, law was substantive; it was as much an education as an instrument of coercion and social order. There was no thinking about commonwealth without thinking about the law, because it was the divine law that taught God's will and what was pleasing to God.[62] In Melanchthon's formulation, there were three uses of the law: the civil, the accusatory, and the pedagogical. The pedagogical use of the law was important even to the regenerate since it taught them what was pleasing to God. The purpose of the law then was to serve not only as a means to realize an ideal state, but as a description of what that ideal state really looks like. The institutionalization of the law—the process of legislating—could have a sophisticated relationship to these uses of the law and to the teachings of the divine law. The aim was to achieve conformity with the divine law while taking account of fallen human nature. This in turn required a view of the moral psychology of unregenerate man.

60　Bucer, *Dialogi*, dialogue 7, sig. L4b: "Plato, Aristoteles, Cicero und andere . . . geben ja allwegen den gesetzen und ordnungen von der religion und Gottesdienst die erste stat." Cited by Kroon, *Studien*, 27n105, who identified the sources as Aristotle, *Politics*, 1328b; Plato, *Laws*, 907d–910d; and Cicero, *De Natura Deorum*, 1.2.3–4.

61　Kroon, *Studien*, 30, citing *Dialogi*, dialogue 7, sig. M4a; Plato, *Gorgias*, 479d.

62　There is some debate over this. Cornel Zwierlein argued that Bucer's approach to the law was essentially positive and historical and that Bucer's criterion was that whatever was true and right was divine law. Thus, "spricht Bucers Hochschätzung des Rechts der 'christlichen Kaiser' und vor allem und ganz grundsätzlich seine lex Dei-Konzeption, wonach eben auch das römische Recht Gottes Gesetz sein kann, also selbst der reformatorische Inhalt ist." Zwierlein, "Reformation als Rechtsreform," 73. This view was based largely on Bucer's works of the late 1520s, principally his commentary on the Psalms. By his Romans commentary of 1536, he preferred Paul's teaching in Romans 12 on morals to the work of other philosophers. Kok, "Influence of Martin Bucer," 143. It may be that both Bucer and Melanchthon were coming to this view by the mid-1530s. In the *Loci*, Melanchthon wrote: "I should like Christians to use that kind of judicial code which Moses laid down and many of the ceremonial laws as well. For since in this life we have to have judicial laws, and, it seems to me, ceremonial ones, it would be better to use those given by Moses than either the Gentile laws or papal ceremonies." Pauck, *Melanchthon and Bucer*, 126. But this seems to capture the direction that Bucer would take in the 1540s, exemplified in *De Regno Christi*, rather than Melanchthon's approach in the same period. Melanchthon continued to explore the parallels between the Decalogue and classical antiquity, an inquiry that, of course, was never abandoned by Bucer either.

Based on their study of classical moral psychology, the Protestants were in agreement that, given the fallen nature of humanity, the Stoics seemed too idealizing and had to be fully rejected.[63] Protestants were thus faced broadly with a choice between Epicureanism and Peripateticism. While many of the humanists of the early sixteenth century were eclectic, the Epicurean arguments for an ethical hedonism were taken very seriously thanks to Lorenzo Valla's *De Voluptate* (*On Pleasure*), which was finalized in 1449.[64] In his spirited defense of Epicureanism, Valla argued that no one pursued virtue for its own sake, but rather for the sake of some pleasure, usually honor.[65] It was extremely difficult to say why a man would give his life for the state, since he would scarcely exchange his life for that of a single other individual.[66] It turned out from a careful study of the great men and women who risked or sacrificed themselves, such as Mucius Scaevola, Regulus, and Lucretia, that they did so for glory, for the approval of others, or at least to avoid shame and disapproval.[67] This was true of *honestas*, which is derived from honor, and can be proven to be true of all the cardinal virtues, including justice and the law, which falls under justice. Valla suggested that the point of the law is to secure pleasure for the ruling class and for the people as a whole, not some abstract virtue. "The legislators themselves, which is to say the kings or chief persons of the state, promulgated the laws so as not to forfeit any of the greatness, stability, and tranquility of their rule (not to mention their fame): on the one hand, they gave rewards to encourage what was to the country's profit; on the other, they discouraged with punishments the introduction of anything harmful."[68]

Valla understood that the pursuit of honor could not be identified simply with social distinction, which obviously would only lead to social ruin and, more to the point, mental anguish. "All desire for fame derives from vanity, pride, and ambition. What is this except to want oneself to be above others or to regard others to be below oneself, which is the seed plot of all discord, hatred, and envy?"[69] This means that one should not take pleasure in the honor of "statues, tombs, funerals, and things of the kind," but rather in being trusted with an office, with leadership. "Why are we glad to be con-

---

63 Starkey referred to "the stoyke phylosophar, who never apperyd yet to the lyght, such vertue & wysdome ys attributyd to hym, that in no mortal man hyt can be found." Starkey, *Dialogue*, 18 (Cowper, 26).

64 Valla, *On Pleasure*, 25.

65 Ibid., 81–3, 129.

66 Ibid., 139.

67 Ibid., 149, 151, 153.

68 Ibid., 184–5: Etenim ipsi legum latores, ut qui essent aut reges aut viri in civitate primarii, ne quid de ipsorum imperii magnitudine, stabilitate, tranquillitate deperiret (missam facio gloriam), leges condiderunt, tum invitantes premiis animos ad prestanda commoda patrie tum deterrentes suppliciis ab importandis incommodis.

69 Ibid., 155.

sidered good, just, active? Surely so as to obtain authority and trust." This could mean being appointed a commander in war as a reward for one's abilities and virtues in battle or being a representative of some kind due to one's eloquence. But it could also mean being appointed to an office of a more conventional kind. "He is careful, hardworking and honest in administrative affairs; how can we do better than to assign the administration of our state to him?"[70]

The Christian humanists followed suit. Erasmus, for instance, explained in his *Adagia* that the logic of honor and preferment was in line with Christian teaching, arguing that the saying from the gospel that a lantern should not be hidden under a heap meant that "a good deed should not be hidden in silence in the dirt" and that the deeds of great men should be preached about as an example to others.[71] (Starkey made much the same point, echoing Erasmus, "For lytyl avaylyth vertue that ys not publysched abrode to the profyt of other, lytyl avaylyth tresore closyd in coffurys which never is communyd to the succur of other.")[72] Thomas More adapted Valla's defense of Epicurean moral philosophy in the political institutions of Utopia. Like Valla, the Utopians rejected Stoicism and embraced the ethical hedonism of Epicurus, acting in accordance with a similar hierarchy of pleasures.[73] They too thought that one should aim at the pleasure of others as a route to the highest mental pleasure: the "gratification of looking back on a well-spent life."[74] The greatest pleasure comes from the sacrifice of our own pleasure for others, since "[n]othing is more humane (and humanity is [the] virtue most proper to human beings) than to relieve the misery of others, remove all sadness from their lives, and restore them to enjoyment, that is, pleasure."[75]

The Utopians subscribed to Valla's philosophy of legislation as well. "They not only deter people from crime by penalties, but they incite them to virtue by public honors." Though the Utopians appreciated Valla's criticism of false honor, "the bent knee or bared head," they erected in the marketplace statues of distinguished men "to preserve the memory of their good deeds and to spur on citizens to emulate the glory of their ancestors," which for Valla was of public utility, if not a direct inspiration to individuals who wanted to be entrusted with authority.[76] In 1526, Erasmus in his *Adagia*

70 Ibid., 159, 166–7.

71 Erasmus, *Omnia Opera*, 2:290: Bonum peractum non esse in terra occultandum silentio.

72 Starkey, *Dialogue*, 4 (Cowper, 5).

73 More, *Utopia*, 163.

74 Ibid., 173.

75 Ibid., 163–5.

76 Ibid., 169, 194. More cited the formula from Aristotle and Valla, which was becoming the classic way of thinking about legislation, in slightly different language: Non poenis tantum deterrent a flagitiis, sed propositis quoque honoribus ad virtutes invitant.

identified this theory of legislation with Cicero's phrase *honos alit artes*.[77] But by identifying it not only with Cicero, but with Aristotle's statement that "honor is the reward for virtue," Erasmus made the view more generally classical than specifically Epicurean, as it was presented by Valla.[78]

The continental Reformers were humanists too, and while they were willing to embrace punishment for the effective maintenance of the commonwealth and the *cura religionis*, they hoped that conformity with the law could be achieved through other means. Erasmus's identification of the doctrine of incentives with Aristotle may have made it easier for Melanchthon to embrace it. For though Melanchthon thoroughly (and explicitly) rejected Valla's Epicureanism as "unworthy for good men, and especially Christians," he allowed the incentive approach to be taken in the law.[79] The reason that men seemed to need pleasure to incite them to virtue is that human nature is corrupt, fallen; in a perfect state, men would naturally be drawn to virtue regardless of any other pleasures.[80] Truly great men, like Socrates or Themistocles, deserved the glory heaped on them, but would have pursued the virtuous course regardless. These rewards might be sought as long as they did not conflict with virtue, for even God in the Bible offers rewards and punishments, though God is to be loved out of faith, not for the sake of reward.[81]

Melanchthon argued that though it is possible to control one's external behavior, "to greet a man or not to greet him," one has no control over emotions such as love and hate. It is, however, possible for "affection to overcome affection. For instance, Alexander of Macedon was a lover of pleasures, but because he was more zealous for glory, he spurned pleasures, and chose hard work, not because he did not love pleasures, but because he loved glory with more intensity."[82] It is possible to act contrary to one's desires, but if one does so, it will be nothing but a cold external show.[83] For genuine compliance, one needs to appeal to the emotions. Since a person's dominant emotion is self-love, and since self-love interprets the good in line

---

77 Cicero, *Tusculan Disputations*, 1.2.4.

78 Erasmus, *Omnia Opera*, 2:290: Et Aristoteles scribit honorem esse praemium virtutis. Ac priscorum leges, non solum comminabantur poenam maleficis, sed & praemiis & honoribus invitabant ad recte agendum. Erasmus, *Collected Works*, 174, adage 1.8.92. The *Collected Works* noted that the Latin translation was taken from Cicero, *Brutus*, 81.281. Aristotle, *Nicomachean Ethics*, 4.7, 1123b35.

79 Melanchthon, *Moralis Philosophiae Epitome*, 14: indigna bonis viris, ac praecipuae Christianis.

80 Ibid., 15.

81 Ibid., 22.

82 Pauck, *Melanchthon and Bucer*, 27.

83 Ibid., 28.

with one's own desires, a person's reasons for conforming with the law will differ according to individual ideas of the good.[84] "[A]s far as those who live outwardly good lives are concerned, is not one man drawn to these ways by an aversion for human affairs, another because of the fear of fate, another by ambition, and another by a love of tranquility?"[85]

So much of the question of the proper role of the state in the commonwealth depends on the extent to which one thinks that the state should be geared toward the regenerate or the unregenerate. For the Reformers, genuine sanctification could only take place as a result of a genuine faith and the subsequent gifts of grace. This meant that there could not be true sanctification in light of the internal emotional aspect of the law without faith. For Melanchthon, the fulfillment of the whole law was impossible without grace. The mistake of the earlier Christian humanists who rejected *sola fideism* was to think that a voluntary, spontaneous, uncoerced relationship between virtuous men of the sort described by the classical authors was truly a Christian commonwealth. Even if this were achievable, it would be a simulation of true Christian virtue, rather than the real thing, since friendship and the other social virtues would still be operating due to self-love.

Given the fallenness of humanity, it was preferable to ensure conformity with the law in its external aspect, and Melanchthon understood the teaching of the classical philosophers in moral philosophy and politics to be geared toward articulating the principles of the natural law with which fallen man could hope to conform. The classical philosophers taught various means of achieving conformity with this natural law—the virtues—but these are summarized in universal justice, which "embraces all of the virtues."[86] Melanchthon thus lavished attention on Aristotle's treatise on justice, book 5 of the *Nicomachean Ethics*, appending a commentary on it in his 1539 edition of the *Moralis Philosophiae Epitome*. Aristotle divided justice into two kinds, commutative and distributive. He explained that commutative justice is concerned with commercial transactions and should treat everyone equally, while distributive justice is concerned with rewards, punishments, and honors and needs to take the degrees of persons into account.[87] It is the latter kind that truly interested Melanchthon and that would prove so important for social and political theory. Indeed, the commentary included much of the vocabulary that would become important in the sermons on the commonwealth in the next decades. Melanchthon, for instance, explained that one of the names for the unjust man was *pleonektes*,

---

84 Ibid., 31–2.
85 Ibid., 35–6.
86 Melanchthon, *Moralis Philosophiae Epitome*, 183: quia complectitur omnes virtutes.
87 Ibid., 202.

"he who wants too much," a phrase that would echo throughout Latimer's sermons during Edward's reign.[88] It is well known that the distribution of goods was at the heart of Protestant appeals to the commonwealth during Edward's reign, but Melanchthon and his readers in England were concerned with the distribution not only of material goods, but of honor and esteem, and with the distribution of punishments as well. The Aristotelian theory of justice was thus not only a guide for the intervention of the state in the economy, but a blueprint for the commonwealth in all its senses, understood as a system of honors, as the arrangment of offices, as the disposition of the penal code.

The implementation of distributive justice was understood by Melanchthon to be both public and private in the insitutional sense, that is, conducted by magistrates holding office in a specifically political organization (*ordo politicus*), and in the moral sense, that is, for one's own ends or for the common good.

Unsurprisingly, it was the magistrates who were responsible for settling the matter of the nature of the penal code in a particular country. On the basis of the behavior of the people, they determined what sorts of punishment and reward were necessary to induce the people to conform with the law.

> The magistrate then is also concerned with distributive justice, since he compares multiple injuries and merits with each other, and arranges the degrees of merit, according to which he then conforms the degrees of rewards and punishments. Therefore both kinds are to be handled by the magistrate. Since in the punishment of a thief only the harm of personal loss is considered, the punishment will not be capital, since the harm was not capital. And since the degrees of harm and punishments are established, there will be many comparisons. Punishments are inflicted not really to cause harm, but to control men through fear. And because light punishments do not deter unruly men, the punishments should be made harder or softer in accordance with the nature of the men, just as a physician adjusts the medicine according to the nature of the patient. Therefore, the degree is set, namely, a light punishment for those crimes which seem to be able to be prevented in some way through a light punishment. Capital punishment is set for those crimes which otherwise could not be prevented among wild men. Such is the audacity of our men that other punishments for theft except for capital punishment would be completely laughable. Thus, while milder nations have milder pun-

---

88 Ibid., 184: qui plus appetit. Cf. Latimer, *Works*, 98; Bucer, *De Regno Christi*, 268, 270.

ishments, our men need harsher punishments on account of their barbarity.[89]

The proper approach of the state depended on the national character and culture.

> A worse crime ought to be controlled by a harsher punishment. Robbing a German is worse than robbing a Jew. For the most wild German nation does not allow itself to be controlled with light bonds. If those raving Germans who have a will to rob are to be prevented, they all have to be restrained by violence at the time they are raving. Therefore, it is necessary that robbing a German be prohibited not through a civil penalty as in the case of the Jews, but through capital punishment.[90]

The distribution of honors was a more complicated issue. It is clear that he often imagined honors as being distributed by the state. "In distributive justice," Melanchthon explained,

> geometric equality is preserved, that is according to proportion, as when a reward of two hundred gold coins is given to a private, and a statue is dedicated to a well deserving general. These are by no means equal. For sometimes a small statue is worth a hundred gold coins. And no amount of money is really equivalent in itself to a deserving leader. For what sufficient thanks can be given to that most brave Prince Frederick,

89 Melanchthon, *Moralis Philosophiae Epitome*, 197: Tunc autem consulit Magistratus distributivam iustitiam, cum multiplices iniurias aut merita inter se comparat, & gradus praemiorum & poenarum accommodat. Utraque igitur species Magistratui tradenda est. Cum in poena furti tantum aestimatur damnum laesae personae, poena non erit Capitalis, quia damnum non erat capitale. At cum gradus iniuriarum & poenarum constituuntur, multae fiunt comparationes. Poenae infliguntur, non proprie ad sarciendum damnum, sed ut metu contineantur homines. Et quia leves poenae non absterrent homines feroces, pro natura hominum poenae duriores aut leviores constituendae sunt, sicut medicus naturae aegrotantium pharmaca attemperat. Itaque constituitur gradus, scilicet poena levis in ea delicta, quae videntur aliquo modo prohiberi posse levi poena. Constituitur capitalis poena in ea delicta, quae aliter non possunt prohiberi inter homines feroces. In tanta audacia nostrorum hominum aliae poenae furti praeter capitalem prorsus irriderentur. Ideo etiam si gentes mansuetiores, habuerunt mitiores poenas, tamen nostris hominibus propter barbariam opus est durioribus poenis.

90 Ibid., 205: Atrocius delictum atrociori poena coherceri debet. Furtum germani est delictum atrocius quam furtum Iudaei. Nam haec ferocissima natio germanica non patitur se levibus vinculis coerceri. Ad haec fures germanici latrocinandi voluntatem habent, omnes enim inter furandum simul de vi cogitant, si deprehendantur. Igitur furtum germani non civili poena, sicut iudaicum, sed capitali poena prohiberi necesse est.

the Duke of Bavaria, Count Palatine, by whose counsel a defense was prepared against the Turks with the greatest speed when they attacked Austria in the year 1529 and Vienna was defended, a huge army was repelled, and removed from our throats. But because rewards are given out of one pile, as it were, they cannot be given so as to be equivalent to the service. For then there would need to be unending resources. Thus it is done in accordance with certain degrees, and a better reward is given to the meritorious of a higher degree.[91]

But this was only part of the story: "Private men use distributive justice when they observe the degrees of duties towards parents, children, friends, guests, gentlemen, commoners, or otherwise distribute proportionally from a given amount of a thing."[92]

Even if institutionally distinct, the use of the organs of the state for the implementation of the penal law was not obviously morally and spiritual public, as was maintained by the Anabaptists, who believed that the use of the courts and the holding of offices by Christians were forbidden. Melanchthon, unlike the Anabaptists, did believe that the establishment of a distinct political order ensured some insulation from the private desires for vengeance condemned by Scripture.[93] A distinct political order was divinely sanctioned and was composed of both the legal rights and duties and the order of magistracies.[94] Melanchthon conceded, however, that public and

---

91 Melanchthon, *Moralis Philosophiae Epitome*, 239: In distributiva iustitia servatur aequalitas geometrica, hoc est iuxta proportionem, ut cum gregario militi datur praemium aureo ducenti, duci praeclare merito decernitur statua. Haec nullo modo sunt paria. Nam & fieri potest, ut statua minoris valeat aureis centum. Et nulla quamlibet magna pecunia par est meritis ducis re ipsa. Quis enim parem gratiam reddere possit fortissimo principi Friderico Duci Bavariae, Comiti Palatino, cuius consilio summa celeritate praesidium contra Turcas cum irrumperent in Austriam Anno 1529 comparatum est, & defensa Vienna, & immanissimus hostis repressus & a cervicibus nostris depulsus. Sed quia velut ex uno acervo dantur praemia, non possunt dari paria meritis. Nam ad eam rem infinita copia opus esset. Ideo fiunt certi gradus, & melius meritis ex superiore gradu decernitur praemium.

92 Ibid., 198: Privati utuntur distributiva iustitia, cum gradus officiorum erga parentes, liberos, amicos, hospites, honestos, plebeios, observant, aut alioqui distribuunt proportione ex certo rerum cumulo.

93 Matthew 5:25, 5:40; Estes, *Peace, Order, and the Glory of God*, 76.

94 *CR*, 16:551: Longissime differunt haec, habere ius seu dominium, et habere defensorem magistratum. Sic in omnibus contractibus ius a Deo traditur iuxta praeceptum: Non furtum facies, item non facias inaequalitatem in emendo, vendendo, ponderibus etc. Sed magistratus est minister Dei ad executionem istius iuris. (Having a right or property is very different from having the defense of magistrates. Thus in all contracts the right is given by God according to the commandment, "thou shall not steal," so you should not introduce inequality into buying, selling, weights, etc. But the magistrate is the minister of God for executing this right.)

private intentions could be mixed up in the use of the public institutions of the state.

As Melanchthon understood it, the penal law was institutionalized in a manner that was all too susceptible to private motivations, namely, the bringing of legal actions in court. In a 1529 pamphlet on "whether it is permitted to Christians to litigate in court," Melanchthon asserted that it was as permissible for a Christian to use the courts as to drink or eat. For Melanchthon there was no theological differences among the various ways in which the "help" (*auxilium*) of a magistrate was enlisted.[95]

> And since it is permitted to a Christian to call for the magistrates in the street for defense against robbers; since it is permitted to call on them to be defended in war against enemies, why only in courts should it be impermissible to call on them? Thus it follows that it is permissible to make a complaint about an injustice with the magistrates, just as Paul appealed to Caesar.[96]

Luke 6 did not mean that it was forbidden to make a complaint in court in order to seek restitution for stolen goods, but it was forbidden to "recoup them through private force."[97] Magistrates in the courts were to be utilized through the "forms of accusation and action," which were the "nerves both of the laws and of the whole human society."[98] Melanchthon admitted, however, that the use of litigation was dangerous, that it was "necessary that there be a great force of charity in he who will litigate without ill will," and that good men would be hesitant to litigate.[99] Though the forms of legal action were a means to achieve justice for the unregenerate, who needed the threat of punishment to achieve conformity, this meant that legal actions were not all that different from the classical virtues, which did much the same.

> Thus the Athenian and Roman actions should be read as the doctrine of the virtues derived from the natural law as it were, or the teaching of our earliest fathers. These laws were very useful for regulating

95 Melanchthon, *Christianis*, sig. A4r: sicut Christiano licet uti cibo & potu, ita licet iuditiis uti.

96 Ibid.: Et cum liceat Christiano petere in publica via a Magistratibus defensionem adversus latrones: cum liceat in bellis petere, ut adversus hostes tegamur, cur in solis iudiciis, non licet defensionem petere? Consequitur igitur licere de iniuria queri apud Magistratus, item Paulus provocavit ad Caesarem.

97 Ibid., sig. A7r: vi privata recuperare.

98 Ibid., sig. A3r: Nervi sunt igitur & Legum & totius humanae societatis.

99 Ibid., sig. A7v: Necesse est magnum robur charitatis esse in eo, qui sine odio litigaturus est.

behavior, because they enjoined punishments, the fear of which compels middling minds and turns them to virtue. I wanted to discuss these actions so that people would really know that they are not only the formulas of litigators, but the philosophy and doctrine of virtue.[100]

Melanchthon's interest in legal actions was not unique in the Protestant camp. Johann Oldendorp, a professor of law who was a leading figure in the Lutheran reform movements in Rostock, Lubeck, and Cologne, emphasized the importance of legal actions a few years later.[101] It seems that some voices sympathetic to the radical Reformation were claiming that set formulas for legal actions only came into use with the early papacy and were outlawed by Constantine at that time. Melanchthon and Oldendorp argued that they were rather a classical instrument, in keeping with apostolic Christianity and the classical ideal. Oldendorp noted that the authority of actions "was given to the Praetors long before the time of the Emperor Constantine."[102] Melanchthon reinforced this message and fulfilled the project set out in the quoted passage above in his *Collatio Actionum Forensium Atticarum and Romanarum Praecipuarum* (*Comparison of the Principal Legal Actions of the Athenians and the Romans*) of 1546. This was not just a comparison of Athenian and Roman legal actions, as it sounds, but a categorization of some of the more notable actions of these traditions according to the Ten Commandments. Bucer had already begun to treat the Roman law in this fashion, though without treating the actions as actions per se.[103]

Both Melanchthon and Bucer correspondingly understood the role of the magistrates as custodians of the law.[104] A neat summary of Melanchthon's mature view of the magistracy (and how he saw it as relating to the classical view), already complete by 1539,[105] appeared in the introduction to one of the editions of the *Collatio*:

> God added magistrates to the laws, who have four chief duties. The first is that they should be the voice of the Decalogue in civil society.

100 Ibid., sig. B1r, v: Sic igitur legantur Atticae & Romanae actiones, tanquam doctrina de virtute sumpta ex lege naturae, seu a primorum patrum doctrina: multumque valebant hae leges ad regendos mores, quia poenae erant additae, quarum metus cohercet mediocria ingenia & ad virtutem flectit. Haec de actionibus praemonere volui, ut sciant studiosi eas non tantum esse formulas litigantium, sed Philosophiam & virtutis doctrinam.

101 For Oldendorp, see Berman, *Faith and Order*, 165.

102 Oldendorp, *Actionum*, 29: Denique & illi falluntur, qui referunt Tit. De formul. & impetra. [C, 2.58] ad tempora Pontificum Romanorum, a quibus primum impetrabantur actiones. Nam eorum authoritas diu ante Constantini Caesaris tempora, ad Praetorem translata fuit.

103 See, for example, Bucer, *Zum Ius Reformationis*, 107.

104 Pauck, *Melanchthon and Bucer*, 361; Bucer, *De Regno Christi*, 268.

105 For this judgment, see Estes, *Peace, Order, and the Glory of God*, 176.

II. That they should be the executors of punishments, and should punish those who commit crimes against the Decalogue, and they should correct many, as it is written: You should not forgive the homicide. For law without punishment is not valued. Thus the saying of Aeschines should be praised: "that there is no merit in a city that is nerveless in its dealings with malefactors."

III. It is the duty of the magistrate to add some of his own laws and interpretations which do not contradict divine law, but should be applications to particular circumstances, for example, the divine law requires that robbers be punished, but the magistrate determines the method of punishment.

IIII. It is a duty that the magistrate should be the executor of the punishments which are decreed in his laws.

These duties are included in the Aristotelian definition, which though short, nevertheless contains many requirements and ought to be understood correctly: The magistrate is the custodian of the law, namely in setting out the Decalogue and his own laws and in executing judgments, punishments, and just wars.[106]

Conceiving of magistrates in this way made it possible, as James Estes explained, for Melanchthon to argue that a magistrate should be the "custodian of both tables" of the divine law and thus for the promotion of the Reformation.[107] This may in part have motivated Melanchthon's interpretation of Aristotle's account of magistracy as an executor of the law rather than as a participant or shareholder in the government, as the usual reading of Aristotle's text suggests.

The precise dating of the influence of Melanchthon and Bucer on English political philosophy and policy is difficult. There is abundant evidence that Thomas Cranmer was heavily engaged with their works at least from

---

106 *CR*, 16.594–5: Addidit autem legibus Deus magistratus, quorum haec quatuor praecipua officia sunt. Primum ut sint vox decalogi in societate civili.

II. Ut sint executores poenarum, et puniant deliquentes contra Decalogum, et coherceant plurimos, sicut scriptum est: Non parcas homicidae. Lex enim sine poenis contemnitur. Quare laudatur dictum Aeschinis: οὐδέν ὄφελος πόλεως, ἥτις μὴ νεῦρ᾽ ἐπὶ τοὺς ἀδικοῦντας ἔχει [Demosthenes, 19.283].

III. Officium magistratus est, ut suas leges quasdam addat, et interpretationes, quae non pugnent cum divinis legibus, sed sint determinationes aliquarum cicumstantiarum, ut lex divina iubet fures punire, sed magistratus determinat modum poenae.

IIII. Officium, ut magistratus sit etiam executor poenarum, quae in suis legibus sanctae sunt. Haec officia comprehenduntur in definitione Aristotelica, quae quamquam brevis est, tamen multas commonefactiones continet, et recte intelligenda est: Magistratus est custos legum, videlicet proponendo Decalogum, et suas leges et faciendo executionem iudiciis, poenis et legitimis bellis.

107 Estes, *Peace, Order, and the Glory of God*, 153–4, 158.

the 1530s and, in the case of Melanchthon, most probably by the mid-1520s. Melanchthon sent Cranmer a copy of his 1525 commentary on Proverbs, and annotations that may be in Cranmer's hand are still visible in it.[108] Cranmer's *Great Commonplaces*, probably begun in the mid- to late 1530s, drew heavily on Melanchthon. Cranmer also owned a copy of Bucer's commentaries on Romans (with a dedication from Bucer himself, dated 1538) and, probably, on the Gospels, as well as the 1539 edition of Melanchthon's *Moralis Philosophiae Epitome*.[109] Moreover, the royal tutor Roger Ascham taught Princess Elizabeth theology from Melanchthon's *Loci Communes*.

The specific question of the role of the penal law in the Reformation of England came to a head in the debate over the Six Articles in 1539, a flashpoint between Stephen Gardiner's camp and that of Cromwell and Cranmer. Disagreement had been simmering for years, perhaps in part due to Gardiner's resentment over Cromwell's rise and Cranmer's appointment to the archbishopric of Canterbury over him.[110] The statute of the Six Articles required that those who denied traditional Catholic teachings on transubstantiation, communion, the marriage of priests, and confession would be punished severely: on the first instance with the confiscation of property, and on the second with death. Cromwell, perhaps wishing to append a poison pill, added a measure that priests and ministers should be punished with death for adultery or fornication.[111] Bucer and Melanchthon had included the punishment of adultery as part of the civil law of antiquity and identified it with the sixth commandment of the Decalogue. In his 1546 *Collatio*, Melanchthon adduced several ancient laws, Roman and Greek, that required the death penalty for adultery:

The accusation of adultery is described by a lex Julia of the Romans, called "an action for adultery" in Greek and the punishment for several old laws of the Athenians was capital punishment, as Pausanius writes. Later, capital punishment was not required by Solon's law for one who corrupted the wife of another through violence, but was rather marked by infamy and punished with whipped buttocks. But he who corrupts the wife of another through persuasion without violence is given capital punishment, as Lysias says clearly, and he gives the reason, that this is because a persuader corrupts both the mind and the body.[112]

108 Selwyn, *Library of Thomas Cranmer*, 62.
109 Ibid., 21, 127, 237–8; MacCulloch, *Thomas Cranmer*, 375.
110 Hudson, *Cambridge Connection*, 45.
111 Foxe, *Fox's Book of Martyrs*, 533.
112 *CR*, 16.604–5: Accusatio adulterii apud Romanos lege Iulia [*D*, 48.5; *C*, 9.9] describitur, Graece vocabatur δίκη μοιχείας, et poena veteribus legibus Atheniensium cuiuscunque adulteri fuit capitale supplicium, ut scribit Pausanias. Posteat lege Solonis, qui per vim

There was more at issue here than a difference over doctrine. Though Gardiner was clearly comfortable with the use of penal law for matters of essential doctrine, he saw a real distinction between his approach and that of the continental Reformers and their sympathizers in England. This difference became clear when Gardiner met Bucer at the Diet of Ratisbon in 1540. The Diet was an attempt by Emperor Charles V to reunite Christendom under his aegis, and Gardiner was there as a representative of England to argue that any such agreement should preserve the terms of Henry VIII's supremacy over the church in England, while Bucer was there as one of the representatives of the Protestants.[113] Gardiner granted Bucer an interview, and the two debated the marriage of priests within the broader context of a debate over the nature of obedience and secular authority. The debate seems to have run over several sessions at the diet, and Gardiner sent Bucer two memoranda during the debate so that his ideas would be clearly set out in writing.[114] The second of these is entitled "The Contempt of Human Law Made by Rightful Authority, Is to Be Punished More Heavily and More Seriously than Any Transgression of the Divine Law," and it is of great significance in distinguishing between the theory of Henrician supremacy and the commonwealth program of the 1540s.[115]

You answer nothing to my proofs, you merely deny that which is clearer than day, namely that the commonwealth is more disordered by the contempt of human laws, than by some transgression of divine law. Slothful, sluggish and idle fellows spoil themselves by their laziness; they infringe God's law, yet they do not touch the commonwealth, nor do they disturb it, still less do they cast it into confusion. But it is you who tread under foot all order, you who trample down the common weal, while you strive by covert ways to impair the authority of prices, and of their edicts, even if in your turn, you are willing to listen to the truth. You adorn the authority of princes

---

corrumpebat alterius uxorem, non afficiebatur capitali supplicio, sed notabatur infamia et puniebatur laceratis natibus. Ille vero, qui persuadendo sine vi corrumperat alterius uxorem, capitali supplicio adficiebatur, ut clare recitat Lysias, et rationem addit, quia persuasor et mentem et corpus corrumpit.

113 Gardiner and Janelle, *Obedience in Church and State*, xlii.

114 Ibid., xlii–xlix.

115 Printed and translated ibid., 173–211. The importance of this tract for understanding the opposition to commonwealth was noted by Jones, *Tudor Commonwealth*, 87: "Stephen Gardiner's main purpose in his Answer to Bucer (1541) appears to be the defence of a relatively circumscribed concept of the functions of government against the attempts of some doctrinaire Protestants—typified by Bucer—to load the temporal authority with the duty of enforcement of the moral precepts of the Church in economic and social matters, and to persuade princes 'to proclaim a penal law against every sin forbidden by divine law.'"

with magnificent words, yet only so long as they accommodate their laws to your own decisions, and follow your judgment in religious matters. You have not abolished the authority of Rome throughout the world, but you have appropriated it to yourselves, and transferred it to Wittenberg.[116]

Both Gardiner and Bucer agreed that the supreme magistrate was responsible for the *cura religionis*, but what this meant looked very different. Gardiner's position, like that of other conservatives who supported Henrician supremacy, embraced "functional specialisation," in which the clergy continued to play their traditional role of fostering spirituality and morality in the citizenry, just at the direction of the king.[117] For Gardiner, this meant that the ecclesiastical courts were responsible for upholding the divine law through their traditional, noncoercive methods. The special domain of the ruler in the *cura religionis*, according to Gardiner, was the determination of the things indifferent, the ceremonies and traditions. The ruler was to use his careful judgment of the attitudes of the people to their traditions and customs in order to legislate common practices for the church in nonessentials, such as fasting. The observance of these "human laws," as Gardiner refers to them, was extremely important, since any infringement was seen as contemptuous, betraying a willful disobedience of a law that the sovereign had explicitly legislated.

The clearest sign that Cromwell's camp had embraced Melanchthon's and Bucer's way of thinking about the state—which would mold the official commonwealth thinking of the Somerset protectorate—was John Hales's *Oration on the Commendation of Lawes* of 1540.[118] Hales had been a client of Cromwell from 1534 and, after his fall in 1540, sought the patronage of the lord chancellor, Thomas Audley, with whom Cromwell had worked closely. Hales hoped that the *Oration* and a translation of Plutarch's *Moralia* would secure it.[119] The *Oration* shows many traces of Melanchthon's influence. Above all, Hales takes the position that the common laws of England were derived from the Ten Commandments, and he understood royal supremacy as "grounded and consonant with the law of nature and the word of God."[120] Though Christopher St. German in the 1520s and Starkey in the early 1530s had certainly held that the exertion of royal prerogative through equity, dispensation, and proclamation was consistent with higher

116 Gardiner and Janelle, *Obedience in Church and State*, 209.

117 Cromartie, *Constitutionalist Revolution*, 71.

118 This work has never been printed. It survives in two manuscripts: BL Harleian MS 4990 and in the Free Library of Philadelphia, Carson Collection, MS LC 14.32(1). Baker, *History of the Laws of England*, 895.

119 Schurink, "Print, Patronage, and Occasion, 94."

120 Hales, *Oration*, fol. 17v, cited in Spelman, *Reports*, 33; Cromartie, *Constitutionalist Revolution*, 55.

law, Hales's arguments in the *Oration* reflected a more precisely tuned legal theory in which divine law had more substantive content, namely, as Gardiner complained in the same year to Bucer, the divine law as understood in Wittenberg. This was suggested in Hales's reading of equity:

> The civil law commandeth and willeth that if I give my knife . . . to another to keep, he shall re-deliver that when I ask it. This is reason. But if in the mean season I fall out of my wit, then saith the civil law ye may keep it, for it is to be thought I would kill myself therewith. And this exception they take for an example geometric, whereunto I agree not for this is but an inferior law.[121]

Here, Hales took the position of Melanchthon, in which equity (*epieikeia*) was understood as a clash between a superior and an inferior law, rather than as it was understood by jurists like Guillaume Budé, who saw equity as the application of "geometric" justice, that is, justice that attended to the particular circumstances of a case.[122] The different legal theories reflected different views of the legal basis of commonwealth and showed where the Cromwellians were headed and how they had come so far from Gardiner. They now viewed the commonwealth not as the best efforts of a monarch to administer justice in accordance with custom and tradition, but as a kingdom of Christ to be realized on earth. And as Melanchthon would add, "And laxities cannot be accepted against natural and divine law."[123]

Yet, even if the approach of Audley and Cromwell to the state was coming to seem similar to that of the continental Reformers, it nevertheless had a different idea of the role of the state. The English legal reforms of 1539–40, which Audley initiated in the House of Lords and which were probably developed in consultation with Cromwell, were not as enthusiastic about legal actions as Melanchthon's and Oldendorp's writings, to say the least.[124] While Audley and Cromwell would not have denied the importance of legal actions, or that they were legitimate for Christians, the point of many of the reforms was to limit the reach of the courts. For instance,

---

121 Quoted in Cromartie, *Constitutionalist Revolution*, 54–5.

122 For the echoes of Melanchthon, cf. *CR*, 16.75: Cum enim concurrunt diversae leges, quae pariter servari non possunt, praeferenda est superior, ut, si quis apud te sanus gladium deposuerit, eumque reposcat furiosus, lex inferior iubet reddere, at lex superior vetat nocere furioso, videlicet: Neminem laedas. Ideo reddi gladium vetat. (For when different laws clash which cannot be equally upheld, the superior is to be preferred, so that, if someone who is sane deposits a sword with you and then becomes insane, the inferior law requires that it be returned, but the superior law prohibits harming a madman, namely, "harm no one." Thus it prohibits returning the sword.) Kisch, *Erasmus*, 207.

123 *CR*, 16.75: Nam contra iura naturae et contra ius divinum non sunt concedendae laxationes.

124 For the reforms, see Lehmberg, *Later Parliaments*, 96–7.

one of Audley's measures, which was successfully taken up in Parliament, extended the rights of tenants in fee tail, so that their leases were as good as those made in fee simple.[125] This measure ensured that the tenant in fee tail could not be ejected from his property as easily as before upon the succession of inheritance of the owner of his lease. The tenant was thus protected from a use of the law, from a legal action that could be taken by the new owner.[126] Moreover, a statute of 1540 imposed limitations on several sorts of action, which now had to be brought within fifty or sixty years. This included the writ *de nativo habendo*, which by this date was essentially exercised by landlords to extort fees for charters of manumission from well-off farmers of villein status.[127] This statute was based on a 1539 proposal of Cromwell to confirm the possession of those whose ancestors had held land for forty years without challenge.[128] The concern was clearly with improving the status of the middling and lower sorts, but status was understood here not so much as the liberty to use the courts but to be more immune from their vexatious use. The attitude toward the state (and its relationship to the Christian commonwealth) reflected in these measures was closer to that of Colet and Erasmus than to the Protestant Reformers.

SOMERSET'S COMMONWEALTH

In the historiography of commonwealth, the golden age has been the protectorate of Somerset in the first few years of the reign of Edward VI before the crises of the summer of 1549. It was in these years that Hugh Latimer thundered about covetousness in his court sermons and John Hales introduced legislation to rectify enclosure. But there are several puzzles in the historical record that have led scholars to conclude that the efforts at social policy and the views of the writers urging them on were a hopeless muddle, to the extent that the proponents of Somerset's policies have been seen as "simpliste" and "grossly impracticable and inept and totally ignorant of what was possible."[129]

One of the first acts in the parliamentary session of November and December 1547 was to pass a harsh law against vagrancy.[130] This seems like an odd beginning for an administration that would become famous for its "popular" politics, but this action illustrates one of the central tensions in how

---

125 Ibid., 96.

126 Holdsworth, *History of English Law*, 4:486–7.

127 Ibid., 3:508.

128 Lehmberg, *Later Parliaments*, 97.

129 Elton, "Reform and the 'Commonwealth-Men' of Edward VI's Reign," 251–3; Bush, *Government Policy of Protector Somerset*, 48; Davies, "Slavery and Protector Somerset," 544.

130 Bush, *Government Policy of Protector Somerset*, 43.

to think about labor in a commonwealth. As C.S.L. Davies explained, the provisions of the vagrancy law were remarkably harsh. It specified that able-bodied men and women who were found "lurking" or "loitering idly" rather than working for three days or more could be brought before two JPs, declared to be vagabonds, branded with the letter V, and made the slave of the informant for two years.[131] The act does not seem to have been the government's initiative, but the law was adopted by Somerset after its passage.[132] Davies must be correct that the inspiration for this law was a Roman law of the Theodosian Code that later appeared in the *Code of Justinian*.[133] The law was the basis for discriminating between the able-bodied poor and the helpless poor for centuries, and it provided the precedent for a series of laws implemented in Paris that required the able-bodied poor to labor in public works.[134] (It was this approach that the authors of the draft law of 1535 surely had in mind.) Melanchthon reported approvingly that the Greeks had several laws against idleness, but they were gentler than the English law of 1547, punishing idleness with infamy, and Melanchthon seems ignorant of a corresponding Roman law.[135]

It is true that Bucer would later urge Edward VI to "renew the law of God and of the emperor Valentinian that no one should be permitted to beg, but that those who are able to sustain themselves by their labors should be compelled to work and not be taken care of by the churches," mentioning this law by name, but it is also clear that he was envisioning a very different approach to poor relief.[136] Bucer was concerned about begging by the able-bodied poor not so much as a threat to disorder, but as an indirect threat to the Reformation in England. He feared that they would draw off church funds that could be used for the education and support of proper ministers to preach the gospel in England, which he thought was sorely lacking.[137]

---

131 Davies, "Slavery and Protector Somerset," 534.

132 Ibid., 537.

133 Ibid., 543–4, citing *C*, 11.26.

134 Lucas de Penna, *In Libros Codicis*, on l. un. C. de mendicant. valid. [*C*, 11.26]; Azo, *Summa*, 252.

135 Melanchthon, *CR*, 16.607.

136 Pauck, *Melanchthon and Bucer*, 311; Bucer, *De Regno Christi*, 147.

137 "If we wish Christ to rule us as he did the ancients and the early church then the church, like all the other groups of men, and the state should each have their own treasuries and their own funds, and this should be sufficient for those things which I listed as necessities." Letter of Bucer to William Bill, November 17, 1550, in Harvey, *Martin Bucer in England*, 155: si volumus Christum apud nos regnare, ut sicut apud veterem populum et priscas ecclesias fuit, et nunc ecclesiae, sicut caetera hominum corpora omnia, et res publica habent suum aerarium, suas proprias opes; et quantae ad eas, quas enumeravi necessitates, satis sint, quas qui invadet, aut aliquid sibi inde venditet, supra quam ei opus sit, ad ecclesiis recte ministrandum, vel ad studia, quibus se ad ecclesiarum ministeria, bona fide, praeparet; aut ad vivendum Domino, cum proprio se labore alere ipse plane non possit, sacrilegium committat,

What is so striking about the literal implementation of the Roman law in this act, aside from the enslavement of the idle, was that they were enslaved to the informers who brought notice of their behavior to the JP. The activity of informers, though deplored by some, had been growing in the previous years, and 1547 set a record for the most informations recorded at the exchequer for some twenty-five years, including a significantly larger number for marketing offenses.[138] The replication of the Roman law may have owed much to the feeling that the enforcement of commonwealth measures was only gaining traction through the use of informers. This required something of an admission that the state needed to appeal to self-love, that it needed to be available as a resource for private profit in order to overcome the substantial burdens, financial and social, that kept men from bringing public-interested suits. Latimer, the greatest of the commonwealth preachers of Edward's reign, would call for this approach a few years later: "For God's sake make new promoters!" These should be used to inform on "transgressors, oppressors of the poor, extortioners, bribers, usurers."[139]

Somerset accepted this compromise with the self-love of informers on behalf of the government, but it was not because he wished to give up on the liberty approach of Cromwell and Audley and the hope that the oppressed could bring their own suits against oppressors. Somerset pursued the liberty approach in his private holdings, upgrading the leases of some of the tenants of will on his lands, who had no recourse in the law against him except concerning the "safety of his crops." In a private parliamentary act of 1548, he converted the leases to customary copyholds, which gave his tenants "the additional protection of manorial custom, a means of personal action at common law and final redress in equity."[140] It was this pursuit of liberty that would be the grounds of Somerset's eventual downfall, since it became associated with undue "popularity." After Somerset's tumble from power, it was claimed that he, now on the outs, meant to rebel if made des-

---

sicut committat peculatum, qui publica bona, in alium usum quam rei publicae convertit, et furtum, aut rapinam, qui privata attrectat bona invito possidente.

138 Beresford, "The Common Informer," 223.

139 Latimer, *Works*, 242, quoted in Beresford, "The Common Informer," 222. I find it more plausible that Latimer was influential in the acceptance of this act by the government, if not its formulation, than in the draft act of c. 1534 on the conservators of the commonweal discussed above, as Beresford argued (222). As Davies, "Slavery and Protector Somerset," 538, noted, there is no evidence that Latimer or the other preachers disavowed this act, despite their criticisms of other government policies, and it seems in line with his later view of promoters. The draft act of c. 1534, on the other hand, was specifically opposed to the use of informers and took care to distinguish the sergeants from the informers. It is possible that c. 1534 Latimer was enthused by the idea of the sergeants as public-spirited promoters, but seeing the effect of the old sort of promoters since then, especially in the mid-1540s, came to embrace them. This seems less likely to me, however.

140 Bush, *Government Policy of Protector Somerset*, 55–6; Jones, *Tudor Commonwealth*, 33.

perate, calling out to the apprentices to rise up by shouting "Liberty!"[141] Somerset's concern for personal status did not mean the dissolution of hierarchy, however. His intent was rather "to give to the subjects a little more reasonable liberty without in any way releasing them from the restraints of proper order and obedience," as he informed the imperial ambassador, and the conversion of the tenancies at will to customary copyholds still meant that his manorial court would be the court of first instance for any complaints made under this new status.[142]

If John Hales was already identifying the approach of the continental Reformers with the commonwealth efforts of Cromwell and Starkey by 1540, this connection was only strengthened during Somerset's protectorate. Somerset's view, for instance, was identified with the Reformers' approach to the Ten Commandments by Thomas Hooper in his *Declaration of the Ten Commandments*, written when Hooper was in exile in Zürich.[143] Hooper's central views on theology were close to those of Zwingli and Bullinger, but his understanding of the social teachings of the church drew from Melanchthon and Bucer as well, and it is likely that the *Declaration* drew on Melanchthon's exposition of the Decalogue in his catechism.[144]

Hooper had formed a relationship from abroad with Somerset as of 1547, and there must have been a sense that he, Hales, and Somerset were embarked on a common project to realize a Christian commonwealth in keeping with Protestant teachings. In the *Declaration*, for instance, he prohibited the keeping of private parks for hunting under the heading of the eighth commandment, "thou shall not steal." He wrote there, "I refer it to the charity of every man, whether the keeping of such beasts be not against God's laws and man's laws, and whether it be not suffered rather for a few men's pleasure, than for many men's profit."[145] The introduction of parks into the more conventional discussion of property contextualized one of the first measures of Somerset's government in 1548, the disparking of the chase at Hampton Court, within the continental Reformers' understanding of the law.[146]

---

141 Pollnitz, *Princely Education*, 195.

142 Davies, "Slavery and Protector Somerset," 537; Bush, *Government Policy of Protector Somerset*, 56.

143 For the relationship between Hooper and Somerset, see Bush, *Government Policy of Protector Somerset*, 68, 108–9.

144 The organization of the *Declaration* tracked that of Melanchthon's *Catechesis Puerilis*, with a discussion of the nature of the law before the exposition of the particular commandments. The discussion of the uses of the law in the *Declaration* (281–5) was especially Melanchthonian, but there were other close verbal resemblances, such as the account of the origin of commerce (*Declaration*, 392; *Catechesis*, 51r) and the responsibility for providing for clergymen under the heading of the prohibition against stealing (*Declaration*, 395; *Catechesis*, 49v).

145 Hooper, *Early Writings*, 390.

146 Bush, *Government Policy of Protector Somerset*, 43.

The disparking was easily achieved by the government, but the broader question of the best way to use the magistracy, the state, to further the goal of realizing a Christian commonwealth continued to be elusive. Providing for the liberty, that is, the expanded legal standing of tenants was insufficient to address the problems of enclosure and the rising prices of foodstuffs. Latimer recalled the difficulty of bringing effective suits: "I remember mine ownself a certain giant, a great man, who sat in commission about such matters; and the townsmen should bring in what had been inclosed, he frowned and chafed, and so hear looked and threatened the poor men, that they durst not ask their right."[147] The result was the introduction in 1548 of the enclosure commissions, which established juries of presentment to inquire into the compliance with several statutes, principally concerned with the conversion of tillage to husbandry. This first round of commissions was barely implemented, even with this limited mandate, and in 1549 a second round of commissions was introduced, which seems to have had the power to hear and determine.[148] The use of offices for the effecting of policy was thus imagined in a number of ways during Somerset's protectorate: the top-down approach of the enclosure commissions, the encouragement of presentments through the use of informers, and the encouragement of bringing lawsuits by tenants. This institutional variation—more or less participatory—was understood in the still broader context of the rewards and punishments of distributive justice.

LOVE AND FEAR

The various attempts to use the state to combat greed and injustice and to require the energetic fulfillment of one's vocation may seem to run from pillar to post, but they were largely the result of the government striving to find an effective approach in the face of a largely uncooperative citizenry. The central tension between coercion and neighborly love, however, was not so much the product of the setbacks in the legislative program of the government, but was a cornerstone of Somerset's approach to politics. This was recognized by Bush, who saw the alternation between indulgent clemency and unrelenting force as the pattern that unified many of Somerset's actions and that so alarmed his critics. Somerset had a "tendency to offer clemency before using force as a means of getting his way, a tactic he used to deal with his brother, peasant rebels, offenders against the agrarian laws, religious dissidents and the Scots."[149] This dynamic has been observed in

147 Latimer, *Works*, 248.
148 Bush, *Government Policy of Protector Somerset*, 46–8.
149 Ibid., 160.

more detail in the alternation between violence and negotiation in Somerset's dealings with Kett's rebels.[150] What might not yet be sufficiently appreciated is that Somerset almost certainly thought that in doing so he was following the instructions of classical antiquity, chiefly Cicero's teaching on love and fear in *De Officiis*.

Somerset's approach was reflected in one of the school orations set for King Edward by his tutor John Cheke, formerly the Regius Professor of Greek at Cambridge, on the famous Ciceronian question of whether it is better for a king to rule by love or fear.[151] Erasmus had weighed in definitively on the side of love in his commentary: "it is most useful for those who are ruling to be loved by all; to be feared is both wicked and less secure."[152] Edward, however, began his oration, probably in 1550 or early 1551, by saying that a ruler needed both love and fear, "since it is necessary and very useful for all those who have at some point the care of either a people, a state, or an army, to be able to know how to attract the minds of men to the good and to deter them from evil."[153] On the other hand, "[f]ear compels them to benefit others and to obey by violence; love attracts them to obey through their will."[154] Edward's explanation was much more psychological than what appears in *De Officiis*. Indeed, as Edward explained, the study of psychology shows that "love is the greater cause" of obedience, since the emotion of love persists as long as the object of love does, while fear lasts only as long as the threatened punishment or evil is directly in front of the subject.[155] His portraits of the emotions of love and fear were, respectively, of a durable sentiment and a fleeting but intense passion. His account of love was Aristotle's theory of friendship: "for love is an emotion of the soul, which arises from some good opinion about some concept or from a familiarity between men which is extended towards him who is loved for his own sake, not for the sake of some profit or pleasure of the one who

---

150 Shagan, "'Popularity' and the 1549 Rebellions," 125–6; Santschi, "Obedience and Resistance," 142.

151 On Edward's education, see Baldwin, *William Shakspere's Small Latine and Lesse Greeke*; Needham, "Sir John Cheke"; Pollnitz, *Princely Education*; Cicero, *On Duties*, 2.23.

152 Cicero, *Ad Marcum Filium de Officiis*, 145r: Utilissimum iis qui cum imperio sunt, ab omnibus amari: metui, tum turpe, tum minime tutum.

153 Baldwin, *William Shakspere's Small Latine and Lesse Greeke*, 251: necessarium est & ualde utile omnibus ijs qui aliquam curam habent, aut nationis, aut ciuitatis, aut exercitus, cognoscere quo modo possint & hominum mentes attrahi ad bonum, & deterreri a malo. For the dating of the orations, see Needham, "Sir John Cheke," 202.

154 Baldwin, *William Shakspere's Small Latine and Lesse Greeke*, 251: Timor eos cogit ad benefaciendum & parendum idque ui; Amor eos allicit ad parendum idque uoluntate.

155 Ibid., 252: unde et uideri potest, amorem tam diu permanere posses, quamdiu ille qui amatur existit, timorem solum manere ad tempus, quamdiu quis habeat supplicium & malum imminens prae oculis.

loves."¹⁵⁶ His account of fear was substantively that of Aristotle's *Rhetoric*, elaborated slightly by Cicero's definition in the *Tusculans*: "But fear is a certain movement of the mind, stirred by some sudden or imminent future evil, by which everyone is deterred from doing evil, and fears, lest if he should commit some evil act, he be punished at once. Hence pallor, agitation, or something similar often arises."¹⁵⁷

Edward understood these emotions in light of the evangelical teaching on sanctification. In his notes for the orations, he listed as arguments twice that "our nature is corrupt," and he argued in line with the evangelical position that the fallen human nature was not made whole once again with the coming of Christ, that people are incapable of following the law of God "out of pure emotions," namely, the love described by Paul in Romans, and that it is not possible for people to live without sin in this life.¹⁵⁸ In 1551, he took the usual anti-Stoic position that the goods of fortune were worth pursuing. Life should not be spent in pursuit of the pleasures of the senses. People should rather pursue the higher pleasures of honor and, even more, of the reward of the next life for a life lived well. "For indeed, there is no one among men who naturally does not take pleasure when he is praised, and is saddened if he should [be] defamed and criticized. Nor should this altogether be attributed to corrupt nature."¹⁵⁹ True glory, which is the praise of good men, is to be pursued. Those who pursue only the simple pleasures and pastimes will not be remembered. "Who can remember anyone for hunting or birding, which are very pleasurable, though there were many who were outstanding at hunting, or who has really attained some good or virtue, when he has spent his whole life occupied with playing, hunting, birding, playing cards, dancing, and other games of this kind which are very often immoderate, wicked, and hateful?"¹⁶⁰

156 Ibid., 251: Amor est animi affectus, qui oritur, ex bona aliqua opinione de aliquo concepta, aut ex familiari consuetudine inter homines, qui extenditur erga eum qui amatur sui causa, non alicuius lucri causa aut uoluptatis eius qui amat.

157 Aristotle, *Rhetoric*, 2.5.1, 1382a. Baldwin, *William Shakspere's Small Latine and Lesse Greeke*, 252: Timor est autem animi quidam impetus, excitatus ex repentino aliquo malo futuro, uel imminenti, quo quis deterretur a male agendo, & ueretur, ne si quid malum perperret [perpetret], statim supplicio afficiatur. Hinc sepe pallor, exanimatio, ceteraque simila oriuntur. For *pallor* and *exanimatio*, see Edward's 1548 excerpts from the *Tusculans*, BL Arundel MS 510, fol. 18r. Compare the Stoic language he recorded in his notes on the *Tusculans*, which suggested the unreality of the emotions, that they were merely opinion, 15r: Metus est opinio magni mali impedentis, & aegritudo praesentis mali; 195, 19r: Aut aegritudo est opinio praesentis mali sic metus futuri.

158 Edward VI, Orations, fol. 222r–v: Natura nostra est corrupta . . . simul cum puris affectibus.

159 Ibid., fols. 38v–39r.

160 Ibid., fols. 2v–3r: Quis enim potest indicare memoriam alicuius venationis & aucupationis in quibus capitur maxima voluptas (quanquam plaereque fuerunt insignes tum venationes), aut quis omnino aliquod bonum aut honestum adeptus est cum totum tempus vitae

Fear cannot explain great works of attachment to the state; because it motivates by fear of punishment, the state can scarcely be said to motivate a person to give his life for the common good. "I have never heard that anyone ever gave his life out of fear, because fear belongs only to punishment, and since death is the extreme and the greatest of all of these, then all fear shuns death, and it is not necessary that he die for the sake of his country."[161] It was the desire for glory that was the incentive to virtue. "Moreover, everyone has a natural love for glory, desiring it, but fleeing from disrepute. Therefore, there can be no greater or more weighty punishment, especially for a virtuous and good man, than to be afflicted by disrepute and shame. Therefore, all who [have] this natural spark of virtue will not be lost in their heinous crimes, and who know that if they were wicked they would be shamed, wish, deterred by this fear, to abstain from these crimes which otherwise they might commit."[162] In keeping with this psychology, Edward recalled the now familiar approach to legislation: "Nothing is more necessary for all of those who govern and have care of commonwealths and great nations than that they should inflict punishment on the wicked and give rewards to the good, so that the good are led to good works through the promise of reward, and the wicked deterred from the bad deeds by the fear of punishment, and in this manner order and quiet are preserved in commonwealths."[163] Kings and other rulers thus act toward their subjects like fathers to their sons, using both love and fear, but love above all. Even when a father punishes his son, it is out of love "lest he should fall into worse crimes on other occasions."[164]

---

contulerit & collocaverit in lusum venationem aucupationem lusum chartarum, saltationem aliosque iocos eosdem generis quae sepissime sunt immoderata mali & odiosi?

161 Baldwin, *William Shakspere's Small Latine and Lesse Greeke*, 252: Timoris autem causa neminem unquam audiui morti se tradere, quia supplicij solum est timor, & cum mors extremu, & omnium maximum sit, tum omnem timorem mortem euitare, & non patriae causa eam oppetere necesse est. For the humanist background, see, for example, Valla, *On Pleasure*, 141–3.

162 Edward VI, Orations, fols. 94v–95r: Praeterea unusquisque habet naturalem quendam amorem erga gloria, eam appetens, infamiam autem fugiens. Quocirca nullum maius aut gravius supplicium, honesto & bono viro praesertim, esse potest, infamia aut ignominia affici. Hi igitur omnes qui hanc naturalem scintillam virtutis, suo nefando scelere non perdiderunt, & qui sciunt se malefacientes hac ignominia fore affectos, volunt hoc timore deterriti, abstinere ab illis sceleribus quae alias fortasse committerent.

163 Ibid., fols. 44–45: Nihil magis est necessarium, his omnibus qui Rerumpublicarum & nationum magnaru[m] gubernacula atque curam tenent quam ut se malos suppliciis afficiant, bonos autem pr[a]emiis donent, ut boni spe praemii ad bona adiciantur; mali metu supplicii a malis deterreantur, et hoc modo in Rebuspublicis ordo et quies servetur.

164 Baldwin, *William Shakspere's Small Latine and Lesse Greeke*, 252: Adhec si tales debent esse reges erga subditos, quales patres erga filios, ut eodem genere officii gubernatores, quo patres, & subditi, quo filij, tum certe alterutra debent uti, sed magis amore.

The attempt to balance the Erasmian approach with the penal approach of the continental Reformers was expressed not only in Somerset's swings in political action, but even in the legal expressions of the government, the proclamations. Bush noted that the proclamations of this period were notable for "the frequency with which they promised rewards and issued terrible threats."[165] Most of these rewards were payoffs for informers where the statutes did not provide for forfeiture; they were really part of the penal process and thus cannot be counted as rewards for good behavior in the sense of love being opposed to fear in the contemporary discussions of the Ciceronian question.[166] There was, however, at least one case of a reward for good behavior: the promise of employment in the Royal Navy for those "honest mariners, soldiers, and others who have so perforce served under the said pirates" who were willing to leave the life of piracy behind.[167]

The use of rewards here cannot really be said to be realizing the ideal of commonwealth; they were either remuneration for information on vagrants and rebels or the buying off of former pirates. This was clearly the attainment of civil order, though perhaps the promise of a new life for the former pirates offered a greater possibility for repentance. The use of fear outside the statutory framework seemed to run even more firmly against the commonwealth ideal of the mutuality of neighborly love. Fear and other negative emotions were understood in the hedonistic moral psychology of the humanists to be paralyzing and fracturing, rather than motivating or redeeming. In the Protestant psychology of the law, fear that was yoked to the legal system nevertheless played a redemptive role through its accusatory and pedagogical functions; it instructed subjects about the nature of humanity and human relations through the use of penalties attached to the divine law.

The use of terror in a nonstatutory, or extralegal, sense was thus highly problematic from the point of view of realizing a Christian commonwealth. It seemed to indicate an abandonment of all hope of the higher uses of the law and a reversion to pure violence for the keeping of civil order. Such violence was nevertheless becoming the frequent practice of princes in the face of rebellions, and it had been sanctioned by Luther, Melanchthon, and many others after the Peasants' Rebellion in Germany in 1525. Erasmus was sorely disappointed by the repression that year and lamented, "I see that human affairs are headed towards a kind of Turkish barbarity, and per-

---

165 Bush, *Government Policy of Protector Somerset*, 156.

166 Cf. ibid. This was the case for Hughes and Larkin, *Tudor Royal Proclamations*, nos. 281 (seditious rumors), 337 (rumormongers), and 339 (western rebels, though this case was more complicated, as I discuss below).

167 Hughes and Larkin, *Tudor Royal Proclamations*, 1:437n317.

haps there are princes who are not displeased by this state of affairs."[168] Luther, Melanchthon, and Johannes Brenz, however, argued that the violent conduct of the peasants meant that they deserved to be treated with violence and their serfdom should be maintained.[169] The rebels in England in 1549 echoed many of the demands made by the German peasants in the Twelve Articles (1525), and they were answered using many of the same arguments.[170]

Thus John Cheke in his *Hurt of Sedicion*, a response to the rebels, simultaneously reminded them of the duties they owed to their king as lord, while stressing their duties as members of a commonwealth.[171] By turning to violence, Cheke argued in an echo of the German Reformers, the rebels had shown that they "lack[ed] reason" and should be responded to in kind.[172]

> When common order of the law can take no place in unruly and disobedient subjects, and all men will of wilfulnesse resist with rage, and think their own violence to be the best justices, then be wise Magistrates compelled by necessity, to seek an extreame remedie, where meane salves help not, and bring in the Martiall law, where none other law serveth. Then must yee be contented to bide punishment without processe, condemnation without witnesse, suspition is then taken for judgement, and displeasure may be just cause of your execution, & so without favour yee finde straitness, which without rule seek violence. Yee think it is a hard law and unsufferable. It is so indeed, but yet good for a medicine.[173]

In fact, there was considerable violence in the putting down of the rebels in 1549. But the Privy Council had hoped to threaten violence more than to use it, or to use it in only an exemplary way. Bush has shown that the council hoped that threats in the proclamations would terrify and pacify the people without having to resort to actual violence or abrogation of the law.[174] Though the council members had threatened to suspend the law and make the goods of the rebels forfeit, they explained in a letter to Lord Russell that this was meant only to distract the rebels and send them into disarray. Property could

---

168 Renaudet, "Erasme Économiste," 136: Video res humanas ad Turcicam quamdam barbariem tendere. Et fortasse sunt principes quibus hic status non displiceret.

169 Dauber, "Deutsche Reformation."

170 A fragment of a catalog in the Cecil Papers, seemingly from the period, includes Brenz, *De Administranda*. See "Portion of the Catalogue of a Library," CP 205/63.

171 Cheke, *Hurt of Sedicion*, reprinted as Cheke, *True Subiect to the Rebell*, 21–2.

172 Cheke, *Hurt of Sedicion*, 54.

173 Ibid., 50.

174 Bush, *Government Policy of Protector Somerset*, 156–9.

not be seized from them indefinitely without due legal procedures. "And howsoever it seme to you nowe, it shall reste a grudge, not only in the heades of the sufferes, but all other mens judgements of that shere and ells where that shall heare of this example of mens goods to be thus taken away without order of any law."[175]

The council wished to avoid entrenching social conflict, but this was still a far cry from the neighborly love of the commonwealth. The expression of neighborly love, often equated with the classical ideal of friendship, was the sharing of views, the frank consideration and criticism of each other's faults, and in general the intimate sharing of minds. Friendship was understood to be fundamental to social solidarity and to personal and communal sanctification through its various effects. It could correct privatistic interpretations and rationalizations and give one a sense of the whole. Edward VI, in an oration on the importance of friendship, explained: "For everyone has a certain *philautia*, or self-love, in accordance with which instinct he thinks that all the wicked deeds he has done were well done, unless he has a friend who warns him when he errs, and leads him to the rule of virtue."[176] Layering humanist psychological hedonism and the Protestant emphasis on the fragility of human nature after the fall onto Aristotle's social theory, it was understood that the love and care of others were necessary for the bearing of the negative emotions. This was usually elaborated in the context of long discussions of the possibility and moral worth of consoling a mourner in Cicero's *Tusculan Disputations*.[177] Edward explained in his oration that not only was it permitted to mourn another, but it was the great work of friendship to ameliorate the pain of a friend.[178]

Politically, the ideal of friendship found expression in the counsel institutionalized in the Privy Council and Parliament but also in informal counsel.[179] As Cheke wrote in a letter to Somerset, "Wherefore, as his Majesties hath alwaies learned, so I trust he laboureth daylie to avoide the grownde of all errour, that self-pleaseing which the Greekes do call φιλαυτία; when a man delighteth in his own reason, and despiseth other mens conseill, and thincketh no mans foresight to be so good as his, nor no man's judgment compared to his owne."[180] While counsel was to be taken openly and humbly, there was disagreement over how freely it could be offered by those who were not entitled to offer it due to their office or social status. The reb-

175 Pocock, *Troubles*, 72.

176 Edward VI, Orations, fol. 94v: Unusquisque enim habet quandam φιλαυτίαν, vel sui amorem, quo instinctus, putat omnia scelesta quae fecit bene fieri, nisi habeat amicum cum qui eum errantem admoneat, et ad virtutis normam traducat.

177 For example, see Valla, *On Pleasure*, 141–3.

178 Edward VI, Orations, fol. 24v.

179 On counsel, see Guy, "Monarchy and Counsel."

180 Harington, *Nugae Antiquae*, 1:44; Alford, *Kingship and Politics*, 45.

els, appealing to the rhetoric of commonwealth, were asserting their right to be heard by presenting demands to the government. Cheke responded in *Hurt of Sedicion* that they showed themselves to have misunderstood the concept of vocation in presuming to offer counsel and to have a poor grasp on the fundamentals of counsel.[181] The rebels, he argued, had no right to demand changes to the administrative system, since they were not kings or magistrates and, invoking the theory of vocation, have not been called to do so. "Gods word teacheth us, that no man should take in hand any office, but he that is called of God like *Aaron*."[182] By relying on their own judgment about what the commonwealth should do, the common people were showing the self-love of which they accused the nobility and gentry.[183] Cheke complained that the rebels neglected the classic features of good counsel: regard for the thing, the manner in which it is done, the person, the time, and a reasonable cause for doing it.[184] In mistreating Edmund, the first baron of Sheffield, they failed to appreciate "his service to the Commonwealth" as they should have, reflecting a more general failure to evaluate actions from the point of view of the commonwealth as a whole.[185] Crowley, on the other hand, argued that he was entitled to offer advice to Parliament, despite not being a member of that body, since it was the essence of Christian friendship "to teach the truth boldly, without any feare of death, and to suffer oure brothers to bee led in erroure," an obligation of all Christians, not only pastors.[186]

From the government's point of view, the "participation" of the commonalty was thus strictly curtailed by their vocation. Their love for the king and their superiors was not to be expressed through counsel, but through gratitude. The poor had no possibility of repaying the rich with similar benefits and so owed them gratitude in return. For Cheke, this was one of the

181 Melanchthon had already noted the danger to the commonwealth of consulting with the commonalty. Noting Cicero's admonishment that the whole commonwealth, including all of the degrees of the people, be consulted, Melanchthon added that this was a "most useful teaching, lest those who will be in charge of government affairs do not embrace the whole commonwealth. For in our time, when the demagogues [*concionatores*] consult only with the commons [*plebs*], the commonwealths are overturned." Cicero, *De Officiis*, 160, s.v. "Omnino qui Reipublicae": Utilissimum praeceptum, ne totam Rempublicam complectantur hi, qui praefuturi sunt rebus publicis. Nam et nostris temporibus dum soli plebi consulunt concionatores, evertunt Respublicas.

182 They had asked for more transparency in article 27 of the Mousehold articles. Santschi, "Obedience and Resistance," 150; Cheke, *Hurt of Sedicion*, 4.

183 Cheke, *Hurt of Sedicion*, 48–9.

184 Ibid., 50.

185 Ibid., 24–5. On the importance to commonwealth theory of being able to evaluate the worth of a man to the commonwealth, see Cicero on the dilemma of the starving wise man. Cicero, *On Duties*, 297.

186 Crowley, *Select Works*, 158.

errors committed by the common people during Kett's Rebellion. In rebelling, the commons showed ingratitude, debasing their only currency in the exchange of mutuality that defined a commonwealth.

> And seeing ye be lesse able by money and liberality, to deserve good will then other be, and your only kind of desert is to shew good will, which honest men doe well accept as much worth as money, have ye not much hindered and hurt your selfe herein, loosing that one kind of humanity which ye have only left, and turning it into cruelty which ye ought most to abhor, not only because it is wicked of it selfe, but also most noysome to you.[187]

THE DEACONATE AND THE NOBILITY: FROM CUSTODIANS OF THE LAW TO ADMINISTRATORS OF THE COMMONWEALTH

Though Cheke's view was the standard Aristotelian view of friendship between inferiors and superiors that had long been part of the medieval commentary literature on the *Ethics* and was in line with the preaching of obedience, it was a fitting description neither of the actual participation of the middling and lower sorts in government nor of how to plausibly express the neighborly love taught in the Bible. The literature of admonishment in the wake of the rebellions of 1549 was, like the proclamations of that summer, hyperbolic and strategic. Even in the literature on admonishment, there were more even-handed approaches, and in these, such as Peter Martyr Vermigli's draft for a sermon on obedience by Cranmer, the crisis was perceived in part as a failure of magistrates to implement the law. Vermigli argued that the magistrates should have upheld the penal law more thoroughly with respect to sins both against God and against their fellow men. "We have suffred periury, blasphemy, and adultery, slandering and lying, gluttony and drunkenness, vagabonds, and ydle performers and other haynouse offendours, lightly punysshed, or else clerely pardonned, either thinking this clemencey for the tyme expedient for the common wealthe, or else not duely waying how grevouse those offences were and how much they offended god."[188]

Without question, members of the government were united in the view that the commonalty were not entitled to counsel. But the landlords had been obstructionist in Parliament and had rejected most of the government's program to achieve a commonwealth. Crowley thus imputed the blame for the ineffectiveness of the government's policy to the disobedience of the

---

187 Cheke, *Hurt of Sedicion*, 54.
188 Kirby, *Zurich Connection*, 152.

landlords: "Yea when there was a law ratified to the contrary, you ceased not to finde meanes either to compel your tenantes to consent to your desire in enclosinge. . . . And what obedience showed you, when the kinges proclamations were sent forthe, and commissions directed for the laying open of your enclosures, and yet you lefte not of to enclose stil?"[189] The law was understood not so much as the product of consultation between the nobility and the king but as an expression of divine law. In this context, the pressing question for the government was once again how to use the nobility and gentry to further its policies. William Paget, the first clerk of the Privy Council and a committed Protestant,[190] advised shifting more of the burden to the local nobility.

In a letter of advice to Protector Somerset on February 2, 1549, Paget explained that he had no wish to abandon the commonwealth men's ideal of realizing the kingdom of God on earth, but thought that careful attention had to be paid to how to implement such reform, which had clearly, to his mind, gone wrong. "For as it is trewe that sekinge fyrst the kingdome of God he wyll furnishe us of all thinges, so yt is trewe that sithens [since] the beginninge yt hathe pleased God to do his thinges by meanes, and the olde proverbe ys not for nought which sayeth, 'Youe maie lye longe ynough in the dytche or God will helpe youe yf youe helpe not your selfe.' "[191] The means in question were a blend of the various tactics used by Cromwell to further reform, namely, commissions, proclamations, and, in general, the enforcement of statute. Paget recommended that gentlemen in potentially unstable locations throughout England be charged with commissions to muster troops, levy the relief, and attend to the watchtowers. This advice of Paget has been seen as the origin of the system of county government under the lords lieutenant by envisioning an expanded role for the lieutenancy, which had previously been used solely in a military capacity as a charge to gentlemen to raise troops for defense or for the pacification of an uprising in a given locality.[192] Paget's view of commonwealth envisioned gentlemen enforcing statutes through their enhanced status as commissioned officials of the Crown; this would in turn reinforce hierarchy, distinction, and authority, making the reform legislation possible. "Do as myche as in your grace shalle lye after the pardon [the act of general pardon] to se the lawes executed without remission except it be for a very great consideration," Paget urged. "For so shall youe bringe in agayn obedience which nowe ys cleane gone, and therby your grace shalbe feared in the service of the kinge, the noblemen shall be regarded, and everie other man in his place abrode in

189 Crowley, *Select Works*, 144.
190 Hawkyard, "Paget, William."
191 Beer, *Letters of Paget*, 24.
192 Thomson, *Lords Lieutenant in the Sixteenth Century*, 14, 25–6.

the world reputed as he ought to be, wherby quyet shall ensue amonge oure selfes."[193]

While the Privy Council turned to self-reflection and a questioning of the approach of Somerset's protectorate, Bucer urged the king to stay the course of Reformation and continue to think of magistrates as "custodians of the divine law." Bucer offered his vision for the continued reform of England in his *De Regno Christi*, which he completed in October 1550, after coming to England a few months earlier at the invitation of Cranmer to be the Regius Professor of Divinity at Cambridge.[194] In this work, Bucer continued to insist on the purity and rigor of the magistracy. Like Hales, he stressed that laws are "of no use to the well-being of the commonwealth unless they are strenuously defended by ordinary magistrates and unless the obedience of all is very strictly exacted."[195] The state was essentially a penal structure, meant to achieve civil order but also through the threat of harsh penalties to evoke "true repentance" and extinguish "all yearning and desire" for wrongdoing.[196] Since—moving beyond Melanchthon's view of the civil and accusatory uses of the law—the threat of penalties can lead to sanctification, the state should implement capital punishment for the crimes specified by the Mosaic law in the Decalogue and elsewhere.[197]

The implementation of justice had to be not only terrifying but scrupulously fair. Bucer addressed many contemporary complaints about miscarriages of justice, including the availability of justice for everyone, speedy trials, and the fair use of detention prior to trial.[198] And he demanded the strictest of standards in the selection of magistrates and in the execution of offices. He warned against patronage, favor, or sale of any kind and criticized the related practices of multiple office holding, absenteeism, and the use of deputies.[199] Offices were not private goods to be sold or given away but "divinely assigned responsibilities," such that, as Zwingli had noted, magistrates were referred to as "gods" in the Psalms, since offices were to be awarded to those who "excel others in both knowledge of and zeal for the Christian religion."[200]

Bucer found a classical precedent for his vision of magistracy above all in the oath given to magistrates preserved in Justinian's *Code* from the time of Theodosius and Valentinian, which stipulated that they would be satisfied with their ordinary wages and preserve the "communion of the most holy,

---

193 Beer, *Letters of Paget*, 24–5.
194 Pauck, *Melanchthon and Bucer*, 158–9.
195 Ibid., 361.
196 Ibid., 383.
197 Ibid., 379.
198 Ibid., 374–8; Bucer, *De Regno Christi*, 282–6.
199 Pauck, *Melanchthon and Bucer*, 366.
200 Ibid., 365.

catholic, and apostolic Church of God."[201] Like Starkey, Bucer specified that the watchmen must be watched, and he advocated for the auditing of officers at the end of their term, as was the practice in Athens.[202] Such auditing was being put in place in England, at least for officers in financial departments, and the Athenian practice was cited widely, including by Melanchthon.[203]

For Bucer, the lesson, even in the fall of 1549, was that "those who really are good and approved will enjoy more trust and authority among the people."[204] He went so far as to suggest that what the Reformation of the country required was royal visitation or delegations closely resembling the commissions of inquiry that had just failed. Magistrates were not only to serve as judges when complaints were brought through legal action, but to inquire after the conduct of subjects throughout the realm. Such visitations were undertaken both by King Jehoshaphat personally and by delegates of his, "because he did not wish to effect the reformation either of religion or of public government by edicts alone."[205] The result of such inspections admittedly could not be said to be true sanctification or the concomitant realization of commonwealth, but it was the realization of civil order of the highest kind, such that "the true worship of God was received by all both publicly and privately, with no one now daring to contravene it in word or in deed. And so if anyone did not do this with a sincere heart but as a pretense, he was harmful to himself only and not also others."[206]

Bucer's discussion of poor relief is a good example of the relationship in his theory between office holding and the commonwealth. It has been noticed that Bucer's advice for how to administer poor relief fit squarely into the Tudor poor law, including features specified in the Henrician legislation, such as the rigorous ban on begging, and anticipating features of the Elizabethan poor law, such as the provision of poor relief by another parish should the resources of the original fail to be adequate.[207] Bucer's approach was premised on the idea of the communion of saints. The poor were not simply to be admonished for their behavior and compelled to work, they were to be considered alien to the communion "for the churches of Christ must exclude from their communion those who, when they can maintain

---

201 Ibid., citing *C*, 9.27.
202 Ibid., 372; Bucer, *De Regno Christi*, 280.
203 Bucer, *De Regno Christi*, 280n18.
204 Pauck, *Melanchthon and Bucer*, 364.
205 Ibid., 371; 2 Chronicles 19:4–11.
206 Ibid., 370. The connection between the effect of the inspections and Bucer's view of the *ordo salutis* is clearer in the Latin, which echoed his discussion in his Romans commentary and the similar discussion in Melanchthon's *Loci*. Bucer, *De Regno Christi*, 278: Si quis itaque non sincero corde fecit, sed simulato, sibi uni, non et aliis noxius fuit.
207 Hopf, *Martin Bucer*, 116–22.

themselves by their own powers, neglect this and live inordinately, accepting borrowed food."[208] The whole approach was permeated by what it meant to be a member in the church community, specifically at the level of the parish. Based on the community of the early apostolic church as described in the book of Acts, Bucer hoped to re-create a community with the "irreligious and unworthy persons removed, so that all present, as they know that through communion with Christ they live and have every hope of eternal life, receive with hearts as eager as possible this communion of Christ offered to them in the Holy Supper."[209]

The purpose of moral and penitential discipline was to help the members of the church behave in a manner that was constitutive of the true Christian community, that is, the discipline would help them act rightly for the right reasons. This meant supplying an official structure for the administration of poor relief in the place of private charity. The concern was that "no ambition for human praise and favor compromise the office of almsgiving" for "when everyone gives alms by his own hand, it is with great difficulty that he will exclude from his heart a desire [for] the appreciation and praise of men; and when he receives this empty reward from men, a real and sure one is not to be expected from God."[210] Bucer insisted that poor relief be administered through a system of officials (deacons), patterned after the primitive deaconate of the apostolic church.[211] The deacons played a role in assisting the presbyters in the implementation of discipline in the church community. Bucer recognized several forms of discipline and envisioned particular roles for the church and state in maintaining them. There was the ceremonial discipline, that is, the sanctification of the holy days and religious buildings, along with religious education for children (teaching the catechism), poor relief, and marriage. All of this roughly conformed to the practices of Strasbourg, where Bucer had been the lead Reformer.[212]

Instead of private charity, the deacons were supposed to oversee the disbursal of funds from a common chest of alms collected in church. The deacons were supposed to keep lists of the poor and to investigate which of the poor were truly deserving and which were not, who was capable of working and providing for himself and who was not, and to "learn more precisely how they are engaging the alms of the faithful, and what things they may be in need of at any given time."[213] Bucer recommended that the deacons be "called to this office through his Spirit" and hoped that they would have authority due to their "good reputation among the people of Christ (Acts 6:3)"

208 Pauck, *Melanchthon and Bucer*, 307.
209 Ibid., 239.
210 Ibid., 257–8.
211 Ibid., xlix.
212 Bucer, *De Regno Christi*, xlviii.
213 Pauck, *Melanchthon and Bucer*, 308.

and the "rank near to that of presbyterial dignity" in the church.[214] It was part of the deacons' duties to approach the poor with sensitivity and to offer relief in a manner that respected "not only the need of various persons but also their faintness of heart" so that "in no case they add the affliction of shame to the affliction of poverty."[215]

Unsurprisingly, Bucer's view was already wearing thin by the time he presented *De Regno* to the king; his top-down approach to Reformation and discipline through godly magistrates and commissions of inquiry needed to be modified. Bucer perceived this cooling, but attributed it to the increasing influence at court of the Zürich party, the followers of Zwingli and Bullinger, who were fiercely opposed to Bucer's views on the eucharist.[216] But this distancing was not only a difference over theological doctrine; there was, as Paget's letter suggested, a rethinking of the role of the magistrates. They could no longer effectively be understood to be "custodians of the law" who could be relied on to execute the divine law. The years 1549–51 saw the emergence of a sophisticated analysis of a socially differentiated account of participation in the commonwealth and of conformity with the law by John Cheke and Thomas Smith and an increasing understanding of what an English version of reform and an English application of the principles of a classical commonwealth would look like.

But first, there was the distraction of the reactionary politics of Somerset's replacement, Warwick, and the attendant analysis of the English state. The events of 1549 had moved the question of the role of the nobility once again to the top of the agenda. The rebels had been suppressed with mercenaries at great cost, and Warwick tried to figure out in 1550 a means of maintaining order in the state that did not require such expenditures. He developed a scheme by which there would be, in Jordan's words, "a kind of standing feudal array," a cavalry of 700 horsemen under the command of thirteen nobles. Eventually warrants were issued for 1,100 men, mustered by nobles who were for the most part serving on the Privy Council. This force proved too expensive at £20,000 a year and was disbanded in 1552 as part of a broader cost-cutting effort.[217]

A glimpse at Warwick's analysis of the state is possible through the writing of one of his clients, William Thomas. Beginning in 1551, Thomas, one of the clerks of the council, wrote a series of memoranda for the king, drawing heavily from Machiavelli's *Discourses* and *The Prince*. These were not yet available in English or Latin, but Thomas had a clear command of Italian, thanks to his travels in the mid-1540s in Italy, where he wrote an English-Italian

214 Ibid., 309–12.
215 Ibid., 313.
216 Amos, "The Alsatian among the Athenians," 109.
217 Jordan, *Edward VI*, 434–6.

dictionary and grammar. He had won his position as something of a tutor to the king by dedicating his *Historie of Italie* to Warwick and by establishing himself as an authority on the Italian political literature of the day. Thomas suggested to the king that he keep these memoranda secret and use them as talking points for meetings of the Privy Council, which Edward was beginning to attend.[218]

Thomas's advice does appear to have been quite Machiavellian in foreign affairs; he recommended that Edward dissemble about his commitment to the Reformation during Charles V's lifetime in order to give Edward time to secure his position.[219] Yet, Thomas's analysis of the domestic scene was a retrogression to a stereotyped view of a renewed nobility, reminiscent of Henrician propaganda, and appeared to take seriously the more hysterical passages of the sermons and pamphlets produced during the recent rebellions. One of the five surviving memoranda addresses the famous Machiavellian question of "whether it be better for a commonwealth, that the power be in the nobility or in the community."[220] Thomas found in this question *the* question of 1549–50: whether to continue with Somerset's politics of popularity or return to the politics of a reformed nobility of the Henrician sort, as was being urged by Warwick. As a client of Warwick, Thomas unsurprisingly sided with his patron, in complete disagreement with Machiavelli, who had argued that it was less dangerous to side with the commons than the nobility.

The memorandum was clearly opposed to Somerset's popular politics and can be said to correspond roughly to the oligarchical or aristocratic civic humanism of the sort developed by the Venetian humanists, like Contarini, and the Florentines, like Guicciardini, who were considering the relevance of the Venetian model to Florence's predicament.[221] Thomas appealed to Warwick's patronage by advertising his combination of expertise in Machiavellian tactics and advocacy for the Venetian model of government in *Historie of Italie*.[222] This sounds like the transformation of civic humanism once more into an oligarchical form suited to England, as Mayer claimed for Starkey. Yet, the arguments that Thomas used in his memorandum were drawn as much from the propaganda of Cheke and Cranmer against sedition as from Machiavelli.[223] Thomas repeated the old argument, dredged up

218 Loades, *Intrigue and Treason*, 64–7; Pollnitz, *Princely Education*, 187.

219 Pollnitz, *Princely Education*, 193.

220 Thomas, "Memoranda"; Strype, *Ecclesiastical Memorials*, 372–7; Machiavelli, *Prince*, chap. 9; Machiavelli, *Discourses*, 1.5.

221 On Guicciardini's response, see Skinner, *Foundations*, 1:161.

222 Pollnitz, *Princely Education*, 188.

223 Cf. Loades, *Intrigue and Treason*, 67, for whom this is "the antithesis of Cheke's approach."

from the responses to the Peasants' War in 1525 and repeated in 1549, that the system of private property that favors the nobility is preferable to the community of property due to "the effects. . . . [F]or if the needy might attain their things without travailing for them, or the wealthy find none ease in the riches that they have travailed for, then should the world become barbarous for lack of travail."[224] Thomas's portrait of the commons—inconstant, wrathful, and ignorant—was the opposite of Elyot's vision of the gentleman, who was said to settle on a policy in advance and pursue it with deliberate, unshakable grace. There cannot be said to be a popular policy; the commons is unaware of what it wants or needs, but is simply an incoherent mess, wracked by emotion and inconstancy, and thus no order can be said to arise from this disorder. "[I]f the multitude prevail once in power, al goeth to confusion: the estate is subverted, every mans property, his possession[s] and goods are altered, and themselves never return to order, but by necessity."[225] Like Elyot's, Thomas's remedy was moral and political education. The commons, however, were not to be taught the virtues of the gentleman but simply to be obedient and, in an echo of Cheke's *Hurt of Sedicion*—and the criticism of Somerset's policies—were not to have "so much liberty as to talk of the princes causes." Even at the close of the memorandum, when Thomas seemed to be conceding something to Machiavelli's endorsement of the tumults, he was merely mouthing the view of Henrician preachers that rebellion, which was completely disallowed by the Bible, was the curse of providence on tyrants.[226]

Thomas's memoranda illustrate the difficulty of classifying certain English versions of Italian political thought as civic humanism. The lines of influence are clear, but Thomas's thinking was a far cry from, for example, Contarini's subtle account of the psychological and theological underpinnings of identification with the state. In Thomas's hands, the Venetian view was reduced to a fairly crude, aristocratic view of authority. If Warwick found this amenable, it was not the only official or government view.

The civic humanist approach appeared much more straightforwardly in Edward's student work. He summarized dutifully from the first book of Cicero's *De Officiis*: "Administrators of the commonwealth ought to care for the welfare of the subjects, their own advantage forgotten, and to care for the whole body of the commonwealth."[227] But the importance of participation

224 Melanchthon, *CR*, 16:432–3; Strype, *Ecclesiastical Memorials*, 372.
225 Ibid.
226 For Thomas's reading of the tumults as the providential punishment of tyrants, see Jones, *Tudor Commonwealth*, 50.
227 Bodleian MS Autogr. E. 2, 32v: Administratores reipublicae debent tueri utilitatem subditorum obliti suorum commodorum, et curare totum corpus reipublicae. Cicero, *De Officiis*, 1.85.

was fully brought out in a set of notes for an oration in May 1551: "it is useful for the commonwealth that the magistracies in the provinces be changed
annually."[228] Edward distinguished between magistrates who had the "care
of the whole commonwealth," who should hold office for a long time since
"the knowledge of it is only acquired through long experience," and the inferior magistrates responsible for the administration of justice in the provinces.[229] The stability of a nation increases if there are many who know civil
science (*civilis scientia*), or at least that which is required for the administration of justice; the concentration of such knowledge in a single person
could lead to a crisis when he passes away.

Edward explained that alternation in office holding could lead to stability through the norming of the young, the wealthy, and the powerful. This
view was essentially that of Contarini, and Edward noted that, as Contarini had argued about broad participation in Venice, such rotation would
"completely remove the ambition and zeal for glory."[230] Edward nevertheless thought that England was beating Venice at its own game. He criticized the Venetians for appointing governors for too long terms in Candia
and Cyprus, whereas the Romans had flourished with many annual positions, such as the consuls, censors, and tribunes. The English were following the classical model more faithfully, then, where certain local officers,
such as sheriffs and mayors, were chosen annually.[231] There were hints of a
slightly different view than that of Venetian civic humanists. The effect of
annual magistracies was said to be one of maturing, of becoming temperate
and serious from office holding. The idea seemed to be closer to civic education through service than simply the satisfaction of the desire for honor
alone. The English gloss on the civil knowledge that Aristotle promised was
that the hallmark of rotation in government would be knowledge of the
law. "For when one stays in a single office for a long time, he thinks that his
charge will be forgotten, if neglecting his own care, he should consult only
himself, since the duties of old magistracies are not well remembered."[232]
The charges that Edward was presumably thinking of were the sort given
to constables at quarter sessions or the legal instructions given to bailiffs by
a recorder. This participatory or civic approach was thus not completely at
odds with the view of magistrates as custodians of the law.

---

228 Edward VI, *Orations*, fols. 20–21, for the title; see the notes at fol. 20r.
229 Ibid., fol. 20r: totius Reipublicae cura . . . eius cognitio non nisi diuturna experientia
acquiritur.
230 Ibid., fol. 20v: ambitio, et studium hoc gloriae maxime tollit.
231 Ibid., fol. 21v.
232 Ibid., fol. 20v: Nam cum diu in uno magistratu quis maneat, oblivioni mandatum iri
putat, si suam curam negligens, sibi solum consuleret, quia vetustarum magistratuum officia,
non bene sciuntur.

A COMMONWEALTH OF ESTEEM

In *A Discourse of the Commonweal of This Realm of England*, which was not published at the time, Thomas Smith took a fresh look at the approach to the commonwealth promoted during Somerset's protectorate and concluded that the trouble was that it essentially proceeded on Stoic lines; advocates of this approach thought that suppression of the emotion of covetousness, of self-love, was possible. Smith reminded readers that, as the Christian humanists and the theologians had admitted, this was impossible: "But can we devise that all covetousness may be taken from men? No, no more than we can make men to be without ire, without gladness, without fear, and without all affections."[233] Thus while self-interest may have been part of the background to the enclosure crisis, it was not an ineradicable obstacle to the realization of the commonwealth ideal.[234] Cicero himself had argued that self-interest was fine as long as it did not harm others and, indeed, had argued further that harming others was against one's self-interest, since in the long run this would hurt one's reputation.[235] And Cicero, as indicated by the Knight in the dialogue, believed that the common good was an aggregate of individual goods. As the Knight put it, "As a great mass of treasure consists of many pence and the penny added to another and so the third and fourth and so further makes up the great sum so does each man added to another make up the whole body of the commonweal."[236] The Doctor agreed as long as the Ciceronian proviso was added, "so it be not prejudicial to any other."[237]

The solution to the problems of enclosure needed to work from this firm premise, which was now summarized in another phrase that, mentioned in Smith's *Discourse* in 1549, seems to have made the rounds at court in the early 1550s: "All are covetous of profit" (*Omnes sunt lucre cupidi*).[238] The 1548–9 approaches were thus flawed because it was unrealistic to believe that people would comply with laws that ran counter to their interests. As the Doctor noted, "it were hard to make a law therein, so many as have profit by that matter resisting it. And if such a law were made yet men studying still

233 Smith, *Discourse*, 118.
234 Ibid., 54: "For every man will seek where most advantage is, and they see there is more advantage in grazing and breeding than in husbandry and tillage by a great deal."
235 Cicero, *De Officiis*, 3.63.
236 Smith, *Discourse*, 51–2.
237 Ibid.
238 Thomas Smith had the Doctor cite it in his *Discourse*, and William Thomas included it as part of his rationale for a reform of the coinage in his secret letter of advice to the king sometime around 1552. The phrase, as Thomas noted, came from the Latin translation of the dialogue of Hipparchus, which was then believed to have been written by Plato, but this conclusion is now thought to be spurious. They were clearly reading Ficino's translation and introduction. Ibid., 118; Strype, *Ecclesiastical Memorials*, 390; Plato, *Omnia Diuini Platonis Opera*, 1–3.

their most profit would defraud the law by one mean or another." It would be preferable to take the love rather than the fear approach to the economy. Summarizing the argument in the margin, Smith noted "[h]ow enclosures might be remedied without the coercion of laws."[239]

For Smith, the commonwealth ought to be composed of economic roles that could offer the material and immaterial rewards (honors) that are naturally sought by men. If this were done, men would feel that they had freely chosen their vocations and would thus be motivated to throw themselves into such roles to the extent required for adequate production.

> For if they see there be not so much profit in using the plow as they see in other feats, think you not that they will leave that trade and fall to others that they see more profitable? Is it not an old saying in Latin *Honos alit artes*, that is to say, "profit or advancement nourishes every faculty," which saying is so true that it is allowed by the common judgment of all men. We must understand also that all things that should be done in a Commonweal be not to be forced, or to be constrained by the straight penalties of the law, but some so and so other by allurement and rewards rather. For what law can compel men to be industrious in travail and labor of his body or studious to learn any science of knowledge of the mind?[240]

The approach taken by Smith was not altogether new, and it was not altogether uncoercive. This was the theory of legislation used in Utopia, cited by Erasmus, and understood to be the reward side of the rewards and punishments that comprised Melanchthon's idea of distributive justice. Edward had even duly noted the sententia *honos alit artes* on September 21, 1548, in the notebook in which he was recording various verbal and nominative phrases from Cicero's *Tusculans*, as Cheke required of him as part of his studies.[241] But the *Discourse* used this approach in a more concrete fashion, offering up an alternative to the frontal attack on the landlords and the merchants that had characterized the government's successive attempts at a social program thus far. Smith's work proposed a three-pronged approach: to halt the debasement of the currency that had made goods more expensive, to address the agrarian crisis, and to address the depopulation of the towns and the decline of industry. The inclusion of a discussion of debasement showed Smith's willingness to take a broader approach to the eco-

239 Smith, *Discourse*, 51, 54.
240 Ibid., 59.
241 Baldwin, *William Shakspere's Small Latine and Lesse Greeke*, 229, citing BL Arundel MS 510: Honos alit artes, omnesq' incenduntur ad studia Gloria.

nomic troubles of England, though this explanation of England's woes may not have been meant for public consumption.[242]

Regardless, Smith did not lay the full blame for the agrarian crisis at the feet of the landlords. The Knight explained early in the *Discourse* that though the landlords were often accused of raising rents unfairly, they needed to do so in order to maintain their households, which were now far more expensive to keep up thanks to the rise in prices.[243] Rather than trying to regulate rents, the aim was, as the Doctor put it, "[t]o make the profit of the plow to be as good, rate for rate, as the profit of the grazier and sheepmaster is."[244] The Doctor had several suggestions for effecting this end: addressing the poor reputation of husbandry; taxing the land used in pasturage and the exports of the fruit of pasturage at twice the rate as those of husbandry; and encouraging the maintenance of the old form of commons rights, which were all intermixed and were thus less amenable to being enclosed for pasturage.[245] The tax was one of the few commonwealth measures successfully passed by the government in that session of Parliament, and Smith apparently thought of it as uncoercive, perhaps because unlike the other bills, which were resisted, it actually passed into law.[246]

Smith's attitude toward covetousness had something of the air of resignation, especially with regard to luxury goods, but it was not quite the full-throated embrace of a political economy in the nineteenth-century sense,

242 Bush argued that, though the publicists of Edward's reign were aware of the effect of debasement of the coinage on inflation, they nevertheless stayed away from this explanation in the main, since it would lay the blame for the economic problems directly at the feet of the government policy of pursuing the wars in Scotland. Thus, "to exculpate itself and to show its concern, the government attributed the damage inflicted by the war to sheep-farming." Bush, *Government Policy of Protector Somerset*, 41. This argument depended heavily on the chronology of the various explanations for inflation in the period. Outhwaite maintained that the theory was discussed already from 1544 and continued to be one of the most characteristic theories until the eventual revaluation of the coinage under Elizabeth in 1560–1. Outhwaite, *Inflation*, 17–8. Bush argued that the debasement theory emerged after the peace of 1550 ended the Scottish and French wars. Bush, *Government Policy of Protector Somerset*, 82. The debasement theory was clearly well understood before 1550, but it was also clear that it should not be spoken about freely in public. It was mentioned approvingly in the 1549 memorandum "Policies to Reduce This Realme of Englande unto a Prosperus Wealthe and Estate," which may have been meant only for the king and council. Tawney and Power, *Tudor Economic Documents*, 3:315. Hugh Latimer preached against it before the king in 1549, but was evidently accused of being a "sedicious fellowe" as a result. This led him to cite Isaiah the prophet against debasement in Jerusalem and to ask rhetorically whether Isaiah too was seditious. Tawney and Power, *Tudor Economic Documents*, 2:181.

243 Smith, *Discourse*, 21–2.
244 Ibid., 54.
245 Ibid., 120.
246 2 and 3 Edw. VI, c. 36.

which has sometimes been suggested.[247] There were hints, survivals, in the *Discourse* of Latimer's condemnation of the desire for "too much," but they were transformed into lamentable, but very human choices.[248] Smith echoed softly the complaints of the previous decades about the covetousness of the various sorts. Everyone in recent years had wanted more in the way of luxuries than they really should. The Knight complained about the frippery of the nobility and the Doctor of the useless luxuries driving men from the countryside into the larger cities.[249] And the Doctor lamented the fraudulent and poor workmanship of English manufactures, by which the clothmakers hoped to turn a tidier profit.[250] Smith's approach to economy and society was still classical; it was Ciceronian, asserting the compatibility of the *honestum* and the *utile*, a Roman understanding in which reputation and virtue coincided, or should, for an orderly and flourishing society.

[C]ertain towns in England . . . were wont to make their cloths of a certain breadth and length and so set their seals to the same. While they kept the rate truly, strangers did but look on the seal and received their wares, whereby those towns had great vent of their cloth and consequently prospered very well. Afterward, some in those towns, not content with reasonable gains and continually desiring more, devised cloths of less length, breadth, and goodness than they were wont to be and yet by the commendation of the seal to have as much money for the same as they had before for good cloths. And for a time they got much and so abased the credit of their predecessors to their singular lucre; which was recompensed with the loss of their posterity, for after these cloths were found faulty, for all their seals, they were not only never the better trusted but much less for their seal. Yea, though their cloths were well made; for when their falsehood and untruth was espied, then no man would buy their cloths till they were searched and unfolded, regarding nothing the seal. And yet, because they found them untrue in some part, they mistrusted them in other and so would give less for those cloths than for any other like, having no seals to the same; whereby the credit of the said towns was lost and the towns utterly decayed.[251]

247 Thus, while I would agree with Neal Wood's judgment that "[m]an is depicted in Republica as a frail vessel readily corruptible by power, selfish by nature, tainted by pride, ambitious and profit-seeking, and always at war within [himself] and with each other," I argue that this was a view common to the evangelical adherents and did not in itself represent a new attitude. Wood, "Avarice and Civil Unity," 32.

248 Latimer, *Works*, 98.

249 Smith, *Discourse*, 82–3, 121–2.

250 Ibid., 76–7.

251 Ibid.

Like Cicero, Smith made the case against covetousness not on the grounds of stewardship, but on the grounds that pursuing the common good was in the end also good business, since having a good reputation was necessary for doing business successfully. Smith's thinking turned on reputation and esteem, on mutual valuation. Esteem clearly was a large category for him, of which esteem in commercial transactions, credit, was simply one species. A just distribution of esteem was also important for productivity and for the appropriate distribution of labor to the necessary categories of work.

Material satisfaction is not sufficient to ground an attachment to one's work, and the division of labor is not sufficient to ground social relations; one must have the sense that this work is valued by the community, that one belongs to a community of esteem. It is the esteem for one's work (for the middling sorts, at least, whose lives, from the viewpoint of the commonwealth, were essentially those of work) and the knowledge that one has freely chosen it that allows one to meet others in an atmosphere of relative equality and fellow feeling. Thus, for example, one of the reasons for a decline in learning in England was that people "see no preferment ordained for learned men, nor yet any honor or estimation given them, like as has been in times past."[252]

The classical roots of this approach are apparent in Smith's discussion of agriculture:

> Also the occupation was had so honorable among the Romans that one was taken from holding the plow to be consul in Rome, who, after his year ended, thought no scorn to resort to the same feat again. What occupation is so necessary or so profitable for man's life as this is? Or what mystery is so void of all craft as the same is? And how little is it regarded? Yea, how much it is vilified that this late nobility reputes them but as villeins, peasants, or slaves by whom the proudest of them have their livings. So that I marvel much there is any, seeing such a vility and contempt, will occupy the feat of husbandry at all; for as honor nourishes all science, so dishonor must needs decay them.[253]

Smith took these claims much more seriously than did some of his contemporaries, who had no patience for grumbling over what to them was simply name-calling. John Véron, in his 1551 translation of Leo Jud's 1535 Latin translation of a 1531 anti-Anabaptist tract by Bullinger, added an aside about this. He noted that there were many among the lower sorts who complained that "they do so bitterly revile us, at everi second word, most despitfully calling us peysauntes, and vilaines." Véron wrote that these were just other names

252 Ibid., 32.
253 Ibid., 120.

for farmers and that, even if they were offensive terms, the lower sorts should heed the teaching of Christ in Matthew 10, where he admonishes the apostles to disregard such name-calling in their work spreading the gospel.[254]

The intermixing of economic imperatives with thinking about the importance of status was of course not original to Smith's analysis, since it was one of the telling features of town life. Thus, when Smith turned to the remedy for the depopulation of the towns, he argued that they should extend the liberty of the towns to those skilled men from abroad who might reinvigorate the craft. So, even though it was usually the case that one needed to be a citizen of a town, usually achieved through membership in a guild, to work in a given trade, Smith advised the towns that such a craftsman should be "gladly admitted for his excellency to the freedom of the same town without burdening of him with any charge for his first entry or setting up." Freedom was essentially the freedom to work and here a status that was to be combined with other economic incentives, such as a "house rent free or some stock lent them of the common stock of such towns," which would lure the craftsmen.[255] In this way of thinking—possibly the thinking of the middling sorts, possibly of Smith, or both, and possibly of Roman morality—liberty was status. Acting in an uncoercive way was acting so as to give more people status, to expand liberty. This was to be done both in the agrarian sector and in the towns, though not through coercive policies. The legal conversions of tenancies had done much of the work in the agrarian sector, but there was more to be accomplished.

Like the choice to act in such a way as to ensure one's own credit, so much of this seems to have been up to the individuals in question. The government could make the best possible policies to balance the sectors of the economy and to correct imbalances in trade, such that individuals could earn a living through their vocation, but there was only so much that could be accomplished through conventional legislation. The residue—the questions of esteem and honor—had to be addressed through a careful consideration of the various sorts of people and their corresponding psychological needs. These would have to be addressed through a careful combination of legislation ensuring legal remedies (and thus conferring status to tenants in the agrarian sector), office holding for the middling and higher sorts, the conferring of titles in an honor system, and encouraging the expansion of citizenship in the towns. The statutes passed under Wolsey and Cromwell were certainly important in this view, and Smith was not so much repudiating this approach as arguing, as was apparent to all observers at the time, that it was insufficient to realize a commonwealth in England.

---

254 Euler, *Couriers of the Gospel*, 213, 227–8; Bullinger, *A Most Necessary and Frutefull Dialogue*, sig. B3r–B4r.
255 Smith, *Discourse*, 125.

CHAPTER 2

A SOCIETY OF ORDERS

Accordingly, it seems that we must account for the origin and development of law itself. 1. The fact is that at the outset of our *civitas*, the citizen body decided to conduct its affairs without fixed statute law or determinate legal rights; everything was governed by the kings under their own hand. 2. When the *civitas* subsequently grew to a reasonable size, then Romulus himself, according to the tradition, divided the citizen body into thirty parts, and called them *curiae* on the ground that he improved his curatorship of the commonwealth though the advice of these parts. And accordingly, he himself enacted for the people a number of statutes passed by advice of the *curiae* [*leges curiatae*]; his successor kings legislated likewise. . . . 6. Then about the same time actions-at-law whereby people could litigate among themselves were composed out of these statutes [the laws of the Twelve Tables]. To prevent the citizenry from initiating litigation any old how, the lawmakers' will was that the actions-at-law be in fixed and solemn terms.

—"The Origin of the Law," *Digest of Justinian**

The most celebrated study of the English state in the sixteenth century was written out of homesickness. Sir Thomas Smith, languishing in France as a badly neglected and to his mind underappreciated ambassador, explained how he came to write it in a letter to Walter Haddon in April 1565: "And because in my absence I feel a yearning for our commonwealth I have put together three books here at Toulouse describing it, taking as the title *De Republica Anglorum*." He explained that the point of the work was to explain the differences between the English commonwealth and those of other countries, "which are administered in accordance with Roman law." His approach was both historical and philosophical, "giving it the shape in which I imagined that Aristotle wrote of the many Greek commonwealths[,] books which are no longer extant."[1]

* Mommsen, Krueger, and Watson, eds., *Digest of Justinian*, vol. 1, 3–5.
1 Dewar, *Sir Thomas Smith*, 111–2.

Smith was not the first to think of comparing the English political tradition with that of the civil law countries. This was becoming a standard topic in the emerging Catholic-Protestant polemics and in the apologies for female rule. John Aylmer in his *An Harborowe for Faithfull and Trewe Subjectes agaynst the Late Blowne Blaste, Concerninge the Gouernment of Wemen* of 1559 had compared the two traditions on a number of points to show that the succession of women was perfectly in line with English traditions and constitutional order and to "shewe that you must brynge our owne weyghtes, to weye our matters by, and not straungers." England needed the legal tradition that fit its people and not those of another nation; as Aylmer put it, "you muste let us alone with our own coate, and geve the great boye his." This included a defense of the evidentiary basis of English criminal law, including the jury of twelve peers and the deposing of witnesses. The civil law tradition that relied instead on confession led—in the eyes of these Protestants—to torture and "rackynge those which have not offended, and dyvinge them for paynes of tormesntes to saye that they never did."[2]

Indeed, the debate between Protestant and Catholic polemicists over the nature of the state continued to rage, and this provides an important background to the *De Republica*, as Anne McLaren has argued.[3] In 1542, Jerónimo Osório da Fonseca, a Portuguese bishop, wrote a work, *De Nobilitate*, that was greatly admired at Elizabeth's court. Years later, in 1563, he wrote an open letter to Elizabeth, which was widely read in Paris, suggesting that Elizabeth rethink her devotion to the new learning of the Protestants.[4] The teaching of the Protestants, he argued, specifically that of liberty, was a form of demagoguery, or "people pleasing" in the translation of Richard Shacklock, which only led to the worst sort of license and rebellion.[5] Walter Haddon, who had been one of Cheke's students at St. John's, a tutor to Elizabeth, and the editor of Elizabeth's Latin prayer book, was chosen to respond to Osório.[6] Smith's *De Republica* was his own response to such attacks on Protestant English liberty.[7]

Smith's response avoided the excesses of the Marian exiles, though he was clearly familiar with them. The *De Republica* built rather on the discussions of the previous decades, as Smith argued that English liberty was the sum product of the legal position of a carefully differentiated society of orders, like the classical commonwealths. As such, it was ordered and far from Osório's "people pleasing" or the charges of popularity that had brought an end

2 Aylmer, *An Harborowe for Faithfull and Trewe Subjectes*, L1r–[L2v].

3 McLaren, "Reading Sir Thomas Smith's *De Republica Anglorum*."

4 Ryan, "Haddon-Osorio Controversy," 143; McLaren, "Reading Sir Thomas Smith's *De Republica Anglorum*," 923–5

5 Osório, *An Epistle to Princesse Elizabeth*, 32.

6 Ryan, "Haddon-Osorio Controversy," 143.

7 McLaren, "Reading Sir Thomas Smith's *De Republica Anglorum*," 923.

to Somerset's protectorate. The *De Republica* is continuous with the blend of mutual esteem and liberties that had marked Smith's approach in the *Discourse on the Commonweal*, but new classical scholarship allowed Smith to model England's commonwealth more precisely on the classical commonwealths and to show how legal standing and the need for esteem and social distinction fit together in a general conceptual model of a society of orders.

This account of *De Republica* represents something of a break with the traditional interpretations of the work, which have tended to evaluate it in constitutional terms, albeit within a participatory framework, rather than in classical terms. Recent scholarly accounts have agreed that the *De Republica* represents a furthering of the position that sees English sovereignty as located in the king-in-parliament. One explanation that has been given is that the understanding of English sovereignty as king-in-parliament evolved as part of the attempts to justify union with Scotland in 1548. King-in-parliament became a way of explaining that the Crown of England had always consulted assemblies and councils in Scotland and that the two countries were thus already incorporated into a single polity.[8] A second possibility is that the doctrine of king-in-parliament actually developed later, in the 1550s or 1560s, to justify the imperfect rule of women and children and was essentially the theory of the king's "two bodies." The second of the monarch's bodies was the body politic in which the ruler was incorporated along with his or her advisers, that is, the council and Parliament.[9] These differing explanations clearly gave the emerging monarchical republicanism different colorations, but they were both essentially accounts of the state as sovereign. By emphasizing the classical approach of the society of orders, the account I develop in this chapter highlights the relationship between state and society and demonstrates the continuities with the debates over the commonwealth in the 1530s and 1540s.

Smith was not wholly satisfied with the theory of the state proposed, or at least implied, by the Marian exiles, who had been self-consciously opposed to what they called the "absolutism" of Mary and her Catholic advisers. While sympathetic to them personally and ideologically, Smith showed no interest in endorsing all of the particulars of their position, which they themselves were scrambling to disavow now that Elizabeth, a Protestant queen, was on the throne.[10] In broad terms, Smith did share their critique of absolutism,

---

8 Hoak, "Sir William Cecil, Sir Thomas Smith, and the Monarchical Republic," 52–4.

9 McLaren, *Political Culture*, 100–1.

10 For his sympathetic rejection of the position of the Marian exiles, see Smith, *De Republica Anglorum*, 51–2: "So when the wealth is evil governed . . . the question remaineth whether obedience of them be just. . . . Certaine it is that is always a doubtful and hasardous matter to meddle with the chaunging of the lawes and governement, or to disobey the orders of the rule or government, which a man doth find alreadie established." For the retreat of the Marian exiles under Elizabeth, see Santschi, "Obedience and Resistance," 271, 281.

and he was sympathetic to criticisms of the sort leveled by John Hales, who wrote in 1559 that Mary had failed to recognize the superiority of parliamentary statute and of the liberty of the House of Commons over royal prerogative.[11] Smith used this type of language in the *De Republica*, though transmuted into classical terms, denying that the absolutist form of rule was any sort of commonwealth at all by identifying it with Aristotle's lordship, or household rule, rather than political rule. The absolutist manner of rule meant a failure to take counsel, which in turn meant a recrudescence of factional politics, which in Smith's account was tantamount to reintroducing lordship and servility. The absolutist state was thus, in Smith's analysis, not a state at all.

Among the chief faults of the tyrant was that he legislated "without the advise of the people, and regardeth not the wealth of his people but the advancement of him self, his faction, and kindred."[12] That this was part of the anti-Catholic polemic is evident from the text. Smith, following the Henricians, argued that religious questions should be settled through councils as they had been in antiquity. The centralized approach of papal decision making, which refused to heed general councils, was a form of absolute power, *potestas absoluta*. "[S]ome men doe judge the same" to be the case of the kings of France and the princes of Italy, since they too acted "by their private Counsell and advise of their friends and favourers only, without the consent of the people."[13]

The charges of absolutism in the 1550s by the Marian exiles threatened to eclipse the more subtle debates of the 1530s and 1540s over the role of the state in realizing the ideals of commonwealth. The exiles criticized the fiscal policies of the Counter-Reformation state, including the use of sin taxes, the debasement of the coinage, the use of forced labor, and the extraction of resources as if all the property of the subjects belonged to the sovereign.[14] Smith resisted raising the volume of the debate. Perhaps because he was implicated in the debasement of the coinage in Edward's reign (though he protested against it in the *Discourse*) and supported indirect forms of raising revenue, he failed to echo these particular complaints or to suggest more generally that it was the use of state power that defined Catholic absolutism. Like in the *Discourse*, Smith's argument in the *De Republica* for a noncoercive approach to government turned not so much on a repudiation of state power, which was helpful but insufficient in realizing the goals of commonwealth, but on the perception of the various sorts of people as to how they fit into a community of mutual honor and esteem.

---

11 Hoak, "Sir William Cecil, Sir Thomas Smith, and the Monarchical Republic," 39–40.
12 Smith, *De Republica Anglorum*, 53.
13 Ibid., 54.
14 Ponet, *Shorte Treatise*, [E8r].

Liberty was a necessary feature of the political community; it was the condition of being a free man that made possible the mutuality that was the underpinning of any real community. Following Aristotle, Smith explained that the lordly way of treating the residents of a country meant that it was not in fact a commonwealth. Smith explained that even one of the old Roman estates with "v. thousande or x. thousande bondmen" was no commonwealth, "for the bondman hath no communion with his master, the wealth of the Lord is onely sought for, not the profit of the slave or bondman." Lordship has "no mutuall societie or parte no law or pleading betwixt the-one and thother," all of which are requirements of a commonwealth (a *respublica* or *politeia*, as the Greeks defined it, he noted).[15]

Framing the contrast between liberty and absolutism as between mutuality and estrangement rather than between limited government and the excessive use of power reflected a deeper difference between Smith's understanding of the commonwealth (*respublica*) and the exiles' understanding of the state. Smith did appreciate their emphasis on the state as a legal order (as opposed to the arbitrary rule of the monarch in the absolutist theory), and he echoed such constitutional sentiments in *De Republica*. He explained, in keeping with the exiles, that the state was not merely composed of the customary constitutional arrangements but included statutory laws as well.[16] Yet, Smith's treatment of the orders or degrees of the commonwealth was completely out of step with the exiles' treatment of the orders as an ephorate or inferior magistracy that grew out of the need to develop a theory of resistance. In Smith's analysis, the exiles were well intentioned, but they essentially provided a factional response to a factional problem, treating the commonalty as a faction rather than as part of the commonwealth. Alternatively, the commonalty was identified in this literature with the *populus* as a whole, as if it were an undifferentiated mass, and this was no better in Smith's eyes. It is clear that he thought such appeals to the *populus* as an undifferentiated whole chiefly had the effect of enabling cynical manipulation of the people at the hands of an absolutist tyrant. "The Emperours claime this tyrannicall power by pretence of that Rogation or *plebiscitum*, which *Caius Caesar* or *Octavius* obtained, by which all the people of Rome did conferre their power and authority unto *Caesar* wholly."[17]

Neither approach maintained the differentiated view of society that had been elaborated in the various commonwealth theories before and after the

---

15 Smith, *De Republica Anglorum*, 57. The word "parte" is difficult. The 1583 edition replaced it with "portion," the Trinity College manuscript with "pacte." The idea that a commonwealth needed to be differentiated and thus have "parts" was very much in keeping with Smith's approach, though given his view that a commonwealth was "united by common accord and covenauntes," "pacte" is plausible as well.

16 Ibid., 53. For Smith's devotion to the legal order, see ibid., 49–50.

17 Smith, *De Republica Anglorum*, 53.

rebellions of the mid-Tudor crisis. The exiles broke with the stratified theory of counsel, which Cheke had so forcefully set out in *The Hurt of Sedicion* and which Smith clearly still upheld. Referring to resistance to tyrants, Smith wrote, "whereof the judgement of the common people in according to the event and successe: of them which be learned, according to the purpose of the doers, and the estate of the time then present."[18] John Ponet, on the other hand, wrote, "That a mannes servaunt maye be wiser than his maister, that he maye be juster than his maister, that he maye see what is more profitable and necessarie to be done than his maister, commonly it happeneth: and therfore he maye have som apparent cause, to altre and breake his maisters commaundment."[19]

Smith's indication that the point of *De Republica Anglorum* was to compare England to those countries that were under Roman law can easily lead the reader astray. The remark implies that Smith was drawing on a common-law tradition, on writers such as Fortescue and St. German, and that his vision of English liberty was somehow unique to England. But Smith had been named the Regius Professor of Civil Law in 1540. Admittedly, this choice had been met with much criticism, since the position was highly paid and Smith had no obvious qualifications at the time. But from 1540 to 1542, he went on a European tour to rectify this situation, visiting Orleans, Paris, and, above all, Padua, which was the center of legal teaching and scholarship during this period. In his inaugural lectures in 1542, when he took up the post, he claimed mastery of the new commentaries on the civil law, including those by Alciato, Zasius, and Johannes Ferrarius, and his time in Europe as evidence of his suitability for the position.[20]

The *De Republica* drew on this literature and on the scholarly reconstruction of Rome to show that England resembled the Roman republic in certain ways at certain times and that, in this, it was more free than the Catholic countries, which were governed in accordance with imperial (and canon) law. In 1562, Smith had undertaken a more specialized version of the project, writing a treatise on the wages of the roman footsoldier at the request of Cecil, which drew on similar legal materials (largely Budé and Alciato) to compare the financing of the military in Rome and in England.[21] In the *De Republica*, Smith worked on a much wider canvas, and the conditions of mutuality that he advertised for England in the title (unlike the absolutist regimes, it was a commonwealth) were explored in comparison with the practices of the ancient Roman republic as reconstructed in the best of the humanist scholarship of the sixteenth century.

18 Ibid., 52.
19 Ponet, *Shorte Treatise*, B4r.
20 Dewar, *Sir Thomas Smith*, 20–2.
21 Dewar, "Authorship of the 'Discourse of the Commonweal,'" 390.

A SOCIETY OF ORDERS

From the *Discourse* of 1549, it is clear that Smith, like so many of his con-temporaries, already thought of their society in terms of degree. Yet it was not until the mid-1570s that he elaborated on the subject. In the spring and summer of 1576, he was ill with throat cancer and at home at Theydon Mount, Essex, where he lived until his death in 1577. It was almost certainly during this period that he drew on a manuscript description "of the degrees of People in the Commonwealth of England" by William Harrison, who had probably been asked to write on the subject by Raphael Holinshed for his *Chronicles*.[22] The chapter was first printed as part of that work in 1577,[23] and it was the draft of this version that Smith used to revise chapters 17–24 of book 1 of the *De Republica*.[24] In Harrison's chapter and Smith's revisions, the commonwealth of England was reimagined as society of orders, a new way of thinking about the parts of a society that combined social and politi-cal factors in a broader theory of citizenship. This was actually a new version of an old way, since it was a reconstruction of how ancient societies were organized.

The reconstruction of this approach was undertaken in the mid-sixteenth century, perhaps above all by the Italian professor Carlo Sigonio. Indeed, in form and title, Smith's book resembled Sigonio's 1564 *De Republica Athe-niensium*, and substantively, Harrison and Smith seem to have drawn inspi-ration from Sigonio's *De Antiquo Iure Civium Romanorum* (1560). Harrison certainly consulted Sigonio in the later version of his *Description*, and he may have owned at least one of his works. There is also some evidence that Smith consulted Sigonio after reading Harrison's manuscript chapter.[25] Har-rison evidently had read through some other accounts by "historiographers

22 Parry, "Harrison and Holinshed's Chronicles," 793.

23 Harrison, "An Historical Description."

24 Mary Dewar argued that Smith consulted a manuscript in 1565, but Parry has shown persuasively that it must have been in 1576 or 1577. Dewar, "A Question of Plagiarism," 921–29; Parry, "Harrison and Holinshed's Chronicles," 803.

25 Harrison closely paraphrased Sigonio's *Historiarum de Regno Italiae* at one point in his discussion "Of Degrees of People," as noted in Harrison, *Description of England*, 101. There are two copies of this work in the Derry and Raphoe Diocesan Library at the University of Ulster, shelf marks E.k.33 (Basel, 1575) and D.II.e.01 (Frankfurt, 1591), where much of Harri-son's library ended up after his son-in-law George Downham became the bishop of Derry in 1616. Though both copies have signatures (those of D.II.e.01 are crossed out), neither clearly shows that of Downham. Though there is no signature proving it, it is possible that Harrison owned one of these works. Edelen, "William Harrison," 257, suggests that "[o]ther works in the library, which has an extensive holding of sixteenth-century books, may have belonged to Harrison. His habit was to sign at the top of the title page in the space often clipped in rebind-ing; some of the extant signatures are truncated." Thanks to Frank Reynolds, sublibrarian for the Faculty of the Arts, Ulster University, for sending images of the title pages and providing invaluable help from afar. See also "Derry Diocesan Library Catalogue"; Edelen, "William

of their own countries," perhaps in preparation for writing descriptions of England and Scotland for the *Chronicles*, perhaps because he had been talked to about writing some of the shorter descriptions of foreign lands for the *Chronicles* before that part of the project was canceled, or perhaps for his own *Chronology*, though it did not include such materials. Regardless, Harrison had read works like Vincent de la Loupe's *Commentarii de Magistratibus et Praefecturis Francorum*, where he would have found frequent comparisons between contemporary and classical institutions. It is likely that he read Sigonio during this period and conceived of England as a society of orders, an idea that Smith then embraced and developed, revising the *De Republica* accordingly.

The theory of a society of orders was understood to be a theory of citizenship. Sigonio explained that the classic division of states—in terms of the rule of the one, the few, or the many—was really a matter of citizenship. The *civitas*, or state, was defined by who held office, the *cives* (citizens). Citizenship in turn was defined in Rome (and by Aristotle as well) in terms of residence, membership in a tribe, and access to honors. Citizenship was thus a concept that encompassed genealogy, geography, social status, and political access.[26] This had profound implications for understanding the political development of the ancient world. According to Sigonio, the history of the Roman republic was divided into two eras. In the first period, from roughly the fifth century to the early third century BC, Rome was marked by constant struggle between the first freeborn citizens of Rome, the patricians, who were attempting to secure control of the religious and secular offices for themselves, and the plebs. By discouraging intermarriage and thus trying to institute a closed caste system, the patricians attempted to close off access to the state to the plebs. During this period, the plebs did produce laws (plebiscites), but these required ratification by the patrician Senate to have the force of law.[27]

Harrison," 256. It seems that D.II.e.01 belonged to Ben Jonson, per Pickwoad, "Derry and Raphoe Diocesan Library Lecture."

26 Sigonio, *De Antiquo Iure Civium Romanorum*, 1r–3r. McCuaig pointed out that there was a tension in Sigonio between the Aristotelian theory of citizenship to which he subscribed and according to which office holding was constitutive, and his view of Roman practice: after the Lex Hortensia, Sigonio believed, all artisans and laborers were counted as full Roman citizens. In short, Sigonio, according to McCuaig, believed that membership in an assembly alone was constitutive of citizenship, without broader office holding. While this was in tension with Aristotle's definition, the broad approach in which participation defined citizenship was certainly upheld by Sigonio. Smith and Zasius shared the Aristotelian outlook, but excluded artisans from citizenship in Rome (Zasius) and from "voice" and "authoritie" in "our commonwealth" (Smith). Zasius, *Lucubrationes*, 20, litt. b, s.v. "Cives"; Smith, *De Republica Anglorum*, 77.

27 McCuaig, *Carlo Sigonio*, 103–4.

In the early third century BC, the plebs successfully pushed back with various forms of resistance, including work stoppages, refusing to serve in the army, and, finally, the famous secession to the Janiculum hill. These actions resulted in a constitutional balance in which the plebs won access to the highest patrician offices, including the consulate, dictatorship, censorship, and priesthoods. In the legislative arena, plebiscites were now binding on all citizens thanks to the Lex Hortensia of 287 BC. This, for Sigonio, was the moment of constitutional balance in Rome, the moment of the mixed constitution, for, as McCuaig summarized, in Sigonio's view, "from the moment the plebeians had independent legislative initiative, they no longer suffered any arbitrary limitations qua citizens because of patrician privilege."[28] This second period was itself divided into two. The first half was characterized by constitutional balance, the second by class rivalry. The constitutional balance lasted until the Gracchan revolution, when the country was torn into the warring factions of *optimates* and *populares*. These factions, however, were not identified with the patricians and plebeians, since the matter of access to office—citizenship—that formed that struggle had now given way to class warfare.[29]

McCuaig explained that, according to Sigonio, true constitutional history only began in the second period, once the conflict between the patricians and plebeians had been settled. "Political history could only begin after the dominant group failed to achieve closure based on purity of blood and had given way to a polislike association in which citizenship entailed the complex of juridical guarantees known as *libertas*."[30] The constitution and the attendant practices of citizenship that emerged in this free state blended hereditary privilege, wealth, and individual talent in complicated ways, and Sigonio explained that the citizens of Rome in the later republic could be classified in three ways: orders, magistrates (nobility), and factions. The division into orders classed the Romans into senators, knights, and plebs; the nobility into nobles and new men; and the factions into *optimates* and *populares*.

When theorizing the commonwealth, and the English commonwealth in particular, Harrison and Smith clearly drew on this sort of material, most likely from reading some combination of Sigonio and French scholars like de la Loupe. Harrison used the language of orders throughout his work. And Smith suggested a number of ways of discussing the parts of the commonwealth in which he added several of Sigonio's categories to the traditional Aristotelian schema (bk. 1, chap. 6). For example, he noted, "Another [way of dividing the commonwealth] was among the Romanes of Patritii and plebei,

28 Ibid., 130–3.
29 Ibid., 130, 135–6.
30 Ibid., 136.

thone striving with another a long time, those that were patricii many yeares excluding those that were plebei from bearing rule, till at last all magistrates were made common unto them."[31] But Smith, like Harrison, was clearly only interested in the sorts of classification that pertained to the balanced constitution after the magistracies were opened to all men of talent, namely, "another division among the Romanes *senatores, equites, plebs.*"[32] Tellingly, Smith did not refer to the *optimates* and *populares* and did not develop a theory of oppositional or factional English politics; factional politics seemed to be confined to Rome. In fact, Harrison and Smith seemed to prefer a period before that considered ideal by Sigonio, perhaps right before the Lex Hortensia. The Lex Hortensia, according to Smith, brought on not the mixed regime, as Sigonio had it, but a "common wealth and rule of the people," the good version of the popular constitution.[33] This was certainly better than a form of democracy in which the rule was only concerned with the benefit of the poor, but the constitutional balance was already in favor of the plebs in Smith's eyes, as in those of many others of his day, including Nicholas Grouchy. England's constitution seems to have been suspended, according to Harrison and Smith, in a moment of balance, resembling a period of Roman history sometime after the patrician and plebeian conflict was settled to the point of allowing new men access to magistracies, but certainly well before the Gracchan revolution. This was reflected in both the approach to citizenship in England and the importance of *libertas.*

Harrison and Smith believed then that the hierarchical approach to citizenship in England resembled the hierarchy of orders of the Roman republic in a number of respects. First, social status and access to office were linked; status was defined in part by the ability to hold high office. Second, the basis of status was service to the state, not purity of bloodline, tribal membership, or wealth alone. Third, status was awarded through recognition by a public authority, not by popular acclaim or self-aggrandizement. Fourth, membership in classes of high status was hereditary. Fifth, as implied by the second point, high status was open to new men, who could rise on account of their service to the state. Sixth, high status required wealth in order to ensure the dignity of the order.

The society of orders was not only a sophisticated mechanism for regulating status and social order. It performed this regulation in the context of service to the state and thus united the system of status with that of citizenship. Moreover, the society of orders in the ancient states managed this regulation—especially in the Roman republic—while fulfilling the functions of the fiscal-military state. Cecil and Smith, like so many others in

---

31 Smith, *De Republica Anglorum*, 65.
32 Ibid.
33 Ibid., 51.

their day, were fascinated by how the Roman republic managed to maintain a reasonable approximation of the commonwealth ideal while at the same time operating a state. This relationship is what made Cecil and Smith so interested in the technical details of the operation of Rome in "The Wages of a Roman Footsoldier" and now, in *De Republica*, the institution of the census.

The census served two purposes. First, it was important for sustaining the honor of the positions and keeping the incentive structure solid.[34] Second, the census was linked to military provisioning, and thus the method of honoring was also the method of securing revenue. Though Smith was clearly interested in the first function of the census classes, he was more interested in the 1570s in the relationship between the census classes and state revenue. While this line of thought was not fully developed in *De Republica*, a few of his additions to Harrison's account are very suggestive of his view in this period. Where Harrison was rather general in his discussion of the application of the census to England, Smith was specific, providing the actual numbers necessary in England to qualify for a degree of honor.[35] Furthermore, Smith added to Harrison's account that such arrangements were fluid and could be changed as necessary, and he also included a more detailed discussion of the present arrangement of the census values for knights, which revealed him thinking through how these institutions functioned in England in his day.

The situation in England was apparently not settled:

Census equester was among the Romanes at diverse times at diverse valew: whosoever may dispende of his free lands 40. l. sterling of yearely revenew by an olde law of Englande either at the coronation of the prince or at the marriage of his daughter, or at the making of the prince, knight, or some such great occasion, may be by the king compelled to take that order and honour, or to pay a fine, which many not so desirous of honour as of riches, had rather do. Some who for causes be not thought worthy of that honor and yet have that abilitie, neither be made knightes though they would, and yet pay the fine. XI. l. sterling, at that time when this order began, maketh now an

---

34 Cf. Sigonio, *De Antiquo Iure Civium Romanorum*, 94v: "But the census in the senatorial order is praised, lest the splendor of the most distinguished order be obscured by limited private wealth" (Laudatur autem census in senatore, ne splendor amplissimi ordinis rei familiaris angustiis obscuretur).

35 For example, Smith replaced Harrison's more general statement ("Also in England no man is created Baron except he may dispende of yerly revenues so much as may fully maintayne and beare out his countenaunce and post") with one more specific ("[A]nd in Englande no man is created barron, excepte he may dispend of yearly revenue, one thousand poundes or one thousand markes at the least"). Holinshed, *Chronicles*, 103v; Smith, *De Republica Anglorum*, 66.

Cxx. l. of currant mony of Englande: as I have more at large declared
in my booke of the diversitie of standards or the valor of monies.[36]

Smith had thus come to the conclusion that the census values should not be
fixed as absolute values constitutionally and can and should change with inflation. But he appears not to have made up his mind about the relationship
between honor and financial contribution. There are several models presented here: one is honored and required to give a financial contribution to
the state; one is not honored but required to contribute some lesser amount;
or one is not honored but is required to contribute the same amount as the
one who is honored. Precisely what the relationship should be among the
society of orders, the commonwealth ideal, and the fiscal-military state was
still being worked out.

This is also apparent in his offhand remark that *"Equites Romani* had
equum publicum. The knightes of England have not so, but finde their owne
horse themselves in peace time."[37] As Sigonio remarked, it is not apparent from the ancient sources what precisely the *equum publicum* was. What
Smith had clearly decided on was that private wealth be mobilized for the
common good in a manner which was as voluntary as possible. While this
has overtones of reason of state and the extraction of resources for the state
on the backs of the citizenry, for Smith there did not seem to be any sense
of trickery. The private wealth of those who could afford to part with it was
to be mobilized for the use of the state.

Since he was concerned with the actual functioning of the state, with the
commonwealth in practice, it was essential that inflation not be allowed to
eat away at the contributions of the census classes to the state. The burdens
of the honored classes must be real burdens in order for this method of or-
ganizing society without coercion to be effective in funding the state. If the
higher degrees of people were simply to give a nominal fee to the state, or
be freed from contributing to the state financially at all, like in France, this
would require the state to operate on completely different fiscal principles:
through a heavier tax burden on the commons, as in France, or through
the debasement of coinage or some other financial trick. Smith by 1565 was
certainly on guard against imposing any sort of undue financial burden on
the commons. The choice was then between a quasi meritocratic, symbolic
system of social stratification and the possibility of mutuality and commonwealth or heavy burdens on the lower income classes with almost certain
factional tension. For Smith (and perhaps the Privy Council more generally)
the approach using honors was not only consistent with the commonwealth

---

36 Smith, *De Republica Anglorum*, 67–8.
37 Ibid., 67.

ideal, but unlike in France, where the nobility was exempt from taxation, it was a source of revenue.

DIFFERENTIATED ATTACHMENT

The second half of the first book of *De Republica* (chaps. 17–24), devoted to the "degrees of the commonwealth," combined Smith's thinking in the *Discourse* about how the different sorts of people have different material and psychological needs with the model of a society of orders found in Sigonio and applied to England by Harrison. This led to a rich portrait of the mentalities that characterize the different degrees of the English people and the corresponding psychological needs that had to be addressed and satisfied in order to achieve political attachment and legitimacy without compulsion. The careful examination and use of the historical Roman model offered several advantages over previous approaches in England: it offered a differentiated theory of office without admitting faction or choosing between a stereotyped nobility and the people, as in Contarini; it retained the hierarchy of the Reformers' view of order without committing England to a view of agrarian labor as servile; and it avoided the excesses of the radical resistance theory of the exiles, which verged on popular sovereignty but entrusted much to the nobility. It was unsurprisingly the closest to the humanism of Cheke, as far as that can be reconstructed, but it moved still further away from the universalizing Christian humanism of Colet and Erasmus, which tinged that theory.

Within the society of orders, Smith showed that there were different motives and ways of relating to the commonwealth. His theory included an awareness of the different ideas of social solidarity, of the sort that recent social historians of politics, such as Keith Wrightson, Ethan Shagan, and Andy Wood, have noted.[38] Sigonio had collated a significant body of material from Livy's and Cicero's letters and speeches on the different orders of the Roman citizen in the *De Iure*, some of which spoke to the mentalities of the orders and their attitudes toward participation in the state.[39] This material was not used in a systematic, comparative way by Harrison and Smith, as the more structural elements of the society of orders like the census had been, but their descriptions of the degrees of the people reveal a similar ambition to describe the orders in terms of institutions and attitudes.

Once again, attitudes toward participation in public life turned on the understanding of honor. Smith, despite his sympathies, could hardly agree with Ponet's analysis of honor, which he must have thought played directly

38 See the introduction to this volume.
39 Sigonio, *De Antiquo Iure Civium Romanorum*, 96–7, 101, 108–9.

into Osório's hands. Indeed, Ponet pictured the virtue of the nobility as the promotion of liberty, as the delivery of the people from tyrants. "Good kings, governours and states in time paste tooke it to be the greatest honour that could be, not to take cities and Realmes to their owne use (whan they were called to aide and releve thoppressed) as princes doo now a daies: but to rescue and deliver the people and countreies from the tiranie of the governours, and to restore them to their libertie."[40] Furthermore, for Ponet, it was not the king who conferred honor but "the people of a grate and thankefull minde, [who] gave them that estimacion of honour."[41]

Osório, writing in the *De Nobilitate*, insisted that the pursuit of such "titles of honour and dygnyty" with the aim of winning popular acclaim was a greatly mistaken approach to life, "for they frame theyr life according to the opinion of the unlearned people, and repose the chiefe payne of true praise and commendation on the vain brute and estimation, of the foolish and rascall multitude."[42] Osório offered a more differentiated approach of his own, which, albeit by his own account, was enthusiastically received by the Elizabethan court. The members of the multitude, he explained, were a poor judge of things because they believed that the good consisted of only bodily pleasure. The commonalty were essentially folk Epicureans and Cyrenaics, according to Osório. True nobility, Christian nobility, for Osório needed to be unhooked from popular acclaim so that it would accord with Christian values, not the passing whim of the people.

The three mentalities that were most fully drawn in *De Republica* were those of the nobility, the gentlemen, and the yeomen. The lowest degrees of the commonwealth—the merchants, craftsmen, and day laborers—were hardly treated. This choice seems to have in part been dictated by Harrison's account, especially in the case of the first two sorts, since his treatment of the nobility was extensive and his remarks about the gentlemen suggestive. But Smith's interest in the yeomen seems to have been largely of his own initiative, perhaps stimulated by the Aristotelian treatment of the question of the best sort of populace.

Smith's discussion of the nobility—taking the higher nobles and the knights together—was the most closely integrated into Sigonio's discussion of the society of orders and the Roman model more generally. It was here that most of the formal features of the society of orders appeared, along with his claim that the members of the nobility acted in line with the Roman model. The nobility in England were seen as the result of recognition by the public authority for public service: "[t]he creation I call the originall donation and condition of the honour given by the Prince for the good

---

40 Ponet, *Shorte Treatise*, [G7v].
41 Ibid., [G7r–G7v].
42 Osório, *Fiue Bookes*, [39v]; Osório, *De Nobilitate*, 225–6.

service done by the first auncestor."[43] Knighthood was perhaps the example par excellence of nobility as the royal recognition of public service. Smith followed Harrison closely here but tightened up the language to emphasize the point: "Knightes therefore be not borne but made, either before the battle to encourage them the more to adventure their lives, or after as an advancement for their hardinesse and manhood alreadie shewed: or out of the warre for some great service done, or some good hope for the vertues which do appeare in them."[44]

Despite the fact that the orders in Rome did in part depend on wealth, this was a necessary but not sufficient cause in both Rome and England. In Rome, membership in a given order did depend in part on one's meeting the census requirement, that is, having one's wealth evaluated at a certain level. Harrison noted, and Smith repeated almost verbatim: "For as *Equites Romani* were chosen *ex censu*, that is according to their substaunce and riches: so be Knightes in Englande most commonly according to their yearleye revenues or substaunce and riches, wherewith to maintaine the estate. Yet all that had *Equestrem censum*, were not chosen to be knights, no more be all made knightes in England that maye spende a knightes landes, but they onelye whom the Prince will honour."[45]

It was virtue, that is, public service or the ability to contribute to the commonwealth, that was the hallmark of the English nobility as it was in Rome after the plebs were integrated into the government. The nobility in England was not about purity of blood or the mere fact of the antiquity of a family. Harrison had slightly muddied the waters here, suggesting that blood or antiquity did still play a role for some families in England who were ennobled before William the Conqueror came. And he suggested that there was a Roman analogy for this: "Gentlemen be those whome their race and bloode doth make noble and knowne . . . for as Gens in latin betokeneth the race and surname . . . therefore kept the name, were also called Gentiles, gentlemen of that or that house and race."[46] Here, Harrison was repeating a widespread view of the origin of the aristocracy in the sixteenth century, the "gentilician theory," based on the claim of the patricians in Livy against the plebs that it was only they who had legitimate lines of descent in kin groups. Harrison probably adopted this view and the parallels

---

43 Holinshed, *Chronicles*, 103v.

44 Smith, *De Republica Anglorum*, 67. Compare Harrison: "Knightes be not borne, neythither is any man a [k]night by succession, no not the Kyng or Prince: but they are made eyther before the battaile to encourage them the more to adventure and trie their manhoode, or after, as an advauncement for their courage and prowesse alreadie shewed, or out of the warres for some great service done, or for the singular vertues which doe appeare in them." Holinshed, *Chronicles*, 103v.

45 Holinshed, *Chronicles*, 103v; Smith, *De Republica Anglorum*, 67.

46 Holinshed, *Chronicles*, 105.

between antiquity and his day from André Tiraqueau (Andreas Tiraquellus), whose *Commentarii de Nobilitate* was widely available and in fact was owned by John Jewel, whose writings Harrison borrowed from and who may have contributed to Harrison's work as it appeared in the *Chronicles*.[47]

For Smith, this was a mistaken view about the nobility in England and a faulty model to point to. This sort of thinking only applied to the Romans before the integration of the plebeians and patricians, as Sigonio had explained. Thus, to Harrison's comment that "the Baronny or degree of Lords doth aunswere to the degree of Senatours of Rome," Smith added, "when patricii did betoken *Senatores aut senatorum filii*."[48] Whatever Smith's view of the origin of the Roman nobility before the third century, he insisted that the criterion in England had to be virtue.[49]

For Smith, the nobles had internalized this ethic. Their chief worry was decay and being shown up for not being "true nobility" in the face of the new men. Commenting on the Roman *nobiles*, who gloried in their ancestors' accomplishments, Smith wrote, "This matter made a great strife among the Romanes, when those which were Novi homines were more allowed, for their vertues new and newly showen, then the olde smoke [stock] of auntient race newly defaced by the cowardice and evill life of their nephewes and discendaunts could make the other to be." The new men—like Smith and many of the other councillors to Edward VI and Elizabeth— raised the question of true nobility continually. There was no possibility of simply assuming the habit of command or constituting a governing class through family tradition alone. Smith made no mention of the approach to the patrician-plebeian *nobilitas* in which the official right to use death masks was tied to several generations of curule office-holding ancestors. The echoes of this in the contemporary French practice in which three generations established hereditary nobility had been pointed out by Guillaume Budé in 1508. But Smith had no use for this, and around the same time John Rainolds insisted in his Oxford lectures on Aristotle's *Rhetoric* that "true nobility does not depend upon ancestral statues, but upon one's own virtues, not upon the titles of one's ancestors, but upon one's own deeds."[50] Smith's conclusion, which reflected the attitude of some of the privy councillors,

---

47 McCuaig, *Carlo Sigonio*, 123, 139n13; Smith, *De Republica Anglorum*, 161; *Private Libraries in Renaissance England*, Ad1.

48 Holinshed, *Chronicles*, 103v; Smith, *De Republica Anglorum*, 66.

49 Smith might have taken either the widespread "natural" aristocratic position of Dionysius and Plutarch, who maintained that the patricians had been chosen by Romulus for their qualities, or Sigonio's position that the patricians were simply a faction, the "earliest free-born of Rome." The first was consistent with his view of the importance of virtue to nobility; the second with his apparent sympathy to Sigonio's antagonism to the patriciate before the third century. McCuaig, *Carlo Sigonio*, 137–9.

50 Ibid., 121–2, 145; Peltonen, *Classical Humanism and Republicanism*, 38.

men like William Cecil and Nicholas Bacon, was that "as other common wealthes were faine to doe, so must all princes necessarily followe, where vertue is to honour it."[51]

The mentality of the gentlemen, the next degree below the knights, was of a completely different sort. The gentlemen were that class who were called "master" so-and-so, who were recorded in court documents with the notation "gentleman" after their names, who studied law or at the university, and who in general lived a life free of manual labor and could afford the lifestyle. The mentality of the gentleman was almost an inversion of that of the higher nobility. The gentleman was not elevated because of his virtue, but rather elevated himself and was virtuous in order to justify the elevation. The procedure by which someone was made a gentleman was not the same by which the nobility were recognized by the monarch. Rather, a man initiated the process by paying a herald to either fabricate an ancestral past or "if he will do it more truely and of better faith," the herald would attest that the man was made a gentleman for his own merits. In either case the herald then would grant him a coat of arms and register the new gentleman in the heraldry.[52]

For Smith, the gentleman's mentality was marked throughout by status anxiety. His every effort was to justify the difference between himself and the degrees immediately below him. Fortunately, the effect of this was to foster a certain public-spiritedness. "In any shew or muster or other particular charge of the towne where he is, he must open his purse wider and augment his portion above others, or else he doth so much diminish his reputation. For other outward shew, a gentleman (if he wil be so accompted) must go like a gentleman, a yeoman like a yeoman, and a rascall like a rascall."[53] Honor here was not a reward for virtue, but virtues were deployed to justify the honor. The gentleman had to act his part on stage, in public, and show the world that he was all the things that he said he was. Thus in military matters, "he must and will (whatsoever it cost him) array himselfe and arme himselfe according to the vocation which he pretendeth: he must shew a more manly corage and tokens of better education, higher courage and more liberalitie than others, and keep about him idle men who shall doe nothing but waite upon him."[54] They were anxious that they might be seen to lack the relevant qualities; gentlemen thus set out to make sure that everyone knew that they had them.

The yeomen by contrast were completely and utterly themselves. "This sort of people confesse themselves to be no gentlemen, but give honour to

---

51 Smith, *De Republica Anglorum*, 71.
52 Ibid., 72–3.
53 Ibid.
54 Ibid., 73.

al which be or take upn them to be gentlemen." They were the better sort of farmers, who had forty shillings freehold annual revenue and who by and large set up their sons to become gentlemen and live without manual labor. They prefixed "goodman" to their last names and were noted with a "yeoman" in court records. When they acted in a public-spirited way, they did so for completely different motives than the gentlemen. They did so not to set themselves apart from the next degree of men, but to live up to the expectations of their lord, who was often both their landlord and the leader of their military unit (Smith may have had lords lieutenant in mind). The mentality of the yeomen was one of obedience, but an obedience shot through with mutuality and a sense of connection. They were men who sought a connection with others and were liable to shame if they disappointed them. They were family men who had no desire to leave their families to fight, but were willing to do so in part "to have the love of their Lorde and his children to be continued towardes them and their children, who hath adventured their lives to and with him and his" when they came home.[55]

This differentiation in mentality differed from that of Osório, who conceived of three different reasons for seeking "preheminence and auctority": the pursuit of "al kinde of pleasures"; so that "they may thereby be thought good and inbued with some notable vertu"; or so that "in greatest affaires may be a great ayde and assistance to all those citizens and neighbours wyth whom he is conversante."[56] The motives of Smith's nobles and gentlemen, the chief office-holding classes, were somewhere between Osório's second and third motives. They were neither wholly altruistic nor selfish, though the nobility were closer to the third mentality and the gentlemen to the second. But in Smith's handling, the motivations were conditioned by the traditions of the orders and the position of the classes vis-à-vis the other orders and the rising new men. The psychology of honor and civic engagement had more to do with the structure of the classes in society than with individual intentions. In a material sense, as I discuss below, all of the degrees of people supported the commonwealth, but in a deeper sense, they were so different from each other and the sorts of recognition they were seeking were so different that it is difficult to say that they were really participating in the same commonwealth. This was of course no less true in Livy's Rome, where the plebs and patricians held very different views of the world, or of the many and the few in Aristotle, with their variant views of justice. For Smith, this was part and parcel of the real teaching of antiquity about the nature of the commonwealth, and harmonizing—or at least coordinating—these different views was perhaps the most important task of the state.

55 Ibid., 75.
56 Osório, *Fiue Bookes*, 40r–[40v].

THE STATE: THE COMMUNITY OF STATUTE AND NEIGHBORLINESS

Commentators on the institutional sections of Smith's *De Republica* have in recent years focused on the question of regime type. They have argued that his description of the state fit into the effort to describe a mixed monarchy of the sort put forward by Aylmer, which responded to the acephalic condition of being ruled by a queen. There were various conciliar projects being formulated in response to the unsecured succession of Elizabeth. In this reading, England was a commonwealth of which the queen was only a part; much of the state was independent of her will and could carry on without her. While there is no doubt that Smith held this view, there was much material in these sections of the work that showed that Smith was concerned not only, and perhaps not even primarily, with the question of constitutional balance, but with the conditions that would make the realization of a commonwealth possible. He wanted to argue that England, with all the richness of its institutions, did in fact approximate the commonwealth ideal of a harmonious working together of all degrees of the people.

Though these sections were concerned with the institutions of government and certainly took note of the broad participation of which England was so proud, the account of participation here layered a solidaristic communalism onto the base of classical republican participatory citizenship. At a background level, the solidarism appealed both to the values of neighborliness, which oriented the everyday practices of the countryside and the provincial towns, and to the learned ideal of brotherhood championed by the Christian humanists, like Erasmus and Colet. But the political analysis that made it possible to understand the participation in magistracies and the use of law courts as cooperative and solidaristic depended on the far more specific account of political development that underlay the understanding of England as a society of orders, namely, that England's constitution was arrested at an ideal point in which factional conflict had given way to the openness of the government to all of the orders, but before developing into a radical democracy. Here, I show this with reference to the Parliament, the judicial system, and the Star Chamber.

The survival of the background attitudes about neighborliness and brotherhood in Smith's account of political institutions appeared in the striking exhortation to avoid participation in the high courts of justice, which were now fixed in London rather than along riding circuits with the king, as in the past. Starkey and others had complained about the cost of bringing suits to London and their use to harass one's neighbors, and the Erasmians had argued against the overuse of the courts in a Christian commonwealth. The point was thus by no means new to the literature on commonwealth, but Smith made it his own by finding a classical source to justify nonparticipation and the limited access to justice.

Cato, he recounted, was petitioned to cover the "pleading place in Rome" with canvas to give the plaintiffs and defendants relief from the hot sun. Cato replied, "Nay . . . for my part I had rather wish that the waies to the place of pleading were cast over with galthrops [thorns], that the feete of such as love so well pleading, should feele as much paine of those prickes in going thither as their heades of the sunne in tarrying there."[57] Smith explained:

> [H]e ment that they were but idle, whot heades, busie bodies, and troublesome men in the common wealth that did so nourish pleading: good labourers and quiet men could bee content to ende their matters at home by judgement of their neighbours and kinsfolke without spending so their money upon procurers and advocates whom we call attournies. . . . Those he accounted profitable citizens, who attended their honest labour and businesse at home, and not stand waiting and gaping upon their rolles and processe in the lawe: those other by his judgement, it made no matter what mischiefe they had.[58]

The Cato of this story may have been linked in Smith's mind with the "Cato" of the popular book of Latin sayings in couplets that was widely used to teach Latin and proper conduct simultaneously, which had been recommended by many of the major Reformers, including Luther, Melanchthon, and Beza, and was accompanied by a commentary by Erasmus. It was used in the teaching of Edward VI and in many Tudor grammar schools.[59] "Cato" explained that litigiousness and controversy were not always to be insisted on and that sometimes you "muste give place and be obsequious to thy friend, though thou maieste overcome him."[60] And when one is done fighting, one ought not to dwell on the past: "the evill tales of the contencion passed, ought no more to be rehersed, but all the former injuries ought to be cleane forgotten."[61]

By and large, Smith found the centralization and nationalization of state institutions to be praiseworthy not for the retreat of government from the lives of citizen-subjects, but because they gave participation in government a more public character. Thus, it was clear from the outset that Smith thought of Parliament not simply as a legislative body, but as an instance of the commonwealth, of the entire community of the realm. He began by comparing the political nation meeting in Parliament to the nation going to war. The

57 Smith, *De Republica Anglorum*, 93.
58 Ibid.
59 Green, *Humanism and Protestantism*, 156–9.
60 *Catonis Disticha Moralia*, 1:[B5v–B6r].
61 Ibid., 2:[C3v].

collaboration of the different orders in Parliament was "as in warre where the king himselfe in person, the nobilitie, the rest of the gentilitie, and the yeomanrie is, there is the force and power of Englande."[62] Parliament was a moment of commonwealth, an event as much as a fixed institution for the making of law. In imagining Parliament in this way, Smith was not simply asserting the legitimacy of legislative sovereignty on the basis of universal consent ("That is the Princes and whole realmes deede: whereupon justlie no man can complaine, but must accomodate himselfe to finde it good and obey it. . . . And the consent of the Parliament is taken to be everie mans consent"). This view of Parliament was an image of the entire commonwealth meeting on a free and independent basis. In his description of the institutions of lawmaking and the administration of justice, this was his primary concern, that is, to understand and legitimate the English commonwealth not simply through an abstract understanding of consent, but in an appeal to the actual experience of social harmony and the meeting of the orders, albeit on an unequal basis. This is the importance of the analogy of going to war, which featured prominently in his account of the yeomen. The experience of going to war was one of social harmony, a moment of a community of fate, and it mirrored the moment of consultation in Smith's model, the *comitia centuriata* or *tributa*.[63]

The *comitia centuriata* and *tributa* had recently been described in endless detail by Grouchy. For Smith, what must have been so important about the *comitia centuriata* was that it was organized according to census group, that is, roughly what would later become the orders; that these groups corresponded to classes of soldiers; that it had judicial functions; and, above all, that it was responsible for statutory legislation. The most famous of its legislative acts was the Twelve Tables, which covered most of the areas that Smith said Parliament legislates and that were found in the *comitia centuriata* and *tributa*.

Particulars aside, what Smith and the other Reformers seeking a model of statutory innovation must have found so compelling in the early Roman republic was the very fact of a legislative assembly. The great humanist lawyer Ulrich Zasius had covered much of this material in the narrative reconstruction of early Roman history in his commentary to the beginning of the *Digest*. Zasius, along with Alciato and Budé, was widely read in England in this period, and his works are well represented in catalogs of legal libraries of the time.[64] Zasius suggested that Rome had initially been guided mostly by customary law, even once the first assembly, the *comitia curiata*,

---

62 Smith, *De Republica Anglorum*, 78.

63 Ibid., 78–9: "The parliament. . . . And to be short, all that ever the people of Rome might do either in Centuriatis comitiis or tributis."

64 Wijffels, "Law Books in Cambridge Libraries," 371.

was founded by Romulus. This assembly made few laws, and those were mostly concerned with religious and public matters: "there were no certain and legitimate judgments, nor were matters in private acts of the citizens governed by certain law; it was, as he says, without law."[65]

According to Zasius this time of customary law belonged to a "feudal" period of early Roman history, which was reflected in other institutions. Rome before Servius Tullius was composed of *curiae* (courts), which were associations of clientage. "Romulus, according to book 2 of Dionysius of Halicarnassus, looking ahead lest there be injuries of the rich against the poor, or on the contrary, envy of the poor of the powerful, giving rise to discord, permitted the plebs to choose for themselves a patron from the patricians."[66] These courts were represented in the *comitia curiata*, which was thus a sort of feudal court assembled of subordinate courts. For Zasius, this history loosely paralleled that of Germany and Europe of his day. Zasius argued that Germany was still quasi feudal, depending in part on the customary law.[67] And while the court structure mostly disappeared from towns and cities, it still remained in villages and manors.[68] In Rome, this condition of clientage was only changed and the problem of uncertain law remedied with Servius Tullius's institution of the *comitia centuriata* and the passage of the Twelve Tables. To say then that the Parliament of England was like the *comitia centuriata* and *tributa* was to say that it was a post-feudal legislative assembly, not that it was a radical democracy.[69]

What this means is that the statutes promulgated by Parliament were understood by Smith neither as the edicts of a feudal lord nor as plebiscites of the sort that had binding power after the Lex Hortensia. Smith envisioned

---

65 Zasius, *Lucubrationes*, 4, litt. d, s.v. "sine certa": Nulla erant iudiciorum, certa, legitimave, nec in privatis civium actis, certa lege res gerebatur: hoc est quod dicit, sine lege.

66 Ibid., 5, litt. h, s.v. "curias": Romulus, ut est apud Dionysium Halicarnassus lib. ii urbe condita, provisurus ne iniuria locupletum in humiles, vel vicissim egenorum invidia in potentes, discordiam pareret, plebeis permisit, quem sibi ex patriciis patronum eligerent.

67 Ibid., 4: Saepe enim in iure nostro non praecise, sed ex frequentia usus deciditur.

68 Ibid., 5: Quondam sua cuique civitati vel municipio curia fuit, a praedictis forsan Romanorum decuriis usurpata, quae hodie magna ex parte abierunt. In pagis tamen & villis Curiae dominicales sunt, quae vetustatis velut umbram referunt.

69 This is to say that I believe that Smith subscribed more to Zasius's account of early Roman history than to Grouchy's. Not that he would deny Grouchy's account per se, but Grouchy's themes were not quite those of Smith. Smith was interested in the Protestant-Catholic polemic and in statutory reform and liberty, not regime type. His discussion of Parliament differed in many respects from Grouchy's account of the *comitia centuriata*, except in the broadest strokes. For Grouchy, legislation was just one of three powers of the *comitia*, the others being the creation of magistracies and judicial functions. He also noted that the *comitia* could definitely declare war, which Smith explained was one of the powers given to the monarch in England. For a narrative stressing the importance of Grouchy, see Tuck, "Hobbes and Democracy."

Parliament as the meeting of the entire commonwealth and its acts as acts of the commonwealth. As I have shown, the commonwealth was not a mass of undifferentiated citizens and in no way was to be mistaken for the commonalty; it was rather the cooperation of the various parts of the commonwealth. Thus when Smith wrote that "the consent of the parliament is taken to be everie mans consent,"[70] he did not mean to invoke some individualized notion. The idea was rather to imagine oneself as represented insofar as one's vocation or order was represented.

Indeed, when Smith invoked consent, he seems to have had two related but distinct ideas in mind: a legal notion, according to which one should feel oneself obligated or sworn, and a psychological sense, according to which one should feel identified with the law. The old legal sense in which consent was obligated as a product of the sworn vow of the vassal, who was *commanded* to give both advice and consent, obviously fit poorly with the commonwealth ideal. In the past, consent could not be withheld at the end of a consultative process, and this norm sat happily with one that required a broad basis of consultation in accordance with the principle of *quod omnes tangit ab omnibus approbetur*. Smith did not abandon this way of thinking entirely, and his language was obviously tinged with it. But where consent formerly had to be given to the lord, it was now to be given to the realm as a whole, to the king-in-parliament. One essentially swore an oath to give one's consent to the product of the deliberative process of the realm rather than to the lord. While this may seem to be an odd way of thinking about legitimacy (rather than, say, solely an appeal to the fairness of the procedure) since it seems to preserve a notion of the commonwealth as a whole as one's lord, presumably this view was consistent with the notion of the law as commandment and stricture (the accusatory sense of the law), which fit better with the Protestant understanding of the law than a more proceduralist approach did. Even more significantly, it invoked the old aristocratic political values, if only implicitly, of the importance of one's word of honor and being sworn to obey.[71] The laws embodied thus a social compromise,

---

70 Smith, *De Republica Anglorum*, 79.

71 It was clearly difficult to fit the old theory of advice and consent to the emerging theory of a free people. Suggesting that such consent could be owed to the king-in-parliament as an embodiment of the commonwealth, while abstract, seems to have been a preferable approach to continuing to admit that subjects were compelled to grant their consent to the lord and that such a legislative body was simply consultative. The coexistence of kings and assemblies in early Rome clearly bothered Zasius, who argued that the legal consent of the people under the kings was given because "there was no hope of liberty." In this combination, lordship was simply wrapped in a legal framework, and statute and the legislative process were in part coerced and thus only in part legally enforceable in an abstract sense. See Zasius, *Lucubrationes*, 22, litt. h, s.v. "Datumque."

not in the sense of a compromise between conflicting interests, but rather in the sense of a blending of the voices of the different parts of the commonwealth, as judged by the monarch. The role of the king-in-parliament was not that of the feudal lord, but rather that of a representative of the commonwealth as a whole, who was capable of evaluating the bills put forward by the House of Lords and the House of Commons.

Psychologically, legitimacy would come from a recognition on the part of all the parts of the commonwealth that they had duly been part of the process, that they had been recognized and included in the deliberations, and thus that an act of Parliament was "the Princes and whole realmes deede: whereupon justlie no man can complaine, but must accommodate himselfe to finde it good and obey it."[72] The logic of legitimacy was clearly in part an appeal to autonomy, but in a corporatist or collective sense; in response to the exclusion the commons felt in 1549, here all the parts of the state were said to be included. One's sense of obligation was thus meant to stem from the sense of a common enterprise, like setting out to war together or, here, participating in the reformation of the state. Ultimately, this sense of identification with the commonwealth and its product of Parliament rested on identification with one's order.

Smith's treatment of the Star Chamber also highlighted the notion of a post-feudal, mutual commonwealth. For Smith, the Star Chamber was an instrument of state building, but was neither a resource for the marginal people of the localities to use royal justice against their local superiors nor an instrument of centralizing paternalist enforcement, but rather a means of bringing the commonwealth together out of a fragmented feudal past.[73] Smith characterized the Star Chamber as a tool for bringing the nobility to heel and integrating them into the commonwealth. Indeed, he claimed that the Star Chamber was strengthened under Henry VIII by Cardinal Wolsey, who used it as a means of reining in the recalcitrant nobility of the north. What is crucial to realize, though, is that this was not simply a portrait of a centralizing institution that replaced the lordship of many with the lordship of a single king. Rather, Smith offered in the account of this institution another aspect of the replacement of feudal lordship with the commonwealth. The chief trouble with nobles was that they resorted to coercion rather than to the law. They were "[g]entlemen which would offer wrong by force to any manner man, and cannot content to demaund or defend their right by order of lawe."[74] The lordly use of force was mirrored in the

---

72 Smith, *De Republica Anglorum*, 78.

73 Cf. Hindle, *State and Social Change*. This difference in approach was no doubt in part due to the fact that many of the activities referred to by Hindle still lay in the future in 1565. The chamber had begun to supervise perjury in 1563, but the supervision of homicide and suicide was still in the future.

74 Smith, *De Republica Anglorum*, 127.

form of the social organization that accompanied it, and such noble men were said to be "banding themselves with their tenaunts and servaunts to doe or revenge injurie one against another as they listed."[75] Such bands of tenants and servants were clearly meant to be compared to the free citizenry of England, who held office and participated in the commonwealth. It was one of the achievements of the Tudors to make this possible, according to Smith, and he praised the law on retainers, which required that "no man should have above a number in his Liverie or retinue." The bands of retainers who characterized the late feudalism of the pre-Tudor period ("Bastard feudalism") were clearly analogous for Smith to the patron-client groups of the early Roman monarchy and republic.[76]

LIBERTY AND THE REJECTION OF LORDSHIP

Much of the second book and the beginning of the third book of the *De Republica* was concerned with how the institutions of public and criminal law embodied (or at least structured) the commonwealth ideal of mutuality. Parliament was an idealized moment of the meeting of the commonwealth; the Star Chamber encouraged mutuality by restructuring the organization of society; and the unavailability of justice in the prerogative courts put a premium on neighborliness. Much of the third book (chaps. 5–8) turned to the question of legal standing in private law. Here he treated wards and children, women, and, most significantly for this study, "bondage and bondmen" (chap. 8). In the discussion of bondmen, Smith sketched an account of political development that asserted the superiority of English liberty to continental practice without playing into the charges of "popularity."[77]

Smith's chapter was clearly written with Zasius's discussion of serfdom in Germany in mind. Zasius argued that the German *homines proprii* were more like the Roman manumitted slaves, the *liberti* or *libertini*, than true Roman slaves. The *libertinus* was a useful category in understanding serfdom and servile conditions more broadly in early modern Europe since

75 Ibid.
76 Ibid.
77 The literature thus far has focused on Smith's claim that there were no bondmen in England. While admitting that "Smith's book was written in France with the patriotic desire of proclaiming the merits of English institutions," Holdsworth wrote that Smith was not straying too far from the truth, since villeinage had been significantly degraded, amounting to little more than a method of extorting fees from tenants. Holdsworth, *History of English Law*, 3:508. MacCulloch has, on the other hand, emphasized the real stigma of serfdom in Smith's day, even if it was of a degraded form, and characterized Smith's claim that there were no such bondmen as the shared attitude of scholars who saw it as out of step with their Christian values and were simply wishing it out of existence. MacCulloch, "Bondmen under the Tudors," 92.

liberti were free in political terms (they were Roman citizens), but neverthe-less were required to act deferentially toward their patrons, who were their former masters.[78] Zasius and Smith argued that there was no tradition of slavery in Germany or England, respectively, that rivaled the cruelty and utter subjection of Roman slavery. Zasius cited Tacitus to the effect that Germans did not really have slaves.[79] Smith argued that when there were bondmen (*servi*, villeins in gross) in England,[80] they were never treated as poorly as the slaves in Rome: they were "not used with us so cruelly," they could possess copyhold property, and they occasionally suffered through harsh taxation. This echoed Zasius's claim that the Germans had never been slaves of the Roman sort, "though some labored by us servilely."[81]

Zasius explained that the *homines proprii* were free men in almost every question of legal status and standing: they could hold property, they lived in their own homes, they were not reckoned as members of the lord's household, they could serve in judicial procedures, they could inherit property, they could testify in court, they could trade their own goods, and they could make their own contracts. Above all, the *homines proprii* were not slaves in that they could not be "struck, beaten, tormented, or tortured."[82] The disabilities of the *homines proprii* resembled those of the Roman *liberti* as well: they were technically only free to marry others of their status, or be fined; they were technically not permitted to be given citizenship in a municipality if on the run from a lord; and they were not allowed to take holy orders unless they were manumitted by their lords. As a sign of their servitude they had various obligations to the lord, some in kind, some in money, and some in service. The lord inherited a share of their goods, ranging from a quarter to a half, when they died. They could be bought or sold to another lord, as long as it was in good faith.[83]

For Smith, as for Zasius, it was crucial to argue that the servile disabilities that continued to exist were no longer personal, but rather were obligations that were tied to the land. These disabilities were discussed in Zasius and Smith in terms of the Roman law concept of servitudes. Servitudes were obligations on a property or person that benefited another piece of real property or a person. It had traditionally been argued (Zasius said it was

78 Mommsen, Krueger, and Watson, *Digest of Justinian*, vol. 1, glossary, s.vv. "Libertinus," "Libertus."

79 Zasius, *Singularia Responsa*, 137.

80 I prefer here (and in the identification of the *adscriptii glebae* with the *villeins regardants* below) the reading of the editor of the 1583 printed edition, who, according to Dewar, must have thought of this as one of the few errors of fact to be corrected. The manuscript version does not seem to make sense of the argument. Smith, *De Republica Anglorum*, 17, 135–6.

81 Ibid., 33: licet aliqui servili apud nos nota laborent.

82 Ibid., 33–4: Caedi verberari, adfligi, torqueri homines nostros non est receptum.

83 Smith, *De Republica Anglorum*, 34.

a *communis opinio* and cited Baldus) that only a servitude that benefited some other property could be considered a *servitudo realis*; if it benefited another person, it had to be a *servitudo personalis*. Zasius rejected this view, since it made no sense of the various rights that Germans held (and had held for a long time) against other possessors of land ("such as when peasants have the right of cutting firewood from a neighboring wood, or the nobles possess the rights of hunting and birding in the woods of others").[84] These rights clearly had nothing to do with a benefit to some other property, since they clearly were benefiting individuals and communities. Yet, it made little sense to claim that these rights were personal rights that held between the beneficiary of the right and the possessor of the land. These were clearly rights that one possessed by virtue of living in that area and had nothing to do with a particular relationship between an individual and a lord or corporate body of some kind. To understand all of these rights, Zasius distinguished between two senses in which a servitude could be said to be a matter of real property: the original sense, in which it related to a benefit to some other piece of property, and a second sense, in which it benefited an individual or a group due to where they lived, "as when the right of pasture, hunting, or fishing, is owed to the community of some city, village, or monastery, or to the inhabitants of a castle."[85]

Smith followed suit, dismissing the first sense of a *servitudo realis* ("a bondage annexed to it . . . not as naturally the lower ground must suffer and receive the water and filth . . . nor such as *Justinian* speaketh of *de servitudinibus praediorum rusticorum & urbanorum*") and embracing a notion of a *servitudo realis* that "doeth bring a certaine kinde of servitude to the possessor."[86] For Smith, this had the significance, only implied in Zasius, of a certain moral progress in which personal relationships of subjection had given way to a contract in which subjection or hierarchy was a matter of the possession of particular land tenures. Thus, he pictured a transition from slavery in antiquity, to an early form of servitude where bondmen were bound personally to particular plots of land in order to cultivate them (*adscriptii glebae*, villeins *regardants*), to finally a state in which "not the men but the land should be bound and bring with it such bondage and service to him which occupieth it, to carie the Lords dung unto the fieldes, to plough his ground at certaine daies, sowe, reape, come to his Court, sweare faith unto him, and in the ende to holde the lande but by copie of the Lords court rolle and at the will of the Lorde."[87] Such an understanding allowed

84 Zasius, *Singularia Responsa*, 51–2.

85 Ibid., 52: ut cum communitati alicuius civitatis, villae, monasterii, habitatoribus castri, ius pascendi, venandi, piscandi, &c. debitum est.

86 Smith, *De Republica Anglorum*, 138.

87 Ibid.

the system to be at once free and servile: "Ye see that wher the persons be free, and the bodies at full libertie and *maxime ingenui*, yet by annexing conditions to the lande, there is meanes to bring the owners and possessors thereof into a certaine servitude or rather libertinitie."[88] Smith's idea was that English copyholders contractually had a status resembling that of the Roman *libertini*. In any permanent sense, however, they were simply free, unlike some of the peasants on the Continent. The English serfs, once free, were not stuck with the disabilities of the German peasants, akin to the *libertini*, but were truly free, "not *libertus manumittentis*, but simply *liber.*"[89]

The English servile tenant, though only put in this position due to contract, was still required to conduct himself more or less like the *libertus* or the *cliens*, in a fashion similar to the German *homo proprius*. "That the tenauntes beside paying the rent accustomed, shal owe to the Lord a certaine faith, duetie, trust, obedience, (as we terme it) certaine service as *libertus*, or *cliens patrono*."[90] Zasius had explained that this attitude of reverence was owed by the *homo proprius* to his lord, just as it was required of the *cliens* to his *patronus*. The *homo proprius* could not call the lord to justice without his permission nor bring accusations of breaches of trust (*actiones famosae*). "The person of the lords should always be regarded by them and spoken of by them as inviolate and worthy."[91] For Smith, this squared the circle, providing for the execution of all the servile work needed for the economy, while insisting on the freedom of the people of England. "Thus necessitie and want of bondmen hath made men to use free men as bondmen to all servile services: but yet more liberally and freely, and with a more equalitie and moderation, than in time of gentilitie slaves and bondmen were woont to be used."[92]

All of this servility was contractual and temporary. This was clear in the case of apprenticehood, which was at once freely chosen and servile. As Smith put it, it was "but by covenaunt, and for a time," nevertheless, "for the time it [was] *vera servitus*." The apprentice must be "obedient to all his masters

88 Ibid., 140.
89 Ibid., 136. This identification between the civil and English legal categories helps explain Holdsworth's puzzle of why some English lawyers, Smith among them, seemed to talk about methods of pleading (in gross and *regardant*) as status categories of villeinage. Holdsworth, *History of English Law*, 3:509–10. Smith identified villeins in gross with *servitudo personalis*, *regardant* with *servitudo realis*, and thought of copyhold as a refinement of the *servitudo realis*, a freer form that existed in England. As I am arguing here, this reading of English institutions in light of the status categories of Roman lawyers with sympathies toward the Reformation made it possible to think of England in the context of the ancient practices of the classical commonwealth.
90 Smith, *De Republica Anglorum*, 140.
91 Zasius, *Singularia Responsa*, 52: semper eis sancta & honesta videri & dici persona domini debet. l.liberto.ff. de obseq. lib. (*D*, 37.15).
92 Ibid., 142.

commandments" and "must suffer such correction as his master shall thinke meete." Conditions were nominally freely entered into, but the apprentice really had no choice but to choose a master. If a young unmarried man did not choose a master, he would be punished with the stock and whipping as "an idle vagabond" in keeping with the latest laws against vagrancy.[93]

THE ROMAN IDEAL OF LIBERTY

As the previous sections have shown, the chief argument of the *De Republica* was that the English system of government and society approximated the best stage in the political development of the commonwealth ideal. Liberty played an important role in this approximation, since it was a necessary precondition for the sort of mutuality that characterized true political community. Since the Roman republic represented the ideal moment for Smith (and for so many others), his argument turned on showing that the liberty of the Englishmen resembled the liberty enjoyed by the Romans at that time. Yet, Smith admitted that many Englishmen lived in a state resembling that of Roman freed slaves, *libertini*, albeit on a contractual basis.

This reality was a compromise required, in Smith's view, by the various sorts of work that needed to be done in a given country. The inequality in work meant that mutuality was bound to be limited regardless of institutional design. Given this sense of the real limits on mutuality, Smith thought it preferable to conceive of liberty as temporarily alienable, since to his mind a relationship of deference and paternal care was preferable to one of resentment and self-interest. And certainly, this was preferable to idleness and a concomitant refusal to participate in the commonwealth at all. This qualification of Smith's endorsement of Roman liberty is evident in a comparison of Smith's account of liberty with that of Sigonio.

Sigonio defined liberty in three senses in his discussion of the *ius libertatis* in Rome. The first was the difference between free men and slaves. "All men who lived in the city or countryside of Rome were either free men or slaves. They were called free men who were naturally suited to it, had the power of doing what each wanted, unless something was prohibited by violence or law. Slaves on the contrary were those who were in the power of masters."[94] Free people were above all not subject to violence in the same manner as slaves. They were, Sigonio explained, "protected from the beatings of

---

93 Ibid., 140–1; Beier, *Masterless Men*, 10, 86, 159.

94 Sigonio, *De Antiquo Iure Civium Romanorum*, 26: Omnes homines, qui urbem, agrumque R. inhabitarunt, liberi fuerunt, aut servi. Liberi vocati, qui naturale adepti, qui cuique liberet, faciendi arbitrium erant, nisi quod aut vi, aut iure prohiberetur. Servi contra, qui in dominorum erant potestate constituti.

private men."[95] The second sense of liberty was the rule of law and the accountability of office holders, that is, "the citizens of Rome freed themselves from the intemperate rule of kings and tyrants, and bound themselves by law and annual magistracies."[96] Finally, liberty is that by which "the Roman citizens protected themselves against the excessive command of the magistrates, and especially the consuls."[97]

Smith stressed heavily the first category of liberty, the second to some extent, and he approached the third gingerly at best. Many of the elements of the third sense of liberty would have extended more power to the commonalty than the English nobility were willing to extend. Sigonio noted that three laws were made in this vein: the first created the tribunes of the plebs to combat the consuls, the second made the tribunes sacrosanct, and the third stated that any office (honor) required the approval of the plebs.[98] There was some limited support for the creation of the tribunes, but the English sources universally suggested that this quickly went wrong. The sources were mostly silent on the second two. For Smith, then, liberty was about status, not the protection of the ability to choose one's life course. These were obviously interconnected in antiquity and the distinction should not be pushed too far, but the fact is that Smith did not conceive of office holding as a protection against potential constraint, but rather as a recognition of the importance of one's counsel and contribution to the commonwealth. He rejected the notion that liberty required institutions to protect it of the sort Sigonio pictured as protecting the plebs. For Smith (and for so many of his contemporaries) this was not liberty, but the protection of narrow class interest, which only risked the unity of the commonwealth.

A "REALISTIC" COMMONWEALTH?

The broadly participatory nature of the Elizabethan theory of the state, that is, the theory of the state held by Elizabeth's counselors and polemicists, has mostly been explained in the context of "perceived monarchical incapacities" or "acephalic conditions" and of "age, gender and/or disputable legitimacy,"

---

95 Ibid., 30: Proprium praeterea fuit eiusmodi libertatis, immunem a privatorum verberibus esse.

96 Ibid.: Alterum genus libertatis fuit, quo se R. cives a regum, & tyrannorum impotenti dominatione liberaverunt, & legibus se, ac magistratibus annuis obstrinxerunt.

97 Ibid., 31: Tertium huic libertatis genus consequens est, quo se Romani cives adversus nimium magistratuum, & praesertim consulum imperium muniverunt.

98 Ibid.: Fuerunt autem multae, quarum tres pro plebis, reliquae pro populi libertate sunt latae. Primae pro plebe fuerunt, una, Ut tribuni plebis quotannis quinque de plebe crearentur, qui auxilis plebi adversus consules essent; altera, Ut iidem tribuni sacrosancti essent; tertia, Ne is honor nisi plebeis pateret.

concerns that plagued not only Elizabeth's reign, but those of her predecessors, Edward VI and Mary I. This may be true if one wishes to generalize and include Aylmer, Smith, and Haddon in one breath. But the differences are telling. The point of Smith's mixed monarchy was not to dilute the threat a queen posed to the polity, but rather to show that the queen *was* as much a part of decision making in England as were any of the other orders. And while Smith did uphold a mixed monarchy, his real interest was not in the restrictions on royal decision making, but in the defense of the English constitution as a commonwealth. Smith certainly was trying to construct a "Protestant politics of association," but not obviously in the mode of ancient constitutionalism or the "elect nation."[99] The constitution he described was not from time immemorial—it had several self-consciously new features, such as the practices of the Star Chamber and the injunctions against vagrancy—and he did not laud the national characteristics of the English, like Aylmer did. This was Protestant polemic, but in a very low-key way. In arguing for the consistency of liberty and commonwealth in England, he was as much on the defensive as on the offensive. Moreover, while he believed that certain Catholic princes were absolutists, and the pope above all, he did not make out the English constitution to be superior to those of civil law countries. His aim was to defend it in a reasonable fashion, in the manner of a scholar rather than a polemicist.

The literature from the Haddon-Osório controversy through the mid-1570s argued that the commonwealth ideal was possible within a Protestant commitment to liberty. In *De Republica*, the argument was mostly in the background: the new description of Rome available from Grouchy and Sigonio showed that Rome flourished as a society of orders that preserved liberty; England resembled Rome; and England could flourish just the same. This was the Roman republic at just the right moment, though one in which Machiavelli's *tumulti* have been edited out. *De Republica* was written "not in that sort as *Plato* made his common wealth, or Zenophon his kingdome of Persia, nor as *Syr Thomas More* his *Utopia* feigned common wealths, such as never was nor never shall be, vaine imaginations, phantasies of Philosophers to occupie the time and to excercise their wittes," but rather as England was "at this day the xxviii of March *Anno* 1565."[100] The implication was that the level of attachment and the mutual sense of care may not be optimal, but they would be realistic.

The "realism" of the argument was mostly polemical and served the conservative retreat from the oppositional politics of the exiles during the 1550s. "Realism" here in part meant that there were no radical protections

---

99 McLaren, "Reading Sir Thomas Smith's *De Republica Anglorum*," 912; Collinson, "Monarchical Republic of Queen Elizabeth I," 36.

100 Smith, *De Republica Anglorum*, 144.

for the commons; this was not the theory of popular sovereignty proposed by the Marian exiles, who had largely stepped back from their more radical positions by this point anyway. Still, it was a way of saying to Catholic critics that the new approach was capable of not only dreaming big, but plodding carefully. Smith's work was not, however, realistic in its description of political behavior. It offered by and large a static constitutional view, a description of practices rather than of actual powers and resistances. This is obvious when Smith is compared to his sources, like Aylmer and Zasius, who criticized the actual operations of the institutions of their day and revealed the ways in which they could be exploited. Smith also did not use all of the descriptive tools available to him; though faction was vital to his historical account of political development, it disappeared as a living force in the operation of politics in his day. Such idealizing of politics meant that it was not truly clear how the commonwealth of England was supposed to solve the perennial problem of sedition.[101]

Indeed, many of the psychological concerns were left unresolved. It was not clear how a free society of orders would work to solve the systematic rebellions that had plagued the Tudors or the conflict of orders that had plagued Rome. In other words, it was not at all clear why Smith believed that England would not be plagued with just the sort of conflict that afflicted Rome. Smith's portrait of the mentalities of the different orders of citizens provided a partial response. Smith meant to argue that these portraits helped to show that the various degrees of England had various reasons for participating and contributing to the commonwealth.

But the psychology was described in a folk or literary way; it was not yet formalized, theorized, or tested. It was not clear how these different mentalities would interact with the old challenge of self-love, whether these orientations would truly be sufficient to counter class interest and self-interest. It was not clear why the orders in Parliament, in the making of law, and in the administration of justice would not pursue their own interests. The old answers still peeked through at times—avoiding idleness and allowing the people to live their vocations and the talented to be recognized—but Smith, even in this static picture of the world, hinted at the reality that was so much clearer in the *Discourse*, namely, the problems of inflation and structural changes to the economy. The talent of the new men must be recognized, he reminded the reader, but he also hinted that some of the higher degrees of men were not carrying their weight due to inflation. Psychologically, envy and ambition were almost completely absent, except in the

101 I thus agree with Mary Dewar's view that Smith's work "is not so much concerned with the actual workings of government as with the formal framework of the constitution.... We are listening to a learned civilian expounding the formal structure of English society, not the experienced Secretary analysing the realities of power." Dewar, *Sir Thomas Smith*, 112.

domesticated form of the gentleman's desire for respect. Perhaps the clearest example of the idealizing of Smith's work was that political change was treated in a stylized, abstract, and unthreatening Polybian fashion.[102]

In part the reason for the idealism of Smith's realistic commonwealth was that his study of England as a society of orders allowed him to rethink the relationship between state and commonwealth. As I showed in the previous chapter, the state was understood in Protestant political theory to be a subsystem of commonwealth with a specialized set of mechanisms—the positive law and the magistracies—to enforce compliance with divine law, which defined the shape of commonwealth as a whole. The state could take account of the degrees of the people, but this was generally limited to the distribution of honors. In general, the law was universalizing, and the expansion of liberty in this context was understood as the widening of access to the legal system. Thus the approach of Cromwell, Audley, and Somerset to securing the rights of tenants could be said to be "popular." Targeting the degrees of the people in a differentiated way in order to make them conform with the law needed to be done through an appeal to affection rather than fear, as through the social distribution of honor and acclaim. The account of political and legal development that enabled the description of Rome as a society of orders, however, made it possible to see law as the expression of status. The liberty of the various degrees of the people, from the servile apprentices and tenant farmers described in *De Republica* to the townsmen described in the *Discourse*, encoded (and idealized) economic and social relationships, including relationships of deference. The state was thus not a subset of the means to conformity with the law but a legal representation or mirroring of the economic and social relationships that defined a particular commonwealth. Smith's realism was thus a kind of positivism and was scarcely justificatory of the distribution of status and office; under the pressure of resistance, it would collapse to naturalism and an invocation of a higher law.

102 Smith argued (bk. 1, chaps. 12–14) that the various sorts of regime could arise naturally, out of good motives, and concluded that "the mutations and changes of fashions of government of common wealthes be naturall, and do not alwayes come of ambition or malice." Smith was of course well aware that a form of government could be the result of such ambition and malice, and he gave an extremely abbreviated version of this usual view in book 1, chapter 4, where inter alia, the usual Livian story of the conflict of orders was presented. Smith, *De Republica Anglorum*, 51, 62.

CHAPTER 3

THE MONARCHICAL REPUBLIC

[I]t is probable that kings existed from the beginning in accordance with nature. For if the slave has obeyed his master, if the wife her husband, if the son his father, if the household its governor, if the village has obeyed the command of nature, it is also probable that the commonwealth has never existed without a king.

—John Case, *Sphaera Civitatis**

The Aristotelian moment in Tudor political thought flourished between 1581 and the early 1590s and can be traced through various activities at Oxford spurred on by the court. It fizzled out soon, though not immediately, after the execution of Mary, Queen of Scots, in 1587 and the securing of the succession in the person of James VI of Scotland.[1] During these years, some of the most important men at court, including Sir Henry Unton, William Cecil, Lord Burghley, and Sir Christopher Hatton, the lord chancellor from 1587 to 1591, encouraged the study of Aristotle's *Politics*. The *Politics* had several advantages for the privy councillors: it provided a public alternative to Machiavelli,[2] whose approach to politics Burghley and the other councillors were accused of adopting in the 1570s and 1580s;[3] it provided training in political argument pro and contra, *in utramquem partem*, the style

* Translated by Dana Sutton, http://www.philological.bham.ac.uk/sphaera/1eng.html, 1.1.5.
1 For periodization, see Guy, "Tudor Monarchy and Its Critiques," 100.
2 Case attacked Machiavelli for atheism in the preface of the *Sphaera*; he allowed that fortune appeared to be a cause of political change, but noted that this was only in the eye of the beholder and that divine providence really was responsible for all political change.
3 Simon Adams has shown that a number of Catholic pamphleteers used the charge of Machiavellism to attack the puritan courtiers on behalf of the old Catholic nobility. In the eyes of the pamphleteers, these courtiers were acting in a Machiavellian fashion by attempting to hijack the state for their own ends and to centralize power in their own hands. In the 1571 *A Treatise of Treasons*, Lord Burghley and Nicholas Bacon, the two new men among Elizabeth's chief councillors, were accused of conspiring to keep Elizabeth unmarried and thus a puppet in their hands and of manipulating the queen to put her at odds with the ancient nobility, which then rose against her in 1569. Adams, "Favourites and Factions at the Elizabethan Court," 265–9.

in which Burghley preferred to frame his policy memoranda; and it provided an alternative to the monarchomachic political theories that leading councillors, like Hatton, believed were being used by presbyterians to threaten the existing order.

The queen's counselors either suggested outright or encouraged the inclusion of politics in the moral philosophy curriculum, which master's students at Oxford were required to study along with natural philosophy for the degree. Richard Hakluyt, the future geographer of the Americas, was at the center of this development. Hakluyt was incepted as a master of arts in 1577 at Christ Church, a college with close ties to the court, and began teaching the *Politics* in 1581. A year later, he was appointed censor of the college with the explicit understanding that he would teach the *Politics* and conduct academic disputations on the subject.[4] Hakluyt's teaching of the *Politics* ended shortly thereafter: in 1583 he was selected to serve as chaplain to the ambassador of France. Here the court's interest is obvious, and it is likely, given Burghley's involvement in arranging Hakluyt's finances, that the patronage went through him.[5] In September 1583, in gratitude for the preferment, he presented to the queen a manuscript, *Analysis*. The *Analysis* is an outline of the *Politics*,[6] based on Donato Acciaioli's breakdown of the arguments, with very occasional marginal notes and additions.[7] The *Analysis* provided a text that the privy councillors could use for their arguments pro and contra, revealing the structure of those arguments of Aristotle that Acciaioli noted were argued *in utramquem partem*, labeling them as objections and responses.[8]

Sometime in the next few years, Burghley suggested to the Oxford philosopher John Case that Aristotle's *Politics* could serve "as a light to the nation and a marvel of wisdom."[9] This suggestion, Case explained in the prefatory

---

4 Ryan, "Richard Hakluyt's Voyage into Aristotle," 74–6; Schmitt, *John Case and Aristotelianism*, 110–1.

5 BL Royal MS 12 G, xiii, fols. 1–47. Quinn, *Hakluyt Handbook*, 280, noted that it was Hakluyt's italic hand.

6 Hakluyt's translation does not match perfectly any of the usual translations of the *Politics*. It echoes some of the unusual choices in Michael Toxites's translation, based on the notes of Johann Sturm, of book 1 of the *Politics* and may be eclectic. See Toxites, *Aristotelis Politicorum Liber Primus*.

7 The procedure by which Hakluyt produced the *Analysis* is apparent from Acciaioli, *Commentarii*, BL, General Reference Collection, 519.b.15. In this copy of the work, the text was broken down in the margins into the chapters used by Hakluyt, and various questions were noted in the margins. This may in fact be the copy used to produce the *Analysis*, or perhaps it was a later copy by a student, approaching the text in a similar way. It included the question on ostracism, which appeared in Case's *Sphaera* in 1588 and was set as a question in 1589, which might suggest a date at the end of the decade, but it might be that it was Hakluyt's and this question was simply not set until later.

8 Alford, *Early Elizabethan Polity*, 16–20.

9 Schmitt, *John Case and Aristotelianism*, 136.

letter to his lengthy study of Aristotelian political theory, the *Sphaera Civita-tis*, was the inspiration for that work. Case dedicated the *Sphaera* to Hatton, and Case referred specifically to Hatton's speech on becoming chancellor in 1587, which encapsulated the values that Case was dedicated to, namely, "justice, equity, favor towards the people, and love of the nation."[10] Case clearly benefited from Hatton's patronage; he received a benefice in Hatton's county of Northamptonshire in 1584, and in 1589 a prebend at Salisbury, also probably due to Hatton's influence.[11] The *Sphaera* was inspired, he wrote, by Lord Burghley and Sir Henry Unton, who "has written much about secrets of state in an Attic and accurate way. If he would publish this-stuff, you would imagine that dead Sidney's soul had migrated into the breast of Unton."[12]

Case's *Sphaera Civitatis*, at 740 pages and 222 questions, is clearly the monument of English Aristotelian political theory. Case was well aware that his book was not an antiquarian study of Aristotle, but a work of political theory in the Aristotelian tradition. "If the reader sometimes sees me to have entered in more arguments than are in my text, let him ascribe this to the interpreters whom I am following, namely Thomas, Donatus, Versor, and Borreus among the older ones, Victorius, Sepulveda, Freigius, Osyrus, Regius, and other more modern and recent writers, both French and Italian."[13] Case drew heavily on his sources but combined them in such a way, reflecting their strengths and his needs, as to make the end result more than the sum of its parts. Case relied most heavily on Johannes Versor's commentary, which structured the choice of many of the topics of the book and usually provided some of the basic arguments, though he supplemented this list of questions with Johannes Thomas Freig's, which supplied more of the material of interest to an early modern state, including questions on magistracies and assemblies of various kinds. Like Hakluyt, Case used Acciaioli for seeing the structure of Aristotle's argument, while he added many parallels to Roman history and literature and more analytic and psychological depth from Piero Vettori, the psychologically, historically, and politically richest source. From Martin Borrhaus, whose commentary was the most theological (and Protestant), Case added a certain flavor of Reformation political thinking, which bridged the gap between an antiquarian approach and contemporary political culture. The net effect was a commentary in a lively and often difficult

10 Case, *SC*, sig. [¶3v]; Case, "Sphaera Civitatis," preliminary matter.

11 Tuck, *Philosophy and Government*, 149.

12 Case, *SC*, sig. ¶4r; Case, "Sphaera Civitatis," preliminary matter; Greengrass, "Unton, Sir Henry."

13 This list of commentaries was essentially identical to that soon to be available in the Bodleian; either Case had consulted whatever he could find in Oxford, or he was responsible for telling Thomas Bodley which commentaries on the *Politics* to add to his collection. *First Printed Catalogue of the Bodleian Library*, 425.

Latin, which must have seemed simultaneously encyclopedic and up-to-date to its readers.

The *Sphaera Civitatis* offered Elizabeth's councillors more than a scholarly resource; through Case's scholarship, it provided a more naturalistic vision of a hierarchical society than Smith had in the *De Republica* while it emphasized the compatibility of the broad office holding Smith had described with an insistence on the monarchical character of the state. These differences were a response above all to the challenge of presbyterianism, as understood by the conformists on the council. Presbyterianism had come to England in the early 1570s when the Englishmen who admired the Genevan model of church government began pushing openly for the adoption of presbyterianism at home. The presbyterians, chiefly Thomas Cartwright in the second of two admonitions to the Parliament, argued that the conformists who were defending the existing form of hierarchical church government were guilty of fostering the worldly commonwealth at the expense of further spiritual renovation, of being "politic Machiavels," and of insisting on episcopacy in order to pursue honors and titles for themselves. The puritans desired instead the presbyterian model of church government, in which the ministers were all equal. Whitgift, who was the head of the lower house of convocation in addition to serving as master of Trinity College, Cambridge, and who had responded to the first admonition, responded to these charges in a lengthy series of exchanges with Cartwright.[14] He had noticed that Cartwright had overstepped his brief of considering the question of church government and had claimed that England was a mixed regime, with the queen representing the monarchy, the council representing the aristocracy, and the Parliament, "assembled of all estates," representing the democracy.[15] Whitgift hammered Cartwright on this point, arguing that he was on dangerous ground in championing popular liberty and portraying the conformist view of government as tyranny.[16]

By the mid-1580s, Elizabeth's Privy Council was dominated by a coalition of conformists. Hatton was increasingly preferred to Robert Dudley, Elizabeth's previous favorite, who had been the champion of the puritan cause. Hatton joined the Privy Council by 1578, and in 1586, to counter the influence of Leicester, whose adventurism in foreign policy was becoming dangerous, Burghley appointed three other conservatives, including Thomas Sackville, Lord Buckhurst (to whom Case would later dedicate his *Thesaurus Oeconomiae*), and Whitgift himself. In the late 1570s and early 1580s, increasing hostility with Spain, the threat of a Catholic succession in the person of Mary, Queen of Scots, and the arrival of the Jesuits in England raised

14 Sheils, "Whitgift, John"; MacCulloch, *Later Reformation*, 33-5.
15 Ibid., 118.
16 Lake, "The Monarchical Republic of Queen Elizabeth I," 138.

tensions between the government and the Catholic citizenry.[17] Led by Catholic peers like Charles Arundell and his second cousin Lord Henry Howard (later the Earl of Northampton), the councillors were now also being accused by the Catholic gentry of being a cabal of new men and practicing a Machiavellian brand of amoral, corrupt patronage politics.[18] Meanwhile, the puritans were still advocating for a presbyterian form of government on increasingly radical grounds although their program failed in Parliament in 1586–7.[19] The councillors were now forced to manage a "three cornered" fight among the Catholic gentry, the bishops, and the puritans.[20]

The councillors tried to answer complaints and attacks from all sides. Burghley, long sympathetic to the furtherance of the Reformation in England, had insisted in *The Execution of Justice* that Catholics were not being singled out for persecution and that it was only treasonous behavior that put the conformity of the state's religious practice at risk that was being punished.[21] The conformists on the council and their clients kept up the attack on the puritans, continuing to claim, despite rather slim evidence, that the presbyterians were arguing for popular sovereignty and a theory of resistance of the sort advocated by theorists like Buchanan and Beza. Hatton argued as much in a speech in 1586–7 defending the Book of Common Prayer against puritan critiques written by his chaplain, Richard Bancroft.[22] Bancroft's line was too hysterical for many and was resisted by some of the governing class, like Francis Bacon, but nevertheless had influence. The issue for Bancroft was not simply that the presbyterians were offering a new understanding of the basis of English sovereignty, nor even that they were threatening rebellion, but that they were envisioning a new form for English government on a narrow class basis. He believed that it was the "aim of the presbyterians to establish parish government by a rabble of 'artisans, shoemakers, tinkers, and tailors.' "[23] Despite his commitment to conformity, Hatton had Catholic sympathies, which Case may have shared,[24] and the *Sphaera* was more obviously opposed to any claims of rule (imaginary or not) of the lowest sorts as described by Bancroft than to the claims of the Catholic gentry.[25] Nevertheless, there are

17 MacCulloch, *Later Reformation*, 38–40; Schmitt, *John Case and Aristotelianism*, 99.

18 Peck, *Leicester's Commonwealth*, 20–31.

19 MacCulloch, *Later Reformation*, 44–6.

20 Ibid., 41.

21 For the official view, see Burgess, *British Political Thought*, esp. 102–3.

22 McGiffert, "Covenant, Crown, and Commons"; MacCaffrey, "Hatton, Sir Christopher."

23 McGiffert, "Covenant, Crown, and Commons," 43.

24 Cf. Schmit, *John Case and Aristotelianism*, 114–5.

25 It is less obviously a work of conformist thought in a narrow sense. It did broadly share Whitgift's view that the bishops could hold office, but he is far from the *iure divino* thinking of the next decade. "Let priests sometimes be endowed with political garments and duties. Yet I urge that they grasp these things with their left hand, not their right, and regard them as a privilege, not as things simply due them because of their office. . . . It is just, since they often perform their offices prudently. It is not according to the essence of their

some features of the book, such as its defense of new men and ambition, which seem pointed at the criticisms of the Arundell-Howard circle.

The topical use of the Aristotelian commentary tradition is evident from the choice of questions set for debate at Oxford during this period. University commentaries on Aristotle's corpus had been arranged for centuries as a series of questions and answers suitable for scholarly debate. The questions selected at Oxford in this period not only served the Oxford curriculum, but reflected the agenda of the Privy Council. Every summer from 1583 to the early 1590s one of the questions was drawn from the *Politics*, and the master's students were required to answer. These questions, preserved in the records of the university, overlap closely with the questions that appear in the margins of the two extant copies of Hakluyt's *Analysis* (there is a more informal copy made in 1588 in addition to the presentation copy of 1583) and the much larger set of questions covered by the *Sphaera*.[26] The questions that appear in the margins of the 1588 manuscript of the *Analysis* (many of which appeared in Case's *Sphaera* as well) are illustrative: "whether magistracies are to be given to the poor," "what is a commonwealth," "which magistracies should be given to the people," "whether nobles are to be borne in a polity," "whether monarchy is the best," "ostracism and excellence in a subject," and "why citizens should be exercised to prepare for war."[27] These questions touched on many of the key issues of Elizabethan governmental institutions and practices: the lord lieutenancy, the militia, and the use of favorites. Other issues, such as the poor law, were treated in passing in a number of questions or, like female rule, were given their own.

A CONFORMIST ARISTOTELIANISM

By the time that Case wrote the *Sphaera*, the classical analysis of the commonwealth—in which citizenship, office holding, and conformity with the law were understood to be a function of socially differentiated attitudes

---

office, since they have undertaken another duty, distinct from the secular one, upon which they should busy themselves and meditate day and night." Case, *SC*, 408–9; Case, "Sphaera Civitatis," 4.15.11.

26 Ryan, "Richard Hakluyt's Voyage into Aristotle," 76–7.

27 BL Sloane 1982: peregrini an augenda civitas (2.7, 12v); An pauperibus dandi magistratus (2.9, 14v); Respublica quid (3.4, 17r; Case, *SC*, 224); qui magistratus populo sint tribuendi (3.7, 18v; cf. Case, *SC*, 251: summum imperium concedatur populo?); An generosi in politia ferendi (3.8, 19r; cf. Case, *SC*, 273: Utrum in ferendis legibus utilitas potius bonorum quam totius multitudinis spectari debeat?); An monarchia optima (3.9, 19v; cf. Case, *SC*, 261: An monarchia sit optimus status reipublicae?); Ostracismus et excellentiam in subjectio (3.9, 20r; cf. Case, *SC*, 275); Adulator (5.2, 40r; cf. Case, *SC*, 455: Utrum adulatores populi permittendi sint in civitate vivere?); Cur cives ad bellum exercendi (7.14, 54r; cf. Case, *SC*, 135: Res militaris pacis tempore exerceri debeat?).

toward the distribution of rewards and punishments—was being pushed and pulled in all directions. On the one hand, Jean Bodin's theory of sovereignty represented a frontal assault on the Aristotelian identification of social and political authority; on the other hand, the new historicized readings of Aristotelian political theory being offered by Italian scholars, such as Sigonio and Vettori, were shifting classical political theory increasingly in a republican direction. In developing an Aristotelian analysis that was acceptable to the conformists on the Privy Council, Case had to find a position in the scholarship that at once upheld the subtle analysis of the broad participation of the degrees of the people of the sort offered by Smith while avoiding any encouragement of a turn to popular government. The result was an eclectic Aristotelianism that drew from a variety of traditions of Aristotelian commentary and, in places, from Bodin himself.

Bodin's analysis of the state was a hot commodity by the mid- to late 1570s. Sir Philip Sidney recommended that his younger brother study this work with Henry Savile at Christ Church; in 1576, the English ambassador, Amias Paulet, was asked by the courtier Sir Edward Dyer to purchase a copy of Bodin's *De Imperio*; and in 1579, Gabriel Harvey reported that Bodin's *De Republica* was to be found everywhere in Cambridge.[28] The understanding of the state among the Elizabethans in the 1580s was nevertheless very different from what Bodin had advised in the summary of his political thought in *Methodus ad Facilem Historiarum Cognitionem* in 1566. Bodin had not found Aristotle's definitions of the state to be useful for describing states other than Periclean Athens, for Aristotle insisted on the participatory nature of the citizen and the deliberative nature of the magistrate. Bodin believed that the view of all writers before him had failed to capture the essence of the state by mistaking the relationship between state and society and the basis of social order. This was the case in his eyes for Machiavelli as much as Aristotle and for even the most impressive of the post-Machiavellian writers on politics, including Gasparo Contarini. Aristotle came in for special criticism, since he was the founder of this line of reasoning and because his definitions implied that a nonparticipatory or nondeliberative government was scarcely a state at all. But all of the authors erred in one way or another by assuming that political power could mean something else aside from the explicit legal power to administer justice.

Bodin found this mistake both empirically confounding and dangerous. It was empirically confounding because one could scarcely analyze the state if it was identified with all of the various social structures of all times and places. There had to be specialized institutions that could be identified and analyzed if one were to speak meaningfully of politics at all and make com-

---

28 Salmon, "Seneca and Tacitus," 172; Jardine and Stewart, *Hostage to Fortune*, 47; Sommerville, *Royalists and Patriots*, 43.

parisons between states. And this mistake was dangerous because it suggested, in treating social forces as a form of power, that there were rival sources of power to that of the central government, allowing for division and anarchy. For a new model Bodin turned to imperial Rome, which offered very different definitions of magistracy and citizenship. The magistrate was to be understood as an official whose power was exclusively legal and derived ultimately from the sovereign power. "Then let a magistrate be a man who has a part of the public authority," defined Bodin. "I add 'public' that it may be distinguished from the authority of a father and of a slaveowner."[29] Citizenship was a matter no longer of participation, but of legal qualification in accordance with stipulated characteristics, as in Roman imperial citizenship.[30]

At bottom, then, there was a fundamental disagreement on the basis of social order. Bodin believed that social order was the result of a well-ordered set of magistrates who were endowed with the necessary powers to compel compliance with the law. Bodin did not allow for any techniques of social control or influence. This must mean, he said, that the definition of a magistrate depended on the power of arrest: "since the smallest part of exercising authority against the unruly is vested in arrest . . . it follows that he who lacks the right to arrest lacks authority." These powers had been granted to those considered magistrates at even the lowest level of government, and even the lowest of the low had the power to levy fines.[31] He specifically rejected the view of the state in which magistracies were understood as honors to be distributed rather than as offices of the administration of legal justice. "For who would call a man a magistrate when he lacks an agent and cannot issue a command? He may be endowed with office and honors, indeed, but not with authority as well." It was legal competency that produced power and authority, not simply the honor and title of office.[32]

In the meantime, Italian classical scholarship was offering a very different but just as rich analysis. As I explained in the previous chapter, the model of a society of orders developed by Sigonio was filtering through to England and was incorporated in Smith's revisions to the *De Republica* in the mid-1570s. In the 1570s and 1580s, the scholarship on Aristotle's *Rhetoric*, *Ethics*, and *Politics* was significantly advanced by the commentaries of the Florentine

29 Bodin, *Method for the Easy Comprehension of History*, 169.

30 Wells, *Law and Citizenship in Early Modern France*. On this distinction, see Brubaker, *Citizenship and Nationhood*, 31–2, esp. 31: "Modern state citizenship differs sharply in this respect from citizenship in the ancient Greek polis or in medieval towns. There it was axiomatic that some persons ought not to be citizens of any city. Persons lacking citizenship were not placeless; their status was not anomalous. Rather, they did not form part of the self-governing or otherwise privileged civic corporation."

31 Bodin, *Method for the Easy Comprehension of History*, 169–70.

32 Ibid., 170.

scholar Vettori, which synthesized the Aristotelian view of ethics and politics with the experience of Rome. This literature was of great importance and influence in the late sixteenth century and the first half of the seventeenth century in England, but it was handled carefully there because of its relatively strong support for more popular forms of government.

Indeed, much of this material was tinged with republican sympathies that threatened the vision of commonwealth as a cooperative society of orders. Indeed, the Italian scholarship on ancient Rome provided a revolutionary outlook on antiquity: Rome had come to be categorized by some as a democracy,[33] and the Roman basis for nobility was increasingly coming under critical scrutiny. Sigonio argued, for instance, that the patricians were simply the first freeborn men in Rome.[34] While the French scholars were more divided, the entire outlook of the Italian strain of this scholarship was premised on the Livian view that Roman history was driven by the conflict of orders and that the institutions of Rome embodied various compromises between these conflicting parties. In this literature, it was the constitutional struggle between the orders that was paramount, and the citizenship of the plebs was understood in terms of liberty.

By the 1580s, the leading privy councillors (at the very least Burghley) must have understood the choice that they were being offered. While they were concerned (though perhaps not to the extent that Bancroft's hysterics suggested) that England was tilting toward democracy, the full-scale abandonment of the ideal of commonwealth (or so it must have seemed to them) of the sort offered by Bodin was too much of a reaction. In the face of the challenge of presbyterianism, they were sympathetic to the claim that there was no such thing as a mixed regime, but they had already assimilated the sophisticated models of ancient society and were confident that there was no need to prematurely abandon the experience of the Greek city-states and the Roman republic in favor of that of the empire, as Bodin had done. This preference for the model of the Greek city-states and the Roman republic does not mean that they were republicans or endorsing the "free state," however. Their idea of commonwealth drew heavily on the republican traditions of antiquity, but they carefully distinguished between various manifestations and epochs within the broadly republican experience of antiquity, especially the history of the Roman republic, and, as I have already shown with Smith, it was only in particular moments in the history of the republic that they believed that their ideal of commonwealth was approximated.

It seems that Case believed that the ideal moment in Roman republican history was just after the introduction of the tribunes when, according to Livy, both the patricians (such as Scaevola) and the plebs were devoted to the

33 Tuck, "Hobbes and Democracy."
34 McCuaig, *Carlo Sigonio*, 138.

common good, but before the tribunate took on too much power.[35] Case rejected the view of the popular party at Rome that the liberty of the Roman citizenry meant that the rulings of the judicial magistrates could be overruled. When the tribunes of the plebs began to obstruct the rulings of judges, Case wrote, that was the beginning of the end, and "the glory of the Roman rule failed." Magistrates must be respected, since "a sitting judge embodies the king's person," and "the person of the king should not be held in contempt."[36] Incidentally, this condemnation echoed the Crown's argument in the recent debates over the Norfolk election case, in which the court of chancery had disagreed with Parliament over who should be able to decide on cases of disputed elections. One MP argued that "albeit they thought very reverently . . . of the said lord chancellor and judges, and know them to be competent judges in their places, yet in this case they took them not for judges in parliament in this House."[37] Case was elsewhere supportive of Parliament as an institution in opposition to the direct voice of the people, but he clearly reflected the position of Hatton and the council that it was getting out of hand.[38]

CITIZENSHIP AND OFFICE HOLDING

Case's account of citizenship and the distribution of office as social stratification in the broad sense (the more technical aspects of office are treated in the next section) was characteristic of the eclectic approach that he was adopting in developing a conformist political analysis. Like Smith and so many others, his approach was to reinforce the folk notion of the commonwealth as a cooperative society of all of the degrees of the people, yet on a more theoretical level, he stepped back from Smith's embrace of the commonwealth of England as a society of orders. In Smith's hands, the society of orders was pacific, but it was the theoretical underpinning of the conflict of orders that characterized so much of early Roman history and was thus a dangerous way of thinking of society in a world where ancient orders

---

35 Case, *SC*, 423; Case, "Sphaera Civitatis," 5.1.5.

36 Case, *SC*, 179–80 [An liceat populo impedire magistratum quo minus in iudicio sententiam ferat?]: Persona principis contemni non debet in civitate: sed iudex in tribunali personam gerit principis: ergo iudex in tribunali contemni non debet. Case, "Sphaera Civitatis," 2.8.6. For the rejection of the liberties of the plebs as a rejection of the citizenship view of magistracies, see McCuaig, *Carlo Sigonio*, 210; Smith, *De Republica Anglorum*, 120–1.

37 Smith, *Emergence of a Nation State*, 128, 395.

38 Case, *SC*, 180, 182–3: [An dissentientibus principibus viris civitatis, litis populo diiudicandae plena potestas detur?]: sed hoc volo, ut ex qualibet civitate selecti viri ad consilium veniant, resque in contentione positas; suffragiorum multitudine, sapienter & expedite definiant. Case, "Sphaera Civitatis," 2.8.6, 2.9.2.

could be understood to be the predecessors to modern estates, entitled to a particular role in government.[39] In resisting the Italian republican under-standing of classical citizenship, Case diverged from Sigonio and Vettori in two important respects. First, he insisted that emulative behavior, that is, the ambition for office and honor, was to be understood as cooperative, not competitive. Second, he approached social stratification in keeping with an older natural law teaching rather than the institutionally conditioned approach of the society of orders. This did not mean that his approach should be thought of as conservative, since the natural law approach was adapted to a meritoc-racy of new men, which was quite at odds with the claims being made by the critics of the conformists. Case's view is rather an account of citizenship that in its pursuit of conformity was in some ways very modernizing.

In abandoning the idea of England as a society of orders, Case chose to operate on a level of abstraction from the fine detail that the Italian scholars had dredged up and that Smith and Harrison had used in the 1570s. He no longer took account of the ascriptive characteristics—such as social and geo-graphic origin, kinship, and wealth—that membership in a status group, or *dignitas*, depended on in Rome and that had been used by those who applied the concept to his day.[40] There were real differences between the Roman re-publican model and the Aristotelian model of citizenship, and in part Case was building on these differences. Sigonio dove to the heart of the distinc-tion between citizenship in a Greek polis and in Rome when he explained that citizenship in a polis depended on office holding, whereas the lower orders were citizens in Rome only by dint of their participation in the var-ious assemblies.[41] This and other differences were sometimes taken note of and sometimes glossed over in contemporary expositions of Aristotle.[42] By emphasizing the Aristotelian conception of citizenship as defined by office

39 Mendle, *Dangerous Positions*, 70-1.

40 McCuaig, *Carlo Sigonio*, 125, 134, 147–8.

41 Ibid., 134.

42 Even introductory textbooks, like Freig's *Quaestiones* (1578), reflected the increasingly sophisticated approach to citizenship, though without clarifying precisely what view was being taken. Commenting on what precisely was wrong with the Platonic commonwealth, Freig explained that it made a mess of social reproduction in a way that indicated he was thinking of orders rather than class per se. "How children are transferred to artisans or farm-ers or guardians, in what manner, by what means, and by whom they are handed over, is arranged in well constituted commonwealths," he explained. "Thus the Romans used to give their adolescent sons the pure or virile toga, and the Greeks would inscribe theirs in the deme registers. But in the Platonic community this is not arranged, but 'involves much con-fusion.'" Freig, *Quaestiones*, 65–6: In recte constitutis Rebuspublicis expeditum est, quomodo filii vel inter artifices vel agricolas vel custodes transferantur, quive quibus & per quos tradan-tur: Sic enim Romani filiis puberibus posita praetexta dabant puram seu virilem: Graeci in ληξιαρχικόν, suos scribebant. At in Platonica illa communione hoc expeditum non est: sed πολλὴν ἔχει ταραχήν [*Politics*, 1268b].

holding, Case reinforced the vision of citizenship in England as a hierarchical experience where different sorts of office were held by the different degrees of the people. Even the experience of legislation, which was imagined by Smith as the *comitia tributa*, took on the overtones of the anti-democratic thinking of Athenian elite political thought.

Yet, Case's hierarchical vision was not meant to be either divisive or exclusive, as it so often had been in the ancient world. His vision of hierarchy, like that of the other conformists, was meritocratic and open to the ambition of well-intentioned and deserving candidates for office. This vision was underpinned in his analysis by a cooperative view of competitive behavior, on which he took a very different position from Vettori. By the 1580s, the role of honor, which was widely seen in the 1530s and 1540s to be a means for achieving conformity with the law, was seen by the Italian commentators to be more fraught and liable to social conflict. Vettori understood honor to be a distributive good, which was regarded just as any other external good would be, where one's satisfaction depended on one's views about the pattern of distribution as a whole. Honor could thus serve as a source of division and envy, even if its recipients were deserving. "But if these same men [the morally worthy] should perpetually bear the command, then the others must necessarily live deprived of it. Thus, they will be hostile to the commonwealth, and always be longing for revolution. For it is not easy for men to bear that the good men have taken for themselves the honors due to them. And thus it is not a just or stable state which afflicts such men with such injuries."[43] The incomplete morality of honor and justice is evident here. The stability of the state required that such honors be shared, though in reality they were due only to the virtuous. The attribution of honors to everyone was a very real necessity for Vettori. Echoing Tacitus, he noted that men who were altogether excluded from office and honor and thus "marked by ignominy" were not only "enemies" of the state, as Aristotle said, but, indeed, "internal enemies, who plot more to harm the commonwealth than external ones."[44]

Case showed that he was well aware of this,[45] but nevertheless he saw honor in much the same way it had been viewed earlier. He rehearsed many of the points that were a standard part of the position: honor was necessary

43 Vettori, *Commentarii in Octo Libros*, 228: Cum autem perpetuo illic imperium iidem gerant, necesse est reliquos orbatos illo vivere. Erunt igitur male animati erga rempublicam, & cupidi semper rerum novarum: non facile enim homines honesti eripi sibi debitos honores patiuntur: non est igitur iustus, firmusque status, qui tanta iniuria ipsos afficit.

44 Ibid., 232: Tamquam ignomini notati . . . necesse est civitatem hanc plenam esse hostium, ac domesticorum quidem hostium, qui magis ad huc quam externi nocere reipublicae consuerunt.

45 Case noted that "fear of sedition" required that honors be distributed broadly. For "what makes the people burn more vehemently than to go long without dignity and honors?" Case, *SC*, 223; Case, "Sphaera Civitatis," 3.3.9.

for productivity, that is, *honos alit artes*; it was a necessary stimulus to virtue; and it must be rendered to all degrees of the people.[46] He summarized much of the theory in a single sentence: "Within the commonwealth this indeed is politic, that not even an excellent cobbler should go without his reward. For honor nourishes the arts, and we are incited to the pursuit of virtue by rewards, as if by goads."[47] Case understood that honor was a distributive good,[48] and he must have understood the expansion of the distribution of offices—as Elizabeth knighted 878 men and increased the number of justices of the peace—in this light.[49] But, for Case, the proper distribution of honors could not lead to disorder. This was because true virtue did not engender competitive instincts, but only imitative ones: "Furthermore, splendor and eminence of virtue is no reason for good men to puff themselves up, but to strive by imitation to be similar and alike to him."[50] It was the "license" of honors, the distribution of them willy-nilly, like the excessive accumulation of wealth among the few, that led to ambition and sedition.[51]

In the theological interpretations of the *Politics*, the hierarchy of the non-political relationships of chapter 1 of the *Politics* was expanded as a means of understanding the work as a whole. The social structure that reflected natural inequality was first described in terms of lordship, which gave way to the idiom of patriarchal relationships of care and obedience. Beginning with Scotus and continuing in the Reformation, most notably in the work of Melanchthon, the *Politics* was interpreted as the natural law for fallen man and political authority as a response to original sin and the fallenness of man. In this vein, Melanchthon had used Aristotle on natural slavery to explain the institution of serfdom (*Leibeigenschaft*).[52] Borrhaus used it to discuss hierarchy more generally. He argued that there was hierarchy, though no "abject servitude," in the state of innocence. "For indeed the state of uncorrupted nature did not lack every duty of commanding and obeying. Indeed, neither the

---

46 Aristotle, *Nicomachean Ethics*, 1095b23ff. Case and Vettori agreed (with virtually everyone else at the time) that the Stoic approach was mistaken, since virtue needed a stimulus. Vettori, *Petri Victorii Commentarii*, 15–16. Case put it vividly: "For though virtue is more valuable than gold, though only virtue survives after death, nevertheless, if it is only in habit and not in activity, if it is in rest and not motion, if finally you keep it [in] your pocket and not in your hand, then certainly it will be less helpful to others as an example, so too it will not be pursued by you as happiness." Case, *Speculum Moralium*, 13: Nam etsi virtus sit pretiosior auro, etsi virtus sola post funera vivat, tamen si illam in habitu non in actu, si in quiete non in motu, si denique in sinu non in manu teneas, certe ut parum prodest aliis ad exemplum, ita sibi deest ad nomen beatitudinis aucupandum.

47 Case, *SC*, 270; Case, "Sphaera Civitatis," 3.8.3.

48 Case, "Sphaera Civitatis," 2.5.6. Case noted that this was treated in depth in book 5 of the *Nicomachean Ethics*.

49 Peck, *Court Patronage and Corruption*, 3, 32.

50 Case, *SC*, 280; Case, "Sphaera Civitatis," 3.9.5.

51 Case, *SC*, 138; Case, "Sphaera Civitatis," 2.5.2.

52 Dauber, "Deutsche Reformation."

marital rule of husbands over their wives, nor of fathers over their children, nor of political officials were to lose their power in the now much increased posterity."[53] There was a further source of inequality in the fallen state due to the variation in the transmission of the "left over seeds of the old reason" from the state of innocence such that "some are more intelligent, some less, some are blessed with better health, some less; some have longer lives, others, shorter; some are free, and others are slaves."[54] Case followed this view closely, departing only in maintaining that hierarchical relationships only occurred after the fall, not beforehand, and only held on average (which made the rule of Elizabeth, an exceptional woman, possible).[55] This hierarchical order was established through the distribution of material goods, which tracked the providential distribution of natural endowments. Thus, he thought that the pursuit of material gain was natural and God-given,[56] and wealth was distributed in accordance with natural abilities, such that nature "has granted more and more ample things to masters for the necessity of life and sustenance than she has to slaves, so she might maintain magnificence in these and obedience in those."[57]

Case believed that there were three factors that explained one's social position: natural endowment, a good will, and luck. The first two were evident in Case's discussion of "true nobility," the middling sort, and the laborers, and the last in his discussion of beggars and vagrants. Case readily agreed with Versor that men's abilities were set according to nature ("Nature has granted many men more divine minds, and many men duller spirits; in these is a kind of nobility, in those a kind of dullness"),[58] but he argued that nature only affected someone's character in conferring a certain disposition to him, not a proper inclination or actual intention. Virtue, and thus nobility, required a good will as well ("So the perfection of nobility is twofold, one, from nature, in the disposition of the mind, the other, from virtue, in the direction of the will").[59] This emphasis on the will reflected Case's views on justification, sanctification, and moral theology; he was not a hard predestinarian,

---

53 Borrhaus, *In Aristotelis Politicorum*, 30: Non enim omne imperandi & parendi officium integrae naturae status recusasset. Etenim neque imperium γαμικόν mariti in uxorem, neque patrium in liberos, neque politicum in iam aucta posteritate vim suam amissurum fuisset.

54 Ibid., 31: Etenim gratiae divinae uno beneficio factum est, ut veteris rationis semina relicta sint, & per peccatum non tota intelligentiae vis extincta si, alii maius mentis lumen habeant, alii minus: alii firmiore corporis valetudine praediti sint, alii infirmiore: aliis longior, aliis brevior contingat vita: quidam liberi sint, quidam servi.

55 Case, *SC*, 37; Case, "Sphaera Civitatis," 1.3.7.

56 Case, *SC*, 61; Case, "Sphaera Civitatis," 1.5.7.

57 Case, *SC*, 124; Case, "Sphaera Civitatis," 2.3.4.

58 Case, *SC*, 46; Case, "Sphaera Civitatis," 1.4.3.

59 Ibid.: Est ergo duplex perfectio nobilitatis, alia a natura in dispositione mentis, alia a virtute in directione voluntatis. Translation altered.

and he believed that free will was a necessary prerequisite for a consciousness of sin.[60]

Case used this psychology to reread Aristotle's understanding of citizenship in meritocratic terms. Though the psychology echoed Catholic moral philosophy, in Case's hands it led to the conclusions of conformist social thought. The Catholic nobility excoriated ambition, which, they argued, led to the introduction of mercantile attitudes toward public service. This was stated in extreme fashion in *Leicester's Commonwealth*, an anonymous pamphlet attacking Leicester that represented the thinking of the Catholic nobility, though perhaps elevated to a hysterical level. Typical is the claim that Leicester "[s]o invaded the whole government himself, to sell, spoil, and dispose at his pleasure. Wherefor this is but natural to my Lord of Leicester by descent to make merchandise of the state, for his grandfather Edmund also was such a kind of copesman [merchant]."[61]

In his discussion of the social ladder, Case took rather the view argued by Whitgift in the admonition controversy, namely, that ambition was justified by one's actual abilities to serve.[62] Case attributed the middling sorts' position in very general terms to the first two causes he outlined: their natural talents and effort (good will). Case took a much more positive view of craftsmen holding office than was traditional in the commentary literature. The voices of the wealthier sort of guildsmen can be heard in Case's observation that "craftsmen bear the republic's greatest burdens, therefore it is unjust if they should have no share in the commonwealth."[63] One can picture the master craftsmen when Case noted that Aristotle called "Zeuxis, Apelles, and Polyclitus wise artisans. Indeed God chose Bezaleel and Aholiab, right noble artisans, for the tabernacle of the Covenant, to the ark of witness, to the place of offering, for the making of all the vessels of the Temple."[64] This was the case for the higher sorts of farmers as well, "for Cincinnatus, Curius, and Fabricius worked the plow, and Cato concerned himself with agriculture."[65] In what might have been a further point of contention between Case and the old Catholic nobility, Case condemned the practice of the Thebans, reported in the *Politics*, which required that merchants desist from trade for ten years before being allowed to hold office. "[I]t is absurd to demand such a space of time and such a burden from an artisan before he is let in to the theater of the commonwealth." In doing so, the Thebans were denying

---

60 On free will, see Case, *Speculum Moralium*, 104–5, 115.

61 Peck, *Leicester's Commonwealth*, 111.

62 For a fuller discussion of Whitgift's view of office holding, see the next chapter of this volume.

63 Case, *SC*, 145–6 [An opifices sint cives?]: Case, "Sphaera Civitatis," 2.5.9–10.

64 Ibid.

65 Ibid.

themselves the qualities of leadership and intelligence of those of humble beginnings.[66]

Nevertheless, Case, echoing the conformist critique of the presbyterians, was not willing to include the lower sorts in the duties and honors of office holding. He specifically excluded "sordid artisans and hirelings," drawing a terrible, though richly imagined, portrait of the lowest class of workers: "But I agree with you in excluding those who wallow about in the sewers and dung of the commonwealth, who feed their hungry guts by handling the unclean and filthy garbage of the commonwealth: these are feeble of intellect or slaves by nature, or, nearest to slaves, are deemed unworthy of the light and the theater of the commonwealth, and are thoroughly incompetent for the performance of offices."[67]

When Case turned to the very bottom of the social scale, he found that his first two causes were inadequate to explain their condition. Reflecting the thinking that underpinned the Elizabethan poor law, he distinguished between the poor "of necessity" and the "dissolute," who were poor by choice, presumably due to a failure in intention or inclination, regardless of their natural dispositions.[68] He compared beggars and vagrants of both kinds to other men living the solitary life outside of the commonwealth, such as hermits and melancholics.[69] Their position outside of society and the cost of addressing them made them a threat to social order. But just as the causes of their position were differentiated, so were the remedies. The poor "of necessity" were to be housed in hospitals at the public expense; the dissolute were to be forced to work or to be punished.[70] The treatment of vagrants and beggars as "solitary men" due to a failure of will represented a serious departure from Aristotle's argument. For Aristotle, the point of discussing solitary men in book 1 was to show the naturalness of political life for rational agents, that one needed to live a political life to be fully human. It was an argument *ad oppositum*. This was the understanding of the passage in the medieval commentaries, where hermits and holy men were understood to be living a sort of supernatural life. For Case, however, the discussion of

---

66 Case, *SC*, 223; Case, "Sphaera Civitatis," 3.3.9. That the old Catholic nobility may have objected to this is suggested by its use in Parliament during the trial of Buckingham in 1626, when John Pym, the spokesman in the Commons for Bedford, admittedly a puritan peer rather than a Catholic one, took the side of the Thebans. This passage may have been a *locus classicus* for disagreement over the proper approach to patronage and the distribution of office. Prestwich, *Cranfield*, 226; Rushworth, *Historical Collections*, 339.

67 Case, *SC*, 145–6 [An opifices sint cives?]: Case, "Sphaera Civitatis," 2.5.9–10.

68 The Elizabethan poor law was composed of four acts of Parliament, three of which (5 Eliz., c. 3; 14 Eliz., c. 5; 18 Eliz., c. 3) preceded the publication of the *Sphaera*. Smith, *Emergence of a Nation State*, 237.

69 Case, *SC*, 21–2 [Solitaria vita sit toleranda in civitate?]; Case, "Sphaera Civitatis," 1.2.3.

70 Case, *SC*, 26; Case, "Sphaera Civitatis," 1.8.

solitary men was used to justify state action and the use of coercion, to justify the preserving of the commonwealth through police measures.

Case's hierarchical structure was not completely fixed; he did leave room for new men on the rise. He believed that the social structure "ought to be fixed regarding the offices and orders in the commonwealth," but the exceptional individual could rise.[71] Again in contrast to the old Elizabethan nobility and their spokesmen, Case thought that there should be some degree of social mobility in a "free commonwealth," which he certainly believed England to be.[72] Plato's myth of metals in which social distinction was fixed by birth would scarcely be psychologically compelling in a free commonwealth. Rather, it required the system of honors once again. "For even if God has distinguished human orders and conditions, nevertheless in a free commonwealth He has extended to all men a reward of virtue, like a victory-palm in a stadium, and if this hope be removed, who will run? Who will strive? For, just as honor nourishes the arts, thus hope of dignity nourishes eager citizens."[73] Upward social mobility was thus crucial to the idea of voluntary attachment to the commonwealth.[74]

71 Case, *SC*, 131; Case, "Sphaera Civitatis," 2.4.5.

72 Laurence Humphrey's *The Nobles*, originally published in Latin in 1560, argued that one might think well of the new nobility, but such new men had always been despised for the fraudulent and grasping means by which they attained their status: "But would we had all Ciceros: who with travaile, industrie, eloquence and wyt, would open themselves pathes to the attayninge of honours. But alas, other engines use they to breake unto it, other mynes and privy policies, to winne this Nobilitie. Who, as they enter by a posterne, and wyndowe on the wronge side: so once entred, prove more fruitful in vyces, covetise, pryde, ambition, crueltie, then the ancientest Nobles. As though, farre longer they had learned in the Schole of noughtines. So blynde fortune theyr promoter, them promoted blynds. Whom it contenteth not, to preferre the yll, unlesse with authorytie shee arme them, to make them more harmefull." Humphrey, *The Nobles*, sig. g7r–v.

73 Case, *SC*, 121–2; Case, "Sphaera Civitatis," 2.3.3.

74 The early modern commentators were aware of another source of individual social mobility, which was more disruptive: downward mobility due to population pressure. Acciaioli had worried about the growth of population in general, and by the 1570s the commentators had come to worry about the effect of the number of children on household poverty. Vettori worried that inheritance laws that favored first-born children would be politically untenable, "for the fathers would not be able to bear that their sons go hungry," but the alternative would have much the same effect, since it would impoverish the family as a whole. This would lead "those who have had to part with their possessions," those who "had previously been wealthy" to rebellion and political unrest. Aristotle, *Politics*, 1266b8. Vettori, *Commentarii in Octo Libros*, 118: Si enim inquit superarit magnitudinem patrimonii numerus liberorum, necesse est legem eam abrogari, neque enim pati poterunt patres filios suos esurire. improbabunt igitur eam legem, qua hoc malum parit: praeterquam quod lex haec illic diuturna non erit, est affine culpae, ac periculosum libertati atque otio, multos in civitate esse. qui e divitibus facti sint pauperes; vix enim coercebuntur, ne remp. perturbent. Recte autem, non omnes pauperes cupidos esse dixit rerum novarum, sed illos, qui amiserint bona, cum antea divites forent: assueti enim large & copiose vivere non possunt pati tantam vitae commutationem, atque in mediam flammam saepe se coniiciunt.

Case's openness to new men was nevertheless not the republican view. The tension between the republican analysis and the Elizabethan analysis is apparent when Acciaioli's commentary on the same passage is contrasted with that of Case. Acciaioli argued that there should be an alteration of offices in a commonwealth to avoid sedition; he rejected Plato's notion that a single class should hold all the offices; and he did not note the role of honor and hope.[75] Case's ideal was not, then, concerned broadly with an openness of all offices to the citizenry understood in a class sense, but rather with the openness of all offices to the citizenry understood as individuals.

The many subtle changes here—the introduction of effort, the use of the naturalistic first book to account for the later political books, the openness to new men—amounted at once to an advance and a retreat in Tudor social and political theory. As I explained in the introduction, in some historians' accounts of Elizabethan social theory, there is said to have been a shift from an understanding of society in terms of estates and citizenship to one in terms of social class. This was meant to reflect the discovery of economic and social forces.[76] The complicated models of citizenship—like the society of orders or Aristotelian citizenship—were not straightforwardly modernizing in this sense. Smith's version of the society of orders, for instance, with its careful attention to the mechanics of the census relied on an understanding of inflation and the way that the desire for distinction interacted with consumer demand and the labor market. The system of citizenship (the set of legally defined orders) capitalized on this understanding of the economy in order to mobilize resources for the state. Citizenship in this model, however, did not reify any particular ideology; mutuality was achieved through an exchange of esteem and the satisfaction of particular needs, which were differentiated in line with the various mind-sets of the different degrees of the

---

Freig noted that it was contemporary practice to bestow equal shares and that classical recommendations varied. Freig, *Quaestiones*, 74. In keeping with his positive outlook toward social mobility, Case downplayed the political effects of downward mobility. He emphasized only that fixed classes were an impossibility due to the variation in number of children. Given that first sons inherited the patrimony, the occupations—if not quite the class—of the other children would depend on the capacity of the family to provide for them. "We English much better bequeath our estates to our firstborn sons, and leave our younger ones some legacy in keeping with our resources (a trade, say, or some money)." Case, *SC*, 128–9; Case, "Sphaera Civitatis," 2.4.3.

75 Acciaioli, *Commentarii*, 56v–57r: Quinta est sententia, ubi Platonem refellit, quia cum diviserit civitate in duas partes, & unam vocavit custodies, alteram agricolas, & artifices, ex altera constituit, qui continue magistratus gereret, alteri nullum tribuit magistratum. Et cum custodibus tribuat magistratus, non omnibus tamen illos concedebat. Hoc autem scilicet quod alii semper dominetur, alii vero semper subiiciantur, videtur esse causa seditionis apud quosque, sed multo magis apud animosos viros. Nam vicissitudo magistratuum est causa concordiae, ut inferius ostendet philosophus.

76 See the introduction to this volume; and Wrightson, "Estates, Degrees, and Sorts."

people. This mirrored the standard commonwealth view that different sorts of men were motivated to external conformity with the law (and, hopefully, eventually to voluntary conformity) on the basis of different appeals.

Case held to a traditional vision of economic forces, but was more modernizing in his introduction of a single standard of effort by which to judge the citizenry as a whole. Case conceded that there was variation in the sorts of goods the different degrees of the people desired,[77] but his emphasis on natural endowment and effort suggested that these had become a standard measure for national citizenship. This may have reflected an emerging late-Elizabethan economics, which was embodied in the poor law legislation and more concerned with individual choice and effort than Smith's recourse to monetary policy, supply and demand, and labor market policies. Case's highly moralized approach to the economy appeared in his 1597 *Thesaurus Oeconomiae*, a commentary on the pseudo-Aristotelian *Oeconomica*. In that work, Case showed himself to be in line with the usual Tudor concerns: he praised agriculture and worried about dearth if not enough people pursued it;[78] and he subscribed to a theory of vocation and considered the choice of one a matter of great importance. But the approach was heavily moralizing and abstracted from market forces in both the market for consumer goods and the labor market.[79] Case distinguished between productive and unproductive labor and consumption, and he suggested that the choice of career was a matter of reflection on one's nature alone. In addition, this was all filtered through the pseudo-Aristotelian figure of the head of the household (Case's *paterfamilias*), which cast the operation of the economy in staunchly patriarchal terms.[80]

---

77 Case emphasized the different types of honor that each sort of the people desired, in a manner reminiscent of Contarini. "For the wealthy have their praise, nobles their pedigree, and both their reward of honor." Artisans should be recognized not only insofar as they might have been made wealthy through their crafts, but in recognition of their handiwork. "Indeed, I add this, that the good of any art, even though it be a trifling one, has its glory. Hence Apelles has deserved his statue for being a famous painter, and Polyclitus a painting for being a famous sculptor." Case, *SC*, 270; Case, "Sphaera Civitatis," 3.8.3.

78 Case, *Thesaurus Oeconomiae*, 32–3.

79 Ibid., 125.

80 Case's conventional approach—but also the important difference in tone—was evident in his discussion about the choice of vocation: "I conclude that every head of the household ought to look often at this table [of vocations], and also reflect diligently with himself about what sort of life [*genus vitae*] is most suitable for himselfe and his; for then he will have goals and flags, as it were, with which to direct himself. He will better understand the direction of the arc of his life, if he considers the natural tendency towards this or that work which needs to be done in either himself or some member of his family. Since, 'contrary to nature,' as they say, no art is learned, no work is taken up, no deed is well and prosperously done. Therefore he should accommodate himself and his son and servant to the will and command of nature to do that towards which he sees himself, his son, and servant have tended by the force of nature. For the force of nature is great and wondrous in the guidance of life, if the growing weeds of the vices are cut down, and if the ground, or talent in which are cast the seeds of the virtues is

If the natural law approach to Aristotelian citizenship encoded a different sort of understanding of the economy, it also reflected a very different understanding of citizenship. Office holding as understood in the republican reading of Aristotle reflected the extent of self-government enjoyed by various parts of the state and was a reflection of "liberties" in the Roman vocabulary. Differentiation was not understood in the sense of the Ciceronian-Aristotelian synthesis in which it was the basis of mutuality, but rather as a source of conflict, in which the varying ideas of justice gave rise to political struggle. The constitutional arrangement by which offices were distributed was a reflection of the compromise achieved at a certain point in time and of the distributive principles of the dominant party or parties.[81] Case's citizenship

---

cultivated." Ibid., 43: concludo omnem patremfamilias debere saepissime intueri hanc tabulam, necnon diligenter secum considerare, quodnam vitae genus sibi suisque maxime conveniat: nam hinc habet quosdam veluti scopos & signa, quibus seipsum dirigat. Cognoscet autem melius, quo tandem arcum suae vitae intendat, si propensionem naturae ad hoc vel illud opus agendum, in se, & in quavis familiae suae parte consideret; quippe invita Minerva (ut aiunt) ars nulla discitur, nullus suscipitur labor, opus nullum bene & fortunate conficitur: accommodet ergo seipsum, & filium, & servum pro nutu & imperio naturae ad id operis, ad quod se, filium, & servum naturae vi propensum videat; vis enim naturae magna & mira est in institutione vitae, si fibrae vitiorum in flore amputentur, & si colatur terra, seu ingenium in quo sparguntur semina virtutum.

81 Case followed this traditional Aristotelian line in many of the questions on particular regime types, but his version of the mixed regime (discussed below) showed a marked departure from this approach. Borrhaus and Freig followed Aristotle closely here, essentially paraphrasing his constitutional relativism. Given how much they adhered to the text, however, it is difficult to draw any conclusions about how their approach to social stratification may have intersected with their understanding of Aristotle's theory of citizenship. Borrhaus, *Annotationes*, 163; Freig, *Quaestiones*, 126–7: eum qui in arte sordida & mercenaria versatur, non licet curam & operam impendere in ea quae virtutis sunt. Praeterea nec in oligarchiis mercenarius civis esse potest (nam ex magnis censibus tribuuntur honores) opificem autem nihili prohibet civem esse. Nam & plerique opifices opulenti sunt. Aristotle, *Politics*, 1278a18.

In the republican versions, such as Vettori's work, a more sympathetic and political approach was taken to the question, in which the attributes of various sorts of people are seen relative to the power structure and the ideas of justice of the ruling class. Vettori thus, for instance, offered a more sympathetic portrait of wage laborers in explaining why they did not qualify for citizenship in an aristocracy: "for those who live such a life are not able to devote themselves to the pursuit of human virtue, because their occupations prevent them, as they require that they are always in their shops or occupied with all their heart in base work which was wanted by those who hired their labor for promised wages." Vettori, *Commentarii in Octo Libros*, 208: Non enim inquit licet incumbere in studia virtutis hominibus, qui vitam talem colunt: impediunt enim artes illae, quae requirunt, ut assidui sint in suis tabernis, aut occupentur toto pectore in tenuibus ministeriis, in quibus esse ipsos volunt, qui eorum operam conduxerint, praebita mercede. Aristotle, *Politics*, 1278a24. Vettori showed a similar sensitivity to how the criterion for active citizenship was applied to social stratification in an oligarchy: "there is no doubt that hirelings are not able to attain honors in such [oligarchies], since hirelings of the lesser sort are not able to grow their patrimonies to amass such considerable wealth." Nevertheless, the "sordid artisans" could hold office in an oligarchy, "for many of them obtain great riches by diligently practicing their crafts." Vettori, *Commentarii in Octo Libros*, 209: non est dubium quin in illis mercenarii homines non perveniant ad honores: ex

can barely be understood to be political in this sense at all. It was rather a reflection of the suitability of an individual for office, in which office was understood more as a commission from the monarch and a reward for conformity than as an expression of belonging and ownership (*dominium*). Case treated citizenship neither as a stipulated, artificial, legal definition of the nation, as in Bodin's imperial model, nor as a reflection of involvement and dedication, as in the republican model, but simultaneously as conformity, a reward for talent, and suitability for service, which reflected the fate of the commonwealth ideal in late Elizabethan conformist thinking.

This vision of citizenship was exemplified in Case's question on "whether bastards are citizens." Bastardy had become an object of Tudor social policy since it was considered at once sinful and a potential liability for the parishes, which would be financially responsible for unclaimed offspring. In fact, shortly after Case's *Sphaera Civitatis* was published, the rate of illegitimacy peaked at 4.5 percent.[82] Citizenship here meant, in keeping with Aristotle, the eligibility to hold office. The trouble with admitting bastards to offices, to honors, was that it would engender emulation, for "what else is it to admit bastards and degenerates to the commonwealth's council and senate than to kindle the torches of lust, and to give free rein to corrupters of virgins, adulterers, those who practice incest, and other monsters of men?"[83] For the voluntary approach to external conformity to work where honor was the sole reward, the exclusion of (and construction of) the dishonorable was required. The inclusion of bastards would also engender the other competitive emotions of envy and indignation. "For, beyond the example of evil which is in this way bequeathed to posterity, a deadly hatred is engendered between these fellows and good citizens, since earnest men will tolerate it grudgingly and with indignation that bastards are made their peers and equals in participation in the commonwealth."[84] The effect of such a policy of exclusion was thus both to norm behavior and to maintain the effectiveness of the motivational system.

MAGISTRACY AND GOVERNMENT BY COMMISSION

Case considered the role of the magistrate in greater depth than many of the preceding commentaries had. In chapters 2–4, he included a number of questions on the nature of the magistrate that were not previously treated,

---

minutis enim illis mercedibus nequeunt ita augere patrimonium, ut census illos amplos conficiant. . . . opifices sordidi: divitias enim inquit magnas multi adipiscuntur, sedulo exercentes has artes.

82 Braddick, *State Formation*, 30–1, 143.
83 Case, *SC*, 347–8 [An nothi sint cives?]; Case, "Sphaera Civitatis," 4.6.3.
84 Ibid.

and in fact, most of his new questions were concerned with this topic.[85] Like his treatment of citizenship, Case's understanding of magistracy was precisely triangulated between the contemporary positions in order to show that it was possible to see the Elizabethan approach to government as consonant with a reconstruction of classical politics without resorting to positions like those of the Italian republican commentators, which would have conceded too much to popular government, or defaulting immediately to Bodin's imperial state. Throughout his handling of the *quaestiones* on magistracy, Case unsurprisingly came down in favor of views that avoided open criticism of the government's practices of patronage while portraying an idealized standard of classical office holding. As in his more general account of citizenship and social stratification, this required drawing some fine lines at times, and, as was the case in that context, his conclusions may not have been wholly convincing to all who disputed them *in utramquem partem*.

Case defined office as a public role "by which a man is transformed from his private condition to being a public personage for the sake of procuring a common good."[86] There is little evidence in the *Sphaera*, however, that Case imagined a true psychological transformation of the kind imagined by Whitgift and Bacon, discussed in the next chapter. Case seems to have been imagining a legal and moral transformation, built on the conventional opposition between public and private, which emphasized the obligations and capacities that came with public office, rather than coming to grips with the ways in which the motivations for seeking office colored the experience of authority for the office holders and those subject to their authority. In thinking of a transformation (*ex conditione privata publica persona fieri*), Case may have imagined the practice of government by commission, which had been used for some time to appoint justices of the peace and had in the years right before the publication of the *Sphaera Civitatis* taken on new importance as it was used to commission lords lieutenant throughout England. The lords lieutenant, which were first suggested by William Paget in Edward's reign as a method to control sedition and further the cause of Reformation, were used in Mary's reign solely for the purpose of keeping the peace, without a confessional purpose. Lords lieutenant were commissioned only infrequently in this period and only in particular hot spots; the militia was mustered by the sheriffs and justices of the peace. In the later part of Elizabeth's reign, the lords lieutenant became responsible for mustering and commanding the local units of the militia in addition to keeping order, and this system was regularized in the years 1585–7, when the rumors of Spanish

---

85 For example, from chapter 2: Ad reddendam officii rationem impelli debeat magistratus? Aliquis cogi possit ad magistratum? Liceat sponte susceptum deserere magistratum? Liceat uni plures una sustinere magistratus? An liceat populo impedire magistratum quo minus in iudicio sententiam ferat? From chapter 3: An liceat magistratum emere?

86 Case, *SC*, 184; Case, "Sphaera Civitatis," 2.9.3.

preparations for war led to the commission of lords lieutenant in all the counties in England.[87]

The commissions themselves were relatively short official letters signed by the queen, which detailed the particular duties and powers being delegated to the commissioned official. There is some evidence that when Case spoke of the transformation of the private individual to a public official, he had royal commissions of this sort in mind. Case transformed a question of Versor's from "Whether it is legal in a good regime to kill wrongdoers and wicked men?" to "whether the king has the power of life and death over his citizens?" This was the manner in which magistracy was discussed in the humanistic legal literature in France and Italy, where it was debated whether the power to execute a citizen in itself defined magistracy in Rome. The question was whether magistracy was fundamentally understood in Rome as a kind of military command. Bodin, following the French humanist Nicholas Grouchy, had essentially argued that this was the case. While Case did not think that this was necessary of all magistracies, he did think that such powers were derived solely from above (as opposed to the republican understanding of magistracy as an expression of self-government). He asked, "Why therefore can judges and others do this? I answer, because they have the same authority granted to them by kings."[88] The commissions of the lords lieutenant from this period explicitly noted that they were being granted this power of life and death. The commission to Christopher Hatton in 1586, for instance, noted that he was being given the power "to save whom you shall think good to be saved, and to slay, destroy and put to execution of death such and as many of them as you shall think meet by your discretion to be put to execution of death."[89]

Though, unlike the republican model of voluntary attachment, Case argued that such men should be compelled to serve.[90] This view of office as a commission from above was understood to be in keeping with the experience and theory of the Roman republic. In the margins to the question of "whether it is permitted to magistrates to accept a salary," Case cited a series of classical sources and noted that "magistracy is a duty to be performed, not to be accepted."[91] Indeed, while the commission was a grant of power to

---

87 Thomson, *Lords Lieutenant in the Sixteenth Century*, 38, 45, 59.

88 Cf. Versor, *Politica*, 3.9 (Queritur, utrum licitum sit in politia bene recta malefactores et viciosos occidere) and (An Rex necis & vitae potentiam in suos cives habeat?). Case, *SC*, 288–9: Cur ergo iudices aliique magistratus hoc ipsum agune? Respondeo, quia eandem authoritatem a regibus concessam habent. Case, "Sphaera Civitatis," 3.10.6.

89 Thomson, *Lords Lieutenant in the Sixteenth Century*, 154.

90 Case, *SC*, 171; Case, "Sphaera Civitatis," 2.7.8.

91 Case cited Cicero, *De Officiis*, bks. 1 and 3; Valerius Maximus, 4.3; Cicero's *De Senectute*. Case, *SC*, 351 [An liceat magistratibus mercedem sumere?]; Case, "Sphaera Civitatis," 4.6.7.

a single individual, the act of mustering the people by a lord lieutenant was a moment that echoed the mutuality of commonwealth. Hatton's commission stated that he was being given the

> full power and authority unto you that you from time to time may levy, gather, or call together, all and singular our subjects, of what estate, degree, or dignity they or any of them be. . . . And them to try, array, and put in readiness and them also, and every of them, after their abilities, degrees and faculties, weel and sufficiently to cause to be armed, and weaponed and to take the musters of them from time to time in places most meet for that purpose.[92]

Like Smith, Case thought of the moment of the defense of the commonwealth as an echo of the involvement of all the classes in the defense of Rome in the early republic. Commissions were naturally viewed in particular as echoes of the call to the patrician class to defend the state, and there was, as I mentioned in the previous chapter, considerable interest in just what it meant for the Roman nobility to be required to provide for the "public horse." Case suggested that the nobility of his day imitate the patrician class of republican Rome, such that "they should feed horses at their own expense, and, when needs be, riding on them they fight stoutly against the enemy, as once did Roman knights."[93] The plebs of this golden moment were also to be praised. Fabricius, for instance, "is commended to posterity with just praises, since, being the poorest of all the magistrates among the Romans, he refused a king's lavish gifts."[94] For Case, Fabricius stood for the willingness of a poor man to serve the state without seeking any financial reward.

The correlate of the powers granted by the commission was the accountability demanded by the Privy Council. The lords lieutenant could be required to present themselves before the council or in the Star Chamber for an accounting of their behavior in office. This was rarely done for lords lieutenant during Mary's and Elizabeth's reigns, but would become an important tool of central control during Charles's reign and seems to have loomed large in the Elizabethan imagination of what an official was in the various corners of the three-cornered fight. For the old nobility, the lack of accountability was the companion of the ambition that characterized the factional patronage of the puritan cabal of new men headed by Leicester.

---

92 Thomson, *Lords Lieutenant in the Sixteenth Century*, 153.

93 Case, *SC*, 328 [An equi ad bellum alendi sint in civitate?]; Case, "Sphaera Civitatis," 4.3.6.

94 Case, *SC*, 351 [An liceat magistratibus mercedem sumere?]; Case, "Sphaera Civitatis," 4.6.7.

Ambition is jealous, suspicious, and fearful of itself, especially when it is joined with a conscience loaden with the guilt of many crimes, whereof he would be loth to be called accompt or be subject to any man that might by authority take reviews of his life and actions when it should please him. In which kind, seeing my Lord of Leicester hath so much to increase his fear, as before hath been showed, by his wicked dealings, it is not like that ever he will put himself to another man's courtesy for passing his audit in particular reckonings which he can no way answer or satisfy, but rather will stand upon the gross sum and general quietus est by making himself chief auditor and master of all accompts for his own part in this life, howsoever he do in the next,· whereof such humors have little regard. And this is for the nature of ambition in itself.[95]

Case argued implicitly that the sort of classical politics to which the conformist councillors were committed required such accountability. Case mentioned approvingly on a number of occasions Aristotle's view that magistrates—and, Case added, even of the highest degree—must submit themselves to judicial examination at the end of their term. Such practices encouraged the proper attitude toward office holding: "For once citizens understand they are going to submit an account of their dignity, they will not be so inflamed for office-hunting by love of self-enhancement, as they will be deterred by fear of submitting an account, lest they conduct themselves amiss in office."[96]

It was a central tenet of the ideology behind government by commission that such offices not be compensated, and Case insisted that this was the teaching of antiquity as well. He rejected paying men to hold office, since it "renders the commonwealth sordid and venal, indeed it destroys all government of justice and equity, for justice has no force where money rules."[97] Case also denied that magistrates should earn a salary (*merces*), since "to have a venal office and prostitute his dignity for base gain like a whore is flatly denied to those performing magistracies."[98] Yet, in keeping with the practices of patronage (which of course all of the parties, conformist and not, participated in), he was willing to countenance the offer of a reward (*praemium*) "to a magistrate justly laboring, since he deserves it,"[99] and even portrayed the heroes of republican Rome as accepting such rewards. Heroes like Horatius Cocles (of "Horatius at the Bridge" fame), "who have infinitely deserved well

---

95 Peck, *Leicester's Commonwealth*, 129.

96 Case, *SC*, 167 [An ad reddendam officii rationem impelli debeat magistratus?]; Case, "Sphaera Civitatis," 2.7.5; Case, *SC*, 411; Case, "Sphaera Civitatis," 4.16.

97 Case, *SC*, 188; Case, "Sphaera Civitatis," 2.9.7. Translation altered.

98 Aristotle, *Politics*, 1293a; Case, *SC*, 349–51; Case, "Sphaera Civitatis," 4.6.6–7.

99 Aristotle, *Politics*, 1293a; Case, *SC*, 349–51; Case, "Sphaera Civitatis," 4.6.6–7.

of their commonwealths, therefore it ought to be permitted them to increase their fortunes infinitely."[100]

Since offices were not to be compensated, it was preferable to give them to men of considerable wealth, like the local magnates who were usually granted Elizabethan commissions. Case treated the issue in his version of Versor's question on why a rich man was to be preferred to a poor one.[101] The two agreed that wealth made a holder of office less corruptible. But where Versor pictured the wealth of the ruler in the lordly idiom of patrimonial management, where personal wealth was to be employed both for the direct use of the commonwealth and for rewarding "good deeds and punishments for crimes," Case saw it in terms of the clientelistic patronage system of his day.[102]

> Furthermore, since a magistrate's life ought to be liberal, splendid and magnificent, nothing is more absurd than to elect to a magistracy a man who is helpless and needy, who has no experience in liberality and magnificence, a man who, when he gives gold to others scarcely has a head of garlic for himself.[103]

Lower offices were also not really treated as true magistracies. While Case conceded that the lower sorts should serve in petty courts, this, in almost a mockery of the republican approach to office holding, was to keep order through allowing the expression of concerns. Even the lower sorts of people had their concerns, "since the fly has its bile and the pauper his spleen," and, reiterating his view that the purpose of a legal system was order, he noted that such concerns must be addressed, for "quarrels not cut off sometimes turn into cruel tragedies."[104]

---

100 Case, *SC*, 142–3 [An cuivis liceat ditescere?]; Case, "Sphaera Civitatis," 2.5.6.

101 Versor, *Politica*, 34rb–vb; Case, *SC*, 166 [An tutius divites quam pauperes in magistratus eligantur?]; Case, "Sphaera Civitatis," 2.7.4.

102 Case did follow Versor closely, so the difference in view is noticeable only in omissions. Case omitted the direct use of an office holder's personal wealth for state action ("Sometimes the republic needs money either for the defense of [the] fatherland or for the maintenance of the state and citizens, and the rich man, not the poor man, can be helpful." Versor *Politica*, 34vb: Res enim publica interdum divitiis indiget. aut propter defensionem patriae. aut propter manutenentiam civitatis et civium. et quo ad hoc dives potest sibi succurrere et non pauper) and omitted the notion that wealth could be useful for the punishment of crimes, only including the reward of virtue. As I noted above in reference to the patricians, Case surely would allow for the use of personal wealth in, say, the mustering of troops. That such material could so seamlessly be used by Case points to the continuity between the honor system in a patrimonial government and the patronage state. Nevertheless the omissions here reveal the differences. Case meant for the wealthy to play a role in the state by participating in the patronage system; Versor meant for the ruler to essentially be the state.

103 Case, *SC*, 169–70 [Distinction of An tutius . . .]; Case, "Sphaera Civitatis," 2.7.8.

104 Case, *SC*, 412–13 [Utrum de minimis inter cives contentionibus forense fieret iudicium?]; Case, "Sphaera Civitatis," 4.16.

The Elizabethan idea of office thus negotiated public and private in Case's view through an eclectic portrait of office holding, which borrowed elements from the contemporary practice of commission and the traditions of the medieval commentaries on Aristotle to offer a vision that justified contemporary practices of patronage while insisting that they fit the classical ideals of devotion to the commonwealth. Yet, despite the frequent reference to classical precedent, his account of magistracy was entirely of his age, engaged with a thinking through of the nature of administration with his continental analogues. Case's account shows that the character of commissioned Englishmen was subtly but significantly different from that envisioned by Grouchy or Bodin. Such men were *not* meant to "live in the city with the citizen like a general with an enemy during tumultuous times of war."[105] They were responsible for maintaining order in their counties, but they were also conductors of sorts, who facilitated the moments of cooperation that made the defense of the realm possible. Accepting the delegate theory of officialdom thus did not entail the excesses of Bodin's sovereignty theory, where all offices were reduced to the threat of coercion and where each magistrate held authority of an undifferentiated military sort, the *imperium* or military command.

THE STATE AS A COMMUNITY OF LAW

Aylmer and Smith had portrayed the law in England as a broadly participatory affair in which the free men of England all played a role in the administration of justice. While Case nowhere directly contradicted this view, his approach to the law was, unsurprisingly, more concerned with hierarchy and conformity. Since the expansion of the justices of the peace under Elizabeth, the community of law was now conceived of as a community governed by honorable and honored magistrates, who enforced order and conformity. This understanding of the rule of law was reflected above all in Case's interpretation of Aristotle's discussion of plebiscites (*psephismata*) where Case emphasized the necessity of turning to the "best men" for legislation.

For Case, the commonwealth was a community of shared norms with a shared understanding of decency, even if there were members who failed to live up to it. Case was not in favor of a sense of the commonwealth as an organic unity. Like many commentators over the years, he embraced Aristotle's critique of Plato, using it to defend private property and distinctions of rank. Case rejected the idea that the commonwealth was a sort of friendship, except in the most attenuated way. When analyzing social relations in terms of the Aristotelian theory of friendship, Case concluded that the only

---

105 Case, *SC*, 423; Case, "Sphaera Civitatis," 5.1.5.

type of friendship that pertained among citizen-subjects as a whole was the consensus of the affect of the will. This sort of friendship was distinguished from the "habit of charity," which only affected a few people at a time and made men more similar in their "morals and pursuits."[106] The unity of a commonwealth was thus more correctly defined as concord, "that easygoing affect of the mind, by which many are moved to harmonious agreement in discussion or in choosing something."[107]

This meant agreement about the law. "The commonwealth is defined as the common association of all men, not because everything within it ought to be common, but because within it is a common consensus for doing things according to the laws."[108] "[D]oing things according to the laws" meant many things: having a reverence for magistrates and judges as representatives of the majesty of the sovereign; an understanding of the rule of law as the ability of magistrates to deviate from the letter of the law under the banner of equity and as the impersonal application of rules and procedures; a dedication to a paternalistic, patriarchal, hierarchical society that taught obedience, thus supporting the role of magistrates in maintaining peace and keeping social order; a distinction between the positive law, which took human frailty into account, and higher norms, which aimed at men's better selves; and the involvement of Parliament in circumscribed conditions.

While the state as a consensus of norms and laws implied broad agreement, Case insisted that it rested on a sense of hierarchy and obedience. The law itself was "dumb and helpless" and could not be considered justice in and of itself. It depended on the work of the magistrates. Case wrote that "it is indeed the voice of justice, but not otherwise than an echo issuing from the voice of the magistrate." It was "a norm of justice," but it turns out that this was "in no other way than a measure is called just" and depended on the magistrates to do the measuring.[109] In this model, respect for the law required the intact social standing of the magistrate. The expansion of the commissions of justices of the peace had been accompanied by a transformation in the cultural valuation of the law, and wealth alone was an insufficient basis for holding office. Though "bakers, tavern-keepers, cobblers, and other men of the basest sort" may hold office once they had been "fattened with filthy lucre," wealth was nevertheless insufficient for legislation or the administration of the law. "Such men dispute better about ale-cups than laws, more fitly about Aesop's fables than the tables and statutes of the commonwealth."[110] As Sir Thomas Elyot had explained years earlier in *The Boke*

106 Case, *SC*, 102, 123; Case, "Sphaera Civitatis," 2.1.9, 2.3.4.

107 Case, *Reflexus Speculi Moralis*, 183: Concordia vero definitur facilis affectio animi, qua plures in consultatione aut electione rerum ad unanimem consensum permoventur.

108 Case, *SC*, 112; Case, "Sphaera Civitatis," 2.2.9.

109 Case, *SC*, 296; Case, "Sphaera Civitatis," 3.11.5. Translation altered.

110 Case, "Sphaera Civitatis," 4.1.4.

Named the Gouernour, becoming a good magistrate and learning the law was now part of what it meant to be a gentleman.[111]

Case treated the question of legislation in the context of Aristotle's discussion of plebiscites.[112] In his discussion of the fifth species of democracy, Aristotle suggested that popular decrees (*psephismata, decreta populi, plebiscita*) were of a different quality than the law (*nomos, lex*). Popular law was generated through the demagogic practices characteristic of extreme democracy: "This arises when decrees have authority instead of laws; and this happens because of popular leaders."[113] This was a locus classicus for thinking about the relationship between social class and law. It was addressed in Peter of Auvergne's literal commentary and in a *quaestio* of Versor and was thus probably widely debated in the late medieval universities.[114] Acciaioli drew parallels between this discussion and the conflict of orders at Rome, and this terminology was echoed by essentially all of the mid-century translations and commentaries, including those of Borrhaus and Joachim Perion.[115] The question was echoed in the antiquarian literature, primarily in the debate between Sigonio and Grouchy over the Roman polity in the 1560s, where the nature of the legislative authority of the plebs, secured by the Lex Hortensia in 287 BC, was debated.[116]

The oldest tradition, from Peter of Auvergne, suggested that popular decrees and the law had different formal qualities: laws were universal while the popular decrees were aimed at particulars. But the commentators soon argued on a variety of grounds that the popular decrees were qualitatively different due to the different political processes that created them. Versor ar-

---

111 Cromartie, *Constitutionalist Revolution,* 34.

112 Richard Tuck called attention to the importance of this passage in "Hobbes and Democracy." Focusing on one part of Vettori's commentary on the passage, that is, the second lemma ("Princeps enim populus fit"), Tuck suggested that extreme democracy formed the basis of Hobbes's theory of sovereignty ("his whole theory of the body politic was designed to show how the union which Aristotle had criticized in that passage was in fact the only legitimate form of political association"; 183). Kinch Hoekstra criticized Tuck on the grounds that Hobbes in the *Elements* was actually critical of the "democratical gentlemen," despite some positive comments. My view is that Hobbes was here drawing on the tradition of commentary, which was carried on in the first lemma on the relevant passage in Vettori. That discussion was focused on the relationship between social class, the law, and the demagogues or flatterers who swayed the people. The first lemma ("Hoc autem fit, cum plebiscita rata fuerint, sed non lex") is the one in which I think Case was interested and on which I focus. Vettori, *Commentarii in Octo Libros,* 314–5; Tuck, "Hobbes and Democracy"; Hoekstra, "Lion in the House."

113 Aristotle, *Politics,* 1292a5.

114 Flüeler, *Rezeption und Interpretation,* 162: Dubitatur primo, utrum populus in democracia dominetur secundum leges vel secundum sententias.

115 Much of this account is drawn from Tuck, "Hobbes and Democracy," 180–1.

116 McCuaig, *Carlo Sigonio,* 103–4, 130–3, 191–2.

gued that the popular decrees were a result of the popular leadership, namely, the demagogues who appealed to the wishes of the people. "The philosopher says that this is because of the demagogues who direct the people as if according to their own opinions. And they say that the people possess lordship (*dominium*) over the laws and over everything. And the people readily listens to this opinion, because it supports the aim at which they are striving, namely, liberty, which the people desires and for the sake of which it rules."[117] There is reason to believe that the question had become newly important in England in the 1580s as the councillors responded to the criticisms of the Catholic nobility. Shortly after *Leicester's Commonwealth* appeared in England in 1584, Hakluyt was dispatched by Leicester back to Paris, where he was serving as the chaplain to the ambassador, to ask the ambassador to figure out who the authors of the pamphlet were.[118] In the 1588 copy of the *Analysis*, but not in the 1583 version, Hakluyt identified this fifth form of democracy, where there is no rule of law, as the "anarchy of the men of the recent past,"[119] and he said that this was the case in Rome.[120] The message seems to have been that the situation brought on by the Arundell-Howard faction, in which flatterers of the people (as the councillors pictured them) were allowed to hold sway, was to be avoided at all costs.

Vettori offered a variant of Versor's view. Picking up on a comment of Aristotle that there is a sort of democracy where the "best citizens preside" and where they "are honored there and have the supreme power and freely oppose the multitude when it serves the public interest," he suggested that the popular decrees in an extreme democracy suffered from a lack of loyal opposition.[121] Borrhaus moralized the passage, arguing that the best citizens were those who were governed by the natural law and not their emotions.[122]

---

117 Versor, *Politica*, 60ra: Dicit philosophus quod hoc est propter demagogos qui dirigant populum quasi secundum opiniones suas. et dicunt quod populus habet dominium supra leges et supra omnia. et istam sententiam libenter audit populus. quia hoc valet ad finem quem intendit scilicet ad libertatem. quam populus appetit et propter quam principatur. Freig offered a Romanized version of this view. Freig, *Quaestiones*, 165–6: sed ita ut dominetur populus, non lex, quod fit cum plebiscita praeferuntur legibus: quod fit propter demagogos . . . sunt demagogoi seu tribuni.

118 Peck, *Leicester's Commonwealth*, 6.

119 BL Sloane 1982, 24v: Sed haec est illa Recentiorum Anarchia.

120 Ryan, "Richard Hakluyt's Voyage into Aristotle," 78, citing Hakluyt, *Analysis*, 35r, BL Sloane 1982.

121 Vettori, *Commentarii in Octo Libros*, 314: Verum inquit in honore illic sunt, summamque potestatem habent optimi cives, qui libere adversantur multitudini, cum publica utilitas postulat.

122 Borrhaus, *Annotationes*, 252: Non popularis. (Qui contra legem factiosae plebi se ducem praebeat, quae multa temere iubet ex affectibus contra honestum. Sed optimates imperant.) Ex legis praescriptione, non affectuum arbitrio.

Sigonio and Grouchy, by contrast, understood the laws of the patricians and the plebs to be formally of the same quality. Substantively the various orders had different agendas, but the laws of the plebs and the laws of the patricians were both the law, *lex*.[123]

In keeping with both the worry about a rogue nobility riling up the people and the worry about the puritan turn to popular government, Case argued that the law of the populace was not really law.[124] Case cited the medieval reading that what was of concern was the possibility of demagogues swaying the populace to a particular position, but it is clear that his real concern was to argue that the law produced by different classes was of differing qualities. Case built on a suggestion in Borrhaus that the difference between the people and the "best men" was expertise. Case characteristically adapted Borrhaus's natural law view in a stratified way, emphasizing once again his view of a hierarchy of talent, but also suggesting a dynamic class tension of the kind found in the Roman sources.[125] Real law was the embodiment, he explained, of considered judgment that was meant to take the long view.[126] This was not the case with "decrees of the people," which were ad hoc measures taken in the heat of the moment, "deemed to be frail always, often unjust, and most chamaeleon-like."[127] This distinction between the two types of law was clearly stratified by class (though the upper classes could be thought to include the new men, men of talent, as well as those of old money and birth). He invoked the old body politic metaphor, suggesting that there were some men who were meant to provide nourishment and motion while others supplied prudence and reason. The different sorts of law that issued from these different classes reflected their class character. "There are many cases and various events, and men's wills are flexible, especially those of the ignorant, such as are most of the multitude. For as often as vicissitudes of this kind in citizens' affairs occur, so often new decrees and fantasies of the people are manufactured."[128]

123 McCuaig, *Carlo Sigonio*, 103–4, 130–3, 191–2.
124 Case, *SC*, 329; Case, "Sphaera Civitatis," 4.4.
125 Borrhaus, *Annotationes*, 252: Propterea quod lege.) Quae multitudinem ut imperitam imperio subiicit, & optimis qui imperandi usum calleant, potestatem permittit. Non pareat.) sed affectibus. Quocirca assentatores.) non lex, & eius ministri & interpretes optimates.
126 The basic analysis here follows Borrhaus. But, again, Case imposed a class analysis on it, which was not quite there. Crucially, Case borrowed the sense of the long-term reasoning of the law versus the short-term thinking of the popular decree. But Borrhaus, citing *Rhetoric*, 1354b7ff., suggested that this logic could apply to a magistrate who was not directly governed by the law. Case could be said to be following Borrhaus insofar as both agreed that what was meant here was the natural law, but if it was the positive law, then Case's emphasis on the independent judgment, the equity, of the magistrate, seemed to contradict Borrhaus's view. This passage from the *Rhetoric* was clearly important for understanding the relationship between the context of decision making and the susceptibility to the passions. Borrhaus, *Annotationes*, 254.
127 Case, *SC*, 333; Case, "Sphaera Civitatis," 4.4.5.
128 Case, *SC*, 332; Case, "Sphaera Civitatis," 4.4.5.

Nevertheless, such popular decrees were permitted, in order to allow the will of the lower classes to be recognized, "lest it be held in contempt and become unruly and seditious." But the popular decrees were to "prevail only temporarily and not have the force of law."[129]

Given Case's hierarchical approach to society, the true law in his view had to be the product of the more esteemed classes. Case claimed that this was true of Rome (perhaps until some unspecified date) and that it would even be the case in a democracy.[130] "For even if the people is called the entire commonwealth, yet within administration there is an order of dignity, so that some preside over others and govern them, and if these men's consent is not granted a decree should not be regarded as having the force of law. Therefore in a popular constitution there is an equality of dignity, not because in fact each and every citizen is equal in participation in dignity (for this would be absurd), but because each and every citizen has the ability to be equal, and this is regarded as just in the first species of democracy."[131] The law of the populace could only be the law in the full sense of the term in a place that was not socially stratified by dignity, which he clearly thought was *not* England—or anywhere else he easily recognized, for that matter.

A (MONARCHICAL REPUBLICAN) ORDER OF OFFICES

Case defined the commonwealth in the traditional Aristotelian mode as an "order," that is, a form or ordering that was superimposed on the "material" of the commonwealth, the populace. The nature of the order depended on who held the highest power in the state and on the distribution of the lower offices.[132] While this captures the notion of the state in some broad sense, exactly what the nature of power was and the relationship between the highest power and the lower offices needed to be interpreted. Through the fifteenth century, the commentators did not elaborate on the relationship between the highest power and the lower offices.[133]

The sixteenth-century commentators offered essentially lordly readings of the state (though they understood that the highest power may in fact be

129 Ibid.

130 Case wrote in the margin: Tribunitiae rogationes non sunt leges. It is not entirely clear what he was thinking of, but presumably it was the situation in Rome before the Lex Hortensia, when the decrees of the plebs had to be ratified by the senators. Case, *SC*, 336.

131 Ibid.; Case, "Sphaera Civitatis," 4.4.8.

132 Aristotle, *Politics*, 1278b9.

133 At least this was the case for Acciaioli, who made no mention of the lower magistracies in his paraphrase of the definition of the state. Acciaioli, *Commentarii*, 88: Respublica est ordinatio civitatis, & circa alios magistratus, & maxime eius, qui dominatur. Est enim ubique dominans, quod est institutum civitatis regimen. Id autem est respublica, veluti in populari statu populus, in regia vel optimatum gubernatione rex, vel optimates.

a group of people), in that the highest power in the state controlled and imposed order on all of the lesser offices. For Borrhaus this image of lordly order mirrored the spiritual order:

> The arrangement of the state is especially perceptible in the magistracy, to whom moreover the others answer, as to the head, and about all things which pertain to the governor of the state. Just as the universal arrangement and right ordering of the state of the heavenly church answers to Christ as its ruler and governor, who alone takes care with the spirit of his gospel that all things are in order and well disposed, such that if he commands and rules, the state of the church is maintained in its best state, but if not, it loses and forgoes it.[134]

Vettori kept the same general understanding of the definition of the state "as the order of the state and some form, as it were, and certainly the arrangement of all offices, but above all the highest of these, by whose authority the commonwealth is governed."[135] In his attempt to wade through the thicket of words that Aristotle used in the definition, he relied on a more lordly understanding: "for the *politeuma* is everywhere the lord and ruler as it were, and the *politeuma* (unless I am mistaken) is what he calls that part of the citizens which has in its hands and power the commonwealth. Indeed, there is no doubt, that, though often outnumbered, it is in some way the state, because it overcomes the others with the powers and law of its government, as it wishes." He concluded that "the *politeuma* is the *politia* itself, that is the commonwealth; indeed, this was the proper name for this thing."[136]

Case reinterpreted Aristotle in terms of the later Elizabethan notion of the highest power being in control of the distribution of offices.[137] He defined the order of the commonwealth as "an order of the state as much of

134 Borrhaus, *Annotationes*, 165: Descriptionem civitatis maxime in magistratu cerni: ad quem nimirum cuncta referantur, ut ad caput, & omnium quae ad rempublicam pertinent administratorem. Veluti quoque Ecclesiae coelestis civitatis universa descriptio atque legitima ordinatio ad Christum tanquam principem & moderatorem refertur: qui unus omnia ut ordine & rite fiant, spiritu evangelii sui procurat. qui si imperet & praesit, Ecclesiae respublica suum optimum statum tuetur: sin minus, eum perdit ac amittit.

135 Vettori, *Commentarii in Octo Libros*, 209: affirmatque rempublicam esse ordinem civitatis, & quasi formam quandam, descriptionemque magistratuum sane omnium: sed in primis summi illius, cuius auctoritate respublica regitur.

136 Vettori, *Commentarii in Octo Libros*, 209: Est enim politeuma ubique quasi dominus ac princeps: politeuma autem (nisi fallor) vocat partem illam civium, quae in sua manu potestateque rempublicam habet: non enim est dubium, quin haec, quamvis saepe vincatur numero, aliquo modo civitas sit, quia vincit ceteros opibus & iure illius administrandae, ut vult. . . . quare politeuma inquit est politia ipsa, idest respublica: hoc enim nomen proprium erat huius rei.

137 James, "English Politics."

other magistrates as of that chiefly to which has been given the highest power and judgment."[138] Though he made slight changes in the Latin translation, suggesting a greater equality between the higher and lower magistrates, the chief alterations were in his discussion of the definition.[139] "It is an order of other magistrates," he explained, "because it justly distributes the lesser grades and degrees of honor to worthier men."[140] Vettori had suggested, obliquely, a lordly version of this, noting that the *politeuma* uses government "as a certain means and support for approving what it wished to uphold."[141] Case's inclusion of the term "justly," however, suggests that his was no longer a lordly reading of the state, but an understanding of the state in terms of the just distribution of offices as honors and rewards for virtue and talent. In general, he offered more of an intersubjective definition of the state, adding a phrase not found in the other commentaries: "it is an order of the state, since it wisely demands, not the opinion of one man, but civil consent."[142]

The more active, bottom-up understanding of the state rather than the lordly view was even reflected in subtle choices in terminology. Some of the previous commentators, such as Acciaioli, had translated τάξις as *ordo*, while others, such as Borrhaus and Vettori, had preferred the more Ciceronian *descriptio*. *Descriptio* suggests more of an arrangement or delineation; it does not in itself have lordly connotations.[143] Case preferred *ordo*, since *descriptio* suggests that the *respublica*, the state, is an abstract, theoretical arrangement of magistracies. He preferred *ordo* for two reasons: it captured better that the state was constituted by the activity of all officials, not simply their arrangement, and it captured better the dynamic relation between the state (*civitas*) and the material that was given order by the commonwealth (*respublica*). The choice of terminology and Case's defense shows that he put more of

---

138 Case, *SC*, 224: Definitur ergo respublica hoc modo, ut sit ordo civitatis cum aliorum magistratuum, tum eius maxime, cui tradita est summa potestas & arbitrium rerum. Case, "Sphaera Civitatis," 3.4.1.

139 The way that different scholars translated and interpreted the *ton . . . kai malista* reflected their understanding of the state and the relationship between sovereign power and the lower offices. Borrhaus used the lemma *cum in caeteris magistratibus* as the opportunity for his discussion of the relationship between the magistracies and the highest power in the state. Case adopted Vettori's *summa potestas*, but replaced Vettori's *caeterumque . . . et* with *cum . . . tum*, which made it more equal.

140 Case, *SC*, 224; Case, "Sphaera Civitatis," 3.4.1.

141 Vettori, *Commentarii in Octo Libros*, 209: utitur autem hoc tamquam medio quodam adminiculoque ad probandum, quod firmare volebat.

142 Case, *SC*, 224; Case, "Sphaera Civitatis," 3.4.1; Vettori, *Commentarii in Octo Libros*, 209: utitur autem hoc tamquam medio quodam adminiculoque ad probandum, quod firmare volebat.

143 E. A. [Ethan Allen] Andrews, *A Latin Dictionary Founded on Andrews' Edition of Freund's Latin Dictionary* (Oxford: Clarendon, 1980), s.v. "descriptio."

an emphasis on the state understood as the actual practices of all office holders *and* the way in which the offices were distributed. The more lordly interpretations were more concerned with the manner in which the offices were distributed in accordance with the wishes of the highest power in the state. *Descriptio* suggests a more top-down approach, *ordo* a more bottom-up one, though this is only the slightest of shades of meaning. Case and the others all thought of offices as being distributed in light of the desires of the highest power, but Case wished to emphasize the role played by the office holders as much as how those offices were arranged and distributed.[144]

Along with Burghley and much of the rest of the Privy Council, Case walked a very fine line, an almost impossibly thin line, in negotiating the relationship between broad-based customs of office holding and popular involvement, on the one hand, and the tradition of monarchy, on the other. This is the famed monarchical republicanism of the Elizabethan period. As Patrick Collinson has explained, there were two sides to monarchical republicanism: the broad practices of office holding in England, which were largely independent of the central monarchy without in any way opposing it, and the willingness to imagine a conciliar interregnum of some kind in the case of a succession crisis.[145] I have already mentioned that Case, like Aylmer and Smith, was closely concerned with the first sense throughout his work. But he also engaged with the second sense in his more precise definition of the state. Writing (or at least revising) in 1588, with the succession crisis averted, he did not strike quite the same notes as the privy councillors and their associates in Parliament did in the memoranda of 1584. Rather, Case created a sort of hybrid political theory of the state based on a particular reading of Aristotle's political theory and on a modified version of Bodin's distinction between the *forma reipublicae* and the *forma gubernandi*, which in some ways preserved the essence of the proposed solution to potential crisis without reproducing the most radical elements or embodying them in high political theory.[146]

Whatever the nuances of his monarchical republicanism, Case was unequivocal in his assertion that England was a monarchy. Case, like the conformist theologians, rejected the idea that England was a mixed regime. He argued in general terms that Aristotle thought that monarchy was the best regime, despite much disagreement among interpreters over the issue, and he claimed, against any sort of ancient constitutional argument to the

---

144 Case, *SC*, 229; Case, "Sphaera Civitatis," 3.4.5.

145 Collinson, "Monarchical Republic of Queen Elizabeth I."

146 Richard Becon, a contemporary of Case from St. John's, took a similar approach, though his defense of the mixed regime lacked the nuances of Case's, which made it more amenable to a hierarchical but participatory republic. Becon, *Solon His Follie*, 84. For Becon's use of Bodin's distinction, see Sommerville, "English and Roman Liberty," 210–1.

contrary, that England had been a monarchy for centuries. This was the case even though, he admitted, "in England there is a mixed *administration* [emphasis added] of the republic by the prince, the nobles, and the tribunes of the people, so much so that no law can be enacted, no custom abrogated and rescinded without the consent of them all." Case explained that this was so since "a single sovereign has the greatest dominion" in England.[147] This closely echoed the words of John Whitgift in *The Defence of the Answer to the Admonition* (1574), a reply to a reply to the presbyterian Cartwright: "I know that all these three kinds of governments may be mixed together after divers sorts; yet still the state of government is named according to that which most ruleth, and beareth the greatest sway. . . . As in this realm in the court of parliament, although all the states be represented, yet because the judgment, confirmation, and determination resteth in the prince, therefore the state is neither 'aristocraty,' nor 'democraty,' but a monarchy."[148]

Case defined the mixed administration by handling the offices that represented the monarchical, aristocratic, and democratic elements in terms of the formal qualities of office rather than in terms of the resulting distribution of power, as was traditional in the Aristotelian analysis of the mixed regime. Case distinguished between three types of office, which would have various term lengths: the royal magistracy, that of the king or queen, should be perpetual "lest sedition arise"; the senatorial should be "continual, but at the king's pleasure"; and the common should be "changed frequently." Thus, the broad participatory character of the English constitution stressed by Aylmer and Smith satisfied the Aristotelian requirements for a stable state, that is, a just distribution of recognition and honor, without flattening its hierarchical character or thinking of it as a constitutional settlement in which power was shared. Mixed administration was psychologically satisfying, justly distributed, and in keeping with English traditions:

> the hopes of the citizens, who are more keenly incited to the pursuit of virtue by the stimuli of honor; the order of the commonwealth, which demands and prescribes that citizens participate in counsel and magistracies in proportion to the merit of their virtue; the custom of our ancestors, who were in the habit of raising and promoting many men from the hoe to the Senate, from the clod to the throne of dignity.[149]

147 Case, *SC*, 233–4, 238, 265; Case, "Sphaera Civitatis," 3.5.1, 6, 3.7.12: quamvis in Anglia mixta sit administratio reipublicae per principem, per nobiles, per tribunos plebis, adeo ut nulla lex sanciri, nulla consuetudo abrogari & rescindi possit sine consensu omnium. Translation modified to reflect the echoes of Livy.

148 Whitgift, *Works of John Whitgift*, 1:393, quoted in Burgess, *British Political Thought*, 100; Mendle, *Dangerous Positions*, 67.

149 Case, *SC*, 98; Case, "Sphaera Civitatis," 2.1.4.

In arguing thus, Case accepted Bodin's argument about how to classify England in terms of regime type, as he did about France (a monarchy) and Venice (an aristocracy).[150] Case, however, was by no means accepting Bodin's understanding of the state wholesale. He (and I imagine that this was the case for his patrons as well) was not interested in defining the common-wealth solely as a function of political power. The state was not simply a union of those who had been cowed into submission by some lord. It was not an *ordo parentium* and *imperantium* in this sense, and it was not the prod-uct of fear, as Machiavelli had urged. (Case opposed Machiavelli's notion that obedience was due to fear. He noted that God commanded that both Saul and David be obeyed, "not just because of fear, as many men do today, but out of conscience, as few today are willing to do.")[151] And so, Bodin had helped Case to classify England as a monarchy, not because the monarch was sovereign in some deep sense, but because the monarch was the most power-ful part of the administration; this was the Aristotelian *summa potestas* rather than Bodinian sovereignty.

The identity of the state as a whole did not, in the councillors' view, de-pend on who had power in the last resort, who was sovereign in Bodin's sense. It depended rather on the norms and attitudes that the populace held about the distribution of offices, that is, the assent and good will of the peo-ple and the various customs of office holding that defined citizenship in the Aristotelian sense.[152] This willingness to analyze the nature of citizenship and office holding independently from administration was a crucial depar-ture from Aristotle's theory of the state. For Aristotle, the identity of the state depended crucially on the form of the constitution. But the council, faced with the Elizabethan succession crisis, was concerned not to define the state in such a way that England would cease to exist if there were an interregnum or if the constitution were changed to redistribute power. The councillors thus adapted Bodin's distinction between the *forma reipublicae* and the *forma gubernandi* to Aristotle, developing a theory of the state that would allow them to maintain the identity of an English state with its consti-tutional traditions of broad office holding and consent of the people.

This was, of course, a departure not just from Aristotle, but from Bo-din, since it suggested that part of the nature of the state depended on the

150 Case, *SC*, 238; Case, "Sphaera Civitatis," 3.5.5; Bodin, *Bodin: On Sovereignty*, 23, 25, 63, 115.
151 Case, *SC*, 265; Case, "Sphaera Civitatis," 3.7.13.
152 Case, *SC*, 197; Case, "Sphaera Civitatis," 3.1.3: Nam ut inter animam & corpus: ita in-ter regem & plebem, inter principem & populum summa debet esse conspiratio . . . nam quod regnum tutum, cuius custos populi metus est? Quae civitas salva, in qua multitude vi & armis oppressa vivit? Iam in qua libertate consultandi, iudicandi, magistratus gerendi privata & spoliata vivit? Est ergo civis pars recte administratae civitatis natus, aut factus, consilii, iudicii, & magistratus particeps.

Aristotelian theory of citizenship rather than on who was sovereign. "From the definition of the citizen, whether born or made, who has a share in counsel, judging, and dignity [i.e., the performance of magistracies], in act or potentiality, and, where liberty remains, these are all present in every just form of a republic. It therefore follows that the citizen remains the same when the constitution has changed."[153] The appeal of such a theory to the English—and the Privy Council in particular—is clear. They could claim that the constitutional traditions of England were largely intact while countenancing extremely large changes in the structure of government. Case spelled out the implications of this view and his departure from Aristotle:

> But you will say that to obey kings and Ephors, to be subject to the government of a single man (as in a monarchy) or the power of a few (as in an aristocracy) is not the same thing. I admit this, but these things argue a change of organization rather than of the citizen, of the mode rather than of the thing. Just as a shoot of an apple or some other plant, when grafted on a pear, is changed in its nature from an apple into a pear, but the root remains the same, thus when a new order of administration is instituted the form of the republic is altered, but the citizen (who is the root and the seed of the commonwealth) exists immutable. Therefore, if liberty, authority, and participation in counsel, judging and dignity remain the same after a change, I do not see a reason why the citizen should not remain the same. But so far these things are my own personal opinion, which does not contradict Aristotle in the text. But if the republic is changed from good to evil, from a just state to a depraved one, such as from monarchy to tyranny, from aristocracy to oligarchy, from democracy to timocracy, from a mixed constitution to anarchy, then I do not think the citizen remains the same.[154]

Case then was willing to suggest that the state remained identical despite massive constitutional changes at the level of the administration, which he seems to have envisioned as the monarch and the two houses of Parliament, as long as the practices of office holding at the lower levels remained the same. This was substantially the position in the memoranda of 1584 of Thomas Digges and Burghley, who maintained that in a succession crisis, all office holders should remain the same. Case did not, however, suggest that any sort of grand council take charge at a moment of transition, and in general he did not emphasize practices of counsel. As Collinson suggested in his remarks about Burghley's lack of enthusiasm for republicanism, by 1588, with the crisis

153 Case, *SC*, 200; Case, "Sphaera Civitatis," 2.1.4. Translation altered.
154 Case, *SC*, 200; Case, "Sphaera Civitatis," 2.1.5.

averted, this may have seemed unnecessarily republican and may have even posed a threat to the power of the Privy Council and the *regnum Cecilianum*. Certainly Case was not interested in a democratic republican regime, and he may have been holding his breath through the earlier part of the decade, dismayed like Digges at the more excessively republican proposals and ideas, such as the Bond of Association, which Digges criticized as "a confused company of all partes of the Realme of all degrees and estates" with "no president, no Judges, no sheriffs, no justices, briefly no officers."[155]

CONCLUSION

Case's Aristotelian commonwealth—which maintained a position on a theoretical level between Italian republicanism and the Bodinian understanding of the state, and on a political level between presbyterian popularity and the aristocracy of the old nobility—was a monarchical republic, neither fish nor fowl. This was not, however, simply a matter of regime type. At the heart of the project was an attempt to reimagine not only how the broad participation of the populace could be squared with monarchy understood as the form of sovereignty, but how the desire for distinction and esteem that underlay the Reformers' theory of attachment to the state could be reconciled with an emphasis on the monarchical form of sovereignty. This was a task for all those sympathetic to conformity, and Case's solution, characteristic of conformist thought, was at once conservative and modernizing. It recalled the traditional natural law readings of Aristotle, but embraced the ambition of new men and a meritocratic set of values. The psychology that was so carefully differentiated by Smith was beginning to be universalized, and the recognition that had been sought from others, above and below, in so many different ways was now becoming reduced to one's suitability on a single scale combining talent and effort. That the judge of this suitability was the monarch, or the monarch's favorite, is obscured in Case's *Sphaera*, which, following Aristotle's *Politics*, surveyed the various sorts of constitution, yet it was the unity of such judgment according to which goods should be distributed that made a monarchical republic imaginable.

155 Collinson, "Monarchical Republic of Queen Elizabeth I," 51, 53, 56.

CHAPTER 4

THE PRIVATE AND THE PUBLIC

There are many places in Court which a mere formal man may perform. . . . And yet in these the choice had need be of honest and faithful servants, as well as of comely outsides, who can bow the knee and kiss the hand, and perform other services of small importance compared to this of public imployment.

—Francis Bacon to George Villiers, Earl of Buckingham, 1618*

Late in Elizabeth's reign, Francis Bacon was still thinking about the relationship of state and commonwealth in ways that would have been familiar in Somerset's protectorate. In the Parliament of 1597, apparently acting in the government's interest, if not directly at its representatives' instigation, Bacon introduced in the House of Commons a motion on the first day of business against enclosure and the depopulation of towns and houses of husbandry, and for the preservation of tillage. A large committee was appointed to consider the matter, and Bacon drafted the bills on tillage and depopulation.[1] The surviving materials from the debates over the bill and its renewal in 1601 suggest that this argument over "motheaten laws," as Bacon referred to the old statutes he had studied in the drafting of the bills, echoed the old debates.[2] The dispute turned mostly on various attempts to exclude particular classes of property and counties from the act. Henry Jackman, a London merchant with ties to the Wiltshire wool trade, echoed the old arguments of Sir Thomas Smith in opposing the use of the penal law to influence tillage: "Men are not to be compelled by penalties but allured by profite to any good exercise."[3] Sir Walter Raleigh, who represented Devon, another exempted county, made a similar argument in the 1601 debate over the renewal of the statute.[4]

---

* Peltonen, *Duel in Early Modern England*, 124.

1 Neale, *Elizabeth I and Her Parliaments*, 337–9; Dean, *Law-Making and Society*, 162–3.

2 Neale, *Elizabeth I and Her Parliaments*, 339, characterized the debate on the second reading as between a "protagonist of the welfare state" and "a disciple of Adam Smith."

3 Ibid., 341–3; McRae, *God Speed the Plough*, 11.

4 Neale, *Elizabeth I and Her Parliaments*, 343.

What Bacon and the government had in mind can be pieced together through the interventions of Elizabeth's secretary of state, Robert Cecil. Insisting that the preservation of tillage was necessary to keep up the population required for defense, Cecil argued against the attempt to exempt Northumberland, Cumberland, and Westmoreland, three of the four northernmost counties in England.[5] The idea of the government, fleshed out further in the second act "against the decaieng of townes and houses of husbandry," which required that every house have twenty acres, was apparently to restore England, or at the very least the border counties, to the old, celebrated conditions of the harmonious but differentiated degrees of the people, the rural ideal of commonwealth, in the hope of building up a middle sort of yeomanry, which would provide foot soldiers for defense.

Not only did it seem that Bacon was helping to rebuild the old structures of commonwealth in the late 1590s, but he and his opponents were still thinking in the old patterns of achieving conformity by overcoming affection with affection. In his 1605 *Advancement of Learning*, Bacon wrote:

> howe I say to sett affection againste affection, and to Master one by another, even as wee use to hunt beast with beaste, and flye byrde with burde, which otherwise percase wee coulde not so easily recover; upon which foundation is erected that excellent use of *Praemium* and *poena*, whereby Civile states Consist imploying the predominante affections of *feare* and *hope*, for the suppressing and brideling the rest.[6]

Nevertheless, while the old moral theory of affection overcoming affection was never as sanguine as often thought, it is still the case that Bacon's mature theory, as has long been recognized, sounded quite different than the mid-Tudor talk of commonwealth. The new attitude has been variously described as the result of absolutism or divine right thinking; of the emphasis on royal prerogative; of a new sort of cynical humanism; or of the very public corruption of the patronage system.[7] As I have demonstrated, this was in part an optical illusion as talk of the classical commonwealth fell out of fashion among the Jacobean courtiers, but there were real differences between the Reformers' treatment of the affections in social and political systems and Bacon's.[8] In the accounts of commonwealth from Contarini and Starkey onward, overcoming affection by affection meant the satisfaction of the needs

---

5 Ibid.

6 Bacon, *Advancement of Learning*, 150.

7 Sommerville, *Royalists and Patriots*; Tuck, "Hobbes and Tacitus"; Tuck, *Philosophy and Government*; Peck, *Court Patronage and Corruption*. For a review of the literature on the impact of neo-Stoicism and Tacitism at court, see Burgess, *Absolute Monarchy and the Stuart Constitution*, 52–7; Bacon, *Historie of the Raigne of King Henry the Seventh*, xli.

8 See the introduction to this volume.

of the different degrees of the people in accordance with distributive justice. As mentioned, Vettori's commentaries of the mid- to late 1570s had begun to call into question the assumption that offices could be distributed in a polity in such a way as to reflect the commonwealth ideal of mutual cooperation and harmony. Drawing on Aristotle's theory of envy, he argued that for such distributions to be stable, they needed to reflect the feelings of the various parts of a society, regardless of their justice. Case had ignored these arguments, supplying instead a patriarchal, natural law account of citizenship. As Bacon's list of points to be investigated in connection with the affections suggests ("*Custome, Exercise, Habit, Educacion, example, Imitation, Emulation, Company, Frinds, praise, Reproofe, exhoration, fame, lawes, Bookes, studyes*"), his understanding of overcoming affection with affection included cooperative and competitive social processes as well as those of socialization.[9]

The roots of this analysis were not in the cynical "court discourse" of the 1590s, but once again in Whitgift's defense of conformity during the admonition controversy.[10] Bacon's attitudes about ambition and public service, and his skepticism toward the claims of common lawyers and idle justices of the peace, if not quite the "oligarchy of Puritan minded gentry"[11] that was taking firmer hold of local government in some of the counties by the end of Elizabeth's reign, echoed what he had heard from Whitgift when Bacon and his brother were students at Trinity College, Cambridge, from 1573 to 1575. Social stratification and differentiated citizenship were in this analysis not the instantiations of a divinely instituted natural hierarchy, as in the divine right accounts of Saravia or Bancroft, but a complex reaction to the natural competitive behaviors of men described by the Reformers. The elucidation of natural competitive behaviors shows how people need to help each other and yet how such mutuality is almost by definition self-defeating, since men compete with one another for distinction. Bacon's theory of the commonwealth, like that of King James before him, was a reflection on how social and political organization could transform and channel these competitive behaviors.

ENVY AND EMULATION

The story of the theological treatment of envy and emulation began in the late 1550s and 1560s, when the Marian exiles and the Swiss Reformers

9 Bacon, *Works*, 3:437–8; Bacon, *Advancement of Learning*, 151.

10 This claim and the discussion of it below builds on the work of Julian Martin, who read Bacon as a student of Whitgift against the "select communities" of the puritans. Martin, *Francis Bacon*, esp. 24–5, 42, 57–60. Phil Withington further developed Martin's interpretation into a contrast between the court and the city commonwealths. Withington, *Politics of Commonwealth*, 53–62.

11 MacCulloch, *Suffolk and the Tudors*, 338, cited in Cogswell, *Home Divisions*, 4; Peltonen, "Bacon, Francis."

began to think through these issues in the context of their commentaries and translations of the Bible, which became widely known in England and Scotland due to Laurence Tomson's English edition of the Geneva Bible. The Reformers read the New Testament as a plan for church and common-wealth, looking to the apostolic community and the early Christian communities of the epistles as examples of how to organize and think about their societies. For example, in chapter 12 of 1 Corinthians, the various members of the church were pictured as contributing to the church in the same way that the parts of the commonwealth were thought to contribute to the common good in the classical ideal of the commonwealth.[12] It was the puzzling final verse of this chapter that introduced the theory of emulation into the mix. The final verse posed a series of textual problems—semantically and grammatically. Above all, it was unclear how to translate the first word of the sentence, ζηλοῦτε. William Whittington, the force behind the new English translation of the New Testament, did not offer a gloss on it in either his 1557 edition or the 1560 Geneva Bible, the New Testament section of which was largely based on his work. The Swiss Reformer Theodore Beza was clearly both intrigued by it and tried to make sense of it. In his 1565 edition of the New Testament, he changed both his interpretation and his translation from his 1559 Latin translation and commentary. In 1559, Beza had argued that the Vulgate and Erasmus were mistaken in thinking that the verse was in the imperative, and that it was better to think of it as in the indicative.[13] He took the verse to be asking a rhetorical question to rally the Corinthians. "As if the Apostle were saying," paraphrased Beza, "[b]ut do you desire to be better than others?" He then explained in the next chapter the ways in which a lawful ambition might be pursued.[14] In 1565, Beza's Latin translation now matched the English translation of the 1560 Geneva Bible: "But desire you the best gifts, and I will yet show you a more excellent way."[15] He had changed his mind (perhaps convinced by Whittington or another of the exiles on the basis of surviving manuscripts) and now considered it an imperative. Now Beza believed that the verse meant: "Dedicate yourselves to those things which are most excellent, as if the Apostle were saying, I see that you are envious of each other, and you ought rather to strive in a kind of holy emulation, to surpass each other in sacred things, and those which contribute to the common good. For anyone who excels in such things is the more

---

12 *Geneva Bible 1560*, 1112–3; *New Testament of Our Lord and Saviour Jesus Christ*, 280–1.

13 Beza, *Novum Iesu Christi Domini Nostri Testamentum Latine*, 550: Ambitis vero dona potiora? [en] insuper etiam quam diligentissime viam vobis indico.

14 Ibid.: Cupitis vero aliis excellere? en qua via & ratione vobis liceat maxima cum laude ambitioni indulgere.

15 Beza, *Iesu Christi D. N. Nouum Testamentum*, 279: Sed ambite dona potiora. Et porro iter at excellentiam vobis indicabo.

useful."[16] In Tomson's 1576 edition of the Geneva Bible, which incorporated Beza's 1565 notes on the New Testament, he paraphrased Beza: "He teacheth them that are ambitious and envyous, a certaine holy ambition and envie, to wit, If they give them selves to the best giftes, and such are most profitable to the Church, and so, if they contend to excel one another in love, which farre passeth al other gifts."[17]

Envy and emulation were treated similarly in the interpretations by the Reformers of the fourth chapter of the Epistle of James. The chapter asks one of *the* questions of political theory, namely, "From whence are warres and contentions among you?"[18] There was some debate over whether the Greek really intended the word "envy" in verse 2: "Ye lust and have not: ye envie, and desire immoderatly, and can not obtaine: ye fight and warre, and get nothing, because ye aske not."[19] But it was broadly agreed that the Greek certainly did in verse 5: "Doe ye thinke that the Scripture saith in vaine, The spirit that dwelleth in us, lusteth after envie?" There was no question that this last line was concerned with envy, but what precisely it meant was a matter of dispute. The question was whether "[t]he spirit" referred to the Holy Spirit working through grace to defeat envy or whether "[t]he spirit" was the human spirit, which was corrupted by envy.[20] Beza's Latin translation and Tomson's English edition were both widely read, and this teaching was evidently spreading throughout the Reformed community.[21] In his 1577 *Ethices Christianae*, the Reformed writer Lambert Daneau cited this verse, explaining that emulation "which is the imitation of the virtue of

---

16 Ibid.: iis vos dedite quae sunt praestantissimis. ut si diceret Apostolus, Video vos alios aliis invidere, atqui danda potius est vobis opera, sancta quaedam aemulatione, ut in rebus sanctis, & ad communem salutem pertinentibus, alii aliis antecellatis. Est enim aliquis eo excellentior quo est utilior.

17 *New Testament of Our Lord Iesus Christ*, 294v.

18 Ibid., 405.

19 Calvin and Beza emended the text to be translated as *invidetis*, "you envy." For what Tomson's Geneva Bible had as "desire immoderatly," Calvin used Erasmus's *aemulamini*, while Beza used *studiose affectatis*, "you desire eagerly," which clearly became the basis for the Geneva Bible's English. Beza explained that this word, *zeloute*, like in 1 Corinthians, "intends here something more that to envy, namely an ambitious desire for that which is coveted." Beza, *Iesu Christi D. N. Nouum Testamentum*, 555: declarat hoc in loco aliquid amplius quam invidere, nempe ambitiosam affectationem rei expetitae. Calvin, *Commentaries on the Catholic Epistles*, 329.

20 This question may have some bearing on the history of political thought, since it matters slightly whether one thinks that the Bible is saying that human nature is naturally envious and thus unsociable, or whether the verse is concerned with describing the ways in which sanctification works through grace. Beza argued the former on the basis of Genesis 8:21, whereas Calvin argued the latter. Beza, *Iesu Christi D. N. Nouum Testamentum*, 555; Calvin, *Commentaries on the Catholic Epistles*, 332–3.

21 Tomson's notes were printed in Scotland in the second vernacular Bible published there, the 1610 edition of the Geneva Bible published by Andrew Hart. Tomson, *The Bible*.

another should be praised."[22] Though these works did not cite Aristotle explicitly, it seems likely, given Beza's and Daneau's opposition of *invidia* and *aemulatio*, the typical translations of Aristotle's terms in their day, that they were drawing on his distinction between envy and emulation in the *Rhetoric*, where envy was defined as pain at the thought of another possessing some good, and emulation as a positive desire to possess goods that one does not possess but others do.[23]

In Scotland, George Buchanan, the poet and scholar who was James's tutor during the regency, used the language of envy and emulation with some regularity in his Latin *History of Scotland*, which was published posthumously in 1582, but not in his *De Iure Regni apud Scotos*, probably written in 1567 and published in 1579, suggesting that he familiarized himself with it between these dates, possibly drawing on the 1579 edition of Vettori's 1548 commentary on the *Rhetoric*, which explained the political significance of the issues.[24] The use of the terminology of envy and emulation (*invidia* and *aemulatio*) in the *History* was in part a reflection of Tacitus's extensive use of them, since Tacitus was one of Buchanan's models in writing that work. Tacitus showed considerable interest in the role of rivalries of different sorts—productive and destructive—and illustrated the consequences of such rivalries vividly. As examples of the good sort of emulation, Tacitus included the suicides of Otho's soldiers in imitation of him after he had lost the war against Vitellius, and the desire for the barbarian Frisian envoys to take seats in the Senate alongside the representatives of the more civilized foreign nations. Examples of the harmful sort of emulation included the rivalry between Bassus and Caecina, resulting in their overthrow of Vitellius; possibly that between Sabinus and Vespasian, which may have kept Sabinus from

---

22 Daneau, *Ethices Christianae*, 367: aemulatio quae est virtutis alienae imitatio laudanda est.

23 Aristotle, *Rhetoric*, in *Complete Works of Aristotle*, 2:2211–2, 1387b21–88b15.

24 Buchanan donated an anonymous 1539 commentary on Aristotle's *Rhetoric* to the University of Glasgow in 1578 (shelf mark: Sp Coll BC2-a.17). This was a fragmentary commentary found in the French royal archives and printed by Conrad Neobar. The University of Glasgow also holds two copies of Vettori's commentary. The 1548 edition is from the Hamilton Collection (Sp Coll BC22-y.9) so probably was not used by Buchanan. The 1549 edition was also likely not used by him, since it is part of the Hunterian Collection. The 1579 edition, which is of uncertain provenance, might have been used by him (Sp Coll Bh4-c.12). Irving, *Memoirs*, 394; Durkan et al., *George Buchanan*. Buchanan may have been inspired by Rainolds to turn to the *Rhetoric*, since Rainolds enjoyed a good reputation among the presbyterians in Scotland in this period, perhaps due to his fame for having convinced the English Catholic John Hart to stay true to his recantation of Catholicism in 1582. When Andrew Melville, the leading Scottish Reformer and one of Buchanan's former students, fled to England in 1584 as a result of his support for the Ruthven raid of 1582, he befriended Rainolds in Oxford. Rainolds, *John Rainolds' Oxford Lectures*, 31; Holloway, *Andrew Melville*, 215–17.

accepting the leadership of Rome in order to keep the *imperium* from his younger brother Vespasian; and, finally, that between Petronius and Tigellinus over who would be the arbiter of pleasures in Nero's court.[25] Buchanan combined this Tacitist view of the causes of historical events as the product of competitive behavior with the Christian emphasis on confining competition to the virtues in his *History.*[26]

In Scotland, the distinction between competition in spiritual and in worldly matters, between holy and profane envy, corresponded to the theory of the distribution of offices in church government developed in Andrew Melville's presbyterianism. Beza had already in the 1560s decried the system of preferment by which church positions were filled from above at the request of the local lords, arguing that ministers should be called by congregations. The presbyterians believed that the old system led to the corruption of the ministry as positions were held at times by so-called civil men with no real vocation for the work. Having returned to Scotland from Geneva in 1574, Melville, who had been a disciple of Beza there, argued that church and state government should be distinct, without clerical representation in Parliament or secular interference in the kirk.[27] Melville described the ordinary calling of an ecclesiastical office holder in the memorandum he submitted to the Scottish Parliament in 1578 about the proper form of the church. All ecclesiastical offices, he argued, should be filled only by ministers who had a calling for the position, as testified internally by their conscience before God and externally by their election to the position by the congregation and the eldership. "Election is the chusing out of one man or person to the Office that is void, by the judgment of the Eldership and the consent of the Congregation to whom the person presented is to be appointed."[28]

THE ARGUMENT FOR SOCIAL LEADERSHIP

For King James, the egalitarianism of the presbyterian approach failed to truly address the problems of envy and ambition. The churchmen who were striving for position in the church and authority in the polity outside of the traditional representation of the estate of the clergy by the bishops in Parliament were just as liable to these emotions as their more worldly brethren.

25 *Histories*, 2.49.4 (Otho); *Annals*, 13.54.4 (Frisians); *Histories*, 2.101.1 (Bassus and Caecina), 3.65.1 (Sabinus and Vespasian); *Annals*, 16.18.3 (Petronius and Tigellinus).

26 See, for example, Buchanan, *History of Scotland*, 1:275, 2:11.12–4, 127–8; Buchanan, *Opera Omnia*, 1:6.3, 165, 370.

27 For the institutional story, see Mendle, *Dangerous Positions*, 68-9.

28 Spottiswood, *History of the Church of Scotland*, 292.

It was the traditional representation of the three estates in the Parliament under their king that ensured order and stability in Scotland.[29]

James's vision of a monarchy composed of the estates of the realm resembled the work of one of the leading theorists of the opposition to presbyterianism in England, the Dutch theologian Adrien Saravia. Saravia had addressed the question in two of his works, *De Diuersis Ministrorum Euangelii Gradibus* (1590) and *De Imperandi Authoritate et Christiana Obedientia* (1593). In looking for a model of state and society that would uphold the monarchy against the monarchomachic claims of Buchanan and company, Saravia struck upon the feudal model. Unlike Bodin, he firmly rejected the Roman imperial model, which, he conceded to his monarchomachic adversaries, was ultimately a popular regime in which the power of the emperor was really that of a magistrate whose authority was based on a grant from the people and the Senate of Rome.[30] There was no cohesive "people" in early Roman history, but a conflict between the patricians and the plebs. Like Case, Saravia argued that the plebs cannot be called a "people" but are simply the multitude.[31]

Saravia reimagined the kingdom as a feudal monarchy in which "the people" was composed of the meeting of estates—representatives—who were called as counselors to the king. "In a kingdom, or an aristocracy in large countries, the estates are called, and those who represent the people come together, but to be present, not to rule, to help with their advice, not to command. If it is necessary that something be done, or changed, and so it seemed useful to them, they attend the king as supplicants, to explain the thing to his majesty, not to command."[32] For Saravia, such a vision of subjection to the monarch did not imply an undifferentiated citizenry. Hierarchy was as important in civil government as it was in ecclesiastical government. Hierarchy was divinely given. As he famously explained in his apology for episcopacy, "Equality as Ministers does not hinder inequality as rulers. Under the Old Testament there was one Priesthood, the same and equal in all Priests, yet in point of government, there were different ranks among the Priests, and divers degrees of honour in respect of government, although the dignity of the Priesthood was one and the same in all." Hierarchy was instituted in the church for "the maintenance of good order, eutaxia, that all thing[s] might be done decently and in order."[33]

---

29 For James's vision of the realm of Scotland as monarchy counseled by three estates, see Mendle, *Dangerous Positions*, 73.

30 Saravia, *De Imperandi Authoritate*, 209.

31 Ibid., 214.

32 Ibid., 215: In regno, vel optimatum imperio amplissimarum regionum convocantur ordines, & conveniunt, qui populum repraesentant; sed ut adsint, non ut praesint; ut consilio suo adiuvent, non imperent. Si quid autem fieri, aut mutari necessarium, atque utile visum ipsis fuerit, regem supplices adeunt, ut rem ipsius maiestati exponant, non ut iubeant.

33 Saravia, *Treatise on the Different Degrees of the Christian Priesthood*, 144–5.

James hoped to restore such an order, and he wrote down his advice on how to do so for his son, the young Prince Henry, in the *Basilicon Doron* (1598). The older issue of the choice of vocations among the middling sorts was not the most pressing; it was now treated as an issue of monetary policy and of supply and demand. Covetousness for material gain was a fault that was restricted to the mercantile element in the commonalty, and it did not pose a real threat to the social order. Such covetousness, it was suggested, was easily remedied by a set of familiar commonwealth economic policies, such as refraining from debasement of the coinage, inviting foreign craftsmen in order to raise the level of luxury goods and correct the balance of trade, and fixing the prices at which goods must be imported or at which threats must be made to open competition from foreign merchants for noncompliance.[34] More serious, he warned Henry, was the sort of envy over office holders that Vettori had described in his commentaries. For instance, James advised Henry to "put never a forrainer, in any principall office of estate: for that will never faile to stirre up sedition and envie in the countrey-mens hearts, both against you and him,"[35] and to "[e]mploy every man as ye thinke him qualified, but use not one in all things, lest he waxe proude, and be envied of his fellowes."[36] The true problem of social order, and thus the role of a monarch, was to coordinate the clergy, the aristocracy, and the commons.

For James, the problem of the clergy was that they believed that the testimony of their consciences allowed them to overstep the bounds of their calling. They were so affected by "Pride, Ambition, and Avarice" that none of the usual means of reconciling them to the state were effective: "no deserts can oblige, neither oathes or promises binde." This was because they were "aspiring without measure, railing without reason, and making their owne imaginations (without any warrant of the word) the square of their conscience."[37] This was, to James's mind, characteristic of the more rebellious sort of presbyterian clergy, who overstepped the limits of their role by believing that they should offer advice to the king as to how to conduct himself. This was acceptable, James believed, as long as their advice was "well warranted by the Word," but if, he warned Prince Henry, "they urge you to embrace any of their fantasies in place of God's word," they should be considered "no other then vaine men, exceeding the bounds of their calling," who needed to be brought back into line.[38]

It was in the context of the hierarchical theory of society that James turned to the theory of emulation. In an exchange between Saravia and the monarchomachs, Saravia argued that the essence of magistracy was leadership. Beza

34 James VI and I, *Political Writings*, 29–30.
35 Ibid., 37.
36 Ibid., 38.
37 Ibid., 25–7.
38 Ibid., 19.

had contended in "De Iure Magistratuum" that "peoples were not created on account of the magistrate, but rather magistrates were created on account of the people, just as a tutor is appointed for the sake of his pupil, not the pupil for the sake of the tutor, and the pastor on account of the flock, not the flock on account of the pastor."[39] Saravia responded by arguing that this was not at all universally true and relating that "a great many leaders brought together a multitude which had been up until then . . . wandering and dispersed, or gathered spontaneously to them, out of which a new people was forged, as happened in the case of Aeneas and Romulus, and many others, who were the authors of new peoples." He noted that this was the case where peoples were conquered in just wars as well. One could conclude from this that "in a free commonwealth, such as were the Athenian and Roman, the people was greater than its magistrate, but in a kingdom and an aristocracy, it was different, there magistrates are created by the will of the princes and they pronounce judgment in their names."[40]

For James, the truth of Saravia's analysis was borne out by the influence that the churchmen were having in Scotland. The presbyterian ministers were an example of leadership gone wrong. James was worried that they might be imitated by other estates. For James, the puritan churchmen were the "evil seed men" who could not be allowed to be imitated in their drive for equality in the church, "[f]or if by the example thereof, once established in the Ecclesiastical government, the Politicke and civill estate should be drawn to the like, the great confusion thereupon would arise may easily be discerned."[41] His fear was that emulation could work across estates; the values of one estate could be adopted by another.

The regulation of emulation thus became a key part of James's understanding of good government. The good king should not rule through an extensive legislative program, since it was better for a commonwealth to be ruled by only a few laws and because such a program would require calling Parliaments, which could be used for particular interests.[42] The king's duties were to execute the law and to serve as an example to his people. James paraphrased Plato: "teach your people by your example: for people are naturally

39 Beza, "De Iure Magistratuum," q. 5, 231: non populos propter Magistratum, sed contra Magistratus propter populum fuisse creatos: sicut tutor pupillo, non pupillus tutori constituitur: & pastor ob gregem, non grex propter pastorem.

40 Saravia, *De Imperandi Authoritate*, 4.24, 227: plerosque duces vagam, atque hinc inde dispersam collegisse multitudinem, aut ad eos eam ultro confluxisse, unde novus conflatus est populus; sicut apparet in Aenea, & Romulo, aliisque pluribus, qui novi populi fuere authores. . . . In libera republica, qualis fuit Atheniensis & Romana, populus maior erat suo magistratu: sed in regno, & optimatum potestate, alia est ratio. ibi magistratus ex arbitrio Principum creantur, & eorum nomine ius dicunt.

41 James VI and I, *Political Writings*, 26.

42 Ibid., 21.

inclined to counterfaite (like apes) their Princes manners."[43] He added, moreover, that "as every one of the people will delite to follow the example of any of the Courteours, as well in evill as in good; so what crime so horrible can there be committed and over-seene in a Courteour, that will not be an exemplare excuse for any other boldly to commit the like?"[44] The king should thus arrange things so that the nobles competed with one another to act humbly and obediently, in the hope both that they would behave accordingly and that they would be imitated by the other estates. James advised Henry that in his treatment of the nobility, he should "so use your selfe lovinglie to the obedient, and rigorously to the stubborne, as may make the greatest of them to thinke, that the chiefest point of their honour, standeth in striving with the meanest of the land in humilitie towards you, and obedience to your Lawes."[45] Emulation was meant to be a process of hierarchical mimesis, of the reproduction of social values through the imitation of one's social betters.

Though this may seem like the same use of honor as in the older commonwealth system, it actually reflected a changing attitude toward the use of honor. The point of the system of honors was now understood to be the creation of an exemplary class that would be emulated by others, not to neutralize the potentially seditious forces of a powerful class of magnates. But in the short term, this distinction and any hope of emulation working as social leadership was completely sidelined as James VI resorted to the use of honors in the old way and awarded a large number of titles in a very short span of time in order to secure his place on the English throne and to satisfy the "pent-up demand" that had built up during Elizabeth's reign.[46] Over time, James turned to correct this freewheeling sale of honors, which has become known—in Lawrence Stone's phrase—as the "inflation of honours."[47]

In 1610, James promised Parliament that he would take greater care in granting honors, but in 1611, after the failure of the Great Contract, he agreed to the creation of the order of baronets in order to raise revenue for the Crown.[48] Some steps were made to uphold the character of the nobility in his attempts to control dueling in 1613–4, which I discuss below in the context of Bacon, and James finally took a more systematic approach by appointing Thomas Howard, the Earl of Arundel, as the earl marshal in 1621, toward the end of his reign. Arundel attempted to reinvigorate the Court of Chivalry by clarifying procedures, establishing a table of fees, and actually

43 Ibid., 20.
44 Ibid., 34.
45 Ibid., 29.
46 Coward, *The Stuart Age*, 122.
47 Stone, *Crisis of the Aristocracy*, chap. 3.
48 Cust, *Charles I and the Aristocracy*, 27–8.

bringing cases. The court was meant to adjudicate claims to nobility and in theory would preside over the integrity of the noble class. In practice, however, the court was opposed bitterly by the royal favorite, Buckingham, who benefited from the sale of honors, and thus Arundel's attempts had very little effect.[49] The methods that James had advised Henry to adopt in the *Basilicon Doron* in order to secure an exemplary class—such as the punishment of poorly behaved nobles—were implemented only later, in the reign of Charles. For the moment, the royal commonwealth was less a society headed by a pristine class of nobles than an overheated, disorderly scramble for place.

FRANCIS BACON AND "THE VANTAGE GROUND TO DO GOOD"

Francis Bacon sought office for much of his adult life. Born in 1561, he tried to attain office after the death of his father, the lord keeper of the Great Seal, in 1579 and then through the Earl of Essex in the 1590s, all without success. He finally won a minor appointment in 1603 (as king's counsel) and then his first major office, as solicitor general, in 1607. Bacon was in some sense forced into the position of the endlessly grasping aspirant; his father had passed away before securing the lands that would have made the younger Bacon comfortable in the social circles to which he was accustomed as the son of the lord keeper. In the midst of this scrambling for a position and between the 1597 and 1612 editions of his *Essays*, Bacon incorporated the theory of envy and emulation into his analysis. Bacon had drawn on the *Rhetoric* on occasion in his 1597 edition, but it was in the 1612 edition that he developed the fuller theory, spread over several essays.[50]

The 1612 edition of the *Essays*, written in the hope of higher office, touched on many of these themes. Bacon had received some favor from Prince Henry and hoped that the *Essays*, which he had planned to dedicate to the prince before Henry's untimely death, would help him attain higher office.[51] While it is difficult to say whether it was the success of the *Essays* that did the trick, Bacon was appointed attorney general in 1613, after asking to be considered for it for a few years. This experience must have confirmed the lesson that Bacon had learned from Whitgift as a young man, namely, that ambition

49 Ibid., 37–9.

50 Bacon, *Complete Essays*, ix–xiv. Bacon's "[i]f a man performe that which hath not been attempted before" (*Works*, 6:531, "Of Honour and Reputation," 1597; Bacon, *Essayes*, 163) was drawn from Aristotle, *Rhetoric*, 1368a10f. I quote from Spedding's transcripts of the 1597 (STC 1137) and 1612 editions (STC 1141, King's College Cambridge, A.8.20, as per Bacon, *Essayes*, lxxvii) in volume 6 of Bacon, *Works*, and the final 1625 edition from Bacon, *Essayes*. Page references to *Works* and *Essayes* are provided throughout for ease of reference.

51 Peltonen, "Bacon, Francis."

could be justified as long as it was directed at service to others. It must have led Bacon to argue in the 1612 edition that ambition was perhaps not as bad as it seemed and that it was not necessarily self-serving.

Whitgift's views were developed during the literary battles of the admonition controversy. As I described in the previous chapter, Whitgift and the conformists were accused by Cartwright in the "Second Admonition" of insisting on episcopacy in order to pursue honors and titles for themselves. In responding to the charge, Whitgift developed many of the themes that would be so important to Bacon, including that titles and offices were fine as long as they were not sought vaingloriously and for reputation alone, and they were to be fulfilled as service to others. In his response to Cartwright, Whitgift explained that Christ did not forbid hierarchy and government to Christians but "such tyrannical kind of government as the gentiles used, and that ambitious desire and affection of the same which ruled in them."[52] Discussing Christ's teaching in Luke 22:25–6 and the parallel passages that "the kings of the Gentiles exercise lordship over them; and they that exercise authority upon them are called benefactors. But ye shall not be so," he wrote: "If either they vain-gloriously desired that name, or were so called, when they deserved rather the names of tyrants and oppressors, doth it therefore follow that they be unlawful names for such as may deserve them?"[53] The bishops and other officers of the church were servants of the public and were doing their best to serve the commonwealth as a whole. They were fulfilling the teaching of Matthew 23:11, "[b]ut he that is greatest among you shall be your servant," as expounded on by the Reformers. "[F]or," as Whitgift explained, "though the name of a prince and of a lord be a name of honour and dignity, yet is it the office of a prince and lord to serve those which be under them in governing of them carefully, and in providing for their wealth and peace."[54] The claim to titles of honor and dignity was transformed from vainglorious striving by the justice of the claims, by the fact that they *deserved* them.

It was in fact the puritans who were really doing what Wolfgang Musculus, Martin Bucer, and the other Reformers understood to be condemned by the Bible, namely, the gentile version of politics, which was ruthlessly and pointlessly ambitious, the *libido dominandi*. Though Cartwright denied that the puritans could be envious of those who held offices they thought were illegal (citing Aristotle's definition of envy in the process), Whitgift argued that such envy was surely possible "as it is not unlike that there are some of you that disdain such as be in place above you, be they deans, bishops, or archbishops, although you say that their offices be unlawful and

52 Whitgift, *Works of John Whitgift*, 1:150.
53 Ibid., 1:152.
54 Ibid., 1:159.

tyrannical."[55] Like the Anabaptists, the puritans were seeking popularity through a kind of pharisaical show of virtuosity, celebrating the "straitness of life."[56] In a sermon at Greenwich, Whitgift elaborated on this strategy, discussing those who "under the pretence of zeal seek their own liberty, under the colour of religion seek confusion, and the shadow of reformation cloak and cover their usury, their ambition, their minds desirous to spoil the church."[57] In the context of conformity, the pursuit of honor and popularity took on a cognitive aspect, such that arrogance "so puffeth up the minds of their teachers with an opinion of themselves, that they dare be bold to propound anything, so that it taste of novelty and please the people, though it tend to the disturbance of the church, the contempt of magistrates, and the breach of good laws and orders."[58]

Though a 1589 memorandum on religious controversy chiefly showed that Bacon disagreed with the harsh measures being carried out against the puritans by Whitgift and Bancroft, it nevertheless revealed that Bacon had absorbed Whitgift's criticisms of the puritans.[59] There were two sorts of men, he explained: would-be leaders, who wished to lord over others by wielding "an inward authority which they seek over men's minds, in drawing them to depend upon their opinion," and "stiff followers," who for "young years and superficial understanding, [were] carried away with partial respect of persons, or with the enticing appearance of goodly names and pretences."[60] Bacon continued to see society as divided into these two categories throughout his life, and they reappeared in his late *History of the Reign of King Henry the Seventh* as Yorkist pretenders and gullible followers, though there the lower sorts of English people took on some of the qualities of Machiavelli's and Guicciardini's *popolo*.

In the *Essays*, Bacon showed that he also accepted Whitgift's defense of ambition and office holding. In doing so, Bacon adapted it to respond not only to James's call for social leadership by the nobility, but to the arguments of the older nobles more generally. The analysis of unsociability, of envy, had become both thoroughly accepted and the basis of a conservative argument about the dangers of ambition and the necessity for social distance. Such arguments against new men had been around for years; I have mentioned that Laurence Humphrey argued against their inclusion in government, and several other Elizabethan writers on nobility, including Gerard Legh in *The Accedence of Armorie* (1562, 1568, 1576, 1591, etc.) and John Ferne in *The Blazon of Gentrie* (1586), argued for the narrowing of the no-

55 Ibid., 1:166–7.
56 Ibid., 1:109–10.
57 Ibid., 3:580.
58 Ibid., 3:579.
59 Collinson, *Richard Bancroft*, 80–1.
60 Bacon, *LL*, 1:82–3.

bility.[61] The arguments against ambition were even captured in the sententiae painted on the walls of Gorhambury, where Bacon had spent his childhood and which he inherited from his brother Anthony in 1602: "Ambition does not look backwards, and is not so pleased to see many behind her, as bitter to see someone ahead of her."[62] Sir Nicholas Bacon, himself a new man, nevertheless saw ambition as a route to unhappiness (or believed that he should). Another sententia read: "If candidates about to seek office were to consult ambitious men who had attained the highest honors, they might change their prayers."[63]

The new Aristotelian arguments, absorbed into the standard Reformed outlook, seemed to offer yet more ammunition for the argument against social mobility. The Aristotelian premise that was of most cultural concern was, as Bartholomaeus Keckermann summarized in his standard textbook of Reformed Aristotelian ethics of 1607, "envy governs above all between equals or men of the same status and condition." The conclusion drawn was that "therefore we do not envy those who are highly placed, beyond our common condition, and those who are commonly judged to be eminent men."[64] The natural implication was that to control envy and achieve social peace, it was best to create significant social distance between the classes and to entrust government offices to the nobility. In the 1612 *Essays*, Bacon conceded all of this in a halfhearted way. He accepted the analysis of unsociability and confessed that strict social stratification could extinguish envy, but his discussion of the usefulness of the nobility to government can hardly be thought of as a ringing endorsement.

Nobilitie of Birth commonly abateth industrie: and hee that is not industrious envieth him that is: Besides noble persons, cannot goe much higher: And he that standeth at a stay when others rise, can hardly avoid motions of envie. On the other side Nobility extinguisheth the passive envie in others towards them; because they are in possession of *Honour*: and Envy is as the sunne beames, that beate more upon a rising ground, then upon a levell. A great *Nobilitie* addeth maiesty to a *Monarch*, but diminisheth power: and putteth life and spirit into the people; but presseth their fortunes. It is well when nobles are not

61 Cust, *Charles I and the Aristocracy*, 13–15.

62 Bacon, *Sir Nicholas Bacon's Great House Sententiae*, 68: Ambitio non respicit, nec tam gaudet, multos post se videre, quam maeret, aliquem ante se. Translation altered. McCutcheon noted that this was drawn from Seneca, *Epistulae*, 73.3.

63 Bacon, *Sir Nicholas Bacon's Great House Sententiae*, 70–1; Seneca, *Epistulae*, 115, 17. For a similar view, see my discussion of Vettori in the previous chapter.

64 Keckermann, *Systema Ethicae*, 232: Invidia potissime regnat inter pares sive homines eiusdem status & conditionis. . . . Itaque summis & extra communem nostram conditionem positis, communique iudicio eminentibus viris non invidemus.

too great for *Sovereaigntie*, nor for *Iustice*; and yet maintained in that height, as the insollency of inferiours may be broken upon them, before it come on too fast upon the maiestie of *Kings*. Certainely *Kings* that have able men of their Nobility, shal find ease in imploying them; and a better slide in their businesse: For people naturally bend to them, as borne in some sort to command.[65]

The nobles were essentially arguing that it was easier for them to be the "public" class in government, since, as Bacon noted, they "cannot goe much higher" and would not be envied by their inferiors. The ambition that makes office holding a "private" goal did not truly apply to them. As Henry Hastings, the fifth Earl of Huntingdon, told his son, "by thy birth thou art a publique person."[66] While Bacon agreed that those at the top of the social scale had relatively little in the way of private ambition, this was not altogether a good thing for the realm: "[i]t is well when nobles are not too great for *Sovereaigntie*, nor for *Iustice*." What he meant is clear from his charge as the lord chancellor to the JPs in the Star Chamber in 1617, where he contrasted England with France and noted that unlike there, where there was a division between the *noblesse du robe* and *noblesse d'épée*, the English commissions of justices of the peace "doth knit the noblemen, and those that are *minores nobiles*, knights and other, in one commission . . . and this makes the noblemen here modest, and the knights and gentlemen well spirited . . . and lastly by this institution those that have voices in Parliament to make laws, they for the most part are those which in the country are appointed to administer the same laws."[67] It was the desire of the minor nobility to emulate the greater nobility that lent energy to the commonwealth.

The conventional understanding of the public man imagined the public and private as fundamentally opposed categories. The ideal of the public man was expressed in Joseph Hall's *Characters* of 1608. Hall, the chaplain to Bacon's niece Anne, Lady Drury, and her husband, made the relationship between the private and the public man the central theme of his character study of the good magistrate.[68] The magistrate faced challenge after challenge as one who was trying to be a public figure, whose "brest is the Ocean whereinto all the cares of priuate men emptie themselues." The contemporary understanding of what the state should be—in the countryside, if not at court—received perfect expression: "His nights, his meales are short and interrupted; all which hee beares well, because hee knowes himselfe made for a publique seruant of

---

65 Bacon, *Works*, 6:549–50 ("Of Nobility," 1612); Bacon, *Essayes*, 41–2.
66 Cogswell, *Home Divisions*, 21.
67 Bacon, *LL*, 6:303-4.
68 McCabe, "Hall, Joseph."

peace and iustice."[69] The magistrate was a public person, not a private individual, when working as a judge for "[o]n the bench he is another from himselfe at home; now all priuate respects of blood, alliance, amitie are forgotten; and if his own sonne come vnder triall, hee knowes him not."[70]

The gentry were often disappointing to the king and council in this regard. The desire for social distinction meant that members of the ruling class often neglected their duties in the hope of favor at court in London or popularity at home. In a charge to the JPs in the Star Chamber in 1608, the lord chancellor before Bacon, Baron Ellesmere, thundered at the gentry:

> for the number of newe & younge knightes, that Come in there braveryes & stande there lyke an Idoll to be gazed upon, & doe nothinge, ys so greate & pressinge for place, Countenaunce & estimacyon: but they must knowe they are not Justices for there Countenaunce onelye; let them remember there oathes & dutyes, that they are for the Justice, peace & governmente of the Cuntrye, & not to be quarter Justices, as many of them are, that lye aboute this towne 3 partes of the yeare, & goe down onelye for there pleasure in hawkinge & huntinge.[71]

Such complaints would recur frequently over the next decade, appearing, for instance, in Hall's *Characters*, in James's speech in the Star Chamber in 1616, and in Samuel Ward's 1618 sermon "Jethro's Justice of the Peace."[72] The range of epithets that officials were called gives some sense of the problem. "Forsooth they will be no pragmaticall fellowes, no busi-bodies to trouble the Countrey. Is there no mean between busi-bodies and tell-clockes, between *factotum* and fay't neant."[73] The "tell clock" was an idler, one who just watched time tick by. The factotum was a busybody, with the implication of a meddling servant who takes care of everything but gets into everyone's business.[74] The busybody "hates constancie as an earthen dulnesse, vnfit for men of spirit: and loues to change his worke and his place."[75]

Bacon's goal was to show that it was possible to surmount the problem of ambition through good intentions, thereby showing, like Whitgift, that private desires could be transformed into public ones. He argued that ambitious men were a nation's blessing and its curse. They represented the talent

---

69 Hall, *Characters*, 57–8.

70 Ibid., 59.

71 Hawarde, *Reportes*, 368.

72 For the sermons and the view of magistracy in Jacobean England, see Peck, *Court Patronage and Corruption*, 165–73.

73 Hall, *Characters*, 65.

74 *Oxford English Dictionary*, s.v. "factotum."

75 Hall, *Characters*, 84.

and promise as well as the source of faction and sedition. The wise prince would be able to perceive the difference between well-intentioned ambitious men of genuine talent who sought "the vantage ground to doe good" in addition to their own "fortunes" and those who were solely self-serving with no genuine merit, committed only to promoting their own reputations.[76] The trouble with ambitious men of little merit was that they had a psychology that undermined the stability of the state. Such vainglorious men were incapable of managing subordinates and, insecure and envious, they were natural springs of faction and violence. "They that are [vain]glorious must needs be factious; for all bravery stands upon comparisons. They must needer be violent, to make good their owne vaunts."[77] They were concerned always to put themselves above others and thus to deride others for their own benefit. Subordinates of this sort were also to be avoided "for they teint businesse through want of secrecy, and they export honor from a man and make him a returne in envy."[78]

Being a public man came through a life of public service, and it was neither an easy thing to bear nor without its faults. Men "of great place" had turned themselves inside out and always looked to others for confirmation of their own happiness.

> Certainely, great persons had need to borrow other mens opinions, to think themselves happy: for if they judge by their owne feeling, they cannot find it; but if they thinke with themselves, what other men thinke of them, and that other men would fain be as they are, then they are happy as it were by report, when perhappes they finde the contrarie within; for they are the first that finde their owne griefes, though they bee the last that finde their own faults.[79]

Such men had forgotten how to live private lives and were "impatient of privatenesse, even in age and sicknesse, which require the shadow."[80] For Bacon, it was merit and the consciousness of having done something good that were the ultimate criteria by which an office holder should be judged.

> But power to doe good, is the true & lawfull end of aspiring. For good thoughts, (though God accept them) yet towards men are little better than good dreams: except they be put in Act; and that cannot be without power and place; as the vantage & commanding ground.

---

76 Bacon, *Works*, 6:465–7 ("Of Ambition," 1612); Bacon, *Essayes*, 116.
77 Bacon, *Works*, 6:503–9 ("Of Vaine-Glory," 1612); Bacon, *Essayes*, 161–3.
78 Bacon, *Works*, 6:494 ("Of Followers and Friends," 1612); Bacon, *Essayes*, 147–9.
79 Bacon, *Works*, 6:398 ("Of Great Place," 1612); Bacon, *Essayes*, 34.
80 Ibid.

Merit is the ende of mans motion; and conscience of merit is the accomplishment of mans rest. For if a man can in any measure be the pertaker of *Gods Theater*, he shall like wise be pertaker of *Gods rest*.[81]

Bacon expanded on Whitgift's argument that deserving an honor transformed its pursuit into a worthy one. Meriting an honor (to now use Bacon's language) was a psychological state, it was a consciousness of one's desert, and it was enabled by the pyschological transformation from a private to a public man in which one looked to others for approval and a sense of worthiness.

The key to saving the government from the crisis of idleness and the pursuit of private ends described by Baron Ellesmere and Hall was then the careful discernment between the two sorts of ambitious candidate. This was reflected in Bacon's advice in 1616 to the king's favorite, Villiers. The role of the favorite was to act as the personnel division of the early modern courtly state; he was petitioned for favors and offices and, weighing merit and mutual benefit, distributed them accordingly. In giving Buckingham advice on how to respond to petitions for favor, Bacon ruled out the view of "some persons of great birth" that they deserved positions as the king's councillors as a matter of honor. Rather, he advised that positions should be allotted according to "the parts of the man and not his person."[82]

LAW, PATRONAGE, AND THE STATE

After Buckingham's ascendancy, the idea that advancement entailed a transformation from a private to a public sensibility was scarcely credible. Buckingham oversaw the sale of honors, arranged for positions to be given to family members, and preferred favor to merit.[83] The psychological transformation was supposed to take place when one turned outward and looked to others for recognition and respect, but what if one turned to a favorite? Or one's kinsman? Or patron? The distribution of office on these grounds scarcely seemed public minded to Buckingham's aristocratic opponents in the Lords or to their clients in the Commons, who, like the Earl of Arundel and John Pym, were arguing for a more purely aristocratic version of the honor system. Without shifting ground entirely, Bacon argued that there was some element of private affection, of affiliation with a patron and his faction, that was ineliminable in either monarchical or aristocratic government, and given that England was a monarchy, it was more public minded

---

81 Bacon, *Works*, 6:399 ("Of Great Place," 1612); Bacon, *Essayes*, 35.
82 Peck, *Court Patronage and Corruption*, 50–1.
83 Ibid., 52; Sharpe, "Opposition to the Duke of Buckingham," 242.

to serve in the national monarchical faction than in an aristocratic or oligarchical one.

While such royal service was in some sense private, it was not arbitrary nor meant to serve the king understood as a private person at the expense of the realm. Service, for Bacon, meant administration of the law. Over the course of his career, Bacon distinguished the legal rule of monarchies from the informal rule of would-be oligarchs and the mockery of the royal rule of law typified by the fiscal patrimonialism of Empson and Dudley in the reign of Henry VII. As early as 1610, the approach of Empson and Dudley had come to stand as the epitome of the wrong approach to government for Bacon.[84] Years later, in *The History of the Reign of King Henry the Seventh*, he explained that supporters of that approach had many means of "preying upon the people." Their chief mechanism was the use of the penal law,

> wherein they spared none great nor small; nor considered whether the law were possible or impossible, in use or obsolete: but raked over all old and new statutes; though many of them were made with intention rather of terror than of rigour; ever having a rabble of promoters, questmongers, and leading jurors at their command; so as they could have any thing found, either for fact or valuation.[85]

Bacon made the question of "whether law were possible or impossible, in use or obsolete," a central issue in his writings on the reform of the law. He opposed the unlawful use of informers,[86] and castigated the use of "professional" jurors, who found whatever they were instructed to find.[87]

The rule of law was not, however, to be celebrated only for its impersonal or formal qualities. It combined these qualities with the demands of ambition and the monarchy's need for stable patronage networks. It is well known that Bacon thought of the judges as being in the service of the monarch; he wrote in "Of Judicature," "Let them be Lions, but yet Lions under the Throne; Being circumspect, that they do not checke, or oppose any Points of *Soveraigntie*."[88] Yet, it is not well appreciated that Bacon thought of judges as serving the monarch through a network of patronage.

The doctrine that a monarchy was a special kind of legal patronage faction was formulated early and was already expressed in his counsel on the jurisdiction of the Marches in 1606:

84 Beresford, "The Common Informer," 232.

85 Throughout, the text of Bacon's *History* is quoted from Kiernan's edition, with references to Spedding's and Weinberger's editions provided for reference. Bacon, *Historie of the Raigne of King Henry the Seventh*, 147 (Bacon, *Works*, 6:219; Weinberger, 185).

86 Beresford, "The Common Informer," 232.

87 Martin, *Francis Bacon*, 120–1.

88 Bacon, *Works*, 6:510 ("Of Judicature," 1612); Bacon, *Essayes*, 169.

But the State, whose proper duty and eye is to the general good, and in that regard to the balancing of all degrees will happily consider this point above law: That Monarchies in name do often degenerate into Aristocraties or rather Oligarchies in nature by two insensible degrees. The first is when prerogatives are made envious or subject to the constructions of laws; the second when law as an oracle is affixed to place. For by the one the King is made accomptable and brought under the law; and by the other the law is over-ruled and inspired by the Judge; and by both all tenures of favour, privy Counsel, nobility and personal dependances (the mysteries that keep up states in the person of the Prince) are quite abolished and magistracy enabled to stand by itself. The states of Venice and Poland might be examples hereof. And the Maires du Palais in France, by making the Law great and themselves masters thereof, supplanted the whole line of their ancient Kings. And what greater strength had the League there of late than the exorbitant greatness of the Parliament of Paris? . . . Whether then these popular titles of limiting prerogatives for subjects' birth-rights and laws may not unawares, without any design or thought of the authors, open a gap unto new Barons' wars, or other alteration and inconvenience in government, the wisdom of the state is best able to discern.[89]

Bacon seems to have applied this Jacobean view of the French monarchs to faction in the Parliament in 1614, when he urged the exclusion of opponents to the king's policies, and the question of whether the king's servants should be included or not was hotly debated.[90] This view may have also come into play in the Parliaments of the early 1620s; it certainly seems to have been fresh in Bacon's mind in the mid-1620s. He added the analysis to his essay "Of Faction" in 1625: "Kings had need beware, how they Side themselves, and make themselves as of a *Faction* or Partie: For Leagues, within the State, are ever pernicious to Monarchies; For they raise an Obligation, Paramount to Obligation of Soveraigntie, and make the King, *Tanquam unus ex nobis*: As was to be seene, in the *League* of *France*."[91]

The issue was debated openly in the 1626 Parliament in the context of Buckingham's trial. Sir Edward Coke admitted, "No king can subsist in an honorable estate without 3 abilities, 1 to maintain himself against sudden invasions; 2 to aid his allies and confederates; 3 to reward his well-deserving servants."[92] Heath, in responding, "presented the fundamental dilemma of

89 Bacon, *LL*, 3:371-2.
90 Russell, *King James his English Parliaments*, 104–5.
91 Bacon, *Works*, 6:499 ("Of Faction," 1625); Bacon, *Essayes*, 156.
92 Peck, *Court Patronage and Corruption*, 127–8.

early Stuart politics," as Linda Peck explained. Heath noted that Buckingham was torn, because "he had two parts to act, one as a private man and the servant of his Majesty; the other as a public man for the public good."[93]

Bacon's view that the servants of the king should be lawyers does not seem to have been particularly appealing to James. In preparing the proclamation to accompany the writs for the Parliament of 1621, Bacon had written a draft advising that "lawyers of mean account and estimation" not be returned, but James rewrote the proclamation, exhorting them not to return "wrangling lawyers" of any sort.[94] Yet Bacon persisted. In 1621, he recalled the feast of the sergeants-at-law in the reign of Henry VII as a moment when the king's subjects were honored for their service as lawyers. "The King, to honour the feast, was present with his Queen at the dinner; being a Prince that was ever ready to grace and countenance the professors of the law; having a little of that, that as he governed his subjects by his laws, so he governed his laws by his lawyers."[95]

The participation of the lower sorts was necessary for justice, but their private motivations and allegiances were of less concern if their leaders were kept in line.[96] Bacon feared that the lower sorts would be easily manipulable as jurors, lacking the independence of the higher sorts. He allowed that the statute from Henry VII's day "for the admission of poor suitors *in forma pauperis*, without fee to counsellor," was a "charitable law," but its effect was that "poor men became rather able to vex than unable to sue."[97] Bacon was concerned with vexatious lawsuits and as lord chancellor hoped to limit access to the chancery for minor lawsuits.[98] He advised that plaintiffs admitted *in forma pauperis* be directed to other jurisdictions or "to some gentleman in the country, except in some special cases of commiseration, or potency of the adverse party."[99]

His insistence that the social basis of monarchy be given a legal character reflected his views about the interpenetration of legal decisions and social organization. Bacon did not complete the statement of his mature legal theory, which he intended to form part of his *Instauratio Magna*, his grand

93 Peck, *Court Patronage and Corruption*, 127–8.

94 Kyle, "Wrangling Lawyers," 132.

95 Bacon, *Historie of the Raigne of King Henry the Seventh*, 100 (Bacon, *Works*, 6:158; Weinberger, 133).

96 See "Of Empire" (1612 and after): "For their Commons; There is little danger from them, except it be, where they have Great and Potent Heads." Bacon, *Works*, 6:419; Bacon, *Essayes*, 62.

97 Bacon, *Historie of the Raigne of King Henry the Seventh*, 103 (Bacon, *Works*, 6:161; Weinberger, 137).

98 Bacon, *Works*, 7:761 ("Ordinances for the Chancery"); Coquillette, *Francis Bacon*, 205.

99 Bacon, *Works*, 7:773 ("Ordinances for the Chancery").

project for revising human knowledge according to his inductive principles.[100] His attempt at a universal jurisprudence appeared rather as a sketch
in a set of aphorisms appended to his *De Augmentis Scientarum* (1623) and in
an earlier draft of the aphorisms entitled *Aphorismi de Jure Gentium Maiore
Sive de Fontibus Justiciae et Juris*.[101] Though the origin of the law in the sense
of a higher or pure law was neutral and egalitarian,[102] Bacon believed that
the content of the law quickly changed as the law began to be applied by
higher judges and by commissioned officers and justices of the peace. The
theoretical statement of this view in the aphorism on the origin of the law
in the *Aphorismi* was somewhat oblique: "But if it should happen that an
offending person should prosper by his alliances, clientships, or by the ubiquity of the crime, so that those whom are protected are not so numerous
or so powerful as those whom are endangered, then a faction subverts the
law, and its destruction is followed by a general enfeeblement, as commonly
occurs."[103] In *De Augmentis*, he wrote that the cause of the subversion was
"through the state of the times, and a communion of guilt."[104] Bacon seems
to have imagined three scenarios: one in which a law endangered a particular patronage or clientelistic faction; one in which the meaning of the law
had changed over time as circumstances shifted; and one in which behavior
had shifted so that what was criminal had become more general practice.

The *Aphorismi* were concise and vague by design in the hope of offering a
universal statement of principles. They nevertheless represented a summary
of Bacon's observations on the nature of the law and social change throughout his career. The first scenario clearly echoed his views on the balancing of
faction, but it is difficult to say precisely where he saw faction subverting the
law. He does seem to have meant particular factions or client groups rather
than fixed social orders as a whole, and he seems to have been thinking
more pointedly about patronage at this time, as I discuss below in the context of his views of sovereignty. While there were moments in which Bacon
saw the law as an instrument of class conflict, these were few and far between in comparison with the classical sources he used. Thus, he criticized
the lawyer Thomas Flammock in *The History of the Reign of King Henry the
Seventh* for inciting rebellion "by telling his neighbours commonly upon

---

100 Coquillette, *Francis Bacon*, 234–7.
   101 It was included in a manuscript presented to William Cavendish, the second Earl of
Devonshire, Hobbes's student and patron. See Malcolm, *Reason of State*, 7; Neustadt, "Making
of the Instauration," 239–99.
   102 Ibid., 275.
   103 Ibid. Translation revised.
   104 Bacon, *Works*, 5:88–9; the Latin is at 1:803–4.

any occasion that the law was on their side."[105] But if Bacon is compared to the classical sources from which he drew his Latin vocabulary, the extent to which he did not think in terms of the society of orders is striking. Unlike Cicero's forensic speeches, Bacon did not portray the law as subject to the envy between orders.[106] The groups that might suffer from any particular law seemed to shift in his analysis, and the use and abuse of the law was not understood to be tied to particular orders. The second scenario, in which change in the meaning of the law tracked changes in circumstances, was at the heart of his *Reading of Uses*. He considered there how the ruling of the Statute of Uses, which had nullified uses (a type of trust) that were employed to evade payments to the Crown, was now being employed to void uses that were meant to secure the income of widows through a secondary trust constructed on top of the trust of the primary heir.[107] Bacon must have seen the third scenario, the "ubiquity of a crime" or "communion of guilt," in the widespread practice of dueling, which showed how the social psychology of envy and emulation resulted in legal change.

Bacon, indeed, was intimately involved in the campaign against dueling under James. James had opposed single combat in Scotland, and in 1612–13 he moved against the growing fashion for dueling in England.The campaign against dueling was a practical development of a broader critique of the Italian view of honor as a courtly or military code of martial valor; the English believed that the pursuit of honor only made disagreement more likely. The Protestant Innocent Gentillet had claimed—in a work available by 1602 in a new English translation—that Machiavelli's argument for the ineradicabiltiy of the desire for revenge was based on a distinctly Italian culture of honor:

> [A]ccording to the honour of his nation, vengeances, and enmities are perpetuall and irreconcilable: and indeed, there is nothing wherein they take greater delectation, pleasure, and contentment, than to execute a vengeance; insomuch as, whensoever they can have their enemie at their pleasure, to be revenged upon him, they murder him after some strange & barbarous fashion.[108]

---

105 Bacon, *Historie of the Raigne of King Henry the Seventh*, 119 (Bacon, *Works*, 6:176; Weinberger, 148).

106 Bacon cited *Pro Rabirio Posthumo* in his essay "Of Riches." Bacon, *Works*, 6:460; Bacon, *Essayes*, 109. His language in the *Aphorismi* (*solvere . . . legem*) and in the aphorisms in *De Augmentis* echoed this speech and its Renaissance commentaries, in particular that of Paolo Manuzio (*periculum creatur*). Manuzio, *In M. Tullii Ciceronis Orationum*, 203.

107 Coquillette, *Francis Bacon*, 48–9.

108 Gentillet, *A Discourse*, 177.

This was understood to be a difficulty not just for Machiavelli's theory, but for Italian political thought more broadly. Lewis Lewkenor had even suggested in the preface to his new English translation of Contarini's *Commonwealth of Venice* in 1599 that the Venetian management of ambition was faulty, since it identified honor with the martial virtues and then applauded itself when it employed mercenaries so as to avoid Venice's gentlemen becoming overly ambitious.[109]

In 1612, Bacon argued in a case at the king's bench that revenge was Italian and that forgiveness was a sign of magnanimity.[110] The earl marshal, Henry Howard, the Earl of Northampton, wrote the official proclamation, published in 1614, and Bacon, who had been appointed attorney general shortly before, began to prosecute cases of challenges in the Star Chamber. Though both were opposed to the practice of dueling, Northampton and Bacon understood the phenomenon very differently. Northampton saw it as the sort of bad behavior that resulted from a long night at an alehouse, which should be replaced by more respectable means of adjudicating questions of honor, namely, through the courts of chivalry. For Bacon, the vogue for Italian courtesy was a potent cultural force, for "it imposeth a necessity upon men of value to conforme them-selves; or else there is no living or looking upon mens faces." Significantly, he thought that social processes, such as emulation, were insufficient to remedy dueling without disastrous unintended consequences. If dueling were left alone to spread, "men of birth and quality will leave the practice, when it begins to bee vilified and come so lowe as to Barbers-surgeons and Butchers, and such base mechanicall persons."[111] Emulation worked, but it worked too well and was ultimately self-defeating.[112] As the values of the upper classes were imitated, those values would be abandoned by the nobility. Obviously in this case, this would only transfer the bloodthirsty habits of the nobility to the masses. The solution was to punish those in the nobility who participated in the practice in the Star Chamber by excluding them from access to the court and office holding, thereby undermining the connection between dueling and honor

109 For Lewkenor's introduction, see Peltonen, *Classical Humanism and Republicanism*, 116–7.

110 Peltonen, *Duel in Early Modern England*, 126.

111 Ibid., 87–8, 92, 113–6, 136.

112 This was evident in Bacon's 1625 essay on custom and education, where he explained that it was custom that was the most predictive about one's behavior, not one's natural disposition or statements. This was even more the case in society, where custom was layered and reinforced, "[f]or there example teacheth, company comforteth, emulation quickeneth, glory raiseth." "But the misery is," Bacon wrote, "that the most effectual means are now applied to ends least desired." Bacon, *Works*, 6:470–2 ("Of Custom and Education," 1625); Bacon, *Essayes*, 122. Bacon's "quickeneth" may be a translation of Goulston's idea of emulation rendering people *promptiores*. Aristotle, *Aristotelis de Rhetorica*, 124, litt. b: Aemulatio . . . ad bona acquirenda promptiores nos facit.

since access to the monarch's person was still considered the height of honor.[113] This proposed solution was in keeping with Bacon's view that judges should correct the reading of a statute in light of the preamble rather than "general opinion and reputation." As a matter of practice, those who acted under some corrupted construction of the law before it was corrected by judges should have a defense in the courts of equity.[114]

This legal theory, which held that the meaning of the law shifted in accordance with various social processes, had significant implications for Bacon's understanding of sovereignty. He used the language of Bodin's theory of sovereignty to some degree but introduced several modifications in keeping with his promise in the preface to the *Aphorismi* not only to introduce "many things entirely of my own devising" but to correct other authors as well.[115] Bacon turned Bodin on his head in thinking about the source of sovereignty.

> Public laws—which define powers, impart order or proportion to things, correct the wicked dispositions of the spirit and its inclinations to do injury, and impress upon the people certain rudiments or exercises of obedience—flow from private rights. For law requires execution, execution magistrates, magistrates imperium, imperium command, and all public order, solemnity and discipline needs arms, habits of obedience, and hence retinues, insignia and arrangements of duties.[116]

Bodin had argued that sovereignty was sharply distinguished from the sort of power wielded over one's family and servants in a household. Sovereignty, or the public and supreme power, was distinguished in his view from private and intermediate power.[117] Bacon argued to the contrary, in keeping with the Reformers' view of the commonwealth, that public power was dependent on the healthy operation of obedience among the orders in their private relationships as patrons and clients. It seems that Bacon was newly impressed with the importance of patronage around this time. This section from the *Aphorismi* echoed strongly the passage in the essay "True Greatness of Kingdomes," which first appeared in the Latin edition that was

---

113 Peltonen, *Duel in Early Modern England*, 140–1.

114 Coquillette, *Francis Bacon*, 205–6.

115 Neustadt, "Making of the Instauration," 274. Richard Serjeantson has noted echoes of Bodin's views on the transplantation of surplus populations to colonies in Bacon's "Speech Touching Naturalization" of 1607. Serjeantson, "Francis Bacon, Colonisation, and the Limits of Atlanticism."

116 Neustadt, "Making of the Instauration," 275–6. Translation revised.

117 Bodin, *Methodus ad Facilem Historiarum Cognitionem*, 214.

included in *De Augmentis* in 1623.[118] An English translation of the passage was then added to the 1625 edition of the *Essays*.[119]

> Nor should that part of the people be passed over (which is almost peculiar to England, nor is elsewhere in use as far as I know, unless perhaps in Poland), namely the *servants of the nobles*, and which in respect to footsoldiery are in no way inferior to the yeomanry. And therefore it is without question that the magnificence and splendor, hospitality, service and great retinues as it were, which the nobles and gentlemen of England are accustomed to, conduce excellently to military greatness.[120]

The description of private rights in the *Aphorismi* was precisely that of a noble affinity or client group, with retainers, insignia, and particular duties.[121] Bacon himself had amassed a great household and seems to have thought that such a system was not inconsistent with military greatness and that it contributed to the authority of the class of magistrates, which made the rule of law possible. It is difficult to say whether this was a new position for him. Robert Cecil had argued for the augmentation of hospitality in 1597 in the debates that are discussed at the beginning of this chapter, and it may be that Bacon kept this view in mind over the intervening years. But it is also possible that reflecting on the laws that apparently were the inspiration for the acts of 1597 in his *History of the Reign of King Henry the Seventh* jogged his memory. In Bacon's retelling, Henry VII and his Parliaments realized that depopulating enclosure meant a decay of the population and a smaller tax base. They did not simply require tillage as a matter of penal law, since "that was to strive with nature and utility," but legislated that houses of husbandry— homes for agricultural tenants that were attached to twenty acres and above

118 This reading thus suggests a different emphasis in the 1620s from earlier drafts. In a 1608 manuscript version of "Of the True Greatness of the Kingdom of Britain," Bacon argued that Britain should follow the model of the Low Countries, which relied on the broad mass of the citizenry for their tax base. In an expanding state, the nobility were insufficient to provide the necessary funds or manpower for war. Bacon wrote, "[T]hose states are least able to defray great charges for wars, or other public disbursements, whose wealth resteth chiefly in the hands of the nobility and gentlemen." Bacon, *Works*, 2:80–1.

119 Ibid., 6:448 ("Of the True Greatness of Kingdoms and Estates," 1625); Bacon, *Essayes*, 93.

120 Bacon, *Works*, 1:796: Neque praetereunda est illa pars populi (quae Angliae fere est peculiaris, nec alibi (quod scio) inusu, nisi forte apud Polonos), famuli scilicet Nobilium. Hujus enim generis etiam inferiores, quoad peditatum, agricolis ipsis minime cedunt. Quare certissimum est, quod magnificentia et splendor ille hospitalis, atque famulitia et veluti satellitia ampla, quae in more sunt apud Nobiles et Generosos in Anglia, ad potentiam militarem apprime conducant. My translation. Cf. Bacon, *Essayes*, 93.

121 On duties, see Thomas Cooper, *Thesaurus Linguae Romanae et Britannicae*, s.v. "munia."

of land—should be preserved in perpetuity. The idea was to create a supply of leases of sufficient extent to constitute a "yeomanry or middle people," since the amount of land necessitated that the "dweller not . . . be a beggar or cottager, but a man of some substance, that might keep hinds and servants, and set the plough on going." These men would become foot soldiers, while in France, "where in effect all is noblesse or peasantry," they had to depend on Swiss mercenaries for foot soldiers.[122]

Other transformations of Bodin's theory of sovereignty in the *Aphorismi* confirm the greater dependency of the state on society in Bacon's theory. Thus Bodin's idea that the sovereign was above the law—absolute—and free to change the law became transmuted into the susceptibility of the law to social change. Bacon began his discussion of "the Authority and obligation of the laws" in the *Aphorismi* by echoing Bodin's thought that there must be an authority (*imperium*) that was absolute: "For this supreme and commanding power can dissolve or transfer itself, but it cannot be bound."[123] He discussed the various attempts to make a perpetual law through legal means in a similar manner to Bodin, but his conclusion was that such attempts were meaningless due to social change, rather than due to the wishes of a sovereign, as in Bodin. Once public opinion shifted, it was trivial to change the law through various clauses or interpretations. "For once the spirit is so inclined that it becomes aware of change in its and others opinions, those fearful things, that at first seemed so formidable, begin to seem ridiculous."[124] Bacon clearly thought that Bodin's notion of sovereignty failed to acknowledge the realities of power and (despite being a legal doctrine) to understand that the law was open to interpretation and social change from the first instance. A theory of sovereignty thus had to have an adequate account of social psychology and social change.

It is tempting to see in Bacon's reimagined commonwealth, presided over by royalist lawyer-landlords, a sort of bureaucratic reform where the magistrates were meant to invoke a sort of rational-legal legitimacy. And in some sense this is correct. But, as in Weber, the notion of legal legitimacy turns out to be more complicated than it first seems. "Legal obligation has little force," Bacon explained, if it only depended on the intellectual recognition of the equity contained in the law. It rather required "religion, custom, and fear . . . since the wills of men are moved by faith and opinions, custom and examples, or by affections."[125] Behind conformity with the law stand affections of the sort that the Reformers had identified. The state, understood

---

122 Bacon, *Historie of the Raigne of King Henry the Seventh*, 54–5 (Bacon, *Works*, 6:95; Weinberger, 84–5).

123 Neustadt, "Making of the Instauration," 281.

124 Ibid., 283–4.

125 Ibid., 297.

again as both legislation and the administration of the law, depended once more on the meeting of the various material and emotional needs of the degrees of the people in order to realize a stable legal order.

The meeting of these needs had a complicated relationship to law. In the divine law version of the Reformers, law was, if not always opposed to one's private affections, often so. And the use of love and fear through penal laws and the distribution of honors was largely external to the content of the law. Bacon repeated the opposition between the penal law and the use of incentives once more in the *Aphorismi*, noting that conformity with the law was chiefly to be achieved through the use of fear. "It is fitting to use laws to entice men to great deeds with money and rewards of riches. It is not surprising though that there are few examples of this, since the nobler sorts of laws are rarely devised. Among men most laws are of a moderate sort, not so much written by flourishing commonwealths, as constructed as boundaries in the course of peacetime and daily use."[126] Yet, Bacon well understood that conformity with the law was not possible through the terror of the rigors of the penal law alone. The legitimacy of the law depended in part on the sense of custom, which ultimately depended on the impression that the origins of the laws were consensual and popular. This did not mean that he was actively for popular sovereignty. Bacon admitted that the original sources of authority may have been in most regimes the consent of the people, but denied "the tribune's opinion taught by lovers of liberty, that in all sorts of commonwealths the supreme power resides with the people."[127] The people's power had been decisively transferred to the new government as an all but irreversible *fideicommissum*.[128] In a peculiar quirk to the theory, surely meant to preserve the status of the common law, Bacon claimed that the old laws were preserved "as ancient boundaries" in the same way that the power of the people was preserved in a transformed way in the new government.[129] This is awkward and seems to contradict his statement in the previous aphorism that "if there were anything that needed to be changed in the new state, it would have to be done by edict or by a legitimate assembly of the new state."[130] But the idea seems to be—as the paraphrase of the idea that appeared in the 1620 "Discourse of Laws," probably written by Cavendish with the assistance of Hobbes, suggested—that "where any form, or Law, had had any long continuance in practice, without any known Author, it then receives the name of an ancient custom. . . . And there is great reason for it, because Laws are in esteem, and authority with

126 Ibid., 299.
127 Ibid., 286.
128 Ibid., 288.
129 Ibid., 286.
130 Ibid., 285.

us, for no other reason, but in respect they have had the reputation to be allowed, and made by the Judgment of the people . . . and this is the reason which makes our common Law originally grounded upon ancient customs, of equal power and authority with our Statutes."[131] The commonalty need not actually be given sovereignty, but they needed to imagine that they had been included in some mythic past. The sovereignty of the rule of law was not so much plebiscitary, but it had the reputation of being so.

HOPE AND FEAR

Though the bulk of the laws were penal and depended on fear, this was not the case for the commonwealth laws, which depended on hope, as indicated in Bacon's heavily revised 1625 essay "Of Seditions and Troubles."[132] Early versions of the essay survive in two manuscripts, one of which Bacon was evidently preparing to present to Prince Henry, written sometime between 1610 and 1612; the other, which included the *Aphorismi*, was presented to Cavendish in 1614 or sometime afterward.[133] The 1625 version reflected the closer study of Aristotle's *Rhetoric* in that edition,[134] almost certainly due to Theodore Goulston's 1619 Latin translation. Reading the 1625 *Essays* along-side it shows that figuring out the precise psychology of envy and emulation continued to be of great interest in Bacon's circles.[135]

131 Hobbes, *Three Discourses*, 118–9. For parallels between the *Aphorismi* and the "Discourse," see Huxley, "The Aphorimsi and a Discourse of Laws."

132 Bacon, *Works*, 6:406–12 ("Of Seditions and Troubles," 1625); Bacon, *Essayes*, 43–50.

133 Bacon, *Essayes*, lxxiv.

134 Between the 1612 and the 1625 editions, Bacon added much about envy, reflected in a new essay on envy, the heavily revised essay on sedition, and many smaller revisions to other essays. For example, Bacon added to his description of "natural malignity" in "Of Goodnesse and Goodnesse of Nature" that "Such Men in other men's Calamities, are, as it were, in season, and are ever on the loading Part: Not so good as the Dogs, that licked *Lazarus* sores; but like Flies, that are still buzzing, upon any Thing that is raw." And to "Of Death," he added that among its benefits was that it "extinguisheth Envie." Bacon, *Works*, 6:380, 404; Bacon, *Essayes*, 11, 40.

135 Attention has focused thus far on the parallels between Bacon's *Essays* and writings of Hobbes or his pupil Cavendish, which were printed in 1620 in the collection *Horae Subsecivae*. Tuck, "Hobbes and Tacitus"; Malcolm, *Reason of State*, 6–11; Rahe, *Against Throne and Altar*, 246–74. There were many parallels between the arguments made in the "Discourse on Tacitus" and the psychology of the *Rhetoric* as commented on by Vettori and Goulston. For instance, Tacitus's remark that the people of Rome were concerned about Agrippa as a possible successor to Augustus because he was "kindled with his disgrace" (*ignominia accensum*) became an opportunity for Cavendish to portray the contemporary political situation in a slightly garbled version of the Aristotelian passions of contempt and revenge. Where, strictly speaking, according to Aristotle, it should be Agrippa who has suffered from the contempt of the leading citizens of Rome, in Cavendish's account, it was Agrippa who held the great men of

The 1625 version of "Of Seditions and Troubles" broke the issue into three parts: the materials of seditions, their motives, and their remedies. The motives were the precipitating causes of civil disturbances and were treated very quickly in a single short paragraph. They included changes in religion, taxes, the "advancement of unworthy persons," dearth, "factions grown desperate," and "whatsoever, in offending people, joineth and knitteth them in a common cause."[136] The essay was really concerned with thinking through the two "materials," namely, poverty and discontentment, and their remedies. Discontentment, as he explained in his essay "Of Envy," was another name for "public envy."[137] Bacon had come to believe that there was a disjunction between the actual material arrangements of a society and the way that its people felt about it, their level of contentment. It seems that what Bacon said was not that poverty in itself cannot cause distress—the fact of poverty alone would be sufficient to motivate rebellions, even quite terrible rebellions ("For the rebellions of the belly are the worst")—but that what he called "discontentment" was a particularly political phenomenon generated by political factors, such as factions and leaders, which played on emotions that may not be rooted in just claims.

> As for *Discontentments*, they are in the Politique Body, like to Humours in the Naturall, which are apt to gather a preternaturall Heat and to Enflame. And let no Prince measure the Danger of them, by this; whether they be Just or Unjust? For that were to imagine People to be too reasonable; who doe often spurne at their own Good: Nor yet by this, whether the Griefes, whereupon they rise, be in fact great or small: For they are the most dangerous *Discontentments* where the Feare is greater than the Feeling. *Dolendi Modus, Timendi non item* [Suffering has its limit, but fears are endless].[138]

Rome in contempt for having slighted him. Cavendish may very well have been inspired to think in Aristotelian terms about Agrippa due to the similarity between Tacitus's wording and Goulston's Latin translation of Aristotle on *contumelia*, or by his marginal note, in which Goulston wrote that "one who imparts contumely to another, by branding him with ignominy, neglects him, in that he believes that he is one who should be reckoned of no value." Hobbes, *Three Discourses*, 62–3. Aristotle, *Aristotelis de Rhetorica*, 88: Contumeliae autem sic definitae est, ignominia afficere: Qui autem ignominia quemquam afficit, is eum negligit; 88, litt. m: Quia contumeliam qui alteri infert, ignominiam inurendo, eum negligit; siquidem nullius illum pretii habendum censeat.

136 Bacon, *Works*, 6:409.

137 Ibid., 6:396: "Now, to speak of public envy. . . . This envy, being in the Latin word invidia, goeth in the modern languages by the name of discontentment; of which we shall speak in handling Sedition." Bacon, *Essayes*, 30.

138 Bacon, *Works*, 6:409 ("Of Seditions and Troubles," 1625); Bacon, *Essayes*, 46. Translation of the Latin phrase provided by Spedding.

While Bacon understood discontentment in terms of envy from his days as a student of Whitgift, if not earlier, with a closer study of Aristotle's *Rhetoric*, he had come to understand it in terms of expectations about the future, hope. By the time of the presentation copy, he had already come to think of hope as important in alleviating discontentment ("And it is a certaine Signe, of a wise Government, and Proceeding, when it can hold Mens hearts by *Hopes*, when it cannot by Satisfaction").[139] But in this analysis hope was not yet linked to envy. In the 1625 version, he argued that hope was necessary to ensure that the social processes that supported stability and social reproduction continued. "And when it can handle things, in such manner, as no Evill shall appeare so peremptory, but that it hath some Out-let of *Hope*: Which is the lesse hard to doe, because both particular Persons and Factions, are apt enough to flatter themselves, or at least to brave that, which they beleeve not."[140] Bacon was referring here to Aristotle's account of the passion of emulation in the *Rhetoric*, where, in Goulston's translation, "those are prone to emulation who judge themselves worthy of those goods which they do not possess, but could. For no one judges himself worthy of those things which clearly cannot happen." Borrowing Vettori's language, Goulston commented, "they readily emulate, then, those who in their own opinion are worthy of those goods, which they hope they will possess."[141] Through Vettori's and Goulston's commentaries, Aristotle's view of a man's expectations about his worthiness to receive various goods became labeled as hope. Bacon then saw emulation's opposite, envy, as a product of hopelessness. If one had the hope of achieving some good or virtue that one perceived in someone else then, according to Bacon, this only expressed itself, at worst, as the feeling of envy. If one had no hope, however, then one "will seeke to come at even hand, by Depressing an others Fortune."[142]

139 Bacon, *Works*, 6:410; Bacon, *Essayes*, 48.

140 Bacon, *Works*, 6:411 ("Of Seditions and Troubles," 1625); Bacon, *Essayes*, 48–9. In the last clause, Bacon meant that at least they pretended that they were worthy for the sake of their glory, even if they did not quite believe that they were worthy. This was clear from the Latin translation in the *Sermones Fideles*, which Spedding cited to clarify the point: aut saltem ostentare, in gloriam suam, quod non omnino credunt.

141 Aristotle, *Aristotelis de Rhetorica*, 124: Necesse igitur est, proclives ad aemulandum esse eos, qui existimant se dignos bonis iis, quae non habent, sed habere possunt: Nemo enim se dignum existimarit iis, quae apparent fieri non posse; litt. d1: Facile aemulantur, tum qui iudicio suo digni sunt bona, quorum sperant se compotes fore. Vettori, *Commentarii in Tres Libros*, 385; Aristotle, *Rhetoric*, 1388a36.

142 Bacon, *Works*, 6:393–6 ("Of Envy," 1625); Bacon, *Essayes*, 27. This was a slight modification of Aristotle's distinction between emulation and envy as expressed by Goulston. Goulston, following Vettori, explained that envy was a wicked desire "since it seeks unjustly that some good be taken from innocent men" regardless of the impact on the envious person, while emulation was a good desire, "which makes [one] more eager to acquire the goods" that one has noticed that others possess. Aristotle, *Aristotelis de Rhetorica*, 124, litt. b, c: Differt Aemulatio ab Invidia, quod illa ad bona acquirenda promptiores nos facit; Invidia, malo

Within this swirling mass of discontentment, the old concerns of commonwealth were still relevant. Bacon's list of remedies would have been familiar decades earlier: "The Cherishing of Manufactures; the Banishing of Idlenesse; the Repressing of waste and Excesse by Sumptuary Lawes; the Improvement and Husbanding of the Soyle; the Regulating of Prices of things vendible; the Moderating of Taxes and Tributes; and the Like."[143] Yet these laws were not to be administered in quite the same way as they had under the Tudors, and this represented in the latest thinking a sense that it was the role of the state to rise to the endlessly changing expectations about the future so as to rein them in. The old problem of how to discipline the justices of the peace in order to enforce the statutes had been addressed earlier in James's reign by expanding the use of articles of inquiry and books of orders and by directly intervening with the JPs,[144] and Bacon proposed a third way: establishing standing commissions tasked with particular portfolios.[145] By 1616, the inefficiency of the justices of the peace had reached a breaking point, and James gave an address in the Star Chamber, requiring written reports and, significantly, changing the personnel. Over the next year, he removed 142 JPs from office, appointed 209 for the first time, and readmitted 44. In these changes, James hoped to add a level of professional competency that had been missing, and so, while the numbers are uncertain, it is possible that up to a third of the new JPs were lawyers. Bacon, following up on such changes, proposed establishing a set of standing commissions composed of judges, who would meet regularly in the Star Chamber to oversee the work of JPs in addressing typical commonwealth policies, such as the regulation of the cloth industry, dearth controls, and depopulation.[146]

The proposed establishment of standing commissions (only one was set up in the end) accompanied an expansion of the scope of royal commissioners' power. In November 1616, Bacon, as attorney general, advised the privy councillors that it was appropriate for them to declare that the actions of the commissioners of the sewers could not be challenged by being sued. This opinion, which was acted upon, reflected the view that royal commissioners were free to expand on the letter of a statute where necessity required, for instance, in levying a local rate or erecting new walls. The government took the position—consistent with older canons of statutory interpretation—

---

semper sit aliis, cum iniuste bonum quodque innocentibus viris detractum cupit. Cf. Vettori, *Commentarii in Tres Libros*, 385: ut ipsarum altera bono nobis sit: altera vero malo semper aliis, innocentibus atque honestis viris. Aristotle, *Rhetoric*, 1388a35.

143 Bacon, *Works*, 6:410 ("Of Seditions and Troubles," 1625); Bacon, *Essayes*, 47.

144 Slack, "Books of Orders"; Quintrell, "Making of Charles I's Book of Orders"; Fletcher, *Reform in the Provinces*.

145 Bacon added an endorsement of standing commissions to his essay "Of Counsell" in 1625. Bacon, *Essayes*, 67.

146 Quintrell, "Making of Charles I's Book of Orders," 559–60.

that laws that were beneficial to the commonwealth and that were not as a whole penal could be interpreted broadly by the commissioners in keeping with the intent of the statute as indicated in the preamble. Coke was meanwhile disputing this claim, arguing that the interpretation of a statute should be adjudicated by the courts.[147] Lord Chancellor Ellesmere put it just as Bacon might have, complaining that "whilest they were in this court disputing of tricks and moote points," they had "suffer[ed] a great part of the realm to be surrounded and overflowen; for the winds nor the sea could not be stayed by such new constructions and moote points."[148] In practice, the commissioners who were to exercise discretion over the "evident publick utility" were local magnates and gentlemen,[149] and the conflict between Coke and Bacon was characteristically a struggle between what Bacon would have perceived as the clients of the king and an attempt by Coke to erect an oligarchy by means of an independent magistracy. Bacon's vision of the state thus combined elements of the personal and the impersonal, the traditional and the modernizing.

Bacon clearly hoped that the institutional solutions he had imposed and proposed would make it possible to solve problems in a rational way, with a clear eye to the actual position, economic and military, of England. But what if such policies were not sufficient? What if people still *felt* opposed, as Tacitus had suggested was possible, regardless of the best efforts of a government to address the real problems of the day? In this case, Bacon admitted, "there is little won by intermingling plausible [i.e., aimed at pleasing] Actions. For that doth argue but a Weaknesse, and Feare of *Envy*, which hurteth so much the more."[150] The role of the state was to satisfy as much of the populace as possible, to strive so that the rest would be hopeful, and, for those who remained disaffected and envious, to ensure as best as possible that they were not in a position to do anything about it. Nevertheless, Bacon held fast to his commitments to the Elizabethan approach to government. England was meant to be in some sense a free commonwealth, where the populace was free to think as it wished. Indeed, "[t]o give moderate Liberty, for Griefes, and *Discontentments* to evaporate, (so it be without too great Insolency or Bravery), is a safe Way. For he that turneth the Humors backe, and maketh the Wound bleed inwards, endangereth maligne Ulcers, and pernicious Impostumations."[151]

---

147 Holmes, "Statutory Interpretation, 108–13."
148 Ibid., 113.
149 Ibid., 111, 115.
150 Bacon, *Works*, 6:396 ("Of Envy," 1625); Bacon, *Essayes*, 30.
151 Bacon, *Works*, 6:411 ("Of Seditions and Troubles," 1625); Bacon, *Essayes*, 48.

The meaning of addressing the emotional needs of the degrees of the people, of overcoming affection with affection, was changing as Bacon had begun to strip away the justice of meeting the emotional needs of the populace. As dismissive as Case was of the concerns of the lower sorts, they were still the characteristic concerns of a particular sort of people. For Bacon, the concerns of the lower sorts were far more fluid and far more subject to the influence and example of the higher sorts. Thus, for all of Bacon's tremendous sophistication, both his social analysis and his vision of the state must have been deeply dissatisfying for those raised on a commonwealth vision of state and society. The desire for social distinction and popularity was ripe for mockery and no doubt did represent in its worst forms the petty tyrannies of thousands of oligarchs (as Bancroft had complained about the presbyterians). But this "court" analysis had not yet opposed these very real social desires for distinction with a vision of a universal class of bureaucrats. Its proponents rather imagined those desiring social distinction as a class of lawyer-clients serving a patron-king. Though select lawyer-clients were offered some discretion in their commissions, the overall vision was of an increasingly tightly controlled legal system, reviewed from above by the conciliar courts. What must have proven most dissatisfying, and what must have wound its way to the civil war, was that Bacon insisted on identifying this vision of government with monarchy. Service of this sort was part of the kind of government appropriate to a monarchy.

In anticipation of the debates of the 1630s and 1640s, Bacon insisted on viewing matters through an older lens of regime analysis, which must have felt at once arbitrary (he readily admitted that there were other quite suitable forms of government) and frustrating. Very real needs, which were satisfied in the older conception, were simply ruled out of bounds in a monarchy. These tensions were evident in a passage about Augustus Caesar from the 1620 "Discourse on the Beginning of Tacitus," which owed much to Bacon and was written either by Hobbes or his patron and former pupil Cavendish:

> The change being now fully settled, and the ancient customs no more hoped for, they find, that striving for equality, is not the best of their game, but obedience, and waiting on the command of him that had power to raise, or keep them low at his pleasure. For though other virtues, especially deep wisdom, great, and extraordinary valor, be excellent ones under any sort of government, and chiefly in a free State, (where therefore they thrive best, because they are commonly accompanied with ambition, and rewarded with honor) yet in the subject of a Monarch, obedience is the greatest virtue, and those before mentioned as they shall serve more, or less unto that, so to be had more or less in estimation. Therefore they study no more the Art of

Commanding, which had been heretofore necessary for any Roman Gentleman, when the rule of the whole might come to all of them in their turns; but apply themselves wholly to the Arts of service, whereof obsequiousness is the chief, and is so long to be accounted laudable, as it may be distinguished from Flattery, and profitable, whilst it turn not into tediousness.[152]

---

152 Hobbes, *Three Discourses*, 60–1.

CHAPTER 5

THE PENAL STATE AND THE COMMONWEALTH OF CONSCIENCE

> [I]t is time for Councillors to care [for] those things that concern government in these loose and dear times, lest mischief follow of it. The diligence of some Justices, and the good fruit of their pains, show that there want no laws to reform all things, but good executioners of laws.
>
> —Henry Montagu, Earl of Manchester, 1630*

In the autumn of 1638, at the Earl of Newcastle's request, Hobbes began writing his first full work of political theory, which would become known as *The Elements of Law*. The book put forward a theory of the state that would become famous: an unsociable state of nature of mutual fear led to the erection of a sovereign through a covenant, which provided a source of common fear to overawe warring parties and compelled them to keep the peace and provide mutual security. In doing so, this work offered a subtle and important commentary on the tradition of commonwealth and its relationship to the state. By the time Hobbes wrote the *Elements*, the ideological landscape within which state and commonwealth were understood was quite a bit more difficult to negotiate than it had been in James's reign, due to the divisiveness caused by Charles's policies, religious sympathies, and unpolitic maneuvers. In the fall of 1626, Charles had imposed a tax on all subsidy payers in order to fund the war with Spain. He did so without securing the assent of Parliament and was thus met with significant resistance, notably by the gentry in Northamptonshire, Lincolnshire, and Gloucestershire and on a broader basis in Essex. It was around this tax, which later became known as the "forced loan," that the ideological lines began to crystallize.[1] The king's line was expounded in a series of sermons by Roger Maynwaring and Robert Sibthorpe, who became known for their "absolutist" position.[2]

---

* HMC *Buccleuch-Whitehall*, vol. 1, London, 1899, pp. 270–1.
1 Cust, "Forced Loan (1626–1627)."
2 Sommerville, *Royalists and Patriots*, 119–24.

The forced loan issue loomed large in Hobbes's Derbyshire. In 1626, Hobbes was working for William Cavendish, the second Earl of Devonshire and lord lieutenant of Derbyshire, as a personal secretary. Cavendish had been Hobbes's pupil in the previous decade, and Hobbes had been attached to the household ever since. Cavendish was opposed to the loan and was noted as one of the leading resisters. He was associated with a group around Southampton, including Sir Edwin Sandys and Sir Dudley Digges, who shared commercial interests and, perhaps for this reason, were opposed to Habsburg power and Buckingham's efforts to secure the Spanish Match in the early 1620s. After Southampton died in 1624, Cavendish moved his support to William Herbert, the third Earl of Pembroke, though this seems to have had as much to do with personal ties and Pembroke's opposition to Buckingham as to any commitment to Pembroke's puritan sympathies.[3] Cavendish's opposition to the forced loan appears to have been in part engineered by Pembroke, who, along with several others, notably Montagu, composed a moderate group on the council that was attempting to mitigate the effects of the forced loan and preserve the traditional arrangement of government by both king and Parliament. Richard Cust has argued that the resistance of Cavendish and other leading members of the gentry from the Pembroke group may have been staged in order to persuade Charles to abandon the more extreme approach being urged by Laud and preached by Sibthorpe and Maynwaring.[4]

The approach of the moderates was at least in part successful. The council took a gentler approach after the resistance of the fifteen peers, including Cavendish, who refused the loan. The peers were not imprisoned, the council abandoned subscription, and it issued an order that the billeting and coat and conduct charges owed by the government as part of the war effort could be counted against the levy.[5] By 1627, Cavendish had become reconciled to the tax, and he employed Hobbes as one of the collectors of the loan.[6] These successes must have emboldened the moderate peers. In the Parliament of 1628, Cavendish was among those who lent their support to the Commons in the debate around the subsidy and the Petition of Right.[7]

Cavendish died in 1628, and Hobbes's patron became Cavendish's cousin, also named William Cavendish, the Viscount Mansfield and soon to be the Earl of Newcastle. Newcastle had been the lord lieutenant of neighboring Nottinghamshire (from 1626) and now, upon his cousin's death, took the position in Derbyshire as well (until 1638). Newcastle had very different

3 Malcolm, *Reason of State*, 79–80.
4 Cust, *Forced Loan and English Politics*, 102.
5 Ibid., 103.
6 Sommerville, *Thomas Hobbes*, 9n15, attributed to Richard Cust.
7 Malcolm, *Reason of State*, 80–6.

politics from his cousin. He was assiduous in his collection of the loan and over the course of his life would show himself to be a strong supporter of the royal prerogative and, indeed, of the royalist cause during the civil war. Noel Malcolm summed up the two approaches: "On the one side there was an exponent of active, oppositional politics, associated with the grand cause of international Protestantism and the more particular interests of trading and colonizing bodies; on the other side there was a supporter of royal power, a lover of tradition and order, someone unmoved by religious idealism and inclined to view religion in instrumental terms."[8]

There is some evidence that by 1629, Hobbes and other clients of the Cavendishes had come to disapprove of the earl of Devonshire's politics, if they had not during his lifetime. They apparently had begun to believe that the position of the moderate peers in the Parliament of 1628 was mistaken.[9] Newcastle would soon be working to collect another extra-parliamentary source of revenue, the compositions for knights' fees, under the supervision of Thomas Wentworth, and it was Wentworth's analysis that Newcastle and Hobbes seem to have adopted.[10] The moderate approach of Pembroke and Manchester, though perhaps well intentioned, was insufficient to overcome the sources of instability in the provinces. The broadest front of resistance was among the puritan laity. They had come to view Charles's policies as the advance of "popery" at court, in which the Arminians were garnering favor with the king by strongly supporting the extra-parliamentary collection of revenue and inflating his prerogative. To the "court," they opposed a purer "country," in which true religion and traditional liberties were upheld. The laity seem to have been encouraged by the clergy, but in private, and there is very little documentary evidence of such efforts, probably due to a concerted attempt to avoid a government crackdown.[11]

In 1626, Pembroke and Manchester had tried to calm the waters by floating a compromise religious position in the form of their client Joseph Hall's *Via Media*.[12] But this had led nowhere, and the "court and country" analysis flourished. It was in opposition to this sort of analysis that the commonwealth

---

8 Ibid., 81.

9 Ibid., 86–9.

10 Milton, "Thomas Wentworth," 154–5. Milton argued that there was a correspondence between the political thinking of Wentworth and Hobbes, but he did so mostly on the strength of their Bodinian opposition to mixed sovereignty. While there is no doubt that both men would have shared this view, my contention is that such a view was a holdover from the Jacobean opposition to presbyterianism rather than an opposition to the noncompliance of the personal rule. It was the penalty and the separation of redress of grievances from subsidy—described by Milton—which, I believe, characterized their distinctive brand of politics, which was based on their experience of local administration in the 1630s as much as on Wentworth's attitudes toward Parliament, also described by Milton.

11 Cust, *Forced Loan and English Politics*, 297–306.

12 Cust, *Charles I*, 90.

was once again invoked. John Pym, perhaps the leading spokesman for the opposition in Parliament, combined an appeal to private property with the godly cause: "those who have more deeply drunke of the cleere fountayn [of] God's word have left a meum and tuum in the world, wittnes the commandment in that behalf."[13] Laud had no patience for this combination of property and godliness, and he appealed to the older traditions of commonwealth and sanctification as the realization of the kingdom of heaven in the here and now of the sort Bucer had envisioned.[14] Laud's impatience with talk of legality in matters that he deemed unjust is evident in a passage cited by Tawney from the articles against Laud:

> Then Mr. Talbot upon oath deposed how the Archbishop did oppose the law in business of inclosures and depopulations; how, when the law was desired to be pleaded for the right of land, he bid them "Go plead law in inferior Courts, they should not plead it before them"; and the Archbishop did fine him for that business two hundred pounds for using the property of his freehold, and would not suffer the law to be pleaded.[15]

Running for Parliament in 1628, Wentworth tried to overcome the rhetoric of court and country in terms of public service, which must have appealed to Newcastle and Hobbes.[16] Wentworth's rhetoric while running for office was but one variant of the view that the king's prerogative was in line with commonwealth. It was this line that Bacon had taken, that Maynwaring had preached, and that Laud thundered in the High Commission. But there were various ways of making the case, some more subtle, some more direct.

Such arguments did not lay the divisions in the state to rest. Though efforts were made on the part of the council to ascertain (and publicize) the legality of the ship money levies, another extra-parliamentary revenue,[17] it was nonetheless resisted in the mid-1630s and required coercion for its successful collection in the Cavendishes' Derbyshire and Nottinghamshire as well as elsewhere. Meanwhile, the fear of Charles's and Laud's "popery" spread, especially in the wake of the trial and brutal punishment of the puritans Prynne, Bastwick, and Burton, in which their ears were cut off, Prynne was branded, and the three were banished to prison islands for the rest of their lives.[18] Though the number of actual puritans in England—godly to the point of eschewing recreations on Sunday, refraining from swearing,

13 Cust, *Forced Loan and English Politics*, 304.
14 Tawney, *Religion and the Rise of Capitalism*, 170–5.
15 Ibid., 311–12n70.
16 Cust, "Wentworth's 'Change of Sides' in the 1620s," 67.
17 Kishlansky, *Monarchy Transformed*, 121–2.
18 Coffey, *Persecution and Toleration*, 128; Sharpe, *Personal Rule of Charles I*, 758.

and so on—seems to have always been rather small,[19] the arguments about the liberties of subjects made by the three men in their works commanded far more sympathy, especially in the wake of such treatment.[20]

By the late 1630s, the puritans were not the only target of the council's propaganda, though perhaps they were still the most conspicuous opponents. This was because the puritans' understanding of sanctification was precisely a series of tests of individual conscience, which raised questions of obedience of the sort faced in the collection of the extra-parliamentary revenues. Indeed, the understanding of sanctification had changed considerably in the years since Bucer and Melanchthon. A Genevan understanding of justification, which maintained that justification was only through God's grace, and Genevan teachings about the doctrines of predestination and limited atonement had become mainstream positions. This embrace of the "absolute decree" of the Genevans was balanced with the "conditional promise" that Swiss Reformers like Zwingli and Bucer had offered in suggesting that sanctification was a process of becoming assured of one's salvific status. Among the English theologians, this assurance was to be achieved through the examination of conscience, and they became known for their extensive works of casuistry, in which they considered various cases of conscience. This method was given a decisive impetus by William Perkins, one of the most influential of the English theologians on the puritans, who had written in a series of works, above all the *Armilla Aurea* (1590) or *A Golden Chaine* (1591), that one could proceed to salvation by working through the various cases of conscience. His pupil William Ames followed suit, explaining in the *Medulla Theologiae* (1623, expanded ed. 1627) that it was by this method that the regenerate sought personal assurance of their salvation.[21]

Laud had singled out the puritans for attack to a point that lost touch with the reality of the situation, and his perspective has been labeled a "conspiracy theory."[22] Laud and his followers condemned the puritans hysterically as seeking the sort of leveling in church government pursued by the presbyterians years earlier.[23] Newcastle and Hobbes certainly agreed with Laud and many of the other councillors that the dictates of private conscience, as the puritans understood them, were insufficient to achieve sanctification, which was evident from the lack of voluntary compliance with both the extra-parliamentary revenues and the commonwealth measures. But while Newcastle, known for his civil or *politique* approach to religion, was no friend of puritanism, he and Hobbes clearly thought that Laud had

19 Sharpe, *Personal Rule of Charles I*, 731–49.
20 Sommerville, *Royalists and Patriots*, 205.
21 McGrath, *Reformation Thought*, chap. 13; Jinkins, "Perkins, William"; Muller, "Covenant and Conscience," 308–11.
22 Cust, *Forced Loan and English Politics*, 328.
23 Cust, *Charles I*, 95.

gone too far and had threatened the unity of the state in his merciless drive for conformity.[24] Their approach was somewhere between Manchester's and Wentworth's. They were not as concerned to preserve the liberties of the subjects as Manchester was,[25] but were sympathetic to his use of coercion and oversight to achieve the aims of commonwealth, and they probably admired his unbiased administration of justice in the Star Chamber for puritans and Catholics alike.[26]

The work of Hobbes and Robert Payne in the 1630s at Newcastle's Welbeck Abbey seems to have been aimed not at refuting the puritans directly, but at allaying the concerns of those of a more orthodox Calvinist leaning who feared "popery" and bought the sort of line laid out by Pym. Hobbes and Payne hoped to erect a theory of obligation on the basis of the new science, which they viewed as consistent with Reformed moral theology. They seem to have been working on this project in a general way in the 1630s, and their thinking was then deployed by Hobbes in *The Elements of Law* when Newcastle asked him to write a work of political theory. It is not clear how concerned Newcastle was that the theory be consistent with a Calvinist understanding of predestination. Newcastle was clearly interested in the question, since in 1645 he asked Hobbes and Bishop John Bramhall to debate the issue, but it is not clear that he had a settled view of his own. While Newcastle was accused throughout his life of being an atheist and "indifferent" to matters of religion, he claimed that he practiced the "true Reformed Religion" of the Elizabethan church, which, if true, would have put him more in line with Hobbes than Bramhall. But this may have been a general statement, without entailing a particular view on salvation.[27] If Hobbes's views in the later 1640s and 1650s reflected his earlier perspective, then Hobbes shared the same view on predestination as the puritan opponents of Bramhall and Laud, believing in double predestination in keeping with Calvin.[28]

The hope seems to have been to show the believers in a more orthodox Calvinism, or at least the *Via Media* of Hall, that the personal rule was in keeping with their views of sanctification and commonwealth, that there was no reason for them to think it necessary to their salvation to judge each moment of policy according to the scruples of their own conscience, as the puritans maintained. The approach of the Welbeck circle thus had several elements: first, an attempt to show that compliance with the personal rule, obedience, was in line with a fairly orthodox Reformed understanding of

24 Hobbes, *Correspondence*, 8, 30; Hulse, "Cavendish, William."
25 Quintrell, "Montagu, Henry."
26 Sharpe, *Personal Rule of Charles I*, 739.
27 Jackson, *Hobbes, Bramhall*, 60–1; Hulse, "Cavendish, William."
28 Martinich, *Two Gods of Leviathan*, 276; Hobbes, *English Works*, 5:104, 115–7; Jackson, *Hobbes, Bramhall*, 13.

moral psychology and soteriology; second, a rehearsal of the Laudian argument that the policies of the personal rule, including its penal aspect, were in keeping with the ideals of commonwealth (and thus sanctification through the realization of the kingdom of heaven on earth) on somewhat different grounds; and third, a demonstration that the private judgment of conscience of the puritan sort was wrongheaded and destructive. The great debates over the expansion of the state have often been reconstructed along the lines the common lawyers set out, emphasizing liberty and property, but the expansion of the state was also being evaluated (and promoted) in terms of commonwealth and sanctification. From the point of view of our day and age, they discussed political affairs in a wide range of idioms, all of which highlighted various aspects of the experience of authority. Viewing the state in terms of commonwealth brings out simultaneously reflection on the institutions of governance, spiritual growth, and the nature of voluntary belonging, which helps put the modernizing state into relief in a different way than the common-law idiom of liberty and property, which emphasizes agency and the limits of state action. A rereading of Hobbes's *Elements* in light of the discourse of commonwealth thus portrays the state in a very different way, and this is especially evident in the most controversial aspects of state building during Charles's personal rule: the forced loan and the collection of ship money.

The Forced Loan Debate

The sermons by Sibthorp and Maynwaring in defense of the forced loan showed that the apology for extra-parliamentary taxation was conducted in terms of the values of the classical commonwealth as understood by the Reformers, but with some significant differences. The point of Maynwaring's 1627 sermons was later summarized by Charles when he conceded to their suppression at the request of Parliament: "The grounds thereof were rightly laid, to perswade obedience from the Subjects to their Sovereigne, and that for conscience sake."[29] Maynwaring's view was simply, as Charles wrote, that the subjects owed their sovereign obedience out of conscience. In broad terms, this was not a controversial position. There was some initial confusion about the position of the earliest Reformers, which seemed, in its embrace of Christian liberty, to veer too far into antinomianism,[30] but later Reformers clarified that the question was not whether civil authority in some broad sense was binding in conscience, but whether particular civil laws were binding. Romans 13 had quite clearly stated that civil magistrates

29 Sommerville, *Royalists and Patriots*, 120–3.

30 For the Catholic point of view on these early Reformers, see Azor, *Institutionum Moralium*, 377d–e: An lex humana habeat vim alligandi civium conscientias?

were to be obeyed, and most commentators read verse 13:5, "Wherefore ye must needs be subject, not only for wrath, but also for conscience sake," as unambiguous. On the question of whether particular civil laws were binding, however, there was a great deal of controversy, and the debate was quite developed by the time Maynwaring addressed it in 1627.

The question had been discussed first in the Middle Ages in the context of whether the rules instituted by leaders of religious communities—say, the abbot of a monastery—for the governing of those communities were really binding in conscience.[31] During the Reformation, the issue took on a new life as the Reformers used the question as a means of debating whether the laws made by the pope bound in conscience.[32] The Reformers were naturally concerned to say that they did not, but at the same time, they did not wish to embrace the antinomianism of which the early Reformers had been accused (which had caused so much chaos in the early years of the Reformation). The various solutions to the problem of whether civil law did or did not bind in conscience were summarized for the men of Hobbes's day in the work of the Heidelberg theologian David Pareus, which was well known in England.[33] The issue was so controversial that as Pareus put it in 1617, "even orthodox theologians seem[ed] to disagree."[34]

Among other positions, Pareus described the one taken by Bucer. Turning to the issue in his 1536 commentary on Romans, Bucer had taken an approach consistent with the classical theory of gratitude and authority. Commenting on verse 13:5, Bucer took "wrath" and "conscience" to be opposing concepts, the one negative, the other positive.

> And hence it is that he adds, "not only for wrath," which is surely to be avoided, "but also for conscience sake," namely of such goods which are provided to us by the Magistrate, such that even if out of contempt for power there should be nothing for us to fear, nevertheless as we are conscious of such benefits to ourselves, which the Magistrate procured and maintained as a benefit for us, our conscience itself, which is the judgment of right reason, rightly compels us to thoroughly subject ourselves to him. . . . As if Paul had said, it is necessary that we submit ourselves to the power, not only so that we might avoid calling forth its vengeance, if we listen to it less this being said, but more therefore that it is the procurer and maintainer of such goods. . . . And

---

31 Daniel, *Purely Penal Law Theory*, 9–11.

32 See, for example, Melanchthon's position as cited by Pauck, *Melanchthon and Bucer*, 68: "We agree that consciences are not bound by human traditions; that is, he who violates a human tradition does not sin unless he gives occasion for offense."

33 Ha and Collinson, *Reception of Continental Reformation*, 143.

34 Pareus, *In Romanos*, 1123: quod etiam orthodoxi theologi sententiis dissidere videntur.

thus it is fitting that you subject yourself lest you should appear not to acknowledge and to be ungrateful towards your benefactor.[35]

As Pareus explained, Bucer was following here the tradition begun by Chrysostom, who "interprets conscience not from the fear of divine displeasure, but from the consideration of the benefits which are extended to the subjects by the magistrate."[36] In keeping with the classical theory of friendship and gratitude of the sort developed in the *Nicomachean Ethics* and Seneca's *De Beneficiis*, Bucer saw the activity of the state as generating gratitude, which made fellow feeling between officials and subjects possible and thus the realization of commonwealth in the here and now.

Maynwaring argued, like Bucer, for obedience from the welfare provided by the king to the people. "The way, they passe by, is the Kings high-way. The Lawes, which make provision for their reliefe, take their binding force from the Supreame will of their Liege-Lord. The bread, that feedes their hungry soules, the poore ragges, which hide their nakednes, al are the fruit and superfluity of that happie plenty and abundance caused by a wise and peaceable gouvernement." In the margin, Maynwaring quoted a passage from Aristotle's *Nicomachean Ethics* on friendship between a king and his subjects— "The friendship of a king for his subjects is one of superiority in beneficence"— as well as the passage from Chrysostom on Romans.[37]

Maynwaring's view that taxation was binding in conscience was that of the Spanish theologians, principally Suárez. Like them, Maynwaring argued that paying tribute was a matter of conscience since it was a matter

---

35 Bucer, *Metaphrasis et Enarratio*, 563: Et hinc est quod addit, non solum propter iram, vitandam nimirum, sed etiam propter conscientiam, tantorum scilicet bonorum, quae nobis per Magistratus constant, ut certe si nihil etiam mali nobis a contemptu potestatis metuendum foret, tamen ut conscii nobis sumus tantorum bonorum, quae nobis beneficio Magistratus & conciliantur & conservantur, ipsa nos nostra conscientia, id est, propriae rationis iudicium merito compellat, ut illi nos subiiciamus quamplenissime. . . . Quasi dixisset Paulus, necesse est ut subiiciamus nos potestati, non hac solum causa, ne nobis ab illa accersamus ultionem, si minus ei dicto audientes sumus, sed magis ideo quod ea tantorum nobis bonorum & conciliatrix est & conservatrix. . . . Et sic oportet ut subiicias te ne videare non agnoscere, & esse ingratus adversus benefactorem.

36 Pareus, *In Romanos*, 1005: Chrystostomus conscientiam interpretatur non de metu offensionis divinae, sed de consideratione beneficiorum, quae subditis praestantur a magistratu.

37 Maynwaring, *Religion and Alegiance*, 15; Chrysostom, "In Epistulam Ad Romanos," 60:617. Maynwaring also cited Musculus, *Loci Communes*, 1051–2, which added little to the debate. Musculus too took the position that tribute should be paid to magistrates as a wage of sorts since they were ministers of God and deserved to be supported in their work. He also maintained that obedience to magistrates was binding in conscience for broadly the reasons stated by Bucer, but he did not make the link to benefit and gratitude as clearly. Maynwaring, *Religion and Alegiance*, 9; Aristotle, *Nicomachean Ethics*, 8.13, 1161a11.

of justice, and not simply a coercive means of controlling the populace.[38] Suárez had distinguished among three sorts of positive law: laws that bound in conscience alone, laws that were purely penal, and laws that were mixed, that is, which bound in conscience but which were accompanied with a punishment. He argued that taxation was not purely penal, since it was not in itself meant to be a punishment; everyone understood that some laws placed "heavy burdens" on the populace that were not meant as punishment, such as military service. Taxes were rather a matter of commutative justice, owed to the king as a "just wage" for "the burdens of his office." Such laws "can by no means be called penal," since the wages of soldiers, for example, were paid for the subjects' own benefit.[39]

Taxes thus were binding in conscience, since it was understood that they must be paid due to a natural sense of the justice or reasonability of such laws. The addition of a penalty to a tax did not make it any less binding in conscience, since one was obligated to pay even if one had been punished. The punishment was in no way a substitute for actually fulfilling the law, which was required as a matter of justice. (For Suárez, the substitutability of the punishment for the fulfillment of the law was a test of whether the law was purely penal.) Suárez explained that the obligation to pay the tax and the possible punishment for not doing so aimed at different ends:

> For tribute is for the maintenance of the prince, or for the payment of the natural obligation to give a just wage to one who is working for our benefit. But the penalty is for compulsion to fulfill the prior obligation or to offense, if it is not done. Therefore, though the tax is just and adequate to its end and the obligation to it remains intact, the threat of penalty and its execution is justly added.[40]

Maynwaring elaborated on how to evaluate the justice of the tax in some depth, paraphrasing the criteria of the Spanish theologians. Particularly, he introduced the three points specified by Alphonsus de Castro and Bartolomé de Medina and cited by Suárez, namely, legitimate power, just cause, and due

38 For William Daniel, this was an example of the insufficiencies of the purely penal theory of the law. It seemed that law in practice must be understood as a matter of "natural" justice. Daniel, *Purely Penal Law Theory*, 162: "Thus in an important test case it may fairly be said that Suárez's general theory breaks down in practice, and the concept of a lawgiver who is indifferent as to whether the subject performs the action laid down in the law or submits to the penalty seems to be a figment of the imagination."

39 Suárez, *Tractatus de Legibus* (1619), 10:300.

40 Ibid., 301: tributum enim est ad sustenationem Principis, seu ad satisfaciendum naturali obligationi dandi stipendium iustum laboranti in nostram utilitatem, poena vero est ad cogendum, ut prior obligatio impleatur, vel puniendum delictum, is omittatur: ergo licet tributum sit iustum & adaequatum fini suo, & obligatio eius integra maneat, iuste additur comminatio poenae, & executio eius.

proportion. Some of the language used by Maynwaring here, in translating these concepts for the purpose of justifying the extra-parliamentary revenues, has been associated with a modern logic of legitimacy for the fiscal-military state.[41] For legitimate power, Maynwaring specified that there be a "Magistrate, that is Supreame," and for just cause, a "Necessity, extreame and urgent." This language seems to correspond to the ideas of unitary sovereignty and reason of state, but the third condition, due proportion, which Maynwaring glossed as "proportion being held respectively to the abilities of the Persons charged, and the Summe, or Quantity so required, surmount not (too remarkeably) the use and charge for which it was levied" fit less well with this picture of the modernizing state, suggesting the older criterion of distributive justice rather than a newer one of the expansion (or maintenance) of power in the face of international competition.[42]

Aside from the elaboration on the theory of taxation through the use of the Spanish theologians, there were two marked differences between Maynwaring and Bucer, which show how the absolutist anti-Calvinist use of the classical commonwealth differed from that of the Reformers. First, Maynwaring transformed the theory of friendship between subject and ruler into a divine right theory. Unlike Bucer, he distinguished between divine and natural grounds of obedience. The sort of gratitude described by Bucer was the natural ground of obedience; the granting of authority to rightful kings was the divine ground. In the text, Maynwaring blended the natural and divine arguments into a single smooth sentence:

> God alone it is, who hath set Crownes on their heads, put scepters, yea and revenging swords into their hands, setled them in their thrones; for this, doe their *Royalties* render to *God* (as a due debt) that great *Care, Paines,* and *Providence* which they sustaine in the ruling over, and preserving of their people in wealth, peace, and godliness: and for this, doe the people render, *as due,* to them againe, by naturall and *originall Iustice, tribute, to whom tribute, custome, to whom custome appertaineth.*[43]

Second, Maynwaring identified the grounds of obedience on the basis of justice as "natural allegiance" which he further equated with voluntary action. "*Obedience* is a willing and *Understanding* act of an *Inferiour,* done at the command, and to the honour of a *Superiour. Reasonable* then, and *Willing* must it be: *Violenced-duties, forced* and *extorted actions,* are not within the

41 Tuck, *Philosophy and Government,* 119.
42 Maynwaring, *Religion and Alegiance,* 26–7; Suárez, *Tractatus de Legibus* (1613), 5.17.1.
43 Maynwaring, *Religion and Alegiance,* 15.

compasse of true *Obedience*."[44] Maynwaring in the margin cited a passage from Juan Azor for the technical side of this argument, which addressed the question of what a genuine human action was. Azor argued, based on an interpretation of Thomas Aquinas, that it was action in accordance with the judgment of the will and in accordance with reason by which acts were praised or blamed. These actions were genuinely human and belonged as much to servants as to freemen.[45] The identification of the natural, the moral, and the voluntary was a hallmark of anti-Calvinist as it had been of Thomist ethics.[46]

The equation of the moral, the natural, and the voluntary was part of the political use of classical ethics and the ideal of the classical commonwealth by the Laudians, and Maynwaring's "natural allegiance" for the king in the payment of taxes was just another thrust in the attack against the "legalism" of their parliamentary opponents. Maynwaring's presentation of Suárez emphasized this natural justice without delving into the procedural or legal detail which made it possible to distinguish between the legitimacy of various sorts of taxation in particular cases.[47] Pym and Robert Mason blasted him in Parliament for misrepresenting his "Jesuit" source to suggest that all taxes were natural and did not require the input of Parliament. Both of these statements were qualified in Suárez's work, they pointed out: a king could be limited by compact with his people to seek consent from an assembly, and the taxes to which Suárez referred as natural were only those on real property.[48]

Commonwealth and Penalty in the Personal Rule   ·

The issue of whether taxation—if not in itself penal—ought to be accompanied by a penalty was not only a live question in the later 1630s in England, but an open one, especially among those charged with administering the law. This was a problem of great concern, for example, for Newcastle in his role as lord lieutenant of Nottinghamshire and Derbyshire, where he took on the task of supervising the collection of fines for knighthood from 1630 to 1632. This was part of a general scheme to raise revenue implemented by the Privy Council, which depended on the old requirement

44 Ibid., 20–1.

45 Ibid., 23–4; Azor, *Institutionum Moralium*, 2b.

46 For a textbook of anti-Calvinist ethics, adopted after Laud became the chancellor in Oxford, see Burgersdijck, *Idea Philosophia Moralis*.

47 Maynwaring's version of Suárez: Penditur tributum ad sustentationem Principis & ad satisfaciendum naturali obligationi in dando stipendium iustum laboranti in nostram utilitatem. Maynwaring, *Religion and Alegiance*, 15, quoting Suárez, *Tractatus de Legibus*, 301, which is translated above.

48 Sommerville, *Royalists and Patriots*, 64–5; *Commons Debates, 1628*, 4:108b–109a.

that those with freehold property worth £40 a year take up the honor of knighthood or pay a fine (a "composition"). Due to inflation this now meant that many yeomen were liable for the fine, and so this became a new means of royal finance. Wentworth, who was supervising the effort, took the view that hard measures were necessary to achieve compliance where it was not otherwise forthcoming.[49] Newcastle followed this line and was extremely energetic in collecting the fines. He wrote that defaulters should be punished, for otherwise authority would be eroded. "[S]ervice" to the Crown was impossible "when Loyall subjectes are punished and obstinate fellowes scapes."[50]

The question remained open in the Cavendish counties during the collection of ship money a few years later, and sheriffs took different approaches to the question. Sir John Byron, the sheriff in Nottinghamshire, was unwilling to use distraint, did not provide the Privy Council with the names of those who refused to pay, and so failed to provide the full amount required by the council. Nottinghamshire was thus officially cited by the Privy Council for failing in the collection of the ship money.[51] The sheriffs of Derbyshire took a firmer line. John Gell was apparently effective due to the use of distraint, and Sir John Curzon, his successor, was cited for unspecified violence in the collection of ship money. None of the sheriffs of Derbyshire were censured for their failure to collect, unlike in Nottinghamshire.[52] If the "Mr. Hobs" who was put forward as a possible candidate for Parliament when it was rumored that there might be an election at the end of 1639 was indeed Thomas Hobbes, as has long been assumed, then there is further evidence of this heavy-handed approach of the Cavendishes to the collection of extra-parliamentary revenues. This Hobs was fiercely (and successfully) opposed by the townsmen of Derby, who bitterly resented the ship money levied on them and identified the Hobs in question with the activist and punitive approach of Newcastle, Gell, and Curzon.[53]

It was not just the compliance of the ratepayer that the Caroline council and gentry was concerned with. They were self-consciously struggling with whether they, as the magistrates responsible for inflicting such penalties at great social cost to themselves, could bear to serve in such a system. In keeping with the old understanding of commonwealth, they hoped to be rewarded for the difficulties they faced and the threats to their local status when they angered their neighbors in the collection of such taxes. Reward would renew their status and authority as well as being materially

49 Milton, "Thomas Wentworth," 138.

50 Dias, "Politics and Administration," 346–7, 352, citing a letter of Newcastle to Wentworth, November 18, 1630.

51 Ibid., 383–6.

52 Ibid., 438–40.

53 Ibid., 443.

worthwhile. The failure to be so rewarded led several of the leading gentry to ask to be relieved of service to the Crown in the future. Wentworth refused one such request, advising Sir Gervase Clifton, an employer of Hobbes, in 1631 that this would be a "disservice" and that he should think "less inwards upon your owne ease, more outwarde upon the duties wee oughe the publicke."[54] Meanwhile, Newcastle was trying to take the more high-minded approach that Wentworth was bruiting about, but was having difficulty maintaining his equanimity given his disappointment over not being rewarded.

The issue of the relationship between the commonwealth and penalty had begun in James's reign. Bacon had hoped that an effective fiscal policy could be combined with the enforcement of commonwealth measures through the judicial oversight of officials, who were charged large fines for failing to comply with royal proclamations. This approach was continued under the Caroline attorneys general, Heath, Noy, and Bankes, with the blessing of Laud and Wentworth. The results were largely considered to be tyrannical and rapacious, as the Star Chamber was considered to be an underhanded means of raising revenue at the expense of the gentry. Enormous fines were levied, and offenders were encouraged to settle, or compound, rather than face the sentence.[55]

The loud complaints about the fiscal side have often led historians to think of the commonwealth measures as mere cover, or at least as hopelessly tainted. There have been some dissenting voices, however. For Tawney, it was the "insistent necessities of an empty exchequer" that perverted the traditionalism of the Laudians, who were otherwise well intentioned, if old-fashioned, in their approach to poverty.[56] Sharpe took a similarly sympathetic approach to the commission on depopulation.[57] And, indeed, Laud seems to have been sincere in his anger toward enclosers. He declared himself "a great hater of depopulations in any kind, as being one of the greatest mischiefs in this kingdom."[58]

That penalty was seen as essential to the maintenance of the commonwealth and not simply as a means of raising revenue emerges from the discussions around the Book of Orders issued in January 1631. The Book of Orders was a set of rules written by a commission of privy councillors headed by Henry Montagu, the first Earl of Manchester, which explained how the

---

54 Ibid., 355–6, citing a letter of Wentworth to Clifton, May 1631.

55 Hindle, *State and Social Change*, 74.

56 Tawney, *Religion and the Rise of Capitalism*, 169.

57 Sharpe, *Personal Rule of Charles I*, 473: "Whilst the benefit to the government of fines should not be discounted, the financial aspects of the commission were not the most important."

58 Laud to Gilbert Sheldon, cited in Tawney, *Religion and the Rise of Capitalism*, 311n69.

JPs were to report to the Privy Council via the sheriffs on a quarterly basis. The orders explained to the magistrates the priorities of the government to which they were to pay particular attention and on which they were to report.[59] When drafting the orders, Manchester, who was a JP in Hertford-shire aside from serving on the council (after holding several high offices), corresponded with his brother Edward, Lord Montagu, a JP in Northampton-shire of puritan leanings. The correspondence highlighted the council's view, in the person of Manchester, that there needed to be more oversight and the country view, in the person of Montagu, that such oversight was unwelcome. When Manchester wrote Montagu that the JPs were to report in writing to a commission of councillors and that there might be deputy commissioners appointed to various counties and boroughs, Montagu doubted their necessity.[60]

In keeping with these efforts to manage the commonwealth measures in the provinces, JPs had been instructed in 1630 to report to the Privy Council on enclosure and depopulation. The initiatives took aim at the magistrates, who were often the enclosers. This was the case in the Cavendishes' Derbyshire, where the JPs were cited by the Privy Council for being sluggish in enforcing the law on the enclosers. This all resulted in some success: a few magnates desisted from enclosing, and one account suggested that two thousand formerly depopulated farms were restored.[61] Poor relief was the target of Caroline initiative as well; the attorneys general decided that the parish poor rates should be levied not just on the basis of land, but on wealth more broadly, and those who refused to comply should be fined.[62]

THE ELEMENTS OF THE LAW

By the time Hobbes wrote the *Elements*, Maynwaring's approach had been officially—by royal proclamation no less—discredited for years. Despite his comment to Aubrey that Maynwaring had preached his doctrine,[63] Hobbes took a different position from Maynwaring, not so much because it was un-popular and officially discredited, though this may have nudged Hobbes's thinking, but because Maynwaring's views in the end must have appeared to Hobbes to be too close to those of the opposition they were both trying to undermine. In hindsight, after Hobbes's work, Maynwaring and Heylin appear to have failed to come to grips with the fundamental premise of

59 Quintrell, "Making of Charles I's Book of Orders," 561.
60 Slack, "Books of Orders," 20.
61 Sharpe, *Personal Rule of Charles I*, 471–3.
62 Ibid., 477.
63 Skinner, *Reason and Rhetoric*, 230.

puritan political theory and to have approached the issue of conformity and political obligation on shaky, and even objectionable, grounds. Maynwaring's approach was from this perspective marred by three mistakes: first, he misunderstood the consequences for stability of appealing to justice; second, he believed that this appeal to justice with the attendant punishment of a bad conscience to be a sufficient motive to conformity with the law; and third, he implied that his approach was consistent with the conditions of commonwealth. The first mistake suggested that obedience was a matter of distributive or commutative justice. This would allow a debate about whether the king really had taken care of and suffered pains for the people and whether they really should be grateful and obedient as a result. It opened the question to Catholic and puritan casuistry. Hobbes met the puritan objections by exploring what the conditions of genuine human community really were without resorting to libertarian (in the metaphysical sense) or Arminian views about free will.

Sanctification and Penal Law

The elaboration of the Reformed theory of sanctification meant that the relationship between the techniques by which the classical commonwealth assured conformity with the law—the virtues, the honor system, penal law—and sanctification became a disputed subject in Reformed ethics. Pareus, like so many others in the Reformed tradition, found philosophical morality to still be sinful and insufficient for sanctification.[64] This view pervaded contemporary Reformed textbooks on ethics. Lambert Daneau, for instance, explained that true good did not come naturally and was impossible to find without God's intervention. Without God's assistance, people would not even will the true good on their own.[65] Plato, Aristotle, and many of the other pagan philosophers were mistaken in thinking that one was good by nature and only acted badly out of ignorance. The pangs of conscience show that we do know otherwise, but nevertheless act badly because of original sin.[66] Daneau wrote that many scholastics and other ecclesiastical writers took a Pelagian or semi-Pelagian position in which a man's reason was a sure guide to discovering the good.[67] In fact, he wrote, people turned away from God's gifts and embraced the physical nature of carnal pleasures rather than the spiritual gifts of God. Nevertheless people were left with the "sparks" of conscience by the light of which they could

---

64 Pareus, *In Romanos*, 494.
65 Daneau, *Ethices Christianae*, 42, citing Philippians 2:13.
66 Ibid., 45b–46b.
67 Ibid., 48–9.

tell right from wrong. Unfortunately, conscience was often obscured by pleasures and bad habits.[68]

Though there was some debate over whether the virtues and the affections which accompanied reward and punishment were a preparation for
sanctification or not, it was agreed that the internal feelings of reward and
punishment awarded by good and bad conscience were a surer guide to
regeneration.[69] Though the evidence is slim for the reasons cited above, it
seems that for some of the opponents to extra-parliamentary taxation and
the personal rule, it was conscience which was to be consulted in determin-
ing obedience to the law.

Certainly Pareus, popular among the puritans in the 1620s, saw conscience as a sufficient sanction for ensuring obedience with the law. Reading
Romans 13:5 straightforwardly, he believed that human laws were binding
in conscience. Fear of coercion actually was insufficient to ensure obedience
and less of a sure guide to obedience than a guilty conscience. "It is a great
thing to avoid the punishment and wrath which follow inobedience, but
the wicked often pay no heed to wrath, and are not intimidated by punishments: 'They'll never lose their heads for it,' or 'They're just having a bad
patch.' . . . So through the contempt of corporal punishment or perhaps the
hope of impunity they fall headlong into wickedness."[70] A bad conscience
was far more effective. It "rises up as an internal tormentor and torturer of
the soul, such that good men turn away from our wickedness, such that
God himself appears to us as our enemy, and right now threatens as a harsh
avenger of sin to cast us down in eternal punishment unless there should
be a pardoning."[71] The opposite of this intense feeling of guilt was the joy
of a good conscience: "Obedience therefore gives rise to a good conscience,
which is the approval of our mind as it judges and testifies to us that we have
acted rightly before God and men, which approval is followed by joy as the
heart delights in this approval of God and men."[72]

Hobbes's response was twofold. On a simple level, Hobbes echoed the
older argument that civil laws could not be binding in conscience since it was

68 Ibid., 49b.

69 For a textbook of Reformed ethics from the period, see Keckermann, *Systema Ethicae*.

70 Pareus, *In Romanos*, 1005: Magnum est evitare poenas & iram propter inobedien-
tiam: sed improbi saepe iram contemnunt, nec poenis absterrentur: Es gist ie nicht Ropf-
fabhauuens. vel: Es ist ihnen umbe eia bose stunde. . . . Ita contemptu poenae corporalis vel
etiam spe impunitatis ruunt in scelera praecipites. Thanks to Alan Swensen for his help in
translating the German phrases.

71 Ibid.: Conscientia mala subit tanquam internus tortor & carnifex animi, quod viri
boni nostram turpitudinem aversentur, quod Deus ipse sit nobis hostis, & iam iamque instet
scelerum severus ultor, abjecturus in aeternas poenas nisi fiat remissio.

72 Ibid.: Obedientia igitur parit bonam conscientiam, quae est approbatio mentis nostrae
recte iudicantis & testificantis nobis, quod recta fecerimus Deo & hominibus probata: quam
approbationem sequitur laetitia cordis acquiescentis in hac approbatione, Dei & hominum.

impossible to know what a man thought "unless it break out into action."[73] This was an echo of the view that the "magistrate does not judge internal matter, nor can see when one sins in accordance with their conscience, but only considers the external action; he can neither see nor judge internal emotion."[74] On a more sophisticated level, Hobbes's response reflected the belief that such a view of the effectiveness of a guilty conscience entailed a vision of spiritual conversion or regeneration that was badly mistaken.

The second argument turned on Hobbes's understanding of the role of the fear of punishment and a guilty conscience in repentance or regeneration. Repentance or penance was of course a long-standing Christian method of moral growth and regeneration. Before the Reformation, repentance had both a spiritual and a sacramental character, including oral confession along with good works and contrition. The Reformers abandoned the sacramental character, but clarified the relationship between regeneration that took place on account of punishment and regeneration based on a genuine love of God. Melanchthon described accordingly a double movement of repentance. In the first instance, sinners were brought to change their behavior through the punishments prescribed by the law. The law and its punishments brought sinners to a consciousness of their sin and a willingness to reform themselves. Once the punishment was over and the sinner had altered his behavior, the second moment of repentance began in which "God himself invites us and draws [us] to himself, and when he has drawn us, he takes away our punishments and declares that he is pleased with us and reconciled to us."[75] The Reformed theologians took a similar position, distinguishing starkly between those who repented on account of punishment and those who repented on account of their love of God.[76] Hobbes referred to this distinction between the fear of punishment and a guilty conscience by the conventional Latin terms, *malum poenae* and *malum culpae.*

Hobbes argued in two ways that the puritans misconceived the *malum culpae.* First, he claimed that the *malum culpae* could not be sufficiently harsh to ensure conformity with the external law without making repentance impossible through the threat of mental collapse. For Pareus, a guilty conscience was sufficient to motivate one to compliance with the law, because it was even more frightening than the threat of corporal punishment. A guilty conscience of this sort was so terrifying that even by Pareus's own

---

73 Hobbes, *EL*, 2.6.3, 146.

74 Ibid., 2.6.3, 145–6. Pareus, *In Romanos*, 1123: Magistratus non iudicat de internis, nec potest videre, an aliquis ex conscientia peccet: sed tantum externum opus expendit, internum affectum nec intueri nec iudicare potest.

75 Pauck, *Melanchthon and Bucer*, 44–5.

76 Heidelberg Catechism, q. 90, day 33, vii.

admission it could threaten the possibility of moral regeneration. As Pareus put it, a guilty conscience could "cast us down in eternal punishment unless there should be repentance."[77] This worry that a guilty conscience could spiral out of control into a state of total abjection was a matter of some discussion in Reformed circles. Keckermann considered this state of depression to be the excessive vice of the virtue of repentance. "In excess is opposed to repentance too much pain, or desperation, through which we are in so much pain on account of a wicked deed that we are not able to restore the soul for virtue."[78] For Hobbes, such a terrifying view of conscience and thus the difficulty of repentance were clearly out of step with the promise of moral regeneration in the Bible. Hobbes treated sanctification as a whole under the heading of repentance, stressing that repentance and reconciliation were "the essence of charity, which is the scope of the whole law."[79]

Second, Hobbes held that the true *malum culpae* was difficult to isolate in the storm of human emotions. For Hobbes, the *malum poenae*, which secured external conformity, offered *nothing* in the way of spiritual regeneration. "And by these dead works, is understood not the obedience and justice of the inward man, but the opus operatum, or external action, proceeding from fear of punishment, or from vain-glory, and desire to be honoured of men; and these may be separated from faith, and conduce no way to a man's justification."[80]

For Hobbes, what was so mistaken about the puritan view was that its account of bad conscience confused the notions of penalty and accusation in a way that made spiritual growth difficult. This was not only because construing bad conscience as a tormentor threatened mental collapse and the end of repentance, but because such a bad feeling was not easily interpreted and could not serve as the basis of self-evaluation and growth. This became apparent in Hobbes's discussion of the interpretation of the feelings of private conscience after a man has ceded his private judgment to the will of the sovereign. Hobbes defined "private conscience" as a deeply held conviction (an "opinion" that one believed not to be "doubtful").[81] As I discuss in greater detail in the next section, Hobbes argued that such private conscience or judgment ("which is all one") must be ceded to the will of the sovereign for the sake of civil peace.[82] After this was done, one might still have the feeling that one formerly identified as the pangs of conscience;

---

77 Pareus, *In Romanos*, 1005: abiecturus in aeternas poenas nisi fiat remissio.

78 Keckermann, *Systema Ethicae*, 240: In excessu opponitur paenitentiae nimius dolor, seu desperatio, per quam ita dolemus ob admissum vitium, ut animum ad virtutem non redintegremus.

79 Hobbes, *EL*, 1.18.8, 97.

80 Ibid., 2.6.10, 156.

81 Ibid., 1.6.8, 27.

82 Ibid., 2.5.2, 139.

a man might still feel discomfort when he obeyed a law against his *private* conscience. But Hobbes explained that this feeling stemmed from the sense of the loss of one's power rather than from any true voice of divine, natural, or moral law (all of which he equated). Since a man chose to covenant away his private judgment with the aim of fulfilling the mandates of divine, natural, and moral law, that is, seeking peace, when he complied with the will of the sovereign, he "doth according to his conscience and judgment."[83] Nevertheless, the feeling of loss was powerful, because before this transfer of private judgment, the "liberty [to judge matters according to one's own conscience] appeareth in the likeness of rule and government over others."[84] This was a misperception, but a powerful one, and it imparted to the people a sense of honor and prestige that was lost when they covenanted with the sovereign. When a man obeyed a law that was opposed by his private conscience, he was reminded of the loss of that feeling of prestige, that false honor he had imparted to himself, and, naturally, it hurt.[85]

One of the great advantages of Hobbes's system then was that it made the feelings of guilt discernible from those of the loss of honor or prestige. It separated out the carnal feelings from the spiritual feelings, in the language of Protestant theology.[86] This was achieved by clearly demarcating the sphere of moral regeneration, the true Christian commonwealth or its approximation, from the institutions of human law, the state, which secured external conformity with the law in accordance with the fear of punishment. The advantage of distinguishing clearly between these two realms for the purpose of sanctification was that it allowed men to critically examine their emotions in light of the sovereign will and thus to parse which of their negative emotions were simply feelings of powerlessness in the face of the judgment of the sovereign and which were genuine feelings of remorse. That is, in Melanchthon's terms, it heightened the accusatory use of the law. Men had told themselves in the state of nature that these feelings were meant to seek peace, but after the conditions of peace were actually set forth by the sovereign, men had to jettison any lies they had told themselves about the peacefulness of dictates of conscience that were contrary to the law. Men had created an apparatus for peace—the state—so that they could use it as a method of criticizing their old intuitions about their feelings. One's ideas in the state of nature might have in fact led to peace, but in a true artificial state, Hobbes argued, it would be at the cost of pride and aggrandizement, and

---

83 Ibid., 2.8.5, 171.

84 Ibid., 2.5.2, 139.

85 Ibid. It is possible that what Hobbes was saying was that the anxiety a man felt over his powerlessness and the pride he felt in his powerfulness relative to others would now be felt relative to the state. This was not so much an overcoming of emotions as a transfer of them into a more constructive and peaceful direction.

86 See Pauck, *Melanchthon and Bucer*, 39, 48, 105.

thus issue in a despotic state. The *mutual* fear that Hobbes talked about was not so much a feeling as an intellectual recognition of the means of seeking peace and the emotional backlash of one's recognition of one's powerlessness in the face of it. The consequence of this was that genuine repentance was possible.

For Hobbes, the residue of true regret after the feelings of powerlessness had been screened out was the true *malum culpae*. Hobbes's process of sanctification was more intellectual and less emotional than the standard accounts. John Rainolds, for instance, in his commentary to Aristotle's *Rhetoric*, and Francis Bacon, as I have mentioned, showed great interest in the means of quieting the passions using other passions, the method Melanchthon prescribed of affection overcoming affection. Among other means of quieting anger, Rainolds mentioned the approach taken by Hobbes, namely, "if he is compelled by necessity, as by the order of a king."[87] For Rainolds, as for Melanchthon, this compulsion presumably substituted one emotion for another and, as Hobbes also sometimes spoke of it, made us "willing" in our obedience and conformity with the law. But for Hobbes, this sort of willingness was of no real significance for sanctification; it remained external. Its use was only to allow people to think for themselves more clearly about their motives and to create a sphere of liberty within the context of conformity with the law in order to experiment in higher forms of still more voluntary charity and peacefulness, the "accommodation and forgiveness of one another," which do have a sanctifying and justificatory power.[88] Once external conformity was secured by the sovereign will, there was no need for extensive congregational discipline of the sort being preached by the puritans, and Hobbes cautioned against a heavy-handed approach to people's behavior. "For after our charity and desire to rectify one another is rejected, to press it further, is to reprehend him, and condemn him."[89] This individual and collective process of sanctification within the framework of the state did not, then, amount to the sort of naive psychological hedonism that, it is sometimes suggested, characterized Hobbes's approach. The condition of living under mutual fear would not always be pleasant or

---

87 Rainolds, marginalia in *Aristotelous Technēs Rhētorikēs*, 91: si compulsus necessitate, ut regis imperio.

88 Hobbes hoped that the transfer of private conscience to the will of the sovereign would be limited to a rather small set of issues. The rest should be free for people to decide for themselves, though this of course was a matter for the sovereign to determine. These were matters of philosophy, not of the state. Hobbes was as disapproving of the coercive enforcement of Laudian innovations as he was of Calvinist discipline. "[A]ll other points that are now controverted, and make distinction of sects, Papists, Lutherans, Calvinists, Arminians, &c., as in old time the like made Paulists, Apollonians, and Cephasians, must needs be such, as a man needeth not for the holding thereof deny obedience to his superiors." *EL*, 2.6.5, 147–8.

89 Ibid., 1.18.8, 97.

psychologically comfortable. Ultimately, however, Hobbes did offer hope and the promise of justification as a result of such realism about one's feelings.[90] The sphere in which divine or natural law bound in conscience was one in which people only must strive to do their best, as "Christ required no more than our best endeavour."[91] A man could take solace in the fact that once he repented and "condemn[ed] the same in his own conscience," he was free from any other punishment.[92]

The consequence of this rigorous distinction between the sorts of fear or bad feeling one can experience is that they are said to play very specific roles in the state. The *malum poenae* provided a scaffolding of coercive law to make coexistence possible and the true claims of conscience discernible. For Hobbes, this might be a fairly minimal scaffolding since he, like Bacon, thought there should be a minimum of laws. In conceptualizing the scaffolding, Hobbes made an argument very similar to Suárez's treatment of penal laws in *De Legibus*. Suárez had distinguished between various sorts of human law, including the penal law. Hobbes argued that all human laws were penal laws such as described by Suárez,[93] except for simple laws, which were too general to really be applied.[94] In thinking about the role of the *malum culpae*, Hobbes, like Suárez, believed that the execution of the penalty was binding in conscience on the magistrates, for "in penal laws the commandment is addressed to the magistrate, who is only guilty of the

---

90 Ibid., 2.6.10, 156.

91 Ibid., 1.18.10, 98.

92 Ibid.; Pauck, *Melanchthon and Bucer*, 45. The importance of repentance to Hobbes was evident in a number of places in the *Elements*. At *EL*, 2.7.2, 160-1, for instance, he noted in passing that Aaron's penitence over questioning Moses's authority led to his forgiveness by God, whereas the unrepentant Miriam was punished with leprosy.

93 Hobbes seems to have changed his position from the *Elements* to *De Cive*. In *De Cive*, he certainly emphasized that all civil laws must have a penalty, but he suggested that civil laws were not purely penal and that they bound in conscience as well. This had the disadvantage of watering down the argument presented here, in which the *malum poenae* and *malum culpae* were strictly distinguished, but he could still more or less hold the same position, simply explaining that a bad "conscience" was still very much the *malum poenae*; it was just not the case that conscience in the absence of a commonwealth meant as much as some thought it did. The revision had the (political) advantage of putting Hobbes in line with Maynwaring, which helps to make better sense of his later comment to Aubrey that Maynwaring had preached his doctrine. On Hobbes's rejection of the view that all civil laws were purely penal, see Brett, *Changes of State*, 158.

94 Hobbes, *EL*, 2.10.6, 187. The approach taken by Hobbes in these sections (2.10.6–8) was very close to John Selden's approach to the relationships among natural law, divine law, and judicial law in the contemporaneous *De Iure Naturali and Gentium, Iuxta Disciplinam Ebræorum* (1640). When Hobbes wrote here that "he that stealeth an ox, shall restore fourfold, is a penal, or as others call it, a judicial law," he was probably equating Suárez's category of "penal" with Selden's "judicial."

breach of it, when the penalties ordained are not inflicted; to the rest apper-
taineth nothing, but to take notice of their danger."[95]

Hobbes's use of Suárez seems to have been in part an attempt to respond
to the sort of arguments that Pym and Mason had drawn from Suárez in
the Parliament of 1628, when they argued (fairly) that Maynwaring had mis-
represented Suárez's views. Hobbes here—granted, only implicitly—seems
to be going another round. Yes, he seems to be saying, the right of conquest
may be circumscribed by pact, but this argument is a failure to see the real
point. The crux was that commonwealth measures needed penalties ad-
joined to them to compel the populace to comply *and* that the magistrates
needed to understand that the imposition of such penalties was their duty
in conscience and must be done. While Hobbes was revising Maynwaring's
view by arguing that it was only the duty to impose the penalty that obligated in conscience, and this only the magistrates' duty, in doing so, he
argued against the whole logic of the Petition of Right. The idea was that
the actual experience of the government in the localities showed that the
policies of the personal rule were justified and necessary for the securing of
commonwealth.

Suárez argued that the need to impose the penalty obligated the magistrate in conscience because a law that specified a punishment clearly intended that the punishment be carried out. The law would be ineffective if
the punishment were not imposed; thus, whether it specified explicitly that
the magistrate had a duty to do so, he did, because "from the nature of the
thing the text of a law is addressed to the judge," and as the "custodian of
the law" punishment was the office holder's duty.[96] Moreover, this was dou-
bly true in cases where the penalties were financial rather than corporal—
like the penalties around the forced loan, enclosure, and ship money with
which Hobbes was concerned. In situations where levying the penalty was
for the benefit of another, whether that be an injured party or the treasury
(as was the case here), "there is an obligation not just as a matter of law, but
even of justice not to lessen it. And this is above all true where the law itself
stipulates the penalty, for thus the right of another is acquired, namely that
of the one who is to be punished by the law, since as soon as the sentence
is declared that it is a crime, at once the law itself transfers the right to the
other party, therefore it would be an injustice to him, if he were to be deprived of such a right."[97]

95 Hobbes, *EL*, 2.10.6, 187.

96 Suárez, *Tractatus de Legibus*, 305, col. a, litt. e–col. b, litt. a: nam ex natura rei ad iudi-
cem diriguntur verba legis . . . quia est custos, & executor legum, & quasi animata lex.

97 Ibid., 305, col. b, litt. d: Quando igitur poena est prioris rationis, intervenit obligatio
non solum legis, sed etiam iustitiae ad non diminuendam illam. Quod maxime verum est, si
talis poena ipso facto per legem imposita sit: nam tunc acquiritur ius alteri, cui talis poena

The Passions and the Critique of Distributive Justice

For Hobbes, then, the idea that people ought to test their consciences in light of what they believed to be distributive justice invited self-deception; justice should not be interpreted in light of subjective feeling. This analysis rested on Hobbes's extensive critique of Aristotle's account of the virtues and of distributive justice in particular. Hobbes rejected the tradition of affection overcoming affection, which made it possible to maintain social order through social processes outside of the state, such as the virtues of civility and the recognition of claims of honor between private men. This view was in part the product of his acceptance of Bacon's view of the world as characterized by a competitive, externalized psychology, but it was also in part a totalizing of the very critique that the Reformers had leveled at Aristotle from the outset, namely, that the justice of the pagan philosophers was not the true justice promised in the Gospels.

Hobbes thus presented a deep critique of the thought that such passions could be satisfied so as to achieve peace without state action. The claims to recognition encoded in the Aristotelian view of the passions were in no sense really claims to justice, and the claims to honor were divisive and prone to conflict. Labeling them as claims of justice would only make matters worse. Hobbes's critique emerged from a comparison of the textbooks he used to teach ethics to Cavendish, most probably in the early 1610s. Hobbes probably employed Keckermann's *Systema Ethicae*, a systematic exposition of Aristotle's ethics, alongside Magirus's *Corona Virtutum*, a bilingual (Latin-Greek) student edition of the *Nicomachean Ethics* complete with an extensive commentary. Both were standard textbooks of Protestant Aristotelianism. A manuscript summary of the Keckermann with marginal references to the Magirus survives in the papers at Chatsworth and was probably the student work of Cavendish.[98]

Hobbes's most explicit critique of Aristotle in the *Elements* was that he could "see no ground for" the Aristotelian view "that virtue consisteth in mediocrity, and vice in extremes."[99] The passions for Hobbes were thus not vices—excesses or deficiencies of some proper amount of emotion—but

---

per legem applicata est, quia post latam sententiam declaratioriam criminis, statim lex ipsa transfert ius in illum; ergo in iustitia illi sit, si tali iure privetur.

98 The manuscript, Chatsworth A8(1), entitled "Parva Moralia," has been mentioned in passing in several accounts of Hobbes, perhaps first by Strauss, *Political Philosophy of Hobbes*, 42–3. I have identified it as a summary of Keckermann with notes to Magirus by comparing it with the works on ethics listed in Hobbes's catalog of the library at Hardwick Hall. The catalog probably dates from the mid- to late 1620s, but these works were likely ordered for Cavendish in the 1610s as school books. Similar books (including Keckermann's *Systema Physicum* and *Politica*) were purchased in 1611, according to Cavendish's account books, as was noted by Malcolm, *Reason of State*, 3.

99 Hobbes, *EL*, 1.17.14, 94.

rather feelings derived from judgments in their own right. But such philosophical mistakes had political ramifications. This above all was the case with those passions (or virtues and vices, in Aristotle's nomenclature) that were concerned with the distribution of honor. According to Hobbes, the trouble with Aristotle's virtues surrounding honor, at least as reconstructed by Reformed Protestants like Keckermann, was that these virtues were really judgments about desert, about the justice of some claim made against others or against the state. They thus encoded claims about distributive goods that were not really moral claims, but political claims, and should be dealt with politically.

This was evident in Hobbes's rereading of the virtues and vices concerned with honor in the *Nicomachean Ethics*. Like Keckermann, Hobbes discussed a cluster of passions that were desires for honor, loosely corresponding to Aristotle's *philotimia*, and a cluster of passions corresponding to the shunning of honors, loosely corresponding to Aristotle's *aphilotimia*.[100] Keckermann explained that *philotimia* could be broken down into two virtues: modesty, which was the desire for middling honors, and magnanimity, which was the desire for great honors. In both cases, these desires were virtues, because they were desires for honors that one in fact deserved.

The political relevance of this disagreement over the interpretation of the passions was perhaps clearest in Hobbes's reading of what he called a pair of opposing passions: magnanimity and pusillanimity. Keckermann treated the two in some depth; magnanimity was the virtue "through which we rightly desire, accept, and maintain great honors due on account of our virtue,"[101] while pusillanimity was one of the defects of magnanimity along with "dejection of the soul," which showed a disregard for the great honors and offices that one deserved.[102] For Hobbes, the trouble was that the magnanimous man on the Aristotelian account interpreted his feelings of desire for honor in a moral way, as a feeling of desert. For Hobbes, magnanimity was a feeling of glory about what one could do in the world, this time "well grounded upon certain experience[s] of power sufficient to attain his end in [an] open manner."[103] It was a feeling based on a judgment of fact, on one's own estimate of one's various abilities and capacities and on others' estimates of those abilities and capacities in the world. To encourage people to think of their feelings as entitlement or desert was to introduce a dangerous moral edge to an already turbulent emotional life. It could create a sense of entitlement in which a sensitivity to desert led to a brittle quickness to

100 Aristotle, *Nicomachean Ethics*, 4.4, 1125b22.
101 Keckermann, *Systema Ethicae*, 144: Magnanimitas, quae est virtus, per quam magnos honores virtuti nostrae debitos legitime appetimus, acceptamus, & conservamus.
102 Ibid., 154.
103 Hobbes, *EL*, 1.9.20, 47.

anger, similar to that which characterized the culture of courtliness Bacon had sought to reform.[104]

COMMONWEALTH AND THE BODY POLITIC

Hobbes's critique of the claims of distributive justice established that society was inadequate to the task of attaining social order. A commonwealth (that is, the union of a people, or *civitas*, as defined by Case) would require the establishment of a political authority—a sovereign. Hobbes imagined that the sovereign could be erected (and the unity ensue) in two ways, both the product of a man subjecting himself to another for "fear of not otherwise preserving himself." The first "natural" means was when a man subjected himself to another without covenanting with others; the result was a patrimonial or despotic body politic. The second was when by means of "mutual agreement" men subjected themselves to another, in which case the resulting body politic was called a "commonwealth."[105] He imagined the process of the formation of a commonwealth as when the individuals of the populace, what he called a "multitude," covenanted as individuals with "some one and the same man, or to some one and the same council" (the sovereign) and in so doing unified themselves as a "body politic," or what the Greeks knew as a polis.[106] The result was that the sovereign composed the individuals into a body: the sovereign was imagined as giving form to the people, who otherwise would have no coherence or permanence at all. This image of the state was pictured in the famous frontispiece to *Leviathan*, where individuals were pictured as united in one body, which wielded the symbols of sovereignty. This was a denial of the view exemplified in John Case's theory that there was a populace that existed apart from the *summum imperium*.[107]

By thinking of the origin of government as the subjection of men out of fear of not being preserved otherwise, Hobbes reimagined the sort of original juridical transfer of political power that had been described by Jesuit political theorists, above all Suárez in the 1613 *Defensio Fidei*. Suárez's political theory was extremely influential and hotly debated in England from 1613 through the 1620s, and presumably through 1640. Suárez's location of the origin of government in an original contract was variously seen as giving room for limited government and as evidence that the populace

104 See chapter 4 in this volume; and Peltonen, *Duel in Early Modern England*, chap. 2.
105 Hobbes, *EL*, 1.19, 105.
106 Ibid., 2.19.7–10, 104.
107 Brett, *Changes of State*, chap. 5, esp. 138–41 (on *Leviathan*'s frontispiece).

had transferred its power wholly to the monarch.[108] In keeping with the Caroline critique of popularity, Hobbes's careful formulation of the simultaneous mutual agreement of individuals to covenant with the sovereign precluded the possibility of any original body of the people who might hold rights against the sovereign.[109]

While this does seem to have been Hobbes's intent, there is still some evidence that he may have thought that there was some residuum of mutuality that differentiated the commonwealth from the patrimonial or despotic body politic. This is suggested by his thinking about the moment of mutual agreement and covenant. This moment, though only a moment, is still of great importance for the understanding of Hobbes's political thought, assuming that he meant there to be a real difference between the erection of a sovereign by institution rather than by conquest.[110] Given that Hobbes was simultaneously confronting and building on Reformed Aristotelianism in much of the early chapters of the *Elements*, he may have been thinking of covenant as understood in the Reformed revision of the classical theory of friendship.

The emerging Reformed tradition was faced with assimilating the classical model of friendship—Aristotelian, Senecan, and Ciceronian—which was chiefly about the mutual exchange of benefit, into a picture of sanctified human relationships worked through grace. In this task, adding the idea of covenant and the testimony of God to the Aristotelian account proved crucial. The Reformed ideal of friendship was exemplified by that between David and Jonathan as described by Lambert Daneau in his *Treatise on Christian Friendship* (1579). Daneau rejected the view of "those who define friendship, as that agreement about goods only in private affairs, thereby making friendship into commerce and a social contract."[111] True Christian friendship was rather "a covenant made between two people witnessed by God, to mutually love, foster and altogether maintain and care for each other and for each other's goods, in so far as it can be done without harming the

---

108 Sommerville, *Royalists and Patriots*, 62–5.

109 For "popularity," see Cust, *Charles I*, 21–5; Brett, *Changes of State*, 138.

110 This moment has been reconstructed in a number of ways. Leo Strauss considered the covenant that founded the artificial state a moment of mutual recognition and an admission of fear of violent death. Strauss, *Political Philosophy of Hobbes*, 22–3, 57. Tuck has described the moment in which men became aware of their obligations under the natural law as a psychological transformation of the sort imagined by Descartes in which one proposes a provisional morality for oneself in the face of an acknowledgment of the subjectivity of morality. Tuck, "Introduction," xxvi–vii.

111 Daneau, *De Amicitia Christiana*, 9: Qui autem sic definiunt Amicitiam, ut illa sit, bonorum inter se consensus in rebus tantum privatis gerendis & tuendis, pene ex amicitia mercaturam faciunt, & societatis contractum.

majesty or glory of God."[112] Reformed moral theology thus added the idea of covenant and the testimony of God to the Aristotelian theory of friendship. It was insufficient for true Christian friendship to be left unexpressed.[113] "For though charity commands generally that there should be between us a real union and agreement of minds, so that we all may speak and think the same, 1 Corinthians 1, verse 10 especially requires of friends in a true friendship that union between them be known and made manifest, not tacit and unknown."[114] David and Jonathan thus declared their love for each other through covenants several times in the first book of Samuel.[115]

The emphasis on covenant in the Reformed understanding of friendship was a means of involving God in the process through swearing one's love to another in God's name, but it was also a reflection of the Reformed sense of the difficulty of securing stable human relationships. For the Reformed theologians, as for generations of commentators on classical social theory, this was due to the challenge of interpreting whether a purported benefit was indeed a benefit, whether the exchange of "goods" reflected true mutuality and was a bond of peace or not. In the context of the Ciceronian-Aristotelian synthesis that was the basis of the Protestant political theory of the period, the question was whether the description of commercial relations that occupied so much of the third book of *De Officiis* reflected the higher type of genuine community and whether the classical commonwealth was really a good model for a Christian community.[116]

These uncertainties were preserved in Reformed accounts of friendship, such as Keckermann's discussion of the Aristotelian friendship of utility, which was broadly understood to be the Aristotelian analogue to Ciceronian commercial relations.[117] Such friendships, Keckermann explained, were "very liable to quarrels, moreover, because each friend is engaged in pleonexia, and

---

112   Ibid.: Pactum inter duos Deo teste factum, de sese suisque mutuo diligendis, fovendis, & omnino conservandis ac tuendis, quatenus illaesa Dei maiestate & gloria id facere licet.

113   The Reformed emphasis on express contracts has been shown to be important for Hobbes's theory of representation developed in *Leviathan*. Martinich, "Interpretation of Covenants," esp. 234–5.

114   Daneau, *De Amicitia Christiana*, 9: Nam praeterquam quod in universum iubet charitas, ut sit inter nos animorum summa coniunctio & consensus, & ut idem omnes & loquamur & sentiamus, 1.Cor.1.vers.10 praesertim exigit vera amicitia hoc ab amicis, ut illa coniunctio inter eos nota sit & patefacta, non autem tacita & ignota.

115   1 Samuel 18:3: "Then Jonathan and David made a covenant, because he loved him as his own soul." Daneau also cited 20:8, 17; 23:18.

116   See, for instance, Pietro Marso's commentary on exchange and benefit in Cicero, *Ad Marcum Filium de Officiis*, 177v–78r.

117   Keckermann repeated the view of the commentaries to *De Officiis* that one who bestowed a benefit in the hope of a greater return was engaged in commerce, not true benefit. And he repeated the saying from Terence that "to accept a benefit, is to sell one's freedom," which also appeared in several of the commentaries. Keckermann, *Systema Ethicae*, 283.

wants more than the other can have or wishe[s] to surpass him."[118] This was because "[q]uarrels chiefly arise when he who has received a benefit has not given in return what the one who gave the benefit was hoping that he would get."[119] Hobbes was clearly aware of this critique of benefit. He explained that if it was the intention of the benefactor to receive the gratitude and support of the recipient, then that was conducive to peace, but if it was the intention of the benefactor simply to make a show of his own power or superiority, that might lead to diffidence and war. "For as when they do it upon trust, the end they aimed at, namely to be well used, is the reward; so also when they do it for ostentation, they have the reward themselves."[120] Ideally, according to the law of nature, one should never appear to be benefiting someone for some ulterior purpose that might in fact harm him.[121]

Keckermann explained that express contracts could reduce such uncertainties. He distinguished between moral and legal friendships of utility. Legal friendships were defined by contract and were less liable to conflict. In moral friendships, where a benefit was offered out of benevolence and free will, people were always giving less in return than expected. Hobbes argued that covenant could play a similar role in the achievement of concord, the Aristotelian *homonoia*, which Keckermann had defined as agreement over practical matters, which could only be reached by those who were friends or who wanted to cultivate friendship between them.[122] Given the difficulties of judging the mutuality of benefit, such a covenant would make concord possible. The problem was that the achievement of concord was notoriously difficult; Aristotle, as Keckermann explained, reserved it only for friendships between good men who were "constant and firm in resolve and persevere in their plans, words, and deeds, nor have wills ebbing and flowing like the channel Euripus."[123] Keckermann explained that there was another sort of concord, *homodoxia*, or agreement about more theoretical matters, which could be reached by those who were not friends and even by those who were enemies.[124] Hobbes suggested something similar in the covenant that established sovereignty and the body politic.

---

118 Keckermann, *Systema Ethicae*, 282: Amicitia vero utilis maxime est exposita querelis, propterea quia uterque amicus laborat pleonexia, & plus appetit, quam alter possit aut velit praestare.

119 Ibid., 283: Tunc autem maxime oriuntur querelae, quando is, qui beneficium accepit, non tantum retribuit, quantum sperabat se recepturum is, qui beneficium dabat.

120 Hobbes, *EL*, 1.16.6, 85.

121 Ibid.

122 Keckermann, *Systema Ethicae*, 267.

123 Ibid., 268: quia viri boni sunt constantes & firmi in proposito & perserverant in suis consiliis, dictis & factis, neque habent voluntates instar Euripi fluentes & refluentes.

124 Ibid., 267.

For Hobbes, this type of covenant, where men gave away their rights, embodied the recognition of the need for a common fear to control men's desires for superiority. As a recognition that those rights were really the source of conflict and inequality, this type of covenant was an intellectual declaration of the conditions necessary to make loving relationships possible rather than a sworn testament of love for one another, as between David and Jonathan. It was, however, a declaration of love and charity in the sense of aiming at this end. Hobbes argued that obedience to the divine law that aimed at peace need not be felt as long as it was understood. Political obligation and obedience were then separated experientially, though not intellectually, from the experience of human community in commonwealth.

While the moment of the formation of the body politic by institution might have embodied the ideal of the Christian commonwealth, once established the operative social psychology was closer to that developed by Bacon. Hobbes in the *Elements* was still very much a disciple of Bacon, and Bacon's insistence in the *Aphorismi* and in the essay on sedition on the dependence of the stability of the state on the contentment of the people was carried over into the *Elements*.[125] The distinction between the freemen of

---

125 The question of whether Hobbes possessed a broad basis of legitimacy has been discussed in great depth in an exchange between Richard Tuck and Kinch Hoekstra on Hobbes and democracy. Tuck, drawing on remarks by Hobbes that democracy was "the first in order of time" (*EL*, 2.2.1, 118) and that "the King is the people" (*De Cive*, 12.8), made the case that Hobbes imagined at least one scenario in which the people retained sovereignty but delegated government to a monarchy. The people then could act as a "sleeping sovereign," awakening periodically to rein in the government (183, 189). Hoekstra conceded that Hobbes, having read Bodin, might have imagined a scenario in which sovereignty belonged to the people and government was entrusted to monarchical or aristocratic institutions, but he doubted that "Hobbes thought that democracy either provided or required special legitimacy" (197). Democracy was always disparaged by Hobbes as the rule of the orators, tantamount to an oligarchy (201). Hoekstra concluded by discussing several passages concerned with liberty and contentment, which seemed to be democratic but with an oddly aristocratic tinge to them (214–17). All of these points strike me as deeply Baconian, as I hope can be inferred from the previous chapter, and thus it seems to me that there need not be much disagreement between Tuck and Hoekstra. Bacon in the *Aphorismi* conceded that government could have its origin in a primitive democracy, though it need not. This did confer a "special legitimacy," but only in the sense that it led the masses to think of age-old customs as consensual. There was no sense in Bacon of the sleeping sovereign. For Bacon, democracy was flawed in all of the ways that Hoekstra detailed, and there is no doubt that Hobbes's classical studies confirmed this. Read in a Baconian light, the memory of an original democracy has no political purchase. Bacon, as I have discussed, altered Bodin's theory of sovereignty considerably, and if Hobbes followed suit, then the transference of power from democracy to monarchy was total. There was no preservation of political organization (contrary to Tuck's emphasis on representation and Suárez's view of original democracy as interpreted by Brett, *Changes of State*, 127n52). The survival would be social, in the sense of the affections—here, a sense of tradition combined with a whiff of consensus—and in a continuing concern for contentment. Tuck, "Hobbes and Democracy"; Hoekstra, "Lion in the House."

the commonwealth and the servants of the patrimonial body politic thus echoed closely Bacon's analysis (and Cavendish's summary of it, quoted at the close of the previous chapter):

> The subjection of them who institute a commonwealth amongst themselves, is no less absolute, than the subjection of servants. And therein they are in equal estate; but the hope of those is greater than the hope of these. For he that subjecteth himself uncompelled, thinketh there is reason he should be better used, than he that doth it upon compulsion; and coming in freely, calleth himself, though in subjection, a FREE-MAN; whereby it appeareth, that liberty is not any exemption from subjection and obedience to the sovereign power, but a state of better hope than theirs, that have been subjected by force and conquest. . . . Freedom therefore in commonwealths is nothing but the honour of equality of favour with other subjects, and servitude the estate of the rest. A freeman therefore may expect employments of honour, rather than a servant. And this is all that can be understood by the liberty of the subject.[126]

As Bacon and Cavendish (almost certainly with the assistance of Hobbes) had written, the principle of monarchy was service to the sovereign. Here, this has been adapted to all commonwealths by institution, though a comparison with democracy later suggested that Hobbes was thinking here of monarchy.[127] Liberty of the subject meant the reasonable hope of advancement and the satisfaction of having one's ambitions satisfied and desires for honor recognized. As in Bacon, hope and fear must be used to manage sedition and the various claims to have ambition satisfied.[128] This careful attention to the needs and affections of the people, as I have mentioned over and over again, was the role of the state.

THE STATE

In thinking about state policy, Hobbes adopted many of the conclusions that followed from the Caroline analysis of "popularity," including the Laudian emphasis on the old commonwealth measures and Charles's embrace of exemplary punishment. The "wealth of people," Hobbes wrote, consisted in "the well ordering of trade, procuring of labour, and forbidding the

126 Hobbes, *EL*, 2.4, 134.
127 Ibid., 2.8.3, 170.
128 Ibid., 2.8, 170.

superfluous consuming of food and apparel."[129] These were the commonwealth measures since the time of Edward VI: the merchandising, labor,
and sumptuary laws. Yet the Caroline vision had its own peculiar emphases.
It tended to idealize the countryside (and to think of the problems of the
commonwealth in agricultural terms), and Hobbes's discussion of the importance of private property reflected this emphasis. In the usual accounts of
commonwealth, this was treated more generally as the capacity of everyone
to make a living through their vocation. Hobbes made it a more restricted
problem of land ownership (implicitly in opposition to the consolidation of
the enclosing class).[130] Like Charles, Hobbes embraced exemplary punishment as a means of social control. Hobbes recommended that the government "ordain severe punishments, for such as shall by reprehension of public
actions, affect popularity and applause amongst the multitude, by which they
may be enabled to have a faction in the commonwealth at their devotion."[131]

Still, Hobbes did not sign on completely to "the paternalistic language
of Caroline social policy."[132] His approach might be called "paternalistic"
in that he shared the old view that sinfulness was at the root of social dis-
ruption and oppression, and he did not take a modernizing approach to
economic problems in the vein of Sir Thomas Gresham or Smith under
Elizabeth. Nevertheless, Hobbes's approach was decidedly not patriarchal
and, as I show in the next section, he showed no sign in the *Elements* (or elsewhere) of sharing the hierarchical approach to the commonwealth of Laud.
His approach was closer to that taken by Wentworth in the late 1620s, which
tried to overcome the rhetoric of the divide between court and country by
describing office holding and parliamentary work as public service on behalf of the king for the people and as the conveyance of grievances from the
people (in part about such service) to the king.[133] The state was neither the
"court" meddling with the commonwealth from above nor the traditional
magistracies of the "country" gentry; it was the service of representatives
and magistrates who executed policies and provided information for the improvement of the commonwealth locally and throughout Britain.

In his framing of office holding and authority in terms of sovereignty
and conscience, rather than in Wentworth's language of service, Hobbes
provided an alternative way of understanding this give-and-take between
center and province. Like Wentworth, Hobbes was not endorsing a program
of professionalization; he rather imagined that offices would continue to be

---

129   Ibid., 2.9.4, 180.
130   Ibid., 2.9.4–5, 180–1.
131   Ibid., 2.9.7, 183; Hindle, *State and Social Change*, 76.
132   Hindle, *State and Social Change*, 75.
133   Cust, "Wentworth's 'Change of Sides' in the 1620s," 67.

held by private men of the ordinary variety, subject to the usual failings of corruption. But Hobbes emphasized the importance of coercion of the magistrates as well as the populace. The magistrates, sheriffs, and constables would provide the threat of coercion necessary to maintain order among the populace, since in Hobbes's view, men's individual consciences could scarcely be trusted in its absence. But these officials themselves needed to be subject to the threat of coercion.[134] For Hobbes, the center provided the localities with the assurance that wayward officials would be punished, and thus the threat of punishment, the *malum poenae*, would make it possible for the officials to overcome their passions and act on their consciences. Significantly, officials were to be threatened from above *and* below.

> It is therefore necessary, that there be a power extraordinary, as there shall be occasion from time to time, for the syndication of judges and other magistrates, that shall abuse their authority, to the wrong and discontent of the people; and a free and open way for the presenting of grievances to him or them that have the sovereign authority.[135]

When considering the threat from above, Hobbes probably had in mind not so much the method of summoning the magistrates for disciplining to the Privy Council, which had been used extensively in the period of the forced loan and which was both effective and feared, but the method of "syndication," or review of magistrates, which was a regular practice in Italy and with which Hobbes would no doubt have been familiar from his travels there in 1614–15. The practice was also mentioned in Contarini's *Commonwealth of Venice*, which could be found in the library at Hardwick Hall.[136] And, at least in Lewkenor's 1599 translation, the Protestant understanding for the need of such review echoed clearly: "For as Aristotle wisely sayeth: They that beare rule, unlesse they depend of others, doe (such is the evill sway and bent of everie mans nature) hardly discharge their office well."[137]

·When considering the threat from below, Hobbes may have been thinking of a couple of processes. In England, the Privy Council could be petitioned directly with grievances about the conduct of officials. Suits could also be brought in the Star Chamber. Both of these methods were used during the 1620s and 1630s, and the prosecution of the powerful had been

134 Hobbes, *EL*, 2.9.6, 182.

135 Ibid.

136 Hobbes showed his admiration for the constitution of Venice at *EL*, 2.5.7, 143, where he explained that an aristocracy like Venice's was "no more apt to dissolve from this occasion, than monarchies, the counsel of state being both in the one and the other alike." In other words, the English Privy Council and other monarchical councils of advisers were similar to the Venetian councils.

137 Contarini, *Commonvvealth and Gouernment of Venice*, 138.

an important part of Laud and Wentworth's program. Hobbes implied that he was willing to encourage such prosecutions on what was called "related information," that is, through the bringing of a suit by a private plaintiff who would share in the fines levied, rather than through suits initiated by the Crown (*pro Rege*) alone. In doing so, Hobbes was in part swimming against the tide, since the councillors had grown frustrated with the "vexatious" suits being brought, to the point that earlier in the decade Sir Thomas Coventry, the lord keeper, had banned informers from the court.[138] Hobbes was thus pushing for less of a top-down, official approach and for a more participatory state.[139]

In his account of fiscal policy, as in his account of the disciplining of officials, Hobbes showed some sensitivity to the complaints about the most hated policies and institutions of the recent past. Hobbes was for an excise tax, which had been debated in the late 1620s but was not enacted until 1643, when it was accepted by both the parliamentarians and the royalists.[140] It had been floated again in the 1630s as one of a number of proposals for more regular means for securing revenue for the Crown, but Charles, perhaps finding it too sharp a break with English tradition, failed to put it in place until the war required a simpler and more universal means of tax collection that could be levied even on one's opponents.[141] For Hobbes, the excise offered a means of taxation that was not as susceptible to the concerns over inequality in rating, which had plagued the collection of ship money.[142] "For there is nothing so aggravateth the grief of parting with money, to the public, as lands or goods to think they are over-rated, and that their neighbours whom they envy, do thereupon insult over them and this disposeth them to resistance, and (after that such resistance hath produced a mischief) to rebellion."[143]

Hobbes's views on taxation—his concerns over the unfairness of rating and the reasons given for the support of the excise—reflected the issues that were raised during the collection of ship money in the 1630s. The ship money writs instructed the sheriffs of the counties to raise a particular

138 Hindle, *State and Social Change*, 66–8, 77–8.
139 Hobbes reiterated his commitment to the importance of the grievances bubbling up from below in *Leviathan*. Hobbes, *English Works*, 3.341: "The best counsel, in those things that concern not other nations, but only the ease and benefit the subjects may enjoy, by laws that look only inward, is to be taken from the general informations, and complaints of the people of each province, who are best acquainted with their own wants, and ought therefore, when they demand nothing in derogation of the essential rights of sovereignty, to be diligently taken notice of. For without those essential rights, as I have often before said, the commonwealth cannot at all subsist."
140 Braddick, *State Formation*, 99.
141 Sharpe, *Personal Rule of Charles I*, 123.
142 For the disputes over rating inequalities, see ibid., 573–5.
143 Hobbes, *EL*, 2.9.5.

amount, which they were to apportion in accordance with the usual rates but which could be altered as they saw fit. This led, naturally, to the feeling that many were unfairly rated or overrated. In Nottinghamshire, for instance, one gentleman, Gervase Markham, complained that his rate of £50 was exceptionally high for those of his rank. The sheriff, Sir John Byron, responded that the rating was reasonable, since Markham spent far less than his peers. He spent only a tiny fraction of his income and wealth, perhaps £40 a year, the sheriff suggested, out of an income of £850 and a savings of some £40,000.[144] Hobbes clearly rejected reasoning of the sort put forward by Byron and defended the entitlement of the gentry to their wealth if spent living "according to their estates and quality," as Byron had put it. For Hobbes, "there is no reason, when two men equally enjoying, by the benefit of the commonwealth, their peace and liberty, to use their industry to get their livings, whereof one spareth, and layeth up somewhat, the other spendeth all he gets, why they should not equally contribute to the common charge."[145]

Hobbes's sympathy for a man like Markham, who saved rather than spent in keeping with his station, is one of the clues that Hobbes had a very different sort of commonwealth in mind than Laud had. Hobbes was unconcerned, to put it mildly, with traditional rank and hierarchy and, like Bacon, believed that this was not the path to stability. Hobbes spent a great deal of time thinking about social stratification in the thirty years that preceded the *Elements*. The library at Hardwick Hall was full of books on the subject of nobility, as befit the home of a nobleman, and they were cheek to jowl with works of political theory of other sorts. Hobbes likely taught various Cavendish children how to be proper noblemen from these works.[146] Moreover, the evidence from the letters is that Hobbes thought at least in broad categories of social stratification, referring on several occasions to the common or "vulgar" people.[147]

Nevertheless, he sidestepped the issue in the *Elements*. His ambiguous views may have reflected the position of people like Sir Gervase Clifton, his sometime employer and one of the leading members of the gentry in Nottinghamshire. Clifton, a close friend of Wentworth, a JP and deputy lieutenant in Nottinghamshire (under Newcastle), and a "staunch supporter of the crown," refrained from acquiring any title of nobility above that of a baronetcy, though it seems from a letter of Robert Pierrepont, the first Earl of Kingston upon Hull, that he well deserved one and could have come by

144 Dias, "Politics and Administration," 382–3.
145 Hobbes, *EL*, 2.9.5.
146 See the letter of 1638 to Charles Cavendish, the son of the second Earl of Devonshire, which drew heavily on this literature. Hobbes, *Correspondence*, letter 28, 1:52–3.
147 Hobbes, *Correspondence*, 1:30, 339.

one rather easily. This is just the sort of behavior that echoes with Hobbes's writings, and if Jill Dias was correct that "this was probably a consequence of Clifton's own modesty,"[148] then one can imagine that Hobbes must have admired such an approach, even if he had not advocated for it himself. It may have seemed to Hobbes, with such examples in mind, that despite Laud's worries that the puritans were for a dangerous leveling in English society, one could be a leading servant of the Crown without seeking rank or superiority.

More of this viewpoint and of how Hobbes's thinking diverged from that of Laud was apparent in his later work. Though the intention here is to think through Hobbes's views of the state and society until the eve of the civil war, given the brevity of *The Elements of Law*, looking ahead to Hobbes's later writings, to *Leviathan* and *Behemoth* in particular, helps to fill in some of the gaps, especially in Hobbes's institutional picture of the state and commonwealth, which was discussed in the chapter in *Leviathan* "Of the Office of the Sovereign Representative," where Hobbes explicitly rejected the older commonwealth theory that emphasized reward and punishment.

Hobbes still maintained that there were various degrees of the people, various vocations, and he referred to them in passing throughout *Leviathan*, but it was the division between the intellectual class and everyone else that came to matter for Hobbes.[149] The distinct mental worlds of the parts of the state described by Smith were no more, dissolved into what was effectively a common culture in which honor and wealth were closely related and were the objects of the ambitious man. Like for James, for Hobbes the ideas of obedience and standards of behavior had become unhooked from traditional social classes and were now firmly in the hands of the clergy. This was not due only to the ambitions of the clergy who wished to have the power and status that the bishops had, just as the gentlemen envied the power of the Privy Council,[150] but to the intellectual indifference of most people—of both the working and leisure classes—such that they "receive the notions of their duty, chiefly from divines in the pulpit, and partly from such of their neighbours or familiar acquaintance[s], as having the faculty of discoursing readily, and plausibly, seem wiser and better learned in cases of law and conscience, than themselves."[151]

The presbyterians (and here Hobbes seemed as much focused on what one would think of as the puritan reformation of manners as any view of church government) had meanwhile bought their position at the price of abandoning a broad Christian vision of interpersonal behavior, the old

148 Dias, "Politics and Administration," 363–5.
149 Hobbes, *English Works*, 3:332.
150 Ibid., 6:192–3.
151 Ibid., 3:331.

evangelical commonwealth vision. The presbyterians, Hobbes averred, "did never in their sermons, or but lightly, inveigh against the lucrative vices of men of trade or handicraft; such as are feigning, lying, cozening, hypocrisy, or other uncharitableness, except want of charity to their pastors and to the faithful: which was a great ease to the generality of citizens and the inhabitants of market-towns, and no little profit to themselves."[152] Here, Hobbes showed himself to share Laud's strategy: the commonwealth was clearly used to bait the puritans, to show up their approach as limited and hypocritical.

The presbyterian preachers concentrated, Hobbes wrote, only on purity, on preaching "against two sins, carnal lusts and vain swearing," neglecting other traditional concerns. This served their ambitions, Hobbes explained, since it allowed them to take advantage of the emotional life of the young:

> And, whereas they did, both in their sermons and writings, maintain and inculcate, that the very first motions of the mind, that is to say, the delight men and women took in the sight of one another's form, though they checked the proceeding thereof so that it never grew up to be a design, was nevertheless a sin, they brought young men into desperation and to think themselves damned, because they could not (which no man can, and is contrary to the constitution of nature) behold a delightful object without delight. And by this means they became confessors to such as were thus troubled in conscience, and were obeyed by them as their spiritual doctors in all cases of conscience.[153]

In the *Elements*, Hobbes argued that the discontentment over one's lack of power could be falsely interpreted by oneself as the dictate of conscience suggesting resistance to a lawfully constituted sovereign. The emotional manipulation in the interest of popularity that was suggested in the *Behemoth* was one step more sophisticated. Here the clergy's valuation of delight as sinful meant that they could establish themselves as essentially Protestant versions of confessors. This, for Hobbes, brought sacramentalism in by the back door and established the clergy as a power over the people. This was why a proper analysis of politics for Hobbes required an analysis of the passions, since the misinterpretation of the passions by an elite could lead to dangerous political effects, even if that were not the conscious goal.[154]

152 Ibid., 6:194–5.
153 Ibid., 6:195–6.
154 It is clear that Hobbes thought that the people often do not consciously strive for the instability that results from their actions; they are led. But this might also be the case with the envious and ambitious clergy, who perhaps should know better but are moved by their envy in ways that they might not be fully aware of: they compensate for their weak position in the commonwealth, for instance, by misinterpreting the passions as sin in order to exert more influence on others.

Hobbes, however, had no wish to turn to a political nobility created along the lines implemented in a haphazard fashion by James and in a more controlled way by Charles. He agreed with Bacon (against Laud) that such a system of honors, where ambitious men were meant to be honored and controlled, was no way to create stability. In discussing rewards and punishments, the two levers that the commonwealth theorists all thought through, Hobbes once more resorted to the analysis of popularity. The people were not to be punished, since they had been manipulated by their leaders into wrongdoing. The leaders themselves needed to be treated very carefully. Even "sons, servants, or favourites of men in authority" needed to be punished; they posed a special risk to the stability of the state, since men tended to lash out "against all power that is likely to protect them."[155] Hobbes seems to have been thinking especially of Strafford here, as he also was when he turned to the discussion of rewards. "To buy with money, or preferment, from a popular ambitious subject, to be quiet, and desist from making ill impressions in the minds of the people, has nothing of the nature of reward," he warned.[156] The trouble with this method was that it would only lead to the proliferation of ambitious popular men who saw that there was a reward to be gained by showing signs of ambition and popularity.[157] Hobbes noted that he had "observed often" the truth "that those princes that with preferment are forced to buy the obedience of their subjects, are already, or must be soon after, in a very weak condition. For in a market where honour and power is to be bought with stubbornness, there will be a great many as able to buy as my Lord Strafford was."[158]

What true service and true reward consisted of was a bit murky in the *Leviathan*, but if his thinking there was in line with that of the *Elements* then he was probably continuing to view them as something like a Reformed version of the mentality of the more active lords lieutenant.[159] Indeed, Hobbes seems to have continued to think that the leading citizenry—now with a more thoroughly theorized definition of those educated at a university in the proper principles of ethics and politics—should serve as what

155 Hobbes, *English Works*, 3:337.

156 Ibid., 3:338.

157 Ibid.

158 Ibid., 6:254. Hobbes had a mixed view of Strafford (perhaps shared with Newcastle). He seems to have believed that Strafford was too ambitious and had pushed the people too far. Nevertheless, he believed that the charges of treason were unsupportable and suggested that the people punished Strafford in part as revenge "for deserting the Parliament's party as an apostate." There is no reason to believe that Hobbes thought of the notion of public service as particularly identified with Strafford nor that Strafford was an exemplary adherent of it. Ibid., 6:247, 249.

159 Hobbes, *EL*, 2.7.4, 161. Hobbes invoked the divine plan of government in the Old Testament in terms that echoed the duties of the lieutenancy. The chieftains of the twelve tribes, he wrote, "were to assist him in the muster of Israel."

Clive Holmes has called "brokers" to the sovereign.[160] Though Hobbes was really quite insistent in his denial of the use of hereditary nobility, he was as equally insistent that there would be some sort of intellectual leadership class that would guide and govern the people who are busy with their economic concerns. There was no reason to believe that men who had the ability to earn money (and thus put themselves in the position to purchase titles) were any better at governing. Governing for Hobbes required knowledge of the science of government.[161] Hobbes may well have thought that much of their service continued to consist of presenting grievances to the national government, as was suggested by his repetition of the idea that grievances must be brought from below.

This view of the state, which was acceptable doctrine among supporters of the prerogative in the 1630s, must have sounded dangerously "parliamentarian" to the more conservative royalists of the exiled court in the 1650s. Hyde had his misgivings early on, and the Laudians had Hobbes made a persona non grata at the court in exile.[162] More to the point, Newcastle seems to have abandoned the nuances of the view of 1640 (only elaborated in print since then). In a letter of advice to Charles II in 1658–9, Newcastle skipped back to the hierarchical analysis of Laud and Hooker, popular at the end of Elizabeth's reign and the beginning of James's. The monarch ought to rely on great men to govern and need not worry about this causing instability, "for the people doth not envey great men as they doe meaner men, and then all their kindred, friends, dependance, servants, tenantes are well pleased and your Majestie safe."[163]

CONCLUSION

With the ability of people to swap out various moralized interpretations of their passions seemingly at will, Hobbes gave up on the old understanding of the social world as composed of certain sorts of people with distinct world views keyed to their positions in life. This accompanied his interpretation of how to evaluate the justice of the state. The justice of the state had been understood in terms of its distribution of goods to the various sorts of people

---

160 Holmes, "Charles I and the Aristocracy"; Holmes, "Charles I: A Case of Mistaken Identity," 180–1.

161 Hobbes, *English Works*, 3:339–40.

162 Dzelzainis, "Edward Hyde."

163 Cust, *Charles I and the Aristocracy*, 64. My interpretation of Newcastle differs considerably from Cust's here. Cust saw this later statement of Newcastle as a reflection of his settled view from the 1630s on; I see it as more of a conservative retreat. It may well be that already in 1640 Hobbes was out ahead slightly of where Newcastle wanted to be and that this became increasingly clear (or less comfortable in public) over time.

in the commonwealth (which in the more subtle versions of the theory varied in accordance with the various sorts' own interpretations of benefit and good). For Hobbes, this was a completely mistaken approach, since it could lead to attempts to interpret the justice of the state and could thus destabilize the state. But this was not really his concern; he thought after all that most men were lazily indifferent and shared a similar outlook. The trouble was not plural versions of the good, but the idea that the justice of the state consisted in distributions according to *any* view of the state. Justice was not a question of distribution but of securing the conditions for conscience to operate, which is to say controlling the conditions that allowed antisocial passions to spin out of control, begging for dangerous moralized interpretations. The business of the state was simply to provide for the life of the individual, and taxes were to be paid for this purpose. The securing of life was not so much a distributive benefit, however, according to Hobbes, but rather the creation of a structure in which people could sort out for themselves what benefiting one another might mean.

How then was moral regeneration possible for Hobbes? It was likely due to ensuring that the state was consistent with the aims of conscience, due to friendship, and due to a framework wherein one could aim to help another without being tormented if it did not quite work. One need not fear excommunication of the sort that was possible in the Old Testament (or in Geneva). Mistakes would be recoverable through repentance and growth. Yet this liberty would not be anarchy nor bring out the worst in men because the penal laws would keep external behavior in check. The union was thus meant to be more subtly human, more alive to error and mistake, and to create a framework—as in the redress of grievances—that made the whole thing possible. Hobbes was not saying to abandon commonwealth, to abandon the sphere of charity and neighborliness, but to embed it within the framework of the state.

CONCLUSION: THE LEGACY
OF COMMONWEALTH

At the heart of the commonwealth theory of state and society was the notion that distributive justice was the basis of peace and mutuality, and at the heart of this view was the idea that the public good could only be achieved by paying attention to the needs and wants of the private individual. The failures of a system of government that was based in large part on the voluntary cooperation of the local gentry and the middling sorts to deliver on this promise led to a genuinely political confrontation of high principles and low recriminations. As Hobbes later complained in the *Behemoth*, this was a misunderstanding of the nature of political obligation. The civil war could have been avoided and the government made effective if the various appeals to justice (and perhaps more damaging, the elaborate moralizations that were superimposed on them) were stopped, and if all the degrees of the people, in their various capacities, submitted themselves to a framework of penal law. The commonwealth could be saved by coming to understand that the incentives for conformity with the law needed to be grounded on mutual fear rather than on the pursuit of honor, and it was only through this shift that truly free and uncoerced relationships, a true commonwealth, could be achieved.

In the event, the various grounds for obedience offered in the civil war years by the king and Parliament seemed incommensurate and utterly confusing to many. The muddle was perhaps best expressed in a petition for neutrality addressed to the king by the quarter sessions in Devon in 1642:

> The lamentable Distractions and Convulsions, whereby each member is drawn from the other, and each loyal Heart rent within itself, makes us fly to Your Majesty as a Physician to cure us, and Fall at Your Feet as a Compassionate Father to relieve us; being confident that Your Majesty owns as well a Will as an Ability to help. The Debt we owe, commands to acknowledge, in the highest Pitch of Thankfulness which either Love or Duty can present, Our Obligation to Your Majesty, for passing so many good Laws, for Your and Your Kingdom's Benefit; and yet the unhappy Differences between Your Majesty and Both Houses

of Parliament have, to our unexpressible Grief, bereaved us of the Fruit which we were ready to reap, and left us nothing but Complaints, Tears and Prayers, to feed on. Your Majesty commands our Obedience to the Commissions of Array; whilst both Houses of Parliament adjudgeth us Betrayers of our Liberty and Property if we do so.[1]

At the center of the petition was the old logic of obligation; it was the "Debt we owe" that ought to yield a "Thankfulness" and thus obedience to the king. But Parliament was speaking a different language of liberty and property, and, faced with these two different claims, the quarter sessions in Devon sought eagerly for a more unitary sovereignty, for a "Unity of King and Parliament."[2] The parliamentary side eventually shifted ground. Writing during the engagement controversy, over whether one was bound in conscience by oaths of allegiance taken to the king, the leading parliamentary propagandist, Marchamont Nedham, urged a "de factoism," and he argued on the basis of the right to conquest that one was obligated to obey whoever was in power.[3] Commonwealth had come to mean in the Interregnum something quite different than it had before: a political community taking its direction from a unitary parliamentary sovereign.[4]

By the eve of the Restoration, posing the question of government as one of sovereignty or control had clearly run its course. The discussions surrounding the reform of the commonwealth, such as Harrington's *Oceana* (1656) and the debates at the Rota Club in London (1659–60), turned back to the sort of reflection on the structuring of society that had preoccupied Burghley and Smith a hundred years earlier. Though Harrington used many of the old sources, including Giannotti on Venice and Sigonio on Rome, his analyses had a naive, utopian flavor.[5] The whole debate in these years paled in comparison to the intellectual richness of the first time around. This was not unnoticed by contemporaries. Matthew Wren was dumbfounded by Harrington's approach to reconciling the individual and the common interest—that one part of the legislative body should divide and the other choose—which, he remarked, was "so facile, that it is obvious to such as have the Green sicknesse."[6]

---

1 Morrill, *Revolt of the Provinces*, 162.

2 Ibid., 163.

3 Nedham, *Case of the Common-Wealth of England*, 16–17.

4 This was of course contested, but it was at least Nedham's "main message" in 1650–1. Woolrych, *Commonwealth to Protectorate*, 35: "Nedham's main message during late November and early December was that the Commonwealth needed no other safeguards against tyranny, corruption, or a return to kingship than successive parliaments, elected by the people at regular intervals."

5 Harrington, *Political Works*, 245.

6 Wren, *Considerations*, 20–2.

The return to "squirearchy" at the Restoration surprisingly did not entail a return to a full-blooded rethinking of the nature of commonwealth.[7] The reason for this may have been, oddly enough, its success. The tensions of the earlier period, the functional breakdown that had caused the Privy Council to intervene in the provinces and that had encouraged Bacon and Hobbes to theorize the need for increased oversight and punishment, had begun to fade away. "Many aspects of social order had been protected by spectacular intervention, or calls for it, in the period before 1640, but in the later period these fears were met through routine, institutionalised and self-activating local means."[8] Local government was now routinized; the sorts of activity that had been thought to require close supervision and the threat of punishment from Hales and Bucer to Bacon and Hobbes were now done routinely through the "force of habit" and at the request of the people themselves. The effect of this seems to have been an institutionalization of government in the localities, accompanied by an "elite withdrawal from the active magistracy."[9]

The vision of the state as embedded in or identified with commonwealth hung on in the eighteenth and nineteenth centuries as a mere shadow of itself. While some of the departments of the government became bureaucratic, most notably the excise and the navy, much of the government and even those departments in spots were riddled with patronage and sinecurists. Sinecures were defended in the eighteenth century in language reminiscent of the old theory, where office was seen as a reward for service.[10] The differentiated view of distributive justice, however, on which the theory rested was largely at an end; patronage now "had to be exercised with an eye to administrative effectiveness."[11]

But commonwealth thinking was not quite over. The turn to class politics in the late nineteenth century and early twentieth meant a more genuine return to the sorts of politics imagined in the commonwealth vision, which of course stimulated the modern study of the commonwealth theorists by Tawney. Modern class politics was on its face quite different from the cooperative vision of commonwealth; it tended to treat the classes as opposing interest groups or hostile factions in a fashion more reminiscent of the republican analysis of politics. Moreover, it seemed that class politics was about material well-being, while the commonwealth analysis was as concerned with questions of status and esteem as with material contentment. Nevertheless, there were voices more redolent of commonwealth themes on both the Right and

7 Braddick, *State Formation*, 166.
8 Ibid., 166.
9 Ibid., 166–71.
10 Aylmer, "From Office-Holding to Civil Service," 105–7.
11 Braddick, *State Formation*, 171.

the Left in the twentieth century. The policies and outlook of the Conservative government and its middle-class supporters after the First World War, for instance, echoed the position of the commonwealth men and councillors of Edward's reign. Alarmed by both manufacturing plutocrats and "sectionalist" working classes, Conservatives sought a deflationary economic policy and espoused a view of free and fair competition where the average man could earn his keep. There were certainly still differences; the "neo-Darwinian individualism" of the 1920s was a far cry from the vision of the cooperative pursuit of vocation under the Tudors, where labor market policies were meant to ensure that a man who followed his vocation would be able to earn a sufficient living and be esteemed for his contribution to the commonwealth in doing so.[12] While the institutional arrangements differed considerably, the echoes of the ideal of commonwealth in the postwar welfare state were remarkable.[13]

These echoes resounded clearly in T. H. Marshall's famous characterization of the postwar welfare state in England, *Citizenship and Social Class*. Marshall argued that material well-being could once more be a question of citizenship; real wages had been compressed to the point where common living standards now could be a basis for a sense of community and shared citizenship, rather than idealizing community and reserving citizenship for a "sphere of sentiment and patriotism."[14] In Marshall's view, what characterized the welfare state was the sense of solidarity in a citizenship that at once expected a "universal right to real income" and delivered hard work in return. The aim of the welfare state, he explained, was to achieve social order and stability, and it was for this reason that there were so many "apparent inconsistencies" in the actual policies, some of which were means tested and some of which were not; some were solidaristic while others were selective. The goal was to be a "unified civilization which makes social inequalities acceptable, and threatens to make them economically functionless."[15]

---

12 For the quoted terms and the ideology of the Conservative Party and its followers, see McKibbin, *Ideologies of Class*, 265–73.

13 This was an obvious motivation and concern of the modern scholars of commonwealth, but they had very different views of the lessons to be learned. Jones concluded his study: "Diversity of national and sectional interests . . . leads to variant interpretations of mercantilism and laissez-faire. But these, in turn, are succeeded by the revival of many Commonwealth ideals, reshaped by a very different political, social and religious background, in the philosophies of collectivism and the Welfare State in the nineteenth and twentieth centuries." Jones, *Tudor Commonwealth*, 227. Elton, having paid close attention to the legislative process and the various amendments that qualified the initial bills, concluded on a very different note: "The dreams of 'social engineering' turned out, as usual, to be only dreams; which, in view of some of the things proposed, was just as well, for carried into effect they might easily have become nightmares." Elton, *Reform and Renewal*, 158.

14 Marshall, *Citizenship and Social Class*, 47.

15 Ibid., 81.

Though of course there were many differences, the similarities with the commonwealth ideal, especially in Thomas Smith's version, are remarkable. They shared the ideal of social order, of class harmony, and hoped to achieve it through the careful satisfaction of the needs for recognition and material well-being of the various classes. The welfare state attempted this by addressing status through "symbolic" wage differentials while the commonwealth state approached it through differential office holding, but both aimed to address individual ambition and status seeking in a way that did not threaten social harmony. The psychological basis was similarly differentiated; the upper classes seeking social distinction were allowed that honor, while the lower classes were assured material contentment and the promise of social mobility. The basis for mutuality was, admittedly, different. Class harmony was possible in the welfare state since the symbolic wage differentials were "economically functionless," that is, everyone shared the same real income and were at some level aware of this, while in the commonwealth ideal, mutuality was made possible by the sense that everyone was doing his part in an organic division of labor, which had been harmonized by the state and to which each individual had been called. Perhaps the key difference was that the state in the narrower sense—the realm of officialdom—had receded into a technical function in the welfare state, whereas it played a central role in the commonwealth. That the commonwealth still echoed soundly, despite this relegation of the state to the margins, confirms that the state in this narrower sense was always meant to be part of the commonwealth rather than above it.

BIBLIOGRAPHY

MANUSCRIPT SOURCES

Bodleian Library
    MS Autogr. E. 2
British Library
    Add. 4724
    Arundel MS 510
    Royal MS 12 G
    Sloane MS 1982
Cecil Papers
Chatsworth House, Derbyshire

PRIMARY SOURCES

Acciaioli, Donato. *In Aristotelis Libros Octo Politicorum Commentarii.* Venice, 1566.
Aristotle. *Aristotelis de Rhetorica Seu Arte Dicendi Libri Tres.* Translated by Theodore Goulston. London, 1619.
———. *The Complete Works of Aristotle: The Revised Oxford Translation.* Edited by Jonathan Barnes. Princeton, NJ: Princeton University Press, 1984.
Aylmer, John. *An Harborowe for Faithfull and Trewe Subjectes agaynst the Late Blowne Blaste, Concerninge the Gouernment of Wemen.* London, 1559.
Azo, Portius. *Summa Aurea.* 1557. Frankfurt: Minerva, 1968.
Azor, Juan. *Institutionum Moralium.* Lyon, 1625.
Bacon, Francis. *The Advancement of Learning.* Edited by Michael Kiernan. Oxford: Clarendon, 2000.
———. *Complete Essays.* New York: Dover, 2008.
———. *The Essayes or Counsels, Civill and Morall.* Edited by Michael Kiernan. Cambridge, MA: Harvard University Press, 1985.
———. *The Historie of the Raigne of King Henry the Seventh and Other Works of the 1620s.* Edited by Michael Kiernan. Oxford: Oxford University Press, 2012.
———. *The History of the Reign of King Henry the Seventh.* Edited by Jerry Weinberger. Ithaca, NY: Cornell University Press, 1996.
———. *The Letters and the Life of Francis Bacon.* Edited by James Spedding. 7 vols. London: Longman, 1861.

————. *Works.* Edited by James Spedding, R. L. Ellis, and D. D. Heath. 7 vols. London: Longman, 1857.

————. *The Works of Francis Bacon.* London: Longmans, Green, Reader, and Dyer, 1858.

Bacon, Sir Nicholas. *Sir Nicholas Bacon's Great House Sententiae.* Edited by Elizabeth McCutcheon. Honolulu: University of Hawaii, 1977.

Becon, Richard. *Solon His Follie; or, A Politique Discourse Touching the Reformation of Common-Weales Conquered, Declined or Corrupted.* Binghamton, NY: Medieval and Renaissance Texts and Studies, 1996.

Beza, Theodore. "De Iure Magistratuum in Subditos, et Officio Subditorum erga Magistratus." In *Vindiciae Contra Tyrannos: Sive, De Principis in Populum, Populique in Principem, Legitima Potestate.* Basel, 1580.

————. *Iesv Christi D. N. Nouum Testamentum, Siue Nouum Foedus.* Geneva, 1565.

————. *Novum Iesu Christi Domini Nostri Testamentum Latine Iam Olim a Veteri Interprete Nunc Denuo à Theodoro Beza Uersum: Cum Eiusdem Annotationibus, in Quibus Ratio Interpretationis Redditur.* Zürich, 1559.

The Bible, That Is, the Holy Scriptures Contained in the Old and New Testament. Translated by Laurence Tomson. Edinburgh, 1610.

Bodin, Jean. *Bodin: On Sovereignty.* Cambridge: Cambridge University Press, 1992.

————. *Method for the Easy Comprehension of History.* Edited by Beatrice Reynolds. New York: Norton, 1969.

————. *Methodus ad Facilem Historiarum Cognitionem.* Lyon, 1591.

Borrhaus, Martin. *In Aristotelis Politicorum, Sive de Republica Libros Octo, Martini Borrhai Annotationes.* Basel, 1545.

Brenz, Johannes. *De Administranda Pie Republica.* Hagenau, 1527.

Bucer, Martin. *De Regno Christi Duo 1550.* Edited by François Wendel. In *Opera Latina.* Vol. 15. Gütersloh: Presses Universitaires de France and C. Bertelsmann, 1955.

————. *Dialogi.* Augsburg, 1535.

————. *Metaphrasis et Enarratio in Epist. D. Pauli Apostoli ad Romanos.* Basel, 1562.

————. *Zum Ius Reformationis.* In *Deutsche Schriften.* Edited by Robert Stupperich. Gütersloh: G. Mohn, 1984.

Buchanan, George. *The History of Scotland.* Edited by James Aikman. 4 vols. Glasgow: Blackie, Fullarton, 1827.

————. *Opera Omnia.* Edited by Thomas Ruddimann. 2 vols. Leiden, 1725.

Bullinger, Heinrich. *A Most Necessary and Frutefull Dialogue, betwene [the] Seditious Libertin or Rebel Anabaptist, and the True Obedient Christia[n].* Translated by John Véron. Worcester, England, 1551.

Burgersdijck, Franco. *Idea Philosophia Moralis.* Oxford, 1631.

Calvin, John. *Commentaries on the Catholic Epistles.* Translated by Rev. John Owen. Edinburgh: Calvin Translation Society, 1855.

Case, John. *Reflexus Speculi Moralis Qui Commentarii Vice Esse Poterit in Magna Moralia Aristotelis.* Oxford, 1596.

————. *Speculum Moralium Quaestionum in Vniversam Ethicen Aristotelis, Authore Magistro Iohanne Caso Oxoniensi, Olim Collegij Diui Iohannis Praecursoris Socio.* Oxford, 1585.

———. "Sphaera Civitatis." Translated by Dana Sutton. *Philological Museum* (March 13, 2002). http://www.philological.bham.ac.uk/sphaera/.

———. *Sphaera Civitatis, Authore Magistro Iohanne Caso Oxoniensi, Olim Collegii Diui Iohannis Praecursoris Socio.* Oxford, 1588.

———. *Thesaurus Oeconomiae, Seu Commentarius in Oeconomica Aristotelis.* Oxford, 1597.

Catonis Disticha Moralia. Translated by Richard Taverner. London, 1562.

[Cecil, William, Baron Burghley]. *The Execution of Justice in England.* London, 1583.

Cheke, John. *The Hurt of Sedicion: Howe Greueous It Is to a Commune Welth.* London, 1549.

———. *The True Subiect to the Rebell; or, The Hurt of Sedition, How Greivous It Is to a Common-Wealth.* Edited by Gerard Langbaine. Oxford, 1641.

Chrysostom, John. "In Epistulam ad Romanos." In *Patrologiae Cursus Completus (Series Graeca)*, 60:391–682. Paris: Migne, 1857.

Cicero, Marcus Tullius. *Ad Marcum Filium de Officiis, Libri Tres.* Edited by Sixt Birck, Desiderius Erasmus, Francesco Maturanzio, and Veit Amberbach. Paris, 1562.

———. *De Officiis, Libri III.* Edited by Desiderius Erasmus, Celio Calcagnini, Philipp Melanchthon, Veit Amberbach, and Francesco Maturanzio. Lyon, 1556.

———. *On Duties.* Translated by Walter Miller. Cambridge,MA: Harvard University Press, 1954.

———. *Tusculan Disputations.* Rev. ed. Cambridge, MA: Harvard University Press, 1945.

Contarini, Gasparo. *The Commonvvealth and Gouernment of Venice.* Translated by Lewis Lewkenor. London, 1599.

Crowley, Robert. *The Select Works of Robert Crowley.* London: Early English Text Society, 1872.

Daneau, Lambert. *Ethices Christianae.* Geneva, 1577.

———. *Tractatus Duo . . . de Amicitia Christiana.* Geneva, 1579.

Elyot, Thomas. *The Boke Named the Gouernour.* London, 1537.

Erasmus, Desiderius. *Collected Works of Erasmus.* Toronto: University of Toronto Press, 1974.

———. *Omnia Opera.* Basel, 1540.

Foxe, John. *Fox's Book of Martyrs: The Acts and Monuments of the Church.* Edited by John Cumming. 3 vols. London: George Virtue, 1844.

Freig, Johannes Thomas. *Quaestiones Oeconomicae et Politicae.* Basel, 1578.

The Geneva Bible. Geneva, 1560.

Gentillet, Innocent. *A Discourse Vpon the Meanes of Vvel Governing and Maintaining in Good Peace, a Kingdome, or Other Principalitie . . . Against Nicholas Machiavell the Florentine.* London: Printed by Adam Islip, 1602.

Hall, Joseph. *Characters of Vertues and Vices: In Two Bookes.* London, 1608.

Harrison, William. "An Historical Description of the Iland of Britaine." In *The First (Laste) Volume of the Chronicles of England, Scotlande, and Irelande* by Raphael Holinshed. London, 1577.

———. *The Description of England.* Edited by Georges Edelen. Ithaca, NY: Published for the Folger Shakespeare Library by Cornell University Press, 1968.

Hobbes, Thomas. *The Correspondence*, vol. 1: *1622–1659*. Edited by Noel Malcolm. Oxford: Clarendon, 1994.

———. *The Elements of Law, Natural and Politic*. 2nd ed. Edited by Ferdinand Tönnies. New York: Barnes and Noble, 1969.

———. *The English Works of Thomas Hobbes of Malmesbury*. Edited by William Molesworth. 11 vols. London: J. Bohn, 1839.

———. *Three Discourses: A Critical Modern Edition of Newly Identified Work of the Young Hobbes*. Edited by N. B. Reynolds and A. W. Saxonhouse. Chicago: University of Chicago Press, 1995.

Hooper, John. "A Declaration of the Ten Holy Commandments of Almighty God." In *Early Writings of John Hooper*, edited by Samuel Carr, 249–430. Cambridge: Cambridge University Press, 1843.

Humphrey, Laurence. *The Nobles; or, Of Nobilitye*. London, 1563.

James VI and I. *Political Writings*. Edited by Johann P. Sommerville. Cambridge: Cambridge University Press, 1994.

Keckermann, Bartholomaeus. *Systema Ethicae*. London, 1607.

Lamond, Elizabeth, ed. *A Discourse of the Common Weal of This Realm*. Cambridge: Cambridge University Press, 1893.

Latimer, Hugh. *The Works of Hugh Latimer*. Edited by George Elwes Corrie. 2 vols. Cambridge, England: Printed at the University Press, 1844.

Magirus, Johann. *Corona Virtutum Moralium*. Frankfurt, 1601.

Manuzio, Paolo. *In M. Tullii Ciceronis Orationum*, vol. 3: *Paulli Manutii Commentarius*. Venice, 1578.

Maynwaring, Roger. *Religion and Alegiance in Tvvo Sermons Preached before the Kings Maiestie*. London, 1627.

Melanchthon, Philipp. *Catechesis Puerilis*. Leipzig, 1547.

———. *Christianis, an Liceat Litigare in Iuditio*. Hagenau, 1529.

———. *Collatio Actionum Forensium Atticarum and Romanarum Praecipuarum*. Wittenberg, 1546.

———. *Moralis Philosophiae Epitome*. Leipzig, 1539.

———. *Opera Quae Supersunt Omnia*. Edited by Karl Gottlieb Bretschneider and Heinrich Ernst Bindseil. 28 vols. Halle: Schwetschke, 1834–1860.

Milles, Thomas. *The Catalogue of Honor*. London, 1610.

More, Thomas. *Utopia: Latin Text and English Translation*. Cambridge: Cambridge University Press, 1995.

Musculus, Wolfgang. *Loci Communes Sacr[a]e Theologiae: Iam Recens Recogniti and Emendati*. Basel, 1563.

Nedham, Marchamont. *The Case of the Common-Wealth of England, Stated*. London, 1650.

The New Testament of Our Lord and Saviour Jesus Christ: A Facsimile Reprint of the Celebrated Genevan Testament, M.D. LVII. London: S. Bagster, 1836.

The New Testament of Our Lord Jesus Christ Translated out of Greeke by Theod. Beza. Translated by Laurence Tomson. London, 1576.

Oldendorp, Johann. *Actionum Iuris Ciuilis Loci Communes, ad Vsum Forensem Secundum Aequissimas Legislatorum Sententias Bona Fide Accomodati: Item, de Formula Libelli per Quem Editur Actio, Adiectis Exemplis*. Cologne, 1539.

Osório, Jerónimo. *De Gloria Libri Quinque: De Nobilitate Civili et Christiana Libri Totidem*. Basel, 1584.

———. *An Epistle of the Reuerend Father in God Hieronymus Osorius Bishop of Arcoburge in Portugale, to the Most Excellent Princesse Elizabeth by the Grace of God Quene of England, Fraunce, and Ireland, &c.* Translated by Richard Shacklock. Antwerp, 1565.

———. *The Fiue Bookes of the Famous, Learned, and Eloquent Man, Hieronimus Osorius, Contayninge a Discourse of Ciuill, and Christian Nobilitie*. London, 1576.

Paget, William. *Letters of William, Lord Paget of Beaudesert 1547–1563*. Edited by Barrett L. Beer and S. M. Jack. London: Camden Society, 1974.

Pareus, David. *Davidis Parei in Divinam ad Romanos S. Pauli Apostoli Epistolam Commentarius*. Geneva, 1617.

Piccolomini, Francesco. *Vniuersa Philosophia de Moribus*. Venice, 1594.

Plato. *Omnia Diuini Platonis Opera*. Translated by Marsilio Ficino. Lyon, 1548.

Ponet, John. *A Shorte Treatise of Politike Power and of the True Obedience*. Strasbourg, 1556.

Rainolds, John. Marginalia in *Aristotelous Technēs Rhētorikēs, Biblia Tria. Aristotelis de Arte Dicendi, Libri Tres*. Paris, 1562. Auct. S 2.29, Bodleian.

Romei, Annibale, and John Kepers. *The Courtiers Academie*. London, 1598.

Rushworth, John. *Historical Collections of Private Passages of State, Weighty Matters in Law, Remarkable Proceedings in Five Parliaments*. London, 1721.

Saravia, Adrien. *De Diuersis Ministrorum Euangelii Gradibus*. London, 1590.

———. *De Imperandi Authoritate et Christiana Obedientia*. London, 1593.

———. *A Treatise on the Different Degrees of the Christian Priesthood*. Oxford: John Henry Parker, 1840.

Selden, John. *De Iure Naturali and Gentium, Iuxta Disciplinam Ebræorum*. London, 1640.

Sharpe, Kevin. "The Earl of Arundel, His Circle and the Opposition to the Duke of Buckingham, 1618–1628." In *Faction and Parliament: Essays on Early Stuart History*, edited by Kevin Sharpe, 209–44. Oxford: Clarendon, 1978.

Sigonio, Carlo. *De Antiquo Iure Civium Romanorum, Libri Duo: Eiusdem de Antiquo Iure Italiae Libri Tres*. 1560; 2nd ed., 1563; rpt., Paris, 1573.

Smith, Thomas. *De Republica Anglorum*. Edited by Mary Dewar. Cambridge: Cambridge University Press, 2009.

———. *A Discourse of the Commonweal of This Realm of England*. Edited by Mary Dewar. Charlottesville: Published for the Folger Shakespeare Library by the University Press of Virginia, 1969.

Spottiswood, John. *The History of the Church of Scotland*. London, 1668.

Starkey, Thomas. *A Dialogue between Reginald Pole and Thomas Lupset*. Edited by Kathleen Burton. London: Chatto and Windus, 1948.

———. *A Dialogue between Pole and Lupset*. Edited by T. F. Mayer. London: Offices of the Royal Historical Society, University College London, 1989.

———. *England in the Reign of King Henry the Eighth . . . : A Dialogue between Cardinal Pole and Thomas Lupset, Lecturer in Rhetoric at Oxford*. Edited by J. Meadows Cowper and Sidney J. H. Herrtage. London: Published for the Early English Text Society by N. Trübner, 1871.

Suárez, Francisco. *Tractatus de Legibus ac Deo Legislatore: In Decem Libros Distributus.* Lyon, 1613.

———. *Tractatus de Legibus ac Deo Legislatore.* Lib. X. Mainz, 1619.

Toxites, Michael. *Aristotelis Politicorum Liber Primus, Graece et Latine, Qui Est Oeconomicus, cum Commentario Utilissimo: A Micaelo Toxite Rhaeto Laureato Poëta Confectus ex Scholis Ioannis Sturmii Matutinis.* Zürich, c. 1554.

[Tuvill, Daniel]. *The Dove and the Serpent.* London, 1614.

Tyndale, William. *The Obedience of a Christian Man.* Edited by David Daniell. London: Penguin, 2000.

Valla, Lorenzo. *On Pleasure.* Translated by Maristella de Panizza Lorch and A. Kent Hieatt. New York: Abaris, 1977.

Versor, Johannes. *Politica.* Cologne, 1492.

Vettori, Piero. *Commentarii in Octo Libros Aristotelis de Optimo Statu Civitatis.* Florence, 1576.

———. *Commentarii in Tres Libros Aristotelis de Arte Dicendi.* Florence, 1579.

———. *Petri Victorii Commentarii in X Libros Aristotelis de Moribus ad Nicomachum: Positis Ante Singulas Declarationes Graecis Verbis Auctoris: Iisdemque ad Verbum Latine Expressis.* Florence, 1548.

Whitgift, John. *The Works of John Whitgift.* Edited by John Ayre. 3 vols. Cambridge: Cambridge University Press, 1851.

Wren, Matthew. *Considerations on Mr. Harrington's Common-Wealth of Oceana: Restrained to the First Part of the Preliminaries.* London: Printed for Samuel Gellibrand at the Golden Ball in Pauls Church-Yard, 1657.

Zasius, Ulrich. *Lucubrationes Aliquot Sane Quam Elegantes Nec Minus Eruditae.* Basel, 1518.

———. *Singularia Responsa Sive Intellectus Iuris Singulares.* Basel, 1541.

SECONDARY SOURCES

Adams, Simon. "Favourites and Factions at the Elizabethan Court." In *Princes, Patronage, and the Nobility: The Court at the Beginning of the Modern Age, c. 1450–1650,* edited by Ronald Asch and Adolf M. Birke, 265–87. London: German Historical Institute, 1991.

Alford, Stephen. *Burghley: William Cecil at the Court of Elizabeth I.* New Haven, CT: Yale University Press, 2011.

———. *The Early Elizabethan Polity.* Cambridge: Cambridge Univeristy Press, 1998.

———. *Kingship and Politics in the Reign of Edward VI.* Cambridge: Cambridge University Press, 2008.

Allen, Elizabeth. "Tuvill, Daniel (d. 1660)." In *Oxford Dictionary of National Biography.* Edited by H. C. G. Matthew and Brian Harrison. Oxford: Oxford University Press, 2004.

Amos, N. Scott. "The Alsatian among the Athenians: Martin Bucer, Mid-Tudor Cambridge and the Edwardian Reformation." *Reformation and Renaissance Review: Journal of the Society for Reformation Studies* 4, no. 1 (June 2002): 94–124.

Aylmer, G. E. "From Office-Holding to Civil Service: The Genesis of Modern Bureaucracy." *Transactions of the Royal Historical Society,* 5th ser., 30 (1980): 91–108.

Baker, John. *The Oxford History of the Laws of England, Volume VI: 1483–1558*. Oxford: Oxford University Press, 2003.

Baldwin, Thomas Whitfield. *William Shakspere's Small Latine and Lesse Greeke*. Mansfield Center, CT: Martino, 2005.

Beier, A. L. *Masterless Men: The Vagrancy Problem in England 1560–1640*. London: Methuen, 1985.

Beresford, M. W. "The Common Informer, the Penal Statutes and Economic Regulation." *Economic History Review*, n.s., 10, no. 2 (January 1957): 221–38.

Berman, Harold J. *Faith and Order: The Reconciliation of Law and Religion*. Grand Rapids, MI: Eerdmans, 1993.

Braddick, M. J. *State Formation in Early Modern England, c. 1550–1700*. Cambridge: Cambridge University Press, 2000.

Brett, Annabel S. *Changes of State: Nature and the Limits of the City in Early Modern Natural Law*. Princeton, NJ: Princeton University Press, 2011.

Brubaker, R. *Citizenship and Nationhood in France and Germany*. Cambridge, MA: Harvard University Press, 2009.

Burgess, Glenn. *Absolute Monarchy and the Stuart Constitution*. New Haven, CT: Yale University Press, 1996.

———. *British Political Thought, 1500–1660: The Politics of the Post-Reformation*. New York: Palgrave Macmillan, 2009.

Bush, M. L. *The Government Policy of Protector Somerset*. Montreal: McGill-Queen's University Press, 1975.

Coffey, John. *Persecution and Toleration in Protestant England 1558–1689*. Oxford: Taylor and Francis, 2014.

Cogswell, Thomas. *Home Divisions: Aristocracy, the State, and Provincial Conflict*. Stanford, CA: Stanford University Press, 1998.

Collinson, Patrick. "The Monarchical Republic of Queen Elizabeth I." In his *Elizabethan Essays*, 30–57. London: Hambledon, 1994.

———. *Richard Bancroft and Elizabethan Anti-Puritanism*. Cambridge: Cambridge University Press, 2013.

Commons Debates, 1628. Edited by Robert C. Johnson. New Haven, CT: Yale University Press, 1977.

Coquillette, Daniel R. *Francis Bacon*. Stanford, CA: Stanford University Press, 1992.

Coward, Barry. *The Stuart Age: England, 1603–1714*. London: Routledge, 2014.

Cressy, David. "Describing the Social Order of Elizabethan and Stuart England." *Literature and History* 3 (1976): 29–44.

Cromartie, Alan. *The Constitutionalist Revolution: An Essay on the History of England, 1450–1642*. Cambridge: Cambridge University Press, 2006.

Cust, Richard. *Charles I*. Oxford: Taylor and Francis, 2014.

———. *Charles I and the Aristocracy, 1625–1642*. Cambridge: Cambridge University Press, 2013.

———. "Forced Loan (1626–1627)." In *Historical Dictionary of Stuart England, 1603–1689*. Edited by R. H. Fritze and W. B. Robison. New York: Greenwood, 1996.

———. *The Forced Loan and English Politics, 1626–1628*. Oxford: Clarendon, 1987.

———. "Wentworth's 'Change of Sides' in the 1620s." In *The Political World of Thomas Wentworth, Earl of Strafford, 1621–1641*, edited by J. F. Merritt, 63–80. Cambridge: Cambridge University Press, 2003.

Daniel, William. *The Purely Penal Law Theory in the Spanish Theologians from Vitoria to Suárez*. Rome: Gregorian University Press, 1968.

Dauber, Noah. "Deutsche Reformation: Philipp Melanchthon." In *Politischer Aristotelismus: Die Rezeption der aristotelischen "Politik" von der Antike bis zum 19. Jahrhundert*, edited by Christoph Horn and Ada Babette Neschke-Hentschke, 173–91. Metzlersche, 2008.

Davies, C.S.L. "Slavery and Protector Somerset: The Vagrancy Act of 1547." *Economic History Review*, n.s., 19, no. 3 (January 1966): 533–49.

Dean, D. M. *Law-Making and Society in Late Elizabethan England: The Parliament of England, 1584–1601*. Cambridge: Cambridge University Press, 1996.

"The Derry Diocesan Library Catalogue." N.d. http://www.derryraphoelibrary.org/historicalcatalogues.html#derry.

Dewar, Mary. "The Authorship of the 'Discourse of the Commonweal.'" *Economic History Review* 19, no. 2 (January 1966): 388–400.

———. "A Question of Plagiarism: The 'Harrison Chapters' in Sir Thomas Smith's De Republica Anglorum." *Historical Journal* 22, no. 4 (1979): 921–29.

———. *Sir Thomas Smith: A Tudor Intellectual in Office*. London: Athlone, 1964.

Dias, Jill R. "Politics and Administration in Nottinghamshire and Derbyshire, 1590–1640." D. Phil., University of Oxford, Faculty of Modern History, 1973.

Donaldson, Gordon. "The Relations between the English and Scottish Presbyterian Movements to 1604." PhD diss., University of London, 1938.

Douglas, Richard M. "Talent and Vocation in Humanist and Protestant Thought." In *Action and Conviction in Early Modern Europe*, edited by E. Harris Harbison, Theodore K. Rabb, and Jerrold E. Seigel, 261–98. Princeton, NJ: Princeton University Press, 1969.

Dreitzel, Horst. *Absolutismus und Ständische Verfassung in Deutschland: Ein Beitrag zu Kontinuität und Diskontinuität der Politischen Theorie in der Frühen Neuzeit*. Mainz: Ph. von Zabern, 1992.

Durkan, John, Stephen Rawles, Nigel Thorp, eds. *George Buchanan (1506–1582): Renaissance Scholar and Friend of Glasgow University: A Quartercentenary Exhibition: Glasgow University Library, 17 May–7 August 1982*. Glasgow: Glasgow University Library, 1982.

Dzelzainis, Martin. "Edward Hyde and Thomas Hobbes's Elements of Law, Natural and Politic." *Historical Journal* 32, no. 2 (June 1989): 303–17.

Edelen, Georges. "William Harrison (1535–1593)." *Studies in the Renaissance* 9 (January 1962): 256–72.

Elton, G. R. *The Body of the Whole Realm: Parliament and Representation in Medieval and Tudor England*. Charlottesville: Published for the Jamestown Foundation of the Commonwealth of Virginia by the University Press of Virginia, 1969.

———. "Reform and the 'Commonwealth-Men' of Edward VI's Reign." In his *Studies in Tudor and Stuart Politics and Government*, 3:234–53. Cambridge: Cambridge University Press, 2003.

———. *Reform and Renewal*. Cambridge: Cambridge University Press, 1973.

———. "Reform by Statute: Thomas Starkey's Dialogue and Thomas Cromwell's Policy." In his *Studies in Tudor and Stuart Politics and Government*, 2:235–58. Cambridge: Cambridge University Press, 1979.

———. *Studies in Tudor and Stuart Politics and Government*. Cambridge: Cambridge University Press, 2003.

Estes, James Martin. *Peace, Order, and the Glory of God: Secular Authority and the Church in the Thought of Luther and Melanchthon, 1518–1559*. Leiden: Brill, 2005.

Euler, Carrie. *Couriers of the Gospel: England and Zurich, 1531–1558: Zürcher Beiträge Zur Reformationsgeschichte*. Zürich: Theologischer Verlag, 2006.

The First Printed Catalogue of the Bodleian Library, 1605: A Facsimile. Oxford: Oxford University Press, 1986.

Fisher, R. M. "Thomas Cromwell, Humanism and Educational Reform, 1530–40." *Historical Research* 50, no. 122 (1977): 151–63.

Fletcher, Anthony. *Reform in the Provinces: The Government of Stuart England*. New Haven, CT: Yale University Press, 1986.

Fletcher, Anthony, and Diarmaid MacCulloch. *Tudor Rebellions*. 5th ed. London: Routledge, 2014.

Flüeler, Christoph. *Rezeption und Interpretation der Aristotelischen Politica im Späten Mittelalter*. Amsterdam: John Benjamins, 1992.

Gardiner, Samuel Rawson. *History of England from the Accession of James I to the Outbreak of the Civil War 1603–1642*. 10 vols. London: Longman, 1883.

Gardiner, Stephen, and Pierre Janelle. *Obedience in Church and State: Three Political Tracts*. New York: Greenwood, 1968.

Goldie, Mark. "The Unacknowledged Republic: Office-Holding in Early Modern England." In *The Politics of the Excluded, c. 1500–1850*, edited by Tim Harris, 153–94. New York: Palgrave, 2001.

Green, I. M. *Humanism and Protestantism in Early Modern English Education*. Farnham, England: Ashgate, 2009.

Greengrass, M. "Unton, Sir Henry (c. 1558–1596)." In *Oxford Dictionary of National Biography*. Edited by H.C.G. Matthew and Brian Harrison. Oxford: Oxford University Press, 2004.

Guy, J. "Monarchy and Counsel: Models of the State." In *The Sixteenth Century*, edited by P. Collinson, 113–44. Oxford: Oxford University Press, 2002.

———. "Tudor Monarchy and Its Critiques." In *The Tudor Monarchy*, edited by J. Guy, 78–110. London: Arnold, 1997.

Ha, Polly, and Patrick Collinson, eds. *The Reception of Continental Reformation in Britain*. Oxford: Oxford University Press for the British Academy, 2010.

Habermas, Jürgen. *The Theory of Communicative Action: Lifeworld and System: A Critique of Functionalist Reason*. Boston: Beacon, 1989.

———. *The Structural Transformation of the Public Sphere: An Inquiry into a Category of Bourgeois Society*. Cambridge, MA: MIT Press, 1989.

Hankins, James. "The 'Baron Thesis' after Forty Years and Some Recent Studies of Leonardo Bruni." *Journal of the History of Ideas* 56 (1995): 309–38.

Harington, John. *Nugae Antiquae*. Vol. 1. London: Vernor and Hood, 1804.

Harrington, James. *The Political Works of James Harrington*. Edited by J.G.A. Pocock. Cambridge: Cambridge University Press, 1977.

Harvey, Andrew Edward. *Martin Bucer in England*. Marburg: B. Heinrich Bauer, 1906.

Hawarde, John. *Les Reportes del Cases in Camera Stellata, 1593 to 1609: From the Original MS of John Hawarde.* London: [Spottiswoode], 1894.

Hawkyard, A.D.K. "Paget, William." In *The History of Parliament: The House of Commons 1509–1558*, edited by S. T. Bindoff. London: Published for the History of Parliament Trust by Secker and Warburg, 1982.

Heal, Felicity, and Clive Holmes. *The Gentry in England and Wales, 1500–1700.* Stanford, CA: Stanford University Press, 1994.

Hindle, Steve. *The State and Social Change in Early Modern England, c. 1550–1640.* London: Palgrave Macmillan, 2002.

Hoak, Dale. "Sir William Cecil, Sir Thomas Smith, and the Monarchical Republic of Tudor England." In *The Monarchical Republic of Early Modern England: Essays in Response to Patrick Collinson*, edited by John F. McDiarmid, 37–54. Farnham, England: Ashgate, 2007.

Hoekstra, Kinch. "A Lion in the House: Hobbes and Democracy." In *Rethinking the Foundations of Modern Political Thought*, edited by Annabel Brett, James Tully, and Holly Hamilton-Bleakley, 191–218. Cambridge: Cambridge University Press, 2006.

Holdsworth, W. S. *A History of English Law.* 3rd ed. 7 vols. London: Methuen, 1923.

Holloway, Ernest R. *Andrew Melville and Humanism in Renaissance Scotland 1545–1622.* Leiden: Brill, 2011.

Holmes, Clive. "Charles I: A Case of Mistaken Identity." *Past and Present* 205, no. 1 (November 2009): 175–88.

———. "Charles I and the Aristocracy, 1625–1642, by Richard Cust." *English Historical Review* 129, no. 537 (April 2014): 455–57.

———. "Statutory Interpretation in the Early Seventeenth Century: The Courts, the Council, and the Commissioners of Sewers." In *Law and Social Change in British History*, edited by J. A. Guy and H. G. Beale, 107–17. Atlantic Highlands, NJ: Humanities Press, 1984.

Hopf, Constantin. *Martin Bucer and the English Reformation.* Oxford: Basil Blackwell, 1946.

Höpfl, Harro. *Jesuit Political Thought: The Society of Jesus and the State, c. 1540–1640.* New York: Cambridge University Press, 2004.

Hudson, Winthrop Still. *The Cambridge Connection and the Elizabethan Settlement of 1559.* Durham, NC: Duke University Press, 1980.

Hughes, Ann. *Politics, Society, and Civil War in Warwickshire, 1620–1660.* Cambridge: Cambridge University Press, 1987.

Hughes, Paul L., and James Francis Larkin, eds. *Tudor Royal Proclamations.* New Haven, CT: Yale University Press, 1964.

Hulse, Lynn. "Cavendish, William, First Duke of Newcastle upon Tyne (bap. 1593, d. 1676)." In *Oxford Dictionary of National Biography.* Edited by H. C. G. Matthew and Brian Harrison. Oxford: Oxford University Press, 2004.

Huschke, Rolf Bernhard. *Melanchthons Lehre Vom Ordo Politicus: Ein Beitrag Zum Verhältnis von Glauben und Politischen Handeln Bei Melanchthon.* Gütersloh: Mohn, 1968.

Huxley, Andrew. "The Aphorimsi and a Discourse of Laws: Bacon, Cavendish, and Hobbes 1615–1620." *Historical Journal* 47, no. 2 (June 2004): 399–412.

Irving, David. *Memoirs of the Life and Writings of George Buchanan*. Edinburgh: Blackwood, 1817.

Jackson, N. D. *Hobbes, Bramhall and the Politics of Liberty and Necessity: A Quarrel of the Civil Wars and Interregnum*. Cambridge: Cambridge University Press, 2007.

James, Mervyn. "English Politics and the Concept of Honour." In his *Society, Politics and Culture: Studies in Early Modern England*, 308–415. Cambridge: Cambridge University Press, 1988.

Jardine, Lisa, and Alan Stewart. *Hostage to Fortune: The Troubled Life of Francis Bacon*. New York: Farrar, Straus and Giroux, 2000.

Jayne, Sears. *Plato in Renaissance England*. London: Kluwer Academic, 1995.

Jinkins, Michael. "Perkins, William (1558–1602)." In *Oxford Dictionary of National Biography*. Edited by H. C. G. Matthew and Brian Harrison. Oxford: Oxford University Press, 2004.

Jones, Whitney Richard David. *The Tudor Commonwealth, 1529–1559*. London: Athlone, 1970.

Jordan, Wilbur Kitchener. *Edward VI: The Threshold of Power*. Cambridge, MA: Belknap, 1968.

Kirby, W. J. Torrance. *The Zurich Connection and Tudor Political Theology*. Leiden: Brill, 2007.

Kisch, Guido. *Erasmus und die Jurisprudenz Seiner Zeit: Studien zum Humanistischen Rechtsdenken*. Basel: Helbing and Lichtenhahn, 1960.

Kishlansky, M. *A Monarchy Transformed, Britain 1630–1714*. London: Penguin, 1997.

Kok, Joel Edward. "The Influence of Martin Bucer on John Calvin's Interpretation of Romans: A Comparative Case Study." PhD diss., Duke University, 1993.

Kroon, Marijn de. *Studien zu Martin Bucers Obrigkeitsverständnis: Evangelisches Ethos und Politisches Engagement*. Gütersloh: Mohn, 1984.

Kyle, Chris R. "'Wrangling Lawyers': Proclamations and the Management of the English Parliament of 1621." In *Managing Tudor and Stuart Parliaments: Essays in Memory of Michael Graves*, edited by Michael A. R. Graves and Chris R. Kyle, 129–41. Chichester, England: Wiley Blackwell for the Parliamentary History Yearbook Trust, 2015.

Lake, Peter. *Anglicans and Puritans? Presbyterianism and English Conformist Thought from Whitgift to Hooker*. London: Unwin Hyman, 1988.

———. *Moderate Puritans and the Elizabethan Church*. Cambridge: Cambridge University Press, 1982.

———. "'The Monarchical Republic of Queen Elizabeth I' (and the Fall of Archbishop Grindal) Revisited." In *The Monarchical Republic of Early Modern England: Essays in Response to Patrick Collinson*, edited by John F. McDiarmid, 129–48. Aldershot, England: Ashgate, 2007.

Lehmberg, Stanford E. *The Later Parliaments of Henry VIII, 1536–1547*. Cambridge: Cambridge University Press, 1977.

Lindenbaum, Peter. "John Milton and the Republican Mode of Literary Production." In *Patronage, Politics, and Literary Traditions in England, 1558–1658*, edited by Cedric Clive Brown, 93–108. Detroit, MI: Wayne State University Press, 1993.

Loach, Jennifer. *Edward VI*. New Haven, CT: Yale University Press, 1999.

Loades, D. M. *Intrigue and Treason: The Tudor Court, 1547–1558*. London: Pearson Longman, 2004.

MacCaffrey, Wallace T. "Hatton, Sir Christopher (c. 1540–1591)." In *Oxford Dictionary of National Biography*, edited by H.C.G. Matthew and Brian Harrison. Oxford: Oxford University Press, 2004.

MacCulloch, Diarmaid. "Bondmen under the Tudors." In *Law and Government under the Tudors: Essays Presented to Sir Geoffrey Elton*, edited by Claire Cross, David Loades, and J. J. Scarisbrick, 91–109. Cambridge: Cambridge University Press, 2002.

———. *The Later Reformation in England, 1547–1603*. 2nd ed. Basingstoke, England: Palgrave, 2001.

———. *Suffolk and the Tudors: Politics and Religion in an English County, 1500–1600*. Oxford: Clarendon, 1987.

———. *Thomas Cranmer: A Life*. New Haven, CT: Yale University Press, 1996.

Malcolm, Noel. *Reason of State, Propaganda, and the Thirty Years' War*. New York: Oxford University Press, 2007.

Marshall, T. H. *Citizenship and Social Class*. Cambridge: Cambridge University Press, 1950.

Martin, Julian. *Francis Bacon, the State and the Reform of Natural Philosophy*. Cambridge: Cambridge University Press, 1992.

Martinich, Aloysius. "The Interpretation of Covenants in Leviathan." In *Leviathan after 350 Years*, edited by Tom Sorell and Luc Foisneau, 217–40. Oxford: Clarendon, 2004.

———. *The Two Gods of Leviathan: Thomas Hobbes on Religion and Politics*. Cambridge: Cambridge University Press, 1992.

Mayer, Thomas F. "Starkey and Melanchthon on Adiaphora: A Critique of W. Gordon Zeeveld." *Sixteenth Century Journal* 11, no. 1 (April 1980): 39–50.

———. *Thomas Starkey and the Commonweal: Humanist Politics and Religion in the Reign of Henry VIII*. Cambridge: Cambridge University Press, 1989.

McCabe, Richard. "Hall, Joseph (1574–1656)." In *Oxford Dictionary of National Biography*, edited by H.C.G. Matthew and Brian Harrison. Oxford: Oxford University Press, 2004.

McConica, James Kelsey. *English Humanists and Reformation Politics*. Oxford: Oxford University Press, 1965.

McCuaig, William. *Carlo Sigonio: The Changing World of the Late Renaissance*. Princeton, NJ: Princeton University Press, 1989.

McDiarmid, John F. "Introduction." In *The Monarchical Republic of Early Modern England: Essays in Response to Patrick Collinson*, edited by John F. McDiarmid, 1–17. Farnham, England: Ashgate, 2007.

McGiffert, Michael. "Covenant, Crown, and Commons in Elizabethan Puritanism." *Journal of British Studies* 20, no. 1 (October 1980): 32–52.

McGrath, Alister E. *Reformation Thought: An Introduction*. 2nd ed. Oxford: Blackwell, 1993.

McKibbin, R. *The Ideologies of Class: Social Relations in Britain 1880–1950*. Oxford: Clarendon, 1990.

McLaren, Anne. *Political Culture in the Reign of Elizabeth I*. Cambridge: Cambridge University Press, 2001.

———. "Reading Sir Thomas Smith's *De Republica Anglorum* as Protestant Apologetic." *Historical Journal* 42, no. 4 (1999): 911–39.

McRae, Andrew. *God Speed the Plough: The Representation of Agrarian England, 1500–1660*. Cambridge: Cambridge University Press, 1996.

Mendle, Michael. *Dangerous Positions: Mixed Government, the Estates of the Realm, and the Making of the Answer to the XIX Propositions*. Tuscaloosa: University of Alabama Press, 1985.

Milton, Anthony. "Thomas Wentworth and the Political Thought of the Personal Rule." In *The Political World of Thomas Wentworth, Earl of Strafford, 1621–1641*, edited by J. F. Merritt, 133–56. Cambridge: Cambridge University Press, 2003.

Mommsen, Theodor, Paul Krueger, and Alan Watson, eds. *The Digest of Justinian*. 4 vols. Philadelphia: University of Pennsylvania Press, 1985.

Morrill, John. *The Revolt of the Provinces*. London: Longman, 1980.

Muller, Richard A. "Covenant and Conscience in English Reformed Theology: Three Variations on a 17th Century Theme." *Westminster Theological Journal* 42, no. 2 (1980): 303–34.

Neale, John Ernest. *Elizabeth I and Her Parliaments, 1584–1601*. London: Cape, 1957.

Needham, Paul Swope. "Sir John Cheke at Cambridge and Court." PhD diss., Harvard University, 1971.

Neustadt, Mark S. "The Making of the Instauration: Science, Politics, and Law in the Career of Francis Bacon." PhD diss., Johns Hopkins University, 1987.

Outhwaite, R. B. *Inflation in Tudor and Early Stuart England*. London: Macmillan, 1969.

Oxford University. *Register of the University of Oxford*. Vol. 2.1. Oxford: Printed for the Oxford Historical Society, 1885.

Parry, G.J.R. "William Harrison and Holinshed's Chronicles." *Historical Journal* 27, no. 4 (December 1984): 789–810.

Pauck, Wilhelm. *Melanchthon and Bucer*. Philadelphia: Westminster John Knox, 1969.

Peck, D. C. *Leicester's Commonwealth: The Copy of a Letter Written by a Master of Art of Cambridge (1584) and Related Documents*. Athens: Ohio University Press, 1985.

Peck, Linda Levy. *Court Patronage and Corruption in Early Stuart England*. London: Unwin Hyman, 1990.

Peltonen, Markku. "Bacon, Francis, Viscount St. Alban (1561–1626)." In *Oxford Dictionary of National Biography*, edited by H.C.G. Matthew and Brian Harrison. Oxford: Oxford University Press, 2004.

———. *Classical Humanism and Republicanism in English Political Thought, 1570–1640*. Cambridge: Cambridge University Press, 1995.

———. *The Duel in Early Modern England: Civility, Politeness and Honour*. Cambridge: Cambridge University Press, 2003.

Pickwoad, Nicholas. "Derry and Raphoe Diocesan Library Lecture." N.d. http://www.derryraphoelibrary.org/web_conference_paper_pickwoad.pdf.

Plucknett, T.F.T. "Some Proposed Legislation of Henry VIII." *Transactions of the Royal Historical Society* 19 (1936).

Pocock, Nicholas. *Troubles Connected with the Prayer Book of 1549: Documents Now Mostly for the First Time Printed from the Originals in the Record Office, the Petyt Collection in the Library of the Inner Temple, the Council Book, and the British Museum.* Westminster: Camden Society, 1884.

Pollnitz, Aysha. *Princely Education in Early Modern Britain.* Cambridge: Cambridge University Press, 2015.

Prestwich, Menna. *Cranfield: Politics and Profits under the Early Stuarts: The Career of Lionel Cranfield, Earl of Middlesex.* Oxford: Clarendon, 1966.

Private Libraries in Renaissance England. http://plre.folger.edu.

Quinn, David Beers. *The Hakluyt Handbook.* Cambridge: Cambridge University Press, 1974.

Quintrell, Brian. "The Making of Charles I's Book of Orders." *English Historical Review* 95, no. 376 (July 1980): 553–72.

———. "Montagu, Henry, First Earl of Manchester (c. 1564–1642)." In *Oxford Dictionary of National Biography*, edited by H.C.G. Matthew and Brian Harrison. Oxford: Oxford University Press, 2004.

Rahe, Paul Anthony. *Against Throne and Altar: Machiavelli and Political Theory under the English Republic.* Cambridge: Cambridge University Press, 2008.

Rainolds, John. *John Rainolds' Oxford Lectures on Aristotle's Rhetoric.* Translated by Lawrence D. Green. Newark: University of Delaware Press, 1986.

Renaudet, A. "Erasme Économiste." In *Mélanges Offerts à M. Abel Lefranc, Professeur Au Collège de France*, edited by Jacques Lavaud, 130–41. Paris: E. Droz, 1936.

Rowan, Steven W. *Ulrich Zasius: A Jurist in the German Renaissance, 1461–1535.* Frankfurt am Main: V. Klostermann, 1987.

———. "Ulrich Zasius on the Death Penalty for Anabaptists." *Bibliothèque d'Humanisme et Renaissance* 41, no. 3 (January 1979): 527–40.

Russell, Conrad. *King James VI and I and His English Parliaments.* Edited by Richard Cust and A. D. Thrush. Oxford: Oxford University Press, 2011.

Ryan, Lawrence V. "The Haddon-Osorio Controversy (1563–1583)." *Church History: Studies in Christianity and Culture* 22, no. 2 (1953): 142–54.

———. "Richard Hakluyt's Voyage into Aristotle." *Sixteenth Century Journal* 12, no. 3 (1981): 73–84.

Salmon, J.H.M. "Seneca and Tacitus in Jacobean England." In *The Mental World of the Jacobean Court*, edited by Linda Levy Peck, 169–88. Cambridge: Cambridge University Press, 1991.

Santschi, David Andrew. "Obedience and Resistance in England, 1536–1558." PhD diss., University of Wisconsin, Madison, 2008.

Schmitt, Charles B. *John Case and Aristotelianism in Renaissance England.* Kingston: McGill-Queen's University Press, 1983.

Schobinger, Jean-Pierre, and Friedrich Ueberweg, eds. *Die Philosophie des 17. Jahrhunderts.* Basel: Schwabe, 1988.

Schurink, Fred. "Print, Patronage, and Occasion: Translations of Plutarch's 'Moralia' in Tudor England." *Yearbook of English Studies* 38, nos. 1–2 (January 2008): 86–101.

Selwyn, David Gordon. *The Library of Thomas Cranmer.* Oxford: Oxford Bibliographical Society, 1996.

Serjeantson, Richard. "Francis Bacon, Colonisation, and the Limits of Atlanticism." Paper presented to the Program in Renaissance and Early Modern Studies, University of California, Berkeley, March 16, 2014. http://rems.berkeley.edu/files/2012/03/Richard-Serjeantson-Bacon-and-the-Limits-of-Atlanticism.pdf.

Shagan, Ethan H. *Popular Politics and the English Reformation*. Cambridge: Cambridge University Press, 2003.

———. "'Popularity' and the 1549 Rebellions Revisited." *The English Historical Review* 115, no. 460 (2000): 121–33.

Sharpe, Kevin. *The Personal Rule of Charles I*. New Haven, CT: Yale University Press, 1992.

Sheils, William Joseph. "Whitgift, John (1530/31?–1604)." In *Oxford Dictionary of National Biography*, edited by H.C.G. Matthew and Brian Harrison. Oxford: Oxford University Press, 2004.

Skinner, Quentin. "Classical Liberty, Renaissance Translation and the English Civil War." In his *Visions of Politics*, 2:308–43. Cambridge: Cambridge University Press, 2002.

———. "From the State of Princes to the Person of the State." In his *Visions of Politics*, 2:368–413. Cambridge: Cambridge University Press, 2002.

———. *The Foundations of Modern Political Thought*. 2 vols. Cambridge: Cambridge University Press, 1978.

———. *Liberty before Liberalism*. Cambridge: Cambridge University Press, 1998.

———. *Reason and Rhetoric in the Philosophy of Hobbes*. Cambridge: Cambridge University Press, 1996.

Slack, Paul. "Books of Orders: The Making of English Social Policy, 1577–1631." *Transactions of the Royal Historical Society*, 5th ser., 30 (1980): 1–22.

Smith, A.G.R. *The Emergence of a Nation State: The Commonwealth of England, 1529–1660*. London: Longman, 1997.

Sommerville, Johann P. "English and Roman Liberty in the Monarchical Republic of Early Stuart England." In *The Monarchical Republic of Early Modern England: Essays in Response to Patrick Collinson*, edited by John F. McDiarmid, 201–16. Farnham, England: Ashgate, 2007.

———. *Royalists and Patriots: Politics and Ideology in England, 1603–1640*. London: Longman, 1999.

———. *Thomas Hobbes: Political Ideas in Historical Context*. New York: St. Martin's, 1992.

Spelman, John. *The Reports of Sir John Spelman*, edited by J. H. Baker. London: Selden Society, 1977.

Spruyt, Hendrik. *The Sovereign State and Its Competitors: An Analysis of Systems Change*. Princeton, NJ: Princeton University Press, 1994.

Stone, L. *The Crisis of the Aristocracy, 1558–1641*. Oxford: Clarendon, 1965.

Strauss, Leo. *The Political Philosophy of Hobbes: Its Basis and Its Genesis*. Chicago: University of Chicago Press, 1996.

Strype, John. *Ecclesiastical Memorials*. Vol. 2, pt. 1. Oxford: Clarendon, 1822.

Tawney, R. H. *Religion and the Rise of Capitalism: A Historical Study*. London: J. Murray, 1926.

Tawney, Richard H., and Eileen Power, eds. *Tudor Economic Documents*. 3 vols. London: Longmans, 1924.

Thomson, Gladys Scott. *Lords Lieutenant in the Sixteenth Century.* London: Longmans, Green, 1923.

Tilly, Charles. *Coercion, Capital, and European States, AD 990–1990.* Cambridge, MA: Blackwell, 1990.

———. "War Making and State Making as Organized Crime." In *Bringing the State Back In,* edited by Peter B. Evans, Dietrich Rueschemeyer, and Theda Skocpol, 169–91. Cambridge: Cambridge University Press, 1985.

Tuck, Richard. "Hobbes and Democracy." In *Rethinking the Foundations of Modern Political Thought,* edited by Annabel Brett, James Tully, and Holly Hamilton-Bleakley, 171–90. Cambridge: Cambridge University Press, 2006.

———. "Hobbes and Tacitus." In *Hobbes and History,* edited by G.A.J. Rogers and Tom Sorell, 99–111. London: Routledge, 2000.

———. "Introduction." In *On the Citizen* by Thomas Hobbes, edited by Richard Tuck, viii–xxxiii. Translated by Michael Silverthorne. New York: Cambridge University Press, 1998.

———. *Philosophy and Government, 1572–1651.* Cambridge: Cambridge University Press, 1993.

Vries, Jan de, and Ad van der Woude. *The First Modern Economy: Success, Failure, and Perseverance of the Dutch Economy, 1500–1815.* Cambridge: Cambridge University Press, 1997.

Wells, Charlotte C. *Law and Citizenship in Early Modern France.* Baltimore: Johns Hopkins University Press, 1995.

Wijffels, Alain. "Law Books in Cambridge Libraries, 1500–1640." *Transactions of the Cambridge Bibliographical Society* 10, no. 3 (January 1993): 359–412.

Withington, Phil. *The Politics of Commonwealth: Citizens and Freemen in Early Modern England.* Cambridge: Cambridge University Press, 2005.

Wood, Andy. "Deference, Paternalism and Popular Memory in Early Modern England." In *Remaking English Society: Social Relations and Social Change in Early Modern England,* edited by Steve Hindle, Alexandra Shepard, and John Walter, 233–53. Woodbridge, England: Boydell and Brewer, 2015.

———. *The 1549 Rebellions and the Making of Early Modern England.* Cambridge: Cambridge University Press, 2007.

Wood, Neal. "Avarice and Civil Unity: The Contribution of Sir Thomas Smith." *History of Political Thought* 18 (1997): 24–42.

———. *Foundations of Political Economy: Some Early Tudor Views on State and Society.* Berkeley: University of California Press, 1994.

Woolrych, A. *Commonwealth to Protectorate.* Oxford: Clarendon, 1982.

Wrightson, Keith. *Earthly Necessities: Economic Lives in Early Modern Britain.* New Haven, CT: Yale University Press, 2002.

———. "Estates, Degrees, and Sorts: Changing Perceptions of Society in Tudor and Stuart England." In *Language, History and Class,* edited by Penelope J. Corfield, 30–52. Oxford: Blackwell, 1991.

———. "Two Concepts of Order: Justices, Constables and Jurymen in Seventeenth-Century England." In *An Ungovernable People? The English and Their Law in the Seventeenth and Eighteenth Centuries,* edited by J. Brewer and J. Styles, 21–46. New Brunswick, NJ: Rutgers University Press, 1980.

————. "The Social Order of Early Modern England: Three Approaches." In *The World We Have Gained: Histories of Population and Social Structure*, edited by Lloyd Bonfield, Richard Michael Smith, and Keith Wrightson, 177–202. Oxford: Blackwell, 1986.

Zeeveld, William Gordon. *Foundations of Tudor Policy.* Cambridge, MA: Harvard University Press, 1948.

Zwierlein, Cornel. "Reformation als Rechtsreform: Bucers Hermeneutik der lex Dei und sein humanistischer Zugriff auf das römische Recht." In *Martin Bucer und das Recht: Beiträge zum internationalen Symposium vom 1. bis 3. März 2001 in der Johannes a Lasco Bibliothek Emden*, edited by Christoph Strohm, 29–81. Geneva: Librairie Droz, 2002.

INDEX

absolutism, 5, 11–12, 23, 83–86, 154, 189
Acciaioli, Donato, 115–16, 131, 142, 145, 147
actions, legal, 26, 47–48, 53–54, 69
adiaphorism, 5
admonition controversy, 117, 128, 165
aemulatio, 158
Aeschines, 49
affection, 113, 165, 171; overcoming of by affection, 16, 26, 42, 154–55, 187, 209, 212. *See also* fear; hope
Agnadello, Battle of, 8–9
Alexander of Macedon, 42
Alford, Stephen, 9
ambition, 26, 32, 34, 40, 43, 74, 112, 119, 124–26, 128, 137–38, 152, 154–56, 159, 164–69, 172, 177, 187, 219, 226, 233
Ames, William, 193
Anabaptism *or* Anabaptists, 7, 38, 46, 166; anti-, 79
Anglo-Scottish union, 11
Anne, Lady Drury, 168
Apelles, 128, 132n77
Aquinas, Thomas, 200
aristocracy, 95, 117, 133, 150–52, 160–63, 221n136. *See also* republicanism, aristocratic
Aristotle: account of magistracy, 49; on auditing magistrates, 138; Bacon on, 182, 184; Bodin on, 120–21; Bucer on, 38; on civil knowledge, 74; constitutional relativism of, 133n81; definition of citizenship, 88, 124–25, 133–34; Edward VI on, 64; on envy, 165; *Ethics*, 18, 43, 66, 212–13; Hobbes's critique of, 212–13; influence of on new humanism, 11, 18, 41–43; and John Case, 23, 115–16, 128–29, 138, 142, 146, 148, 150–52, 155; on justice and stability, 17; and lordship, 84; natural law reading of, 24; on natural slavery, 126;

Politics, 18, 23, 114–16, 126, 152; *Rhetoric*, 18, 60, 96, 182–84, 209; theory of friendship of, 59. *See also* commonwealth; competitive behavior; concord; friendship; honor; justice; magistracy; office; office-holding; power, highest; virtue
Arminianism, 191, 204, 209
Armstrong, Clement, 31
Army Council, 12
Arundel, Thomas Howard, fourteenth earl of, 163–64, 171
Arundell, Charles, 118–19, 143
Ascham, Roger, 9, 50
assurance, doctrine of, 193
Aubrey, John, 203, 210n93
Audley, Thomas, 52–54, 56, 113
Augustine, St., 16
Augustus, Emperor, 85, 182, 187
Aylmer, John, 82, 99, 111–12, 140, 148–49
Azor, Juan, 200

Bacon, Sir Francis, 118, 135, 155; on affection overcoming affection, 154, 187; *Aphorismi de Jure Gentium Maiore Sive de Fontibus Justiciae et Juris*, 175–76, 178–82, 218; appreciates competitive behavior, 183–84; and commonwealth legislation, 24, 153–54; *De Augmentis Scientarum*, 175; and dueling, 163, 177; *Essays*, 15, 164, 167; establishes standing commissions, 185; fiscal policies, 202; imagines renewed commonwealth in terms of patronage of lawyer-landlords, 179–80; law, 174–76, 181, 210; and nobility, 167–68; "Of Seditions and Troubles," 182–83; on office-holding, 170–72; prefers lawyers for public service, 185; on royal service, 172; seeks office and titles, 164–65; transforms Bodin's sovereignty into commonwealth, 178–80; use of classical